Frommer's®

P9-DUB-376

Rome

18th Edition

by Darwin Porter & Danforth Prince

Here's what the critics say about Frommer's:

"Amazingly easy to use. Very portable, very complete."

—*Booklist*

"Detailed, accurate, and easy-to-read information for all price ranges."
—*Glamour Magazine*

"Hotel information is close to encyclopedic."

—*Des Moines Sunday Register*

"Frommer's Guides have a way of giving you a real feel for a place."
—*Knight Ridder Newspapers*

1807
WILEY
2007

Wiley Publishing, Inc.

Published by:

Wiley Publishing, Inc.

111 River St.
Hoboken, NJ 07030-5774

Copyright © 2007 Wiley Publishing, Inc., Hoboken, New Jersey. All rights reserved. No part of this publication may be reproduced, stored in a retrieval system or transmitted in any form or by any means, electronic, mechanical, photocopying, recording, scanning or otherwise, except as permitted under Sections 107 or 108 of the 1976 United States Copyright Act, without either the prior written permission of the Publisher, or authorization through payment of the appropriate per-copy fee to the Copyright Clearance Center, 222 Rosewood Drive, Danvers, MA 01923, 978/750-8400, fax 978/646-8600. Requests to the Publisher for permission should be addressed to the Legal Department, Wiley Publishing, Inc., 10475 Crosspoint Blvd., Indianapolis, IN 46256, 317/572-3447, fax 317/572-4355, or online at http://www.wiley.com/go/permissions.

Wiley and the Wiley Publishing logo are trademarks or registered trademarks of John Wiley & Sons, Inc. and/or its affiliates. Frommer's is a trademark or registered trademark of Arthur Frommer. Used under license. All other trademarks are the property of their respective owners. Wiley Publishing, Inc. is not associated with any product or vendor mentioned in this book.

ISBN: 978-0-470-00868-3

Editor: Elizabeth Heath
Production Editor: Michael Brumitt
Cartographer: Andrew Murphy
Photo Editor: Richard Fox
Anniversary Logo Design: Richard Pacifico
Production by Wiley Indianapolis Composition Services

Front cover photo: Piazza di Trevi: One of Neptune's tritons at Rome's famous Trevi Fountain
Back cover photo: Roman Forum: The Temple of Saturn and Santi Luca e Martina in the heart of ancient Rome

For information on our other products and services or to obtain technical support, please contact our Customer Care Department within the U.S. at 800/762-2974, outside the U.S. at 317/572-3993 or fax 317/572-4002.

Wiley also publishes its books in a variety of electronic formats. Some content that appears in print may not be available in electronic formats.

Manufactured in the United States of America

5 4 3 2 1

Contents

6 Where to Stay in Rome   73

7 Where to Dine in Rome   102

8 Exploring Rome   133

9   Strolling Through Rome

10   Shopping

11   Rome After Dark

12   Side Trips from Rome

Appendix A: Rome in Depth

Appendix B: Molto Italiano

Appendix C: Useful Toll-Free Numbers & Websites

Index

List of Maps

About the Authors

As a team of veteran travel writers, **Darwin Porter** and **Danforth Prince** have produced numerous titles for Frommers, including best-selling guides to Italy, France, the Caribbean, England, and Germany. Porter, a former bureau chief of *The Miami Herald,* is also a Hollywood biographer, his most recent book being *Brando Unzipped,* devoted to the tumultuous life of Marlon Brando. Prince was formerly employed by the Paris bureau of the *New York Times,* and is today the president of Blood Moon Productions and other media-related firms.

An Invitation to the Reader

In researching this book, we discovered many wonderful places—hotels, restaurants, shops, and more. We're sure you'll find others. Please tell us about them, so we can share the information with your fellow travelers in upcoming editions. If you were disappointed with a recommendation, we'd love to know that, too. Please write to:

Frommer's Rome, 18th Edition
Wiley Publishing, Inc. • 111 River St. • Hoboken, NJ 07030-5774

An Additional Note

Please be advised that travel information is subject to change at any time—and this is especially true of prices. We therefore suggest that you write or call ahead for confirmation when making your travel plans. The authors, editors, and publisher cannot be held responsible for the experiences of readers while traveling. Your safety is important to us, however, so we encourage you to stay alert and be aware of your surroundings. Keep a close eye on cameras, purses, and wallets, all favorite targets of thieves and pickpockets.

Other Great Guides for Your Trip:

Frommer's Florence, Tuscany & Umbria
Frommer's Italy
Frommer's Northern Italy
Frommer's Sicily
Frommer's Portable Florence
Frommer's Portable Venice
Italy For Dummies
Frommer's Irreverent Guide to Rome
Frommer's Rome Past & Present
Suzys Gershman's Born to Shop Italy

Frommer's Star Ratings, Icons & Abbreviations

Every hotel, restaurant, and attraction listing in this guide has been ranked for quality, value, service, amenities, and special features using a **star-rating system.** In country, state, and regional guides, we also rate towns and regions to help you narrow down your choices and budget your time accordingly. Hotels and restaurants are rated on a scale of zero (recommended) to three stars (exceptional). Attractions, shopping, nightlife, towns, and regions are rated according to the following scale: zero stars (recommended), one star (highly recommended), two stars (very highly recommended), and three stars (must-see).

In addition to the star-rating system, we also use **eight feature icons** that point you to the great deals, in-the-know advice, and unique experiences that separate travelers from tourists. Throughout the book, look for:

Then&Now	A look back at the early days of Frommer's, highlighting timeless bits of travel wisdom as well as hotels and restaurants that have stood the test of time
Finds	Special finds—those places only insiders know about
Fun Fact	Fun facts—details that make travelers more informed and their trips more fun
Kids	Best bets for kids and advice for the whole family
Moments	Special moments—those experiences that memories are made of
Overrated	Places or experiences not worth your time or money
Tips	Insider tips—great ways to save time and money
Value	Great values—where to get the best deals

The following **abbreviations** are used for credit cards:

AE	American Express	DISC	Discover	V	Visa
DC	Diners Club	MC	MasterCard		

Frommers.com

Now that you have this guidebook to help you plan a great trip, visit our website at **www.frommers.com** for additional travel information on more than 3,500 destinations. We update features regularly to give you instant access to the most current trip-planning information available. At Frommers.com, you'll find scoops on the best airfares, lodging rates, and car rental bargains. You can even book your travel online through our reliable travel booking partners. Other popular features include:

- Online updates of our most popular guidebooks
- Vacation sweepstakes and contest giveaways
- Newsletters highlighting the hottest travel trends
- Online travel message boards with featured travel discussions

What's New in Rome

Today a newer and brighter Rome awaits visitors. It's gotten a bit dusty since everything was dusted off for the millennium, but ruins and decay are what you expect in such an ancient city. Augustus boasted that he found Rome a city of brick and left it one of marble. In the historic core, the emperor's claim largely rings true. Museums are better lit, hotels vastly improved, the food as good as ever, transportation modernized, and the "second Renaissance" proclaimed that the millennium is in full swing.

Here are some of the latest developments in the city that always changes but is still "eternal."

ACCOMMODATIONS Close to the Spanish Steps, **Fontanella Borghese,** Largo Fontanella Borghese 84 (*©* **06-68809504**), has been much renovated and improved, and few hotels in Rome occupy such a central position. On the third and fourth floors of a palace dating from the end of the 18th century, the building was once a possession of the Borghese princes.

Only a few minutes' walk from the Basilica of St. Peter's, **Starhotel Michelangelo,** Via della Stazione di S. Pietro 14 (*©* **06-398739**), has been much improved and is recommendable again after a long slumber. Its rooms date from the 1950s but are now up to date with modern amenities and a glamorized decor. The on-site restaurant with its regional and international menu also has been considerably upgraded. You'll dine elegantly.

DINING The "House of Fish," **Hosteria dei Pesce,** Via di Monserrato 32 (*©* **06-6865617**), close to the Piazza Campo de' Fiori, has become one of Rome's finest seafood restaurants, and is today a coveted table reservation. The freshness of the fish is among the best in the city, and the catch of the day is laid out for your inspection. Once you choose from the freshly harvested baby squid, sea bass, or whatever, the chefs will prepare the bounty to your specifications, and they do so with considerable skill.

One of Rome's chicest cafes, serving complete meals, is **Caffeterria Canova Tadolini,** Via del Babuino 150 A/B (*©* **06-32110702**). It's installed in a section of a museum dedicated to Antonio Canova, the neoclassical sculptor. Serving Roman specialties, and doing so exceedingly well, the cafe lies near Piazza del Popolo.

Management opened **Glass,** Vicolo del Cinque 58 (*©* **06-58335903**), in "an attempt to give Trastevere back to the Romans." Lots of glass (including the floors) gives this place a modernist aura, but its food is strictly Roman with many time-tested old favorites not seen on menus in a long time—such as the pigeon in a berry sauce encased in chicory pie.

Casina Valadier, Villa Borghese, Piazza Bucarest (*©* **06-69922090**), was once one of the hottest dining tickets in Rome. It's back, and is better than ever, serving the savory Roman specialties that once made it the favorite choice of the glitterati. In addition to a sublime cuisine, you are also treated to some of the most panoramic views of Rome itself in the heart of the Villa Borghese gardens.

Incidentally, it's now possible to have a romantic picnic in these same Villa Borghese gardens by ordering the picnic from **Gina,** Via San Sebastianello 7A (© **06-6780251**), complete with thermos, glasses, and linen.

EXPLORING ROME At a private palazzo, open only one morning a week, you can see one of the city's most celebrated art collections at **Galleria Colonna,** Piazza SS. Apostoli 66 (© **06-6794362**). Most of the paintings were acquired after the Renaissance, the finest art dating mainly from the 17th century, including works by such old masters as Jan Brueghel the Elder.

SHOPPING Bargain hunters are leaving Rome and heading for the hills, in this case the town of Castel Romano, lying 10km (6 miles) east of Rome. Here they are discovering **McArthurGlen Designer Outlet,** Via Ponte di Piscina Cupa 51 (© **06-5050050**), where 90 vendors display their wares, including clothing, footwear, sportswear, and other accessories. Many designer labels, such as Versace, are on sale at 35% to 75% discounts.

Italians have long been known for their quality eyewear, and one of the best new outlets is **Mondello Ottica,** Via del Pellegrino 98 (© **06-6861955**), found near Campo de' Fiori. A wide selection of Italian designs, along with foreign brands, is for sale.

Degli Effetti, Piazza Capranica 75–79–93 (© **06-6790202**), has opened near the Pantheon. This series of designer boutiques mainly stocks labels from designers not able to afford their own showcase outlets because of the stupendously high rentals in Rome.

AFTER DARK Testaccio is becoming the hippest nighttime district of Rome. A lot of revelers are drawn to the Latin music, especially salsa, played at the **Caruso Café de Oriente,** Via Monte Testaccio 36 (© **06-5745019**). Performers from Italy and abroad appear here, as an attractive, young crowd gyrates to the sounds of Caribbean or Brazilian music.

When the weather gets hot, many Romans flee to Fregene, 38.5km (24 miles) west of the city. Here from May to September, they patronize **Gilda on the Beach,** Lungomare di Ponente 11 (© **06-66560649**), with its four dance floors and first-class restaurant.

Back in Rome itself, **Jonathan's Angels,** Via della Fossa 14–16 (© **06-6893426**), decorated with colorful kitsch, offers live piano music by local musicians. This is a great spot to hit after you stroll around Piazza Navona.

SIDE TRIPS FROM ROME At Palestrina, the **Galleria Nazional d'Arte Antica,** Palazzo Barberini (© **06-32810**), has been renovated and much improved. Although most visitors come here to look at the ancient Nile Mosaic, more and more people are discovering the museum's array of paintings, which are strong not only in Italian works, such as paintings by Fra Angelico and Filipo Lippi, but Dutch and Flemish art as well.

The Best of Rome

Rome is a city of vivid and unforgettable images: the view of the city's silhouette from Janiculum Hill at dawn, the array of broken marble columns and ruins of temples of the Roman Forum, St. Peter's dome against a pink-and-red sunset, capping a gloriously decorated basilica.

Rome is also a city of sounds, beginning early in the morning with the peal of church bells calling the faithful to Mass. As the city awakens and comes to life, the sounds multiply and merge into a kind of urban symphony. The streets fill with cars, taxis, and motor scooters, all blaring their horns as they weave in and out of traffic; the sidewalks become overrun with bleary-eyed office workers rushing to their desks after stealing into crowded cafes for the first cappuccino of the day. The shops lining the streets open for business by raising their protective metal grilles as loudly as possible, seeming to delight in their contribution to the general din. Before long, fruit and vegetable stands are abuzz with activity as homemakers, maids, cooks, and others arrive to purchase their day's supply of fresh produce, haggling over prices and clucking over quality.

By 10am, the tourists are on the streets, battling crowds and traffic as they wind their way from Renaissance palaces and baroque buildings to the famous ruins of antiquity. Indeed, Rome often appears to have two populations: one of Romans and one of visitors. During the summer months especially, the city plays host to a horde of countless sightseers who converge on it with guidebooks and cameras in hand. To all—Americans, Europeans, Japanese—Rome extends a warm and friendly welcome, wining, dining, and entertaining them in its inimitable fashion. (Of course, if you visit in August, you might see only tourists, not Romans, because the locals flee the summer heat of the city. Or, as one Roman woman once told us, "Even if we're too poor to go on vacation, we close the shutters and pretend we're away so neighbors won't find out we couldn't afford to leave the city.")

The traffic, unfortunately, is worse than ever. As the capital, Rome also remains at the center of the major political scandals and corruption known as *Tangentopoli* (bribe city), which sends hundreds of government bureaucrats to jail each year.

Despite all this chaos, Romans still know how to live the good life. After you've done your duty to culture by wandering through the Colosseum and being awed by the Pantheon, after you've traipsed through St. Peter's Basilica and thrown a coin in the Trevi Fountain, you can pause to experience the charm of the Roman evening. Find a cafe at summer twilight and watch the shades of pink turn to gold and copper before night finally falls. That's when another Rome comes alive; restaurants and cafes grow more animated, especially if you've found one on an ancient hidden piazza or along a narrow alley deep in Trastevere. After dinner, you can have a gelato (or an espresso in winter) and stroll by the fountains through Piazza Navona, and the night is yours.

In chapter 8, we'll tell you all about the ancient monuments and basilicas. But monuments are only a piece of the whole. Here we've tried to capture the special experiences that might well be the highlights of your visit.

1 Frommer's Favorite Rome Experiences

- **Walking Through Ancient Rome.** A vast, almost unified archaeological park cuts through the center of Rome. For those who want specific guidance, we have a walking tour in chapter 9 that will lead you through these haunting ruins. But it's fun to wander on your own and let yourself get lost on the very streets where Julius Caesar and Lucrezia Borgia once trod. A slice of history unfolds at every turn: an ancient fountain, a long-forgotten statue, a ruined temple dedicated to some long-faded cult. A narrow street suddenly opens to a view of a triumphal arch. The Roman Forum and the Palatine Hill are the highlights, but the glory of Rome is hardly confined to these dusty fields. If you wander long enough, you'll eventually emerge onto Piazza della Rotunda to stare in awe at one of Rome's most glorious sights, the Pantheon.

- **Hanging Out at the Pantheon.** The world's best-preserved ancient monument is now a hot spot—especially at night. Find a cafe table out on the square and take in the action, which all but awaits a young Fellini to record it. The Pantheon has become a symbol of Rome itself, and we owe our thanks to Hadrian for leaving it to the world. When you tire of people-watching and cappuccino, you can go inside to inspect the tomb of Raphael, who was buried here in 1520. (His mistress, "La Fornarina," wasn't allowed to attend the services.) Nothing is more dramatic than being in the Pantheon during a rainstorm, watching the sheets of water splatter on the colorful marble floor. It enters

through the oculus on top, which provides the only light for the interior. See "The Pantheon & Attractions near Piazza Navona & Campo de' Fiori," in chapter 8.

- **Taking a Sunday Bike Ride.** Only a daredevil would try this on city streets on a weekday, but on a clear Sunday morning, while Romans are still asleep, you can rent a bike and discover Rome with your own two wheels. The Villa Borghese is the best place to bike. Its 6.5km (4-mile) borders contain a world unto itself, with museums and galleries, a riding school, an artificial lake, and a grassy amphitheater. Another choice place for Sunday biking is the Villa Doria Pamphili, an extensive park lying above the Janiculum. Laid out in the mid-1600s, this is Rome's largest park, with numerous fountains and some summer houses.

- **Strolling at Sunset in the Pincio Gardens.** Above the landmark Piazza del Popolo, this terraced and lushly planted hillside is the most romantic place for a twilight walk. A dusty orange-rose glow often colors the sky, giving an otherworldly aura to the park's umbrella pines and broad avenues. The ancient Romans turned this hill into gardens, but today's look came from the design of Giuseppe Valadier in the 1800s. Pause at the main piazza, Napoleone I, for a spectacular view of the city stretching from the Janiculum to Monte Mario. The Egyptian-style obelisk here was erected by Emperor Hadrian on the tomb of his great love, Antinous, a beautiful male slave who died prematurely. See "The Spanish Steps, the

Trevi Fountain & Attractions Nearby," in chapter 8.

- **Enjoying Roma di Notte.** At night, ancient monuments, such as the Forum, are bathed in a theatrical white light; it's thrilling to see the glow of the Colosseum with the moon rising behind its arches. Begin your evening with a Roman *passeggiata* (early evening stroll) along Via del Corso or Piazza Navona. There's plenty of action going on inside the clubs, too, from Via Veneto to Piazza Navona. Club kids flock to the colorful narrow streets of Trastevere, the area around the Pantheon, and the even more remote Testaccio. The jazz scene is especially good, and big names often pop in. An English-language publication available at newsstands, *Wanted in Rome*, will keep you abreast of what's happening.

- **Exploring Campo de' Fiori at Mid-morning.** In an incomparable setting of medieval houses, this is the liveliest fruit and vegetable market in Rome, where peddlers offer their wares as they've done for centuries. The market is best visited after 9am any day but Sunday. By 1pm the stalls begin to close. Once the major site for the medieval inns of Rome (many of which were owned by Vanozza Catanei, the 15th-century courtesan and lover of Pope Alexander VI Borgia), this square maintains some of its old bohemian atmosphere. We often come here when we're in Rome for a unique, lively view of local life. Often you'll spot your favorite *trattoria* chef bargaining for the best and freshest produce, everything from fresh cherries to the perfect vine-ripened tomato. See "The Pantheon & Attractions near Piazza Navona & Campo de' Fiori," in chapter 8.

- **Attending the Opera.** The Milanese claim that Roman opera pales in comparison with La Scala, but Roman opera buffs, of course, beg to differ. At Rome's Teatro dell'Opera, the season runs between December and June, and programs concentrate on the classics: Bellini, Donizetti, Puccini, and Rossini. No one seems to touch the Romans' operatic soul more than Giuseppe Verdi (1813–1901), who became a national icon in his support for Italian unification. See "The Performing Arts" in chapter 11.

- **Climbing Janiculum Hill.** On the Trastevere side of the river, where Garibaldi held off the attacking French troops in 1849, the Janiculum Hill was always strategic in Rome's defense. Today, a walk in this park at the top of the hill can provide an escape from the hot, congested streets of Trastevere. Filled with monuments to Garibaldi and his brave men, the hill is no longer peppered with monasteries, as it was in the Middle Ages. A stroll will reveal monuments and fountains, plus panoramic views over Rome. The best vista is from Villa Lante, a Renaissance summer residence. The most serene section is the 1883 Botanical Gardens, with palm trees, orchids, bromeliads, and sequoias—more than 7,000 plant species from all over the world. See "More Attractions," in chapter 8.

- **Strolling Along the Tiber.** Without the Tiber River, there might have been no Rome at all. A key player in the city's history for millennia, the river flooded the capital every winter until it was tamed in 1870. The massive *lungotevere* embankments on both sides of the Tiber check the waters and make a perfect place for a memorable stroll. You can not only walk along the river from which Cleopatra made her grand entrance into Rome, but you'll also see the riverside life of Trastevere and the Jewish Ghetto. Start at Piazza della

Bocca della Verità in the early evening; from there, you can go for some 3km (1¾ miles) or more. For a stroll that takes you to sites along the river, see the "Renaissance Rome" walking tour in chapter 9.

- **Picnicking on Isola Tiberina.** In ancient times, this boat-shape island stood across from the port of Rome and from 293 B.C. was home to a temple dedicated to Aesculapius, the god of healing. A church was constructed in the 10th century on the ruins of this ancient temple. You can reach the island from the Jewish Ghetto by the Ponte Fabricio footbridge, which dates from 62 B.C. and is the Tiber's oldest original bridge. Romans come here to sunbathe, sitting along the river's banks, and to escape the traffic and the crowds. Arrive with the makings of a picnic, and the day is yours. See the "Trastevere" walking tour in chapter 9.

- **Following in the Footsteps of Bernini.** One of the most enjoyable ways to see Rome is to follow the trail of Giovanni Lorenzo Bernini (1598–1680), who left a greater mark on the city than even Michelangelo. Under the patronage of three different popes, Bernini "baroqued" Rome. Start at Largo di Santa Susanna, north of the Stazione Termini, at the Church of Santa Maria della Vittoria, which houses one of Bernini's most controversial sculptures, the *Ecstasy of St. Teresa,* from 1646. Walk from here along Via Barberini to Piazza Barberini, in the center of which stands Bernini's second most dramatic fountain, the Fontana del Tritone. From the piazza, go along Via delle Quattro Fontane, bypassing (on your left) the Palazzo Barberini, designed by Bernini and others for Pope Urban VIII. At the famous crossroads of Rome, Le Quattro Fontane, take Via del Quirinale to see the facade of Sant'Andrea, one of the artist's greatest churches. Continue west, bypassing the Pantheon, to arrive eventually at Piazza Navona, which Bernini remodeled for Pope Innocent X. The central fountain, the Fontana dei Fiumi, is Bernini's masterpiece, although the figures representing the four rivers were sculpted by others following his plans.

- **Spending a Day on the Appian Way.** Dating from 312 B.C., the Appian Way (Via Appia) once traversed the whole peninsula of Italy and was the road on which Roman legions marched to Brindisi and their conquests in the East. One of its darkest moments was the crucifixion in 71 B.C. of the rebellious slave army of Spartacus, whose bodies lined the road from Rome to Capua. Fashionable Romans were buried here, and early Christians dug catacombs through which to flee their persecutors. Begin at the Tomb of Cecilia Metella and proceed up Via Appia Antica past a series of tombs and monuments (including a monument to Seneca, the great moralist who committed suicide on the orders of Nero; and another to Pope St. Urban, who reigned A.D. 222–230). The sights along Via Appia Antica are some of Rome's most fascinating. You can go all the way to the Church of Domine Quo Vadis. See "The Appian Way & the Catacombs," in chapter 8.

- **Enjoying a Taste of the Grape.** While in Rome, do as the Romans do and indulge in a carafe of dry white wine from the warm climate of Lazio. In restaurants and *trattorie* you'll find the most popular brand, Frascati, but try some of the other wines from the Castelli Romani, too, including Colli Albani, Velletri, and Marino. All these wines come from one grape: trebbiano. Sometimes a dash of malvasia grape is added for greater flavor and an aromatic bouquet. Of course, you don't have to wait until dinner to sip wine; you can sample it at any of hundreds of wine bars throughout Rome, which offer a selection of all the great reds and whites of Italy.

- **Savoring Gelato on a Summer Afternoon.** Having a gelato on a hot summer day is worth the wait through the long winter. Tubs of homemade ice cream await you in a dazzling array of flavors: everything from candied orange peels with chocolate to watermelon to rice. *Gelaterie* offer *semifreddi* concoctions (made with cream instead of milk) in such flavors as almond, *marengo* (a type of meringue), and *zabaione* (or *zabaglione,* eggnog). Seasonal fresh fruits are made into ice creams of blueberry, cherry, and peach. *Granite* (crushed ice) flavored with sweet fruit is another cool delight on a sultry night. Tre Scalini at Piazza Navona is the most fabled spot for enjoying *divino tartufo,* a chocolate concoction with a taste to match its name.

- **Dining on a Hidden Piazza.** If you're in Rome with that special someone, you'll appreciate the romance of discovering your own little neighborhood trattoria that opens onto some forgotten square deep in the heart of ancient Rome. And if your evening dinner extends for 3 or 4 hours, who's counting? The waiters won't rush you out the door even when you've overstayed your time at the table. This is a special experience, and Rome has dozens of these little restaurants. Sample the menu at **Vecchia Roma,** Via della Tribuna di Campitella 18 (© **06-6864604**), with a theatrical setting on a lovely square. Order spaghetti with double-horned clams and enjoy the old-fashioned ambience while you rub elbows with savvy local foodies.

- **Hearing Music in the Churches.** Artists such as Plácido Domingo and Luciano Pavarotti have performed around Rome in halls ranging from churches to ancient ruins. Churches often host concerts, although by decree of Pope John Paul II, it must be sacred music—no hip-grinding, body-slamming stuff. When church concerts are performed, programs appear not only outside the church, but also on various announcements posted throughout Rome. The top professionals play at the "big-name" churches, but don't overlook those smaller, hard-to-find churches on hidden squares. Some of the best music we've ever heard has been by up-and-coming musicians getting their start in these little-known churches. The biggest event is the RAI (national broadcasting company) concert on December 5 at St. Peter's—even the pope attends. Other favorite locations for church music include Sant'Ignazio di Loyola, on Piazza di Sant'Ignazio, and San Paolo Fuori le Mura, at Via Ostiense 186.

- **Walking from Fountain to Fountain.** On summer nights you'll find Romans—especially those who live in crowded apartments without airconditioning—out walking from fountain to cooling fountain. Every visitor makes at least one trip to Bernini's fountain on Piazza Navona, after stopping off at the Trevi Fountain to toss in a coin (thus ensuring their return to Rome), but there are hundreds more. One hidden gem is the Fontana delle Tararughe, in tiny Piazza Mattei. It has stood there since 1581, a jewel of Renaissance sculpture showing youths helping tortoises into a basin. Our favorite Bernini fountain is at Piazza Barberini; his Fontana del Tritone is a magnificent work of art from 1642 showing the sea god blowing through a shell. Unfortunately, it's now against the law to jump into these fountains and paddle around as Anita Ekberg did in *La Dolce Vita.*

- **Hanging Out in the Campidoglio at Night.** There is no more splendid place to be at night than Piazza del Campidoglio, where Michelangelo designed both the geometric paving and the facades of the buildings. A broad flight of steps, the Cordonata, takes you up to this panoramic site, a citadel of ancient Rome from which traitors to the empire were once tossed to their deaths. Home during the day to the Capitoline Museums, it takes on a different aura at night, when it's dramatically lit, the measured Renaissance facades glowing like jewel boxes. The evening views of the brilliantly lit Forum and Palatine are also worth the long trek up those stairs. There's no more stunning cityscape view at night than from this hill. See "The Colosseum, the Roman Forum & Highlights of Ancient Rome," in chapter 8.

- **Shopping in the Flea Markets.** We've never discovered an original Raphael at Rome's Porta Portese flea market (which locals call *mercato delle pulci*). But we've picked up some interesting souvenirs over the years. The market, the largest in Europe, began after World War II when black marketers needed an outlet for illegal wares. Today the authentic art and antiques once sold here have given way to reproductions, but the selection remains enormous: World War II cameras, caviar from immigrant Russians, luggage (fake Gucci), spare parts, Mussolini busts, and so on. Near Porta Sublicio in Trastevere, the market has some 4,000 stalls, but it's estimated that only 10% of them have a license. Sunday from 5am to 2pm is the best time to visit, but beware of pickpockets at all times. See "Shopping A to Z" in chapter 10.

2 Best Hotel Bets

- **Best Historic Hotel:** The truly grand **St. Regis Grand,** Via Vittorio Emanuele Orlando 3 (© **06-47091;** www.stregis.com/grandrome), was created by César Ritz in 1894, with the great chef Escoffier presiding over a lavish banquet. It was the first hotel in town to offer "a private bathroom and two electric lights in every room." Its roster of guests has included some of the greatest names in European history, including royalty, naturally, but also such New World moguls as Henry Ford and J.P. Morgan. This lavish hotel is within walking distance of many of Rome's major sights. See p. 76.

- **Best Recycled Hotels:** A real discovery and a charmer, **The Inn at the Spanish Steps,** Via dei Condotti 85 (© **06-69925657;** www.atspanish steps.com), is the former Roman residence of Hans Christian Andersen. It has been transformed into one of the most desirable little upscale inns of Rome, with each bedroom furnished in gorgeous, authentic period decor. Not far away, the brilliantly restored **Hotel de Russie,** Via del Babuino 9 (© **800/323-7500** in North America, or 06-328881; www. roccofortehotels.com), was a retreat for artists, including Picasso and Stravinsky. Reclaiming its 1890s style, it's been remade as a stunning little boutique hotel with a fabulous location right off the Piazza del Popolo and excellent service. See p. 92 and 91.

- **Best for Business Travelers:** The restored neoclassical palace, **Exedra,** Piazza della Repubblica 47 (© **06-489381;** www.boscolohotels.com), stands right in the heart of Rome near the Termini. A government-rated five-star hotel, it is equipped with all the amenities, including a well-run business center. Executives will also find a helpful, multilingual staff ready to help ease their adjustment to the Eternal City. See p. 76.

- **Best for a Romantic Getaway:** A private villa in the exclusive Parioli residential area, the **Hotel Lord Byron,** Via G. de Notaris 5 (© **06-3220404;** www.lordbyronhotel.com), is a chic hideaway. It has a clubby ambience, and everybody is oh-so-very-discreet here. You get personal attention in subdued opulence, and the staff definitely respects that DO NOT DISTURB sign on the door. You don't even have to leave the premises for dinner; the hotel's Sapori del Lord Byron is one of the finest and most romantic restaurants in Rome. See p. 101.

- **Best Classic Choice:** Ernest Hemingway and Ingrid Bergman don't hang out here anymore, but the **Hotel Eden,** Via Ludovisi 49 (© **06-478121;** www.hotel-eden.it), remains grand and glamorous. Views over the city are stunning, the hotel restaurant (La Terrazza dell'Eden) is one of the city's best, and everything looks as if it's waiting for photographers from *Architectural Digest* to arrive. See p. 81.

- **Best for Families:** Families gravitate to the **Hotel Ponte Sisto,** Via dei Petinari 64 (© **06-6863100;** www. hotelpontesisto.it), near the Piazza Navona and the Campo de'Fiori in the heart of Rome. It's a restored Renaissance palazzo offering reasonably priced family suites on its top

floor with terraces overlooking the rooftops of the ancient city. See p. 85.

- **Best Moderately Priced Hotel:** So you don't have a bottomless expense account? We've got a couple of wonderful values for you. Consider the **Hotel Columbia,** Via del Viminale 15 (© **06-4744289** or 06-4883509; www.hotelcolumbia.com), one of the newest properties in the neighborhoods surrounding Stazione Termini; everything is well-maintained and comfortable. We also like **La Residenza,** Via Emilia 22–24 (© **06-4880789;** www.hotel-la-residenza. com), with a convenient location near the Villa Borghese and Piazza Barberini. Here you'll get a good price on a homey, spacious guest room. See p. 77 and p. 83, respectively.

- **Best Service:** Both management and staff at the **Hotel de la Ville Inter-Continental Roma,** Via Sistina 67–69 (© **800/327-0200** in the U.S. and Canada, or 06-67331; www. interconti.com), are highly professional and exceedingly hospitable. The staff is particularly adept at taking messages, giving you helpful hints about what to see and do in Rome, and fulfilling any special room-service requests. Their general attentiveness to your needs, quick problem solving, good manners, and friendly helpfulness make this place exceptional. Room service is available 24 hours daily. See p. 90.

- **Best Location:** Everybody knows about the astronomically expensive **The Hassler,** Piazza Trinità dei Monti 6 (© **800/223-6800** in the U.S., or 06-699340; www.hotelhasslerroma. com), a grand old hotel set right at the top of the Spanish Steps. But given its high prices and the fact that it's gotten a bit dowdy, we'll send you instead to the **Hotel Scalinata di**

Spagna (© **06-6793006;** www.hotel scalinata.com), which is across the street at no. 17 on the same piazza and isn't so breathtakingly pricey. This intimate, upscale inn has a roof garden with a sweeping view of the dome of St. Peter's across the Tiber. When you step out your door, the heart of Rome, including its best shopping streets, is at your feet. See p. 90 and 93.

- **Best Views:** A great place to book a room with a view is the **Albergo Del Sole al Pantheon,** Piazza della Rotonda 63 (© **06-6780441;** www. hotelsolealpantheon.com), where you can gaze out at the Pantheon from your bedroom window. See p. 88.

- **Best for Understated Elegance:** Of course, it's not as elegant or as grand as the Excelsior, the Eden, or The Hassler, but the **Hotel d'Inghilterra,** Via Bocca di Leone 14 (© **06-699811;** http://hoteldinghilterra. warwickhotels.com), has its own unique brand of low-key opulence. Plus, it's just 2 blocks west of the Spanish Steps. The hotel's public rooms feature black-and-white checkerboard marble floors, and its upholstered lounges are filled with antiques. The fifth floor has some of the loveliest terraces in Rome, and the romantic restaurant below has trompe l'oeil clouds that give the impression of a courtyard terrace open to the sky. See p. 92.

- **Best in a Real Roman Neighborhood:** You can't get more Roman than the **Hotel Teatro di Pompeo,** Largo del Pallaro 8 (© **06-68300170;** www.hotelteatrodipompeo.it), which offers rooms with charming touches such as hand-painted tiles and beamed ceilings. The hotel is actually built on top of the ruins of the Theater of Pompey, where Caesar met his fate. It's on a quiet piazzetta near the Palazzo Farnese and Campo de' Fiori, whose open-air market makes this one of Rome's most colorful neighborhoods. Shopping and nightlife abound in this fascinating section of Renaissance Rome, and restaurants and pizzerias keep the area lively at all hours. See p. 86.

- **Best Value:** Rated three stars by the government, the **Hotel delle Muse,** Via Tommaso Salvini 18 (© **06-8088333;** www.hoteldellemuse.com), lies .5km (⅓ mile) north of the Villa Borghese. It's run by the efficient, English-speaking Giorgio Lazar. The furnishings are modern and come in a wide range of splashy colors. In summer, Mr. Lazar operates a garden restaurant serving a reasonably priced fixed-price menu, and the bar is open 24 hours a day. This is one of Rome's best bargains, and you should consider checking in before he wises up and raises his rates. See p. 100.

3 Best Dining Bets

- **Best for Romance:** A great place to pop the question or just enjoy a romantic evening is **Sapori del Lord Byron,** in the Hotel Lord Byron, Via G. de Notaris 5 (© **06-3613041**), a stunner of a place that also just happens to serve the best Italian cuisine in town. The decor is as romantic as the atmosphere; it's all white lattice and bold Italian colors highlighted by masses of fresh flowers. The setting is in a Relais & Châteaux–member hotel, an Art Deco villa set on a residential hilltop in Parioli, an area of embassies and exclusive town houses at the edge of the Villa Borghese. See p. 131.

- **Best of the Best:** Food critics can never agree on the best restaurant in Rome. But the more discerning cite **La Pergola,** in the Cavalieri Hilton, Via Cadolo 101 (✆ **06-35092152**), opening onto a panoramic view at night from its perch atop Monte Mario. The talented chef's take on Mediterranean cuisine is sublime. See p. 131.

- **Best Seasonal Menus:** Market-fresh ingredients await you at **Il Convivio,** Vicolo dei Soldati 31 (✆ **06-6869432**), one of Rome's most acclaimed restaurants. The Troiano brothers are truly inspired, shopping the markets for the best in any season and adjusting their menus accordingly. The location is in walking distance of Piazza di Spagna. See p. 115.

- **Best Offbeat Choice:** A lay sisterhood of missionary Christians from five continents operates **L'Eau Vive,** Via Monterone 85 (✆ **06-68801095**), where various popes have dined. A fine French and international cuisine is served in a subdued, refined atmosphere under frescoed ceilings. You never know what will be on the menu. See p. 117.

- **Best for a Celebration:** Romans have been flocking to **Checchino dal 1887,** Via di Monte Testaccio 30 (✆ **06-5743816**), since the early 19th century for fun and hearty food. With a bountiful array of wine and foodstuffs, every meal seems like a party. The tables are packed nightly, and the place is a local legend. You'll have fun while still enjoying some of the best cuisine in town. See p. 130.

- **Best Decor:** By night, chic Romans and savvy foreign visitors alike show up at **El Toulà (The Hayloft),** Via della Lupa 29B (✆ **06-6873498**), an elegant establishment set near the fabled Caffé Greco and some of the most upscale boutiques in Rome. It's no bargain, but once you see the sumptuous setting and, more important, enjoy the cuisine, you'll think you've gotten your money's worth. Haute cuisine is served in a subdued, tasteful setting of antiques, paintings, ever-so-discreet lighting, and to-die-for flower arrangements. See p. 121.

- **Best View:** The stars really do come out at night at **Les Etoiles (The Stars),** in the Hotel Atlante Star (✆ **06-6873233**), which has been called "the most beautiful rooftop in Italy." This restaurant is a virtual garden in the sky, with a 360-degree view of Roman landmarks, including the floodlit dome of St. Peter's. Try for an alfresco table in summer, but even in winter, the same incredible view can be seen through picture windows. Fortunately, the food—delicately prepared Mediterranean cuisine using the freshest of ingredients—lives up to the setting. See p. 125.

- **Best Pizzeria:** Even the hardest-to-please Roman pizza lovers head for **Pizzeria Baffetto,** Via del Governo Vecchio 114 (✆ **06-6861617**). This is a popular and fun place, drawing a young crowd. The crusts are delightfully thin. See p. 121.

- **Best Wine List:** The food is secondary to the fabulous wine list at the **Trimani Wine Bar,** Via Cernaia 37B (✆ **06-4469630**). One of the best tasting centers in Rome for both French and Italian vintages, this elegant wine bar offers a dazzling array of wines at reasonable prices. The Trimani family has had a prestigious name in the wine business since 1821; just sit down and let the pouring begin. See p. 106.

- **Best Value:** Twenty dollars gets you one of the finest fixed-price menus in Rome at the **Ristorante del Pallaro,** Largo del Pallaro 15 (✆ **06-68801488**). Each dish is prepared by the chef-owner, Paola Fazi, who sternly urges her diners to *"Mangia!*

Mangia!" The moment you're seated at the table, the dishes start to arrive—first a selection of antipasto; then the homemade, succulent pastas of the day; followed by such meat courses as tender roast veal. Everything's included, even a carafe of the house wine. See p. 114.

- **Best for the Kids:** After their tour of the Vatican or St. Peter's, many savvy Roman families head for the **Ristorante Il Matriciano,** Via dei Gracchi 55 (② **06-3212327**). It's not fancy, but the price is right, and in summer you can opt for a sidewalk table. Let your kids feast on good, reasonably priced homemade fare that includes such crowd pleasers as ricotta-stuffed ravioli. At the next table you're likely to see some priests from the Vatican dining. See p. 126.

- **Best Continental Cuisine:** The city's finest restaurant is now **La Terrazza dell'Eden,** in the Hotel Eden, Via Ludovisi 49 (② **06-478121**), edging out a position long held by Sans Souci. You'll dine on Continental cuisine that is both bold and innovative. The seasonal menu offers the most polished, sophisticated cuisine in Rome; perhaps you'll choose a "symphony" of seafood or a warm salad of grilled vegetables. See p. 108.

- **Best Emilia-Romagna Cuisine:** The area around Bologna has long been celebrated for serving the finest cuisine in Italy, and the little trattoria **Colline Emiliane,** Via Avignonesi 22 (② **06-4817538**), maintains that stellar reputation among Romans. The pastas here are among the best in Rome, especially the handmade *tortellini alla panna* (with cream sauce) with truffles. You can order less expensive pastas as well, all of them good. The prosciutto comes from a small town near Parma and is considered by many the best in the world. See p. 109.

- **Best Roman Cuisine:** The tempting selection of antipasti alone is enough to lure you to **Al Ceppo (The Log),** Via Panama 2 (② **06-8419696**). Try such appetizers as stuffed yellow or red peppers, or finely minced cold spinach blended with ricotta. Only 2 blocks from the Villa Borghese, this is a dining address jealously guarded by Romans, who often bring friends from out of town here. They feast on the succulent lamb chops, charcoal-grilled to perfection, or other grilled meats, such as quail, liver, and bacon. See p. 131.

- **Best Seafood:** In the heart of ancient Rome, **Quinzi & Gabrieli,** Via delle Coppelle 5–6 (② **06-6879389**), serves the city's finest and freshest seafood from a restored and elegant building dating from the 1400s. The fish is simply cooked and presented, and it's heavenly. Expect everything from deep-sea shrimp to sea urchins and octopus. See p. 115.

- **Best Nuova Cucina:** Near the Vittorio Emanuele monument, **Agata e Romeo,** Via Carlo Alberto 45 (② **06-4466115**), serves one of Rome's most inventive and creative cuisines in a striking dining room done in Liberty style. If you'd like a sampling of the best selections of the day, you can order one of the fixed-price menus, available with or without wine. The menu reflects the agrarian bounty of Italy, with ample choices for everyone: meat eaters, fish fanciers, and vegetarians. See p. 105.

- **Best in the Jewish Ghetto:** For centuries, Romans have flocked to the Jewish Ghetto to sample Jerusalem artichokes. No one prepares them better than **Piperno,** Via Monte de' Cenci 9 (② **06-68806629**), which serves savory (though nonkosher) Roman food. Of course, you can order more than these deep-fried artichokes here. A full array of delights includes everything from stuffed squash blossoms to succulent pastas. See p. 113.

- **Best Alfresco Dining:** In Trastevere, Piazza Santa Maria comes alive at night. If you reserve a sidewalk table at **Sabatini,** Piazza Santa Maria in Trastevere 13 (© **06-5812026**), you'll have a view of all the action, including the floodlit golden mosaics of the church on the piazza, Santa Maria, in Trastevere. At the next table you're likely to see . . . well, just about anybody (on our most recent visit, Roman Polanski). In addition to the view, you can enjoy terrific grilled fish and Florentine steaks here. See p. 127.

- **Best for People-Watching:** Join the beautiful people—young actors, models, and artists from nearby Via Margutta—who descend at night on Piazza del Popolo. Young men with their silk shirts unbuttoned alight from sports cars to go on the prowl. At **Dal Bolognese,** Piazza del Popolo 1–2 (© **06-3611426**), not only can you take in this fascinating scene, but you'll also enjoy fine Bolognese cuisine as enticing as the people-watching; see p. 122. In the 1950s, Via Veneto was the place to be for Elizabeth Taylor, Frank Sinatra, and other Hollywood types. Today the celebs are long gone, and Via Veneto is more about overpriced tourist traps than genuine hip. But lots of folks like to stroll this strip anyway, or

enjoy the passing parade from a table at the **Café de Paris,** Via Vittorio Veneto 91 (© **06-4815631**). See p. 228.

- **Best for a Cappuccino with a View:** The best-located cafe in Rome is **Di Rienzo,** Piazza della Rotonda 8–9 (© **06-6869097**), which stands directly on Piazza della Rotonda, fronting the Pantheon. On a summer night, there's no better place to be than "the living room" of Rome, as the square before you has been dubbed, as you sit and slowly sip your cappuccino. See p. 230.

- **Best Picnic Fare:** When the weather is cool and the day is sunny, it's time for an alfresco meal. For the makings of a picnic, head for the **Campo de' Fiori** open-air market, between Corso Vittorio Emanuele II and the Tiber. The luscious produce of Lazio is on display here right in the heart of the old city. If you wish, you can purchase vegetables already chopped and ready to be dropped into the minestrone pot. There are also several excellent delicatessen shops on the square. Visit one of the shops selling freshly baked Roman bread, pick up a bottle of wine and a companion— and off you go. See p. 218.

- **Best for Celebrity-Spotting:** A chic choice is **Café Riccioli,** Piazza delle Coppelle 10A (© **06-68210313**), where you'll often spot models and other beautiful people having a light dinner of sashimi. See p. 117.

2

A Traveler's Guide to Roman Art & Architecture

by Reid Bramblett

The art of Rome ranges from Roman mosaics and Renaissance masterpieces by Michelangelo and Leonardo to baroque statues by Bernini and modern still lifes by Morandi. Its architecture is equally wide ranging, from Roman temples and Byzantine basilicas to Renaissance churches, baroque palaces, and postmodern stadiums that take their cues from the ancient Colosseum. This brief overview should help you make sense of it all.

1 Art 101

CLASSICAL: ETRUSCANS & ROMANS (6TH CENTURY B.C. TO 5TH CENTURY A.D.)

The **Etruscans,** who became Rome's pre-Republican Tarquin kings, arrived from Asia Minor with their own styles. By the 6th century B.C., however, they were borrowing heavily from the Greeks in their sculpture and importing thousands of Attic vases, which displayed the most popular and widespread painting style of ancient Greece.

Painting in ancient **Rome** was used primarily for decorative purposes. Bucolic *frescoes* (the technique of painting on wet plaster) adorned the walls of the wealthy. Rome's sculptures tended to glorify emperors and the perfect human form, copying ad nauseum from famous Greek originals.

Examples of classical art include:

- **Etruscan.** Etruscan artistic remains are confined to the Villa Giulia and Vatican Museums; the best is the Villa Giulia's terra-cotta sarcophagi covers of reclining figures. Some tomb paintings also survive at Tarquinia in northern Lazio.
- **Roman.** Along with an army of also-ran statues and busts gracing most archaeological collections in Italy, you'll find a few standouts: the marble *bas-reliefs* (sculptures that project slightly from a flat surface) on the Arch of Constantine; the sculptures, mosaics, and remarkable fresco collections at the various branches of the Museo Nazionale Romano; and such sculptures as the gilded equestrian statue of Marcus Aurelius and *The Dying Gaul* at the Capitoline Museum. The reliefs on the Ara Pacis are a great example of 1st-century A.D. art as imperial propaganda.

BYZANTINE & ROMANESQUE (5TH TO 13TH CENTURIES)

Artistic expression in the Dark Ages and early medieval Rome was largely church related. Because Mass was recited in Latin, images were used to communicate the Bible's most important lessons to the illiterate masses. Bas-reliefs around the churches' main doors, along with wall paintings and altarpieces inside, told key tales to inspire faith in God and fear of sin (*Last Judgment*s were favorites). Otherwise, decoration was spare, and what little existed was often destroyed, replaced, or covered over the centuries as tastes changed and cathedrals were remodeled.

The **Byzantine** style of painting and mosaic was very stylized and static. The iconographic tradition was imported from the eastern half of the Roman Empire centered at Byzantium (the empire's major political outposts in Italy were Ravenna and Venice). Faces (and eyes) were almond-shaped with pointy little chins, noses were long with a spoonlike depression at the top, and folds in robes (always blue over red) were represented by stylized cross-hatching in gold leaf.

Romanesque sculpture was somewhat more fluid but still far from naturalistic. Often wonderfully childlike in its narrative simplicity, the work frequently mixed biblical scenes with the myths and motifs of local pagan traditions that were being slowly incorporated into early medieval Christianity. Romanesque art was seen as crude in most later periods and, as such, was usually replaced or destroyed over the centuries; it survives mostly in scraps.

Good examples of this era include:

- **Byzantine mosaics.** The oldest paleo-Christian mosaics (5th–7th centuries) are in Santa Maria Maggiore, Santa Sabina (which also preserves remarkable 5th-century wood doors carved with biblical reliefs), and San Giovanni in Laterano's San Venanzio and Santa Rufina chapels (the main church's apse mosaic is 13th c.). Later Byzantine and Romanesque mosaics decorate Santa Maria d'Aracoeli, San Clemente Basilica, and San Paolo Fuori le Mura.
- **Romanesque painting.** San Clemente Basilica's lower church has some of the few remaining early medieval paintings in Rome.
- **National Museum of Palazzo Venezia.** Here you'll find Rome's best collection of medieval art, including the oldest painted wood statue (13th c.), numerous Byzantine crosses, ivories, and an unusual enameled metal *Christ* (13th c.).

INTERNATIONAL GOTHIC (LATE 13TH TO EARLY 15TH CENTURIES)

Late medieval Italian art continued to be largely ecclesiastical. In both Gothic painting and sculpture, figures tended to be more natural than in the Romanesque (and the colors in paintings more varied and rich) but remained highly stylized. The figures' features and gestures are exaggerated for symbolic or emotional emphasis. In painting especially, late-Gothic artists such as Giotto started introducing greater realism, a sense of depth, and more realistic emotion into their art—characteristics that would later define the Renaissance. However, when the pope fled Rome for Avignon, France, in 1308, the Eternal City became a provincial town, and art languished.

The best Gothic artists with work in Rome include:

- **Giotto** (1266–1337). The greatest Gothic artist, Giotto lifted painting from its Byzantine funk and set it on the road to the realism and perspective of the Renaissance. His best works are fresco cycles in Assisi, Padua, and Florence, but in Rome you can see the *Stefaneschi Triptych* (1315) in the Vatican Pinacoteca.
- **Pietro Cavallini** (1250–1330). He designed the *Life of the Virgin* apse mosaics in Santa Maria in Trastevere, but his only painting to survive is the top half of a *Last Judgment* (1295–1300) on the entrance wall of Santa Cecilia in Trastevere (you have to make an appointment to see it).
- **Arnolfo di Cambio** (1245–1302). This Tuscan sculptor and architect left a venerated bronze *St. Peter* in St. Peter's Basilica.

RENAISSANCE (EARLY 15TH TO MID–17TH CENTURIES)

From the 14th to 16th centuries, the popularity of the Humanist movement in philosophy prompted princes and powerful prelates to patronize a generation of innovative young artists. These painters, sculptors, and architects experimented with new modes in art and broke with static medieval traditions to pursue a greater degree of expressiveness and naturalism, using such techniques as linear perspective. The term *Renaissance,* or "rebirth," was only later applied to this period in Italy (from where it spread to the rest of Europe).

This list of Renaissance giants merely scratches the surface of the masters Italy gave rise to in the 15th and 16th centuries:

- **Fra Angelico** (1400–55). This Tuscan monk and early master was invited to Rome by the pope to paint the Vatican's Nicholas V chapel (1448–50).

- **Leonardo da Vinci** (1452–1519). A true "Renaissance man," Leonardo used his genius to experiment in a range of disciplines, from art to philosophy to science (on paper, he even designed machine guns and rudimentary helicopters). Little of his remarkable painting survives, however, because he often used new pigment mixes that proved to lack the staying power of traditional materials. Leonardo invented such painterly effects as the fine haze of *sfumato,* which softens outlines and progressively blurs background landscapes and objects to create a sense of realism and vast distance within the painting. Unfortunately, nothing in Rome shows this; the only major Leonardo here is an unfinished *St. Jerome* in the Vatican Pinacoteca.

- **Raphael** (1483–1520). Rightfully considered one of Western art's greatest draftsmen, Raphael produced a body of work in his short lifetime (he died at 37) that influenced European painters for generations to come. You'll find his ethereal *Transfiguration* (1520), almost finished when he died, in the Vatican Museums. Also in the Vatican are perhaps his greatest works, a series of frescoed rooms (1508–20) including the *School of Athens,* at once a celebration of Renaissance artistic precepts, the classical philosophers whose rediscovery spurred on the Renaissance, and Raphael's contemporaries (the various "philosophers" are actually portraits of Leonardo, Michelangelo, Raphael himself, and Bramante, an architect).

- **Michelangelo** (1475–1564). The heavyweight contender for the title of world's greatest artist, Michelangelo was a genius in sculpture, painting, architecture, and poetry. His work marked the apogee of the Renaissance. A complex, difficult man—intensely jealous, probably manic-depressive, and certainly homosexual—Michelangelo enjoyed great fame in a life plagued by a series of never-ending projects commissioned by the Medici in Florence and Pope Julius II in Rome—the Sistine Chapel frescoes (ceiling 1508–12;) *Last Judgment* (1535–41), and the tomb of Julius II, of which he finished only the powerful *Moses* (1513–15) in San Pietro in Vincoli and some *Slaves* in Florence. He sculpted the *Pietà* (1500) in St. Peter's at age 25.

  Michelangelo worshiped the male nude as the ultimate form and twisted the bodies of his figures (art historians call this *torsion*) in different, often contradictory directions (a positioning called *contraposto*) to bring out their musculature. When forced against his will to paint the Sistine Chapel, he broke almost all the rules and sent painting headlong in an entirely new direction—called mannerism—marked by nonprimary colors, impressionistic shapes of light, and twisting muscular figures.

BAROQUE & ROCOCO (LATE 16TH TO 18TH CENTURIES)

The **baroque,** a more theatrical and decorative take on the Renaissance, mixes a kind of super-realism based on using peasants as models and an exaggerated use of light and dark, called *chiaroscuro,* with compositional complexity and explosions of dynamic fury, movement, color, and figures. **Rococo** is this later baroque art gone awry, frothy and chaotic.

The baroque period produced many fine artists but only a few true geniuses, including:

- **Caravaggio** (1571–1610). Caravaggio started as a street urchin, rose to fame through the graces of a Borghese cardinal, became an honorary Knight of Malta, and ended his life on the run from murder charges in Rome. In between, he reinvented baroque painting, using peasants and commoners as models and including their earthy realism (dirty bare feet were a favorite) in his works. He added his chiaroscuro technique of playing areas of harsh light off deep, black shadows (which helps explain the deeply wrinkled faces he loved to paint). Among his masterpieces are the *St. Matthew* (1599) cycle in San Luigi dei Francesi, a series of paintings in the Galleria Borghese and Palazzo Corsini, and the *Deposition* (1604) in the Vatican Museums.

- **Pietro da Cortona** (1596–1669). This Tuscan painter moved to Rome and became the progenitor of a fluffy, pastel baroque style, which he used to decorate the ceilings of Palazzo Barberini with an allegorical *Glorification of the Reign of Urban VIII* (1635).

- **Bernini** (1598–1680). Bernini was the greatest baroque sculptor, a fantastic architect, and no mean painter. Among his finest sculptures are several in the Galleria Borghese: his youthful *Aeneas and Anchises* (1613), *Apollo and Daphne* (1624), *The Rape of Persephone* (1621), and *David* (1623–24)—the last a resounding baroque man of action rather than a Renaissance man of contemplation like Michelangelo's famous *David* in Florence. His other masterpiece is the *Fountain of the Four Rivers* (1651) in Piazza Navona.

LATE 18TH TO 20TH CENTURIES

After carrying the banner of artistic innovation for more than a millennium, Italy ran out of steam with the baroque. Nevertheless, the country did produce a few fine **neoclassical** sculptures in the late 18th century.

Italy did not play an important role in late-19th- or 20th-century art, although a few great artists did emerge. In 1909 Italian artists living in Paris made a spirited attempt to take the artistic initiative back into Italian hands, but what the **Futurist** movement's **Umberto Boccioni** (1882–1916) came up with was largely cubism—the "fractured" style, made famous by Picasso, in which objects are depicted from several perspectives at once—with an element of movement added in. **Gino Severini** (1883–1966) contributed a sophisticated take on color that rubbed off on the core cubists. You can see work by both artists in the National Gallery of Modern Art.

The greatest Italian artists of the modern era include:

- **Antonio Canova** (1757–1822). Italy's top neoclassical sculptor, Canova was popular for his mythological figures and Bonaparte portraits (he even sculpted both Napoleon and his sister Pauline as nudes). You'll find his work in the Galleria Borghese.

- **Amadeo Modigliani** (1884–1920). A sickly boy, and only moderately successful in his short lifetime, Modigliani helped reinvent the portrait in painting and sculpture after he moved to Paris in 1906. He's known for his mysterious, elongated heads and rapidly painted nudes. Check them out at the National Gallery of Modern Art.
- **Giorgio de Chirico** (1888–1978). De Chirico founded freaky *pittura metafisica* (metaphysical painting), a forerunner of surrealism wherein figures and objects are stripped of their usual meaning though odd juxtapositions, warped perspective, unnatural shadows and other bizarre effects, and a general spatial emptiness. Look for them in the National Gallery of Modern Art and the Collection of Modern Religious Art in the Vatican Museums.
- **Giorgio Morandi** (1890–1964). In the painting of his eerily minimalist, highly modeled, quasi-monochrome still lifes, Morandi was influenced by *pittura metafisica*. His paintings decorate the National Gallery of Modern Art and the Collection of Modern Religious Art in the Vatican Museums.

2 Italian Architecture at a Glance

Keep a couple of points in mind when considering a building's style, particularly for structures built before the 20th century. First, very few buildings (especially churches) were actually built in only one style. Massive, expensive structures often took centuries to complete, during which time tastes changed and plans were altered. Second, while each architectural era has its own distinctive features, some elements, general floor plans, and terms are common to many; features might appear near the end of one era and continue through several later ones.

From the Romanesque period on, most churches (see "Church Floor Plan" illustration) consist of either a single wide **aisle** or a wide central **nave** flanked by two narrow aisles. The aisles are separated from the nave by a row of **columns** or by square stacks of masonry called **piers,** usually connected by **arches.**

Church Floor Plan

This main nave/aisle assemblage is usually crossed by a perpendicular corridor called a **transept** near the far east end of the church so that the floor plan looks like a **Latin cross** (shaped like a crucifix). The shorter, east arm of the nave is the holiest area, called the **chancel;** it often houses the stalls of the **choir** and the **altar.** If the far end of the chancel is rounded off, it's called an **apse.** An **ambulatory** is a curving corridor outside the altar and choir area, separating it from the ring of smaller chapels radiating off the chancel and apse.

Some churches, especially after the Renaissance, when mathematical proportion became important, were built on a **Greek cross** plan, with each axis the same length, like a giant +. By the baroque, funky shapes became popular, with churches built in the round or as ellipses, for example.

CLASSICAL (6TH CENTURY B.C. TO 4TH CENTURY A.D.)

The **Romans** made use of certain **Greek** innovations, particularly architectural ideas. The first to be adopted was *post-and-lintel construction* (essentially, a weight-bearing frame, like a door). Inventive engineers, the Romans then added the load-bearing arch and also developed hoisting mechanisms and a specially trained workforce.

Identifiable features of classical architecture include:

- **Classical orders** (see illustration). The orders are most easily recognized by their column capitals, with the least ornate capital used on a building's ground level and the most ornate used on the top: Doric (a plain capital), Ionic (a capital with a scroll), and Corinthian (a capital with flowering acanthus leaves).

Corinthian Order   Ionic Order   Doric Order

Classical Orders

- **Brick and concrete.** Although marble is traditionally associated with Roman architecture, Roman engineers could also do wonders with bricks or even simple concrete—concrete seating made possible such enormous theaters as Rome's 6-acre, 45,000-seat Colosseum.

Roman architecture includes the sports stadium of the **Colosseum** (1st century A.D.; see illustration), which perfectly displays the use of the classical orders; Hadrian's marvel of engineering, the temple of the **Pantheon** (1st century A.D.); and the public brick **Baths of Caracalla** (3rd century A.D.).

Colosseum

Another good example is the **Basilica of Constantine and Maxentius** in the Roman Forum (4th century A.D.). Roman **basilica** served as law courts. They were rectangular in shape and contained a wide nave, two rows of columns supporting arches, and an apse at one or both ends; the style was adopted by early Christians for their first grand churches.

Rome's ancient seaport, **Ostia Antica,** has been preserved with its street plan and even some virtually intact buildings.

ROMANESQUE & GOTHIC (7TH TO 15TH CENTURIES)

The **Romanesque** took its inspiration and rounded arches from ancient Rome (hence the name). The first major churches in Rome were built on the basilica plan of Roman law courts. Architects constructed large churches with wide aisles to accommodate the masses who came to hear the priests say Mass but who were largely there to worship at the altars of various saints. To support the weight of all that masonry, the walls had to be thick and solid (meaning they could be pierced by few and rather small windows) and supported by huge piers, giving Romanesque churches a dark, somber, mysterious, and often oppressive feeling.

Flying Buttress

By the late 12th century, the development of the pointed arch and exterior *flying buttress* (see "Cross-Section of Gothic Church" illustration) freed architecture from the heavy, thick walls of Romanesque structures and allowed ceilings to soar, walls to thin, and windows to proliferate in the **Gothic** style, of which there's only one surviving example in Rome.

Cross-Section of Gothic Church

Identifiable Romanesque features include:

- Rounded arches. These load-bearing architectural devices allowed architects to open up wide naves and spaces, channeling all the weight of the stone walls and ceiling across the curve of the arch and down into the ground via the columns or pilasters.
- Thick walls.
- Infrequent and small windows.
- Huge piers.

The great early basilicas, each at least partly altered in decor over the ages, include **Santa Maria Maggiore, San Giovanni in Laterano,** and **San Paolo Fuori le Mure.** Other less grand Romanesque churches include **Santa Maria in Cosmedin** (see illustration) and **Santa Sabina.**

Santa Maria Sopra Minerva is Rome's only **Gothic** church, all pointy arches and soaring ceilings. (However, because it is hemmed in by other buildings, its interior is atypically dark.)

Santa Maria in Cosmedin

RENAISSANCE (15TH TO 17TH CENTURIES)

As in painting, Renaissance architectural rules stressed proportion, order, classical inspiration, and mathematical precision to create unified, balanced structures.

Some identifiable Renaissance features include:

- A sense of proportion
- A reliance on symmetry
- The use of classical orders

Bramante (1444–1514) was perhaps the most mathematical and classically precise of the early High Renaissance architects. This is evident in his (much altered) plans for **St. Peter's Basilica** (his spiral staircase in the Vatican has survived untouched) and his jewel of perfect Renaissance architecture, the textbook **Tempietto** (1502; see illustration) at San Pietro in Montorio on the slopes of Rome's Gianicolo Hill, where Christians once believed St. Peter had been crucified (as a plus, the little crypt inside is a riotous rococo grotto).

Tempietto

Renaissance man **Michelangelo** took up architecture later in life, designing the **dome atop St. Peter's Basilica;** the sloping approach, 12-pointed star courtyard, and trio of palace facades that together make up **Piazza del Campidoglio,** atop the Capitoline Hill; and the facade of the **Palazzo Farnese** (1566), which was otherwise built by **Antonio da Sangallo** (1483–1546).

Baldassare Peruzzi (1481–1537) designed the lovely **Villa Farnesina** (1508–11; he also painted a tromp l'oeil fresco in an upstairs room).

Vignola's (1507–73) monumental barrel-vaulted **Chiesa del Gesù** (1568–75), with its graceful facade by **Giacomo della Porta** (1533–1602), became a Catholic Counter-Reformation model for churches throughout Europe.

BAROQUE & ROCOCO (17TH TO 18TH CENTURIES)

More than any other movement, the **baroque** aimed toward a seamless meshing of architecture and art. The stuccoes, sculptures, and paintings were all carefully designed to complement one another—and the space itself—to create a unified whole. This effect was both aesthetic and narrative, with the various art forms all working together to tell a single biblical story (or often to subtly relate the deeds of the commissioning patron to great historic or biblical events). Excessively complex and dripping with decorative tidbits, **rococo** is baroque gone awry.

Some identifiable baroque features include:

- **Classical architecture rewritten with curves.** The baroque is similar to the Renaissance, but many of the right angles and ruler-straight lines are exchanged for curves of complex geometry and an interplay of concave and convex surfaces. The overall effect is to lighten the appearance of structures and to add movement of line and vibrancy to the static look of the classical Renaissance.
- **Complex decoration.** Unlike the sometimes severe and austere designs of the Renaissance, the baroque was playful. Architects festooned structures and encrusted interiors with an excess of decorations intended to liven things up—lots

of ornate stuccowork, pouty cherubs, airy frescoes, heavy gilding, twisting columns, multicolored marbles, and general frippery.

- **Multiplying forms.** The baroque asked, "Why make do with one column when you can stack a half-dozen partial columns on top of each other, slightly offset?" The baroque loved to pile up its forms and elements to create a rich, busy effect, breaking a pediment curve into segments so that each would protrude farther out than the last, or building up an architectural feature by stacking short sections of concave walls, each one curving to a different arc.

The baroque flourished across Italy, but some of the best examples include **Sant'Ivo alla Sapienza** (1640s) by **Borromini** (1599–1667), with its interplay of concave and convex ovals, interlocking truncated triangles, and an elliptical ramplike dome that looks like soft-serve ice cream (as scooped by a mathematician).

Though relatively sedate, **St. Peter's** facade by **Carlo Maderno** (ca. 1556–1629) and sweeping elliptical colonnade by **Bernini** make for one of Italy's most famous baroque assemblages. The two also collaborated (along with Borromini) on the **Palazzo Barberini** (1620–30s). The painter **Pietro da Cortona** designed the distinctive semicircular portico on **Santa Maria della Pace** (1656–57).

For the rococo—more a decorative than architectural movement—look no farther than the **Spanish Steps** (1726), by architect **Francesco de Sanctis** (1693–1740), or the **Trevi Fountain** (1762; see illustration), by **Nicola Salvi** (1697–1751).

Trevi Fountain

NEOCLASSICAL TO MODERN (18TH TO 20TH CENTURIES)

As a backlash against the excesses of the baroque and rococo, by the middle of the 18th century, Italian architects began turning to the austere simplicity and grandeur of the Classical Age and inaugurated the **neoclassical** style. Their work was inspired by the rediscovery of Pompeii and other ancient sites.

From the 19th century through the 20th century, Italian architects constructed buildings in a variety of styles. Italy's take on the early-20th-century Art Nouveau movement was called **Liberty** style. Mussolini made a spirited attempt to bring back ancient Rome in what can only be called **fascist** architecture. Since then, Italy, like the rest of the world, has mostly erected concrete and glass skyscrapers.

Some identifiable features for each of these movements include:

- **Neoclassical.** The classical ideals of mathematical proportion and symmetry, first rediscovered during the Renaissance, are the hallmark of every classically styled era. Neoclassicists reinterpreted ancient temples as buildings with massive colonnaded porticos.

- **Liberty.** Like Art Nouveau practitioners in other countries, Italian artists rebelled against the era of mass production and stressed the uniqueness of craft. They created asymmetrical, curvaceous designs based on organic inspiration (plants and flowers) and used such materials as wrought iron, stained glass, tile, and hand-painted wallpaper.

- **Fascist.** Deco meets Caesar. This period produced monumentally imposing and chillingly stark white marble structures surrounded by classical statuary.

Of the **neoclassical**, the **Vittorio Emanuele Monument** (see illustration), which has been compared to a wedding cake and a Victorian typewriter, was Italy's main monument to reaching its Risorgimento goal of a unified Italy.

Liberty style never produced any surpassingly important buildings, although you can glimpse it occasionally in period storefronts.

Fascist architecture still infests all corners of Rome (although most of the Right Wing reliefs and the repeated engravings of "DVCE"—Mussolini's nickname for himself—have long since been chipped out). You can see it at its, er, best in Rome's planned satellite community called **EUR** (including a multistory "square Colosseum" so funky it has been featured in many films and music videos) and the **Stadio Olimpico** complex.

The **mid–20th century** was dominated by **Pier Luigi Nervi** (1891–1979) and his reinforced concrete buildings, including the **Palazzeto dello Sport** stadium (1960).

Vittorio Emanuele Monument

3

Planning Your Trip to Rome

This chapter is devoted to the where, when, and how of your trip—the advance planning required to get it together and take it on the road. A little planning will help you steer clear of disappointment and stay open to unanticipated pleasures.

1 Visitor Information

For information before you go, contact the Italian Government Tourist Board.

In the United States: 630 Fifth Ave., Suite 1565, New York, NY 10111 (© **212/245-4822;** fax 212/586-9249); 500 N. Michigan Ave., Suite 2240, Chicago, IL 60611 (© **312/644-0996;** fax 312/644-3019); and 12400 Wilshire Blvd., Suite 550, Los Angeles, CA 90025 (© **310/820-1898;** fax 310/820-6357).

In Canada: 175 Bloor St. E., South Tower, Suite 907, Toronto, ON, M4W 3R8 (© **416/925-4882;** fax 416/925-4799).

In the United Kingdom: 1 Princes St., London W1R 8AY (© **020/7408-1254;** fax 020/7399-3567).

On the Web, the Italian National Tourist Board sponsors the sites **www.italiantourism.com** and **www.enit.it**.

For information on the **Vatican,** check out **www.vatican.va**.

In Italy, www.initaly.com not only contains solid information on Italy and Rome presented in a very personal and friendly way, but it also has one of the best sets of links to other Italy-related sites on the Web.

Another good site, **www.enjoyrome. com**, contains information about walking tours, accommodations, restaurants, side trips from Rome, useful links, and maps. Other helpful sites are **www.roma turismo.com** and **www.romeguide.it**.

2 Entry Requirements & Customs Regulations

ENTRY REQUIREMENTS

U.S., Canadian, U.K., Irish, Australian, and New Zealand citizens with a **valid passport** don't need a visa to enter Italy if they don't expect to stay more than 90 days and don't expect to work there. If after entering Italy you want to stay more than 90 days, you can apply for a permit for an extra 90 days, which, as a rule, is granted immediately. Go to the nearest *questura* (police headquarters) or to your home country's consulate. If your passport is lost or stolen, head to your consulate as soon as possible for a replacement.

For information on how to get a passport, go to the "Fast Facts" section of chapter 5—the websites listed provide downloadable passport applications as well as the current fees for processing passport applications. For an up-to-date country-by-country listing of passport requirements around the world, go to the "Foreign Entry Requirement" Web page of the U.S. State Department at **http:// travel.state.gov**.

Traveling with Minors

It's always wise to have plenty of documentation when traveling in today's world with children. For changing details on entry requirements for children traveling abroad, keep up to date by going to the U.S. State Department website: http://travel.state.gov/foreignentryreqs.html.

To prevent international child abduction, E.U. governments have initiated procedures at entry and exit points. These often (but not always) include requiring documentary evidence of your relationship with your child and permission for the child's travel from the parent or legal guardian not present. Having such documentation on hand, even if not required, facilitates entries and exits. All children must have their own passport. To obtain a passport, the child must be present—that is, in person—at the center issuing the passport. Both parents must be present as well. If not, then a notarized statement from the parents is required.

Any questions parents or guardians might have can be answered by calling the National Passport Information Center at © **877/487-6868** Monday to Friday 8am to 8pm Eastern Standard Time.

CUSTOMS REGULATIONS

WHAT YOU CAN BRING INTO ITALY Foreign visitors can bring along most items for personal use duty-free, including fishing tackle, a pair of skis, two tennis racquets, a baby carriage, two hand cameras with 10 rolls of film, and 400 cigarettes or a quantity of cigars or pipe tobacco not exceeding 500 grams (1.1 lb.). There are strict limits on importing alcoholic beverages. However, for alcohol bought tax-paid, limits are much more liberal than in other countries of the European Union.

There are no restrictions on the amount of local currency you can bring into Italy, although you should declare the amount. Your declaration proves to the Italian Customs office that the currency came from outside the country, and, therefore, you can take out the same amount or less. Foreign currency taken into or out of Italy may not exceed 12,500€ ($15,000). No declaration is needed up to this amount.

WHAT YOU CAN BRING HOME Rules governing what you can bring back duty-free vary from country to country and are subject to change, but they're generally posted on the Web.

Returning **U.S. citizens** who have been away for at least 48 hours are allowed to bring back, once every 30 days, $800 worth of merchandise duty-free. You'll be charged a flat rate of 4% duty on the next $1,000 worth of purchases. Any dollar amount beyond that is dutiable at whatever rates apply. On mailed gifts, the duty-free limit is $200. Be sure to have your receipts or purchases handy to expedite the declaration process. *Note:* If you owe duty, you are required to pay upon your arrival in the United States, by either cash, personal check, government or traveler's check, or money order, and, in some locations, a Visa or MasterCard.

With some exceptions, you cannot bring fresh fruits and vegetables into the United States. For specifics on what you can bring back, download the invaluable free pamphlet *Know Before You Go* online at **www.cbp.gov**. (Click on "Travel" and then on "Know Before You Go.") Or request the pamphlet from the **U.S. Customs & Border Protection (CBP)**, 1300

Pennsylvania Ave., NW, Washington, DC 20229 (© **877/287-8667**).

For a clear summary of **Canadian** rules, ask for the booklet *I Declare,* issued by the **Canada Border Services Agency** (© **800/461-9999** in Canada, or 204/983-3500; www.cbsa-adrc.gc.ca). Canada allows its citizens a C$750 exemption, and you're allowed to bring back duty-free 1 carton of cigarettes, 1 can of tobacco, 40 imperial ounces of liquor, and 50 cigars. In addition, you're allowed to mail gifts to Canada valued at less than C$60 a day, provided they're unsolicited and don't contain alcohol or tobacco (write on the package "Unsolicited gift, under C$60 value"). All valuables should be declared on the Y-38 form before departure from Canada, including serial numbers of valuables you already own, such as expensive foreign cameras. *Note:* The C$750 exemption can be used only once a year and only after an absence of 7 days.

Citizens of the U.K. who are **returning from a European Union (E.U.) country** will go through a separate Customs exit (called the "Blue Exit") especially for E.U. travelers. In essence, there is no limit on what you can bring back from an E.U. country, as long as the items are for personal use (this includes gifts) and you have already paid the necessary duty and tax. However, Customs law sets out guidance levels. If you bring in more than these levels, you may be asked to prove that the goods are for your own use. Guidance levels on goods bought in the E.U. for your own use are

3,200 cigarettes, 200 cigars, 400 cigarillos, 3 kilograms of smoking tobacco, 10 liters of spirits, 90 liters of wine, 20 liters of fortified wine (such as port or sherry), and 110 liters of beer.

The duty-free allowance in **Australia** is A$900 or, for those under 18, A$450. Citizens can bring in 250 cigarettes or 250 grams of loose tobacco, and 2.25 liters of alcohol. If you're returning with valuables you already own, such as foreign-made cameras, you should file Form B263. A helpful brochure available from Australian consulates or Customs offices is *Know Before You Go.* For more information, call the **Australian Customs Service** at © **1300/363-263,** or log on to www.customs.gov.au.

The duty-free allowance for **New Zealand** is NZ$700. Citizens over 17 can bring in 200 cigarettes, 50 cigars, or 250 grams of tobacco (or a mixture of all three if their combined weight doesn't exceed 250g), plus 4.5 liters of wine and beer, or 1.125 liters of liquor. New Zealand currency does not carry import or export restrictions. Fill out a certificate of export, listing the valuables you are taking out of the country; that way, you can bring them back without paying duty. Most questions are answered in a free pamphlet available at New Zealand consulates and Customs offices: *New Zealand Customs Guide for Travellers, Notice no. 4.* For more information, contact **New Zealand Customs Service,** The Customhouse, 17–21 Whitmore St., Box 2218, Wellington (© **04/473-6099** or 0800/428-786; www.customs.govt.nz).

3 Money

CURRENCY

The Italian lire disappeared into history on March 1, 2002, replaced by the **euro,** the single European currency, whose official abbreviation is "EUR." Exchange rates of participating countries are locked into a common currency fluctuating against the dollar.

For more details on the euro, check out **www.europa.eu.int/euro.**

Foreign Currencies vs. the U.S. Dollar

Conversion ratios between the U.S. dollar and other currencies fluctuate, and their differences could affect the relative costs of your holiday. The rounded-off figures in the currency chart below were valid at the time of this writing, but they might not be valid by the time of your departure. This chart would be useful for conversions of small amounts of money, but if you're planning on any major transactions, check for more updated rates prior to making any serious commitments.

The U.S. Dollar and the Euro. One U.S. Dollar was worth approximately .83€ at the time of this writing. Inversely stated, that means that 1€ was worth approximately US$1.20.

The British pound, the U.S. Dollar, and the Euro. At press time, £1 equaled approximately US$1.71, or approximately 1.46€

The Canadian dollar, the U.S. Dollar, and the Euro. At press time, C$1 equaled approximately US85¢, or approximately .72€.

Euro €	US$	UK£	C$	Euro €	US$	UK£	C$
1.00	1.20	0.68	1.38	75	90.00	51	103.50
2.00	2.40	1.36	2.76	100	120.00	68.00	138.00
3.00	3.60	2.04	4.14	125	150.00	85.00	172.50
4.00	4.80	2.72	5.52	150	180.00	102.00	207.00
5.00	6.00	3.40	6.90	175	210.00	119.00	241.50
6.00	7.20	4.08	8.28	200	240.00	136.00	276.00
7.00	8.40	4.76	9.66	225	270.00	153.00	310.50
8.00	9.60	5.44	11.04	250	300.00	170.00	345.00
9.00	10.80	6.12	12.42	275	330.00	187.00	379.50
10.00	12.00	6.80	13.80	300	360.00	204.00	414.00
15.00	18.00	10.20	20.70	350	420.00	238.00	483.00
20.00	24.00	13.60	27.60	400	480.00	272.00	552.00
25.00	30.00	17.00	34.50	500	600.00	340.00	690.00
50.00	60.00	34.00	69.00	1,000	1200.00	680.00	1,380.00

EXCHANGING MONEY

Exchange rates are more favorable at the point of arrival. Nevertheless, it's often helpful to exchange at least some money before going abroad (standing in line at the *cambio* [exchange bureau] in the Rome airport could make you miss the next bus leaving for downtown). Check with any of your local American Express or Thomas Cook offices or major banks. Or, order euros in advance from American Express (© 800/673-3782; www.americanexpress.com) or **Thomas Cook** (© 800/223-7373; www.thomas cook.com).

It's best to exchange currency or traveler's checks at a bank, not a *cambio*, hotel, or shop. Currency and traveler's checks (for which you'll receive a better rate than cash) can be changed at all principal airports and at some travel agencies, such as American Express and Thomas

Cook. Note the rates and inquire about commission fees; it can sometimes pay to shop around.

ATMS

The easiest and best way to get cash away from home is from an ATM (automated teller machine), called a Bancomat in Italy. The **Cirrus** (© **800/424-7787;** www.mastercard.com) and **PLUS** (© **800/843-7587;** www.visa.com) networks span the globe; look at the back of your bank card to see which network you're on, then call or check online for ATM locations at your destination. Be sure you know your personal identification number (PIN) before you leave home and be sure to find out your daily withdrawal limit before you depart. Also keep in mind that many banks impose a fee every time a card is used at a different bank's ATM, and that fee can be higher for international transactions (up to $5 or more) than for domestic ones (where they're rarely more than $1.50). On top of this, the bank from which you withdraw cash may charge its own fee. To compare banks' ATM fees within the U.S., use www.bankrate.com. For international withdrawal fees, ask your bank.

You can also get cash advances on your credit card at an ATM. Keep in mind that credit card companies try to protect themselves from theft by limiting the funds someone can withdraw outside the home country, so call your credit card company before you leave home. And keep in mind that you'll pay interest from the moment of your withdrawal, even if you pay your monthly bills on time.

TRAVELER'S CHECKS

Traveler's checks seem less necessary these days because most Italian cities and towns have 24-hour ATMs, allowing you to withdraw small amounts of cash as needed. But if you prefer the security of the tried and true, you might want to stick with traveler's checks—provided that you don't mind showing an ID every time you want to cash a check.

You can buy traveler's checks at most banks. They are offered in denominations of $20, $50, $100, $500, and sometimes $1,000. Generally, you'll pay a service charge ranging from 1% to 4%.

The most popular traveler's checks are offered by **American Express** (© **800/807-6233,** or 800/221-7282 for card holders—this number accepts collect calls, offers service in several foreign languages, and exempts Amex gold and platinum cardholders from the 1% fee); **Visa** (© **800/732-1322**)—AAA members can obtain Visa checks for a $9.95 fee (for checks up to $1,500) at most AAA offices or by calling © **866/339-3378;** and **MasterCard** (© **800/223-9920**).

American Express, Thomas Cook, Visa, and **MasterCard** offer **foreign currency traveler's checks,** which are useful if you're traveling to one country, or to the Euro zone; they're accepted at locations where dollar checks may not be.

⌒Tips **Easy Money**

You'll avoid lines at airport ATMs by exchanging at least some money—just enough to cover airport incidentals and transportation to your hotel—before you leave home.

When you change money, ask for some small bills or loose change. Petty cash will come in handy for tipping and public transportation. Consider keeping the change separate from your larger bills, so that it's readily accessible and you'll be less of a target for theft.

> **(Tips** **Dear Visa: I'm off to Rome!**
>
> Some credit card companies recommend that you notify them of any imp_ _ ing trip abroad so that they don't become suspicious when the card is us_ numerous times in a foreign destination and block your charges. Even if you don't call your credit card company in advance, you can always call the card's toll-free emergency number (see "Fast Facts," in chapter 5) if a charge is refused—a good reason to carry the phone number with you. But perhaps the most important lesson here is to carry more than one card with you on your trip; a card might not work for any number of reasons, so having a backup is the smart way to go.

If you carry traveler's checks, keep a record of their serial numbers separate from your checks in the event that they are stolen or lost. You'll get a refund faster if you know the numbers.

CREDIT CARDS

Credit cards are a safe way to carry money. They also provide a convenient record of all your expenses, and they generally offer relatively good exchange rates. You can also withdraw cash advances from your credit cards at banks or ATMs, provided you know your PIN. If you've forgotten yours, or didn't even know you had one, call the number on the back of your credit card and ask the bank to send it to you. It usually takes 5 to 7 business days, though some banks will provide the number over the phone if you tell them your mother's maiden name or some other personal information. Keep in mind that when you use your credit card abroad, most banks assess a 2% fee above the 1% fee charged by Visa, MasterCard, or American Express for currency conversion on credit charges. But credit cards still may be the smart way to go when you factor in things such as exorbitant ATM fees and higher traveler's check exchange rates (and service fees).

4 When to Go

April to June and **late September to October** are the best months for traveling in Italy—temperatures are usually mild and the crowds aren't quite so intense. Starting in mid-June, the summer rush really picks up, and from **July to mid-September** the country teems with visitors. **August** is the worst month: Not only does it get uncomfortably hot, muggy, and crowded, but the entire country goes on vacation at least from August 15 to the end of the month—and many Italians take off the entire month. Many hotels, restaurants, and shops are closed (except at the spas, beaches, and islands, which are where 70% of the Italians head). From **late October to Easter,** most attractions go on shorter winter hours or are closed for renovation. Many hotels and restaurants take a month or two off between **November and February,** spa and beach destinations become padlocked ghost towns, and it can get much colder than you'd expect (it might even snow).

WEATHER

It's warm all over Italy in summer; it can be very hot in Rome. The high temperatures begin in Rome in May, often lasting until sometime in October. In Rome the weather is warm year-round, averaging 50°F (10°C) in winter.

's drier in Italy
o high tempera-
d because the
e, temperatures
s, but nights are
omfortable.

The average high temperatures in central Italy and Rome are 82°F (28°C) in June, 87°F (31°C) in July, and 86°F (30°C) in August; the average lows are 63°F (17°C) in June and 67°F (19°C) in July and August.

Average Daily Temperature & Monthly Rainfall

	Jan	Feb	Mar	Apr	May	June	July	Aug	Sept	Oct	Nov	Dec
Temp. (°F)	49	52	57	62	72	82	87	86	73	65	56	47
Temp. (°C)	9	11	14	17	22	28	31	30	23	20	13	8
Rainfall (in.)	2.3	1.5	2.9	3.0	2.8	2.9	1.5	1.9	2.8	2.6	3.0	2.1

HOLIDAYS

Offices and shops in Italy are closed on the following **national holidays:** January 1 (New Year's Day), Easter Monday, April 25 (Liberation Day), May 1 (Labor Day), August 15 (Assumption of the Virgin), November 1 (All Saints' Day), December 8 (Feast of the Immaculate Conception), December 25 (Christmas Day), and December 26 (Santo Stefano).

Many offices and business also close on June 29, for the feast day of Sts. Peter and Paul, the city's patron saints.

ROME CALENDAR OF EVENTS

For major events in which tickets should be procured well before arriving, check with **Keith Prowse** in the United States at ℂ **800/669-8687;** www.keithprowse.com.

January

Epiphany celebrations, nationwide. All cities, towns, and villages in Italy stage Roman Catholic Epiphany observances. One of the most festive celebrations is the Epiphany Fair at Rome's Piazza Navona. Usually January 5 to 6.

Festa di Sant'Agnese, Sant'Agnese Fuori le Mura. During this ancient ceremony, two lambs are blessed and shorn, and their wool is used later for palliums (Roman Catholic vestments). Usually January 21.

February

Carnevale, Piazza Navona, Rome. This festival marks the last day of the children's market and lasts until dawn of the following day. Usually 3 days before Ash Wednesday.

March

Festa di Santa Francesca Romana, Piazzale del Colosseo near Santa Francesca Romana in the Roman Forum. A blessing of cars is performed at this festival. Usually March 9.

Festa di San Giuseppe, the Trionfale Quarter, north of the Vatican. The heavily decorated statue of the saint is brought out at a fair with food stalls, concerts, and sporting events. Usually March 19.

April

Holy Week observances. Processions and age-old ceremonies—some from pagan days, some from the Middle Ages—are staged throughout the country. The most notable procession is led by the pope, passing the Colosseum and the Roman Forum up to Palatine Hill; a torch-lit parade caps the observance. Beginning 4 days before Easter Sunday.

Easter Sunday (Pasqua). In an event broadcast around the world, the pope gives his blessing from the balcony of St. Peter's.

Festa della Primavera, Rome. The Spanish Steps are decked out with banks of azaleas and other flowers; later, orchestral and choral concerts are presented in Trinità dei Monti. Dates vary.

May

Concorso Ippico Internazionale (International Horse Show), Piazza di Siena in the Villa Borghese. Usually May. Call tourist office for information.

June

Son et Lumière. The Colosseum, the Roman Forum, and Tivoli areas are dramatically lit at night. Early June to end of September.

Festa di San Pietro, St. Peter's Basilica, Rome. This most significant Roman religious festival is observed with solemn rites. Usually around June 29.

July

Festa di Noantri. Trastevere, Rome's most colorful neighborhood, becomes a gigantic outdoor restaurant, with tables lining the streets, and merrymakers and musicians providing the entertainment. After reaching the quarter, find the first empty table and try to get a waiter—but keep a close eye on your valuables. For details, contact the **Ente Provinciale per il Turismo,** Via Parigi 11, 00185 Roma (✆ **06-36004399**). Mid-July.

August

Festa delle Catene, San Pietro in Vincoli. The chains of St. Peter are shown to the faithful during prayer. August 1.

Ferragosto. Beginning on August 15, most city residents not directly involved with the tourist trade take a 2-week vacation (many restaurants are closed as well). This is a good time *not* to be in Rome.

September

Sagra dell'Uva, Basilica of Maxentius, the Roman Forum. At this harvest festival, musicians in ancient costumes entertain, and grapes are sold at reduced prices. Dates vary, usually early September.

December

Christmas Blessing of the Pope. Delivered at noon from the balcony of St. Peter's Basilica, the pope's words are broadcast around the world. December 25.

5 Travel Insurance

Because Rome for most of us is far from home, and because a number of things can go wrong—lost luggage, a cancelled trip, or a medical emergency—consider taking out insurance.

Check your existing insurance policies and credit card coverage before you buy travel insurance. You may already be covered for lost luggage, cancelled tickets, or medical expenses. The cost of travel insurance varies widely, depending on the cost and length of your trip, your age, your health, and the type of trip you're taking, but expect to pay between 5% and 8% of the vacation itself. You can get estimates from various providers through **InsureMyTrip.com.** Enter your trip cost and dates, your age, and other information, for prices from more than a dozen companies.

TRIP-CANCELLATION INSURANCE Trip-cancellation insurance will help you get your money back if you have to back out of a trip, if you have to go home early, or if your travel supplier goes bankrupt. Allowed reasons for cancellation can range from sickness to natural disasters, to the State Department declaring your destination unsafe for travel.

Travel in the Age of Bankruptcy

Airlines go bankrupt, so protect yourself by **buying your tickets with a credit card.** The Fair Credit Billing Act guarantees that you can get your money back from the credit card company if a travel supplier goes under (and if you request the refund within 60 days of the bankruptcy). **Travel insurance** can also help, but make sure it covers against "carrier default" for your specific travel provider. And be aware that if a U.S. airline goes bust midtrip, a 2001 federal law requires other carriers to take you to your destination (albeit on a space-available basis) for a fee of no more than $25, provided you rebook within 60 days of the cancellation.

For more information, contact one of the following recommended insurers: **Access America** (✆ 866/807-3982; www.accessamerica.com); **Travel Guard International** (✆ 800/826-4919; www.travelguard.com); **Travel Insured International** (✆ 800/243-3174; www.travelinsured.com); or **Travelex Insurance Services** (✆ 888/457-4602; www.travelexinsurance.com).

MEDICAL INSURANCE For travel overseas, most health plans (including Medicare and Medicaid) do not provide coverage, and the ones that do often require you to pay for services up front and reimburse you only after you return home. Even if your plan does cover overseas treatment, most out-of-country hospitals make you pay your bills up front and send you a refund only after you've returned home and filed the necessary paperwork with your insurance company. As a safety net, you may want to buy travel medical insurance, particularly if you're traveling to a remote or high-risk area where emergency evacuation is a possible scenario. If you require additional medical insurance, try **MEDEX Assistance** (✆ 410/453-6300; www.medexassist.com) or **Travel Assistance International** (✆ 800/821-2828; www.travelassistance.com; for general information on services, call the company's **Worldwide Assistance Services, Inc.,** at ✆ 800/777-8710).

LOST-LUGGAGE INSURANCE On international flights (including U.S. portions of international trips), baggage coverage is limited to approximately $9.07 per pound, up to approximately $635 per checked bag. If you plan to check items more valuable than the standard liability, see if your valuables are covered by your homeowner's policy or get baggage insurance as part of your comprehensive travel-insurance package. Don't buy insurance at the airport, as it's usually overpriced. Be sure to take any valuables or irreplaceable items with you in your carry-on luggage, as many valuables (including books, money, and electronics) aren't covered by airline policies.

If your luggage is lost, immediately file a lost-luggage claim at the airport, detailing the luggage contents. For most airlines, you must report delayed, damaged, or lost baggage within 4 hours of arrival. The airlines are required to deliver luggage, once found, directly to your house or destination free.

6 Health & Safety

STAYING HEALTHY

In general, Rome is viewed as a fairly "safe" destination, although problems, of course, can and do occur anywhere. You don't need to get shots, most foods are safe, and the water in Rome is potable. If you're concerned, just order bottled water. It is easy to get a prescription filled, and Rome has English-speaking doctors at hospitals with well-trained medical staffs.

Vegetarians can go into almost any restaurant in Rome, even those specializing in meat and fish, and order a heaping plate of fresh antipasti made with fresh vegetables.

WHAT TO DO IF YOU GET SICK AWAY FROM HOME

If you worry about getting sick away from home, consider purchasing **medical travel insurance** and carry your ID card in your purse or wallet. In most cases, your existing health plan will provide the coverage you need. See "Medical Insurance," above, for more information.

Any foreign consulate can provide a list of area doctors who speak English. If you get sick, consider asking your hotel concierge to recommend a local doctor— even his or her own. You can also try the emergency room at a local hospital; many have walk-in clinics for emergency cases that are not life-threatening. You may not get immediate attention, but you won't pay the high price of an emergency room visit. We list hospitals and emergency numbers under "Fast Facts" in chapter 5.

If you suffer from a chronic illness, consult your doctor before your departure. For conditions such as epilepsy, diabetes, or heart problems, wear a **Medic Alert Identification Tag** (℗ 888/633-4298; www.medicalert.org), which will immediately alert doctors to your condition and give them access to your records through Medic Alert's 24-hour hot line.

Keep **prescription medications** in their original containers, and pack them in your carry-on luggage. Also bring along copies of your prescriptions in case you lose your pills or run out. Carry the generic name of prescription medicines, in case a local pharmacist is unfamiliar with the brand name.

And don't forget sunglasses and an extra pair of contact lenses or prescription glasses.

Contact the **International Association for Medical Assistance to Travelers** (**IAMAT;** ℗ **716/754-4883** or, in Canada, 416/652-0137; www.iamat.org) for tips on travel and health concerns in the countries you're visiting, and for lists of local, English-speaking doctors. The United States **Centers for Disease Control and Prevention** (℗ **800/311-3435;** www.cdc.gov) provides up-to-date information on health hazards by region or country and offers tips on food safety. The website **www.trip prep.com**, sponsored by a consortium of travel medicine practitioners, may also offer helpful advice on traveling abroad. You can find listings of reliable clinics overseas at the **International Society of Travel Medicine** (www.istm.org).

In Canada, contact **Health Canada** (℗ **613/957-2991;** www.hc-sc.gc.ca).

The following government websites offer up-to-date health-related travel advice.

- **Australia:** www.dfat.gov.au/travel
- **Canada:** www.hc-sc.gc.ca/index_e. html
- **U.K.:** www.dh.gov.uk/PolicyAnd Guidance/HealthAdviceFor Travellers/fs/en
- **U.S.:** www.cdc.gov/travel

STAYING SAFE

The most common menace, especially in large cities, particularly Rome, is the plague of pickpockets and roving gangs of Gypsy children who surround you, distract you in all the confusion, and steal your purse or wallet. If accosted by a group of children, even though they're children, don't be polite. Never leave valuables in a car, and never travel with your car unlocked. A U.S. State Department travel advisory warns that every car (whether parked, stopped at a traffic light, or even moving) can be a potential target for armed robbery. In these uncertain times, it is always prudent to check the U.S. State Department's travel advisories at http://travel.state.gov.

7 Specialized Travel Resources

TRAVELERS WITH DISABILITIES

Laws in Italy have compelled rail stations, airports, hotels, and most restaurants to follow a stricter set of regulations about **wheelchair accessibility** to restrooms, ticket counters, and the like. Even museums and other attractions have conformed to the regulations, which mimic many presently in effect in the United States. Always call ahead to check on the accessibility in hotels, restaurants, and sights you want to visit.

Many travel agencies offer customized tours and itineraries for travelers with disabilities. **Flying Wheels Travel** (© 507/ 451-5005; www.flyingwheelstravel.com) offers escorted tours and cruises that emphasize sports and private tours in minivans with lifts. **Access-Able Travel Source** (© 303/232-2979; www.access able.com) offers extensive access information and advice for traveling around the world with disabilities. **Accessible Journeys** (© 800/846-4537 or 610/521-0339; www.disabilitytravel.com) caters specifically to slow walkers and wheelchair travelers and their families and friends.

Organizations that offer assistance to travelers with disabilities include **Moss Rehab** (www.mossresourcenet.org), which provides a library of accessible-travel resources online; **SATH (Society for Accessible Travel & Hospitality;** © 212/ 447-7284; www.sath.org; annual membership fees: $45 adults, $30 seniors and students), which offers a wealth of travel resources for all types of disabilities and informed recommendations on destinations, access guides, travel agents, tour operators, vehicle rentals, and companion services; and the **American Foundation for the Blind (AFB;** © 800/232-5463; www.afb.org), a referral resource for the blind or visually impaired that includes information on traveling with Seeing Eye dogs. **AirAmbulanceCard.com** is now partnered with SATH and allows you to pre-select top-notch hospitals in case of an emergency.

For more information specifically targeted to travelers with disabilities, the community website **iCan** (www.icanonline. net/channels/travel/index.cfm) has destination guides and several regular columns on accessible travel. Also check out the quarterly magazine *Emerging Horizons* ($14.95 per year, $19.95 outside the U.S.; www.emerginghorizons.com); and *Open World Magazine,* published by the SATH (see above; subscription: $13 per year, $21 outside the U.S.).

GAY & LESBIAN TRAVELERS

Since 1861, Italy has had liberal legislation regarding homosexuality, but that doesn't mean it has always been looked on favorably in a Catholic country. Homosexuality is much more accepted in Rome than in the south, especially in Sicily, although Taormina has long been a gay mecca.

The **International Gay and Lesbian Travel Association (IGLTA;** © 800/448-8550 or 954/776-2626; www.iglta.org) links travelers up with gay-friendly hoteliers, tour operators, and airline and cruiseline representatives. It offers monthly newsletters, marketing mailings, and a membership directory that's updated once a year.

Many agencies offer tours and travel itineraries specifically for gay and lesbian travelers. **Above and Beyond Tours** (© 800/397-2681; www.abovebeyond tours.com) is the exclusive gay and lesbian tour operator for United Airlines. **Now, Voyager** (© **800/255-6951;** www.now voyager.com) is a well-known San Francisco–based gay-owned and -operated travel service. **Olivia Cruises & Resorts** (© **800/631-6277;** www.olivia.com) charters entire resorts and ships for exclusive lesbian vacations and offers smaller group experiences for both gay and lesbian travelers.

Gay.com Travel (© **800/929-2268** or 415/644-8044; www.gay.com/travel or www.outandabout.com) is an excellent online successor to the popular *Out & About* print magazine. It provides regularly updated information about gay-owned, gay-oriented, and gay-friendly lodging, dining, sightseeing, nightlife, and shopping establishments in every important destination worldwide. It also offers trip-planning information for gay and lesbian travelers for more than 50 destinations, along various themes, ranging from Sex & Travel to Vacations for Couples.

The following travel guides are available at many bookstores, or you can order them from any online bookseller: *Frommer's Gay & Lesbian Europe* (www.frommers. com), an excellent travel resource to the top European cities and resorts; *Spartacus International Gay Guide* (Bruno Gmünder Verlag; www.spartacusworld.com/ gayguide) and *Odysseus: The International Gay Travel Planner* (Odysseus Enterprises Ltd.), both good, annual, English-language guidebooks focused on gay men; and the *Damron* guides (www. damron.com), with separate, annual books for gay men and lesbians.

SENIOR TRAVEL

Mention the fact that you're a senior when you make your travel reservations. Although all of the major U.S. airlines except America West have cancelled their senior discount and coupon book programs, many hotels still offer discounts for seniors. In most cities, people over the age of 60 qualify for reduced admission to theaters, museums, and other attractions, as well as discounted fares on public transportation.

Members of **AARP** (formerly known as the American Association of Retired Persons), 601 E St. NW, Washington, DC 10049 (© **888/687-2277;** www.aarp. org), get discounts on hotels, airfares, and car rentals. AARP offers members a wide range of benefits, including *AARP: The Magazine* and a monthly newsletter. Anyone over 50 can join.

Many reliable agencies and organizations target the 50-plus market. **Elderhostel** (© **877/426-8056;** www.elderhostel. org) arranges study programs for those ages 55 and over (and a spouse or companion of any age) in more than 80 countries around the world. Most courses entail 2 to 4 weeks abroad, and many include airfare, accommodations in university dormitories or modest inns, meals, and tuition. **ElderTreks** (© **800/741-7956;** www. eldertreks.com) offers small-group tours to off-the-beaten-path or adventure-travel locations, restricted to travelers 50 and older. **INTRAV** (© **800/456-8100;** www. intrav.com) is a high-end tour operator that caters to the mature, discerning traveler, not specifically seniors, with trips around the world that include guided safaris, polar expeditions, private-jet adventures, and small-boat cruises down jungle rivers.

Recommended publications offering travel resources and discounts for seniors include: the quarterly magazine *Travel 50 & Beyond* (www.travel50andbeyond. com); *Travel Unlimited: Uncommon Adventures for the Mature Traveler* (Avalon); *101 Tips for Mature Travelers,* available from Grand Circle Travel (© **800/221-2610** or 617/350-7500; www.gct.com); *The 50+ Traveler's Guidebook* (St. Martin's Press); and *Unbelievably Good Deals and Great Adventures That You Absolutely Can't Get Unless You're Over 50* (McGraw-Hill), by Joann Rattner Heilman.

8 Planning Your Trip Online

SURFING FOR AIRFARES

The most popular online travel agencies are **Travelocity** (**www.travelocity.com**, or www.travelocity.co.uk); **Expedia** (**www.expedia.com**, www.expedia.co.uk, or www.expedia.ca); and **Orbitz** (www.orbitz.com).

In addition, most airlines now offer online-only fares that even their phone agents know nothing about. For the websites of airlines that fly to and from your destination, go to "Getting There," p. 37.

Other helpful websites for booking airline tickets online include:

- www.biddingfortravel.com
- www.cheapflights.com
- www.hotwire.com
- www.kayak.com
- www.lastminutetravel.com
- www.opodo.co.uk
- www.priceline.com
- www.sidestep.com
- www.site59.com
- www.smartertravel.com

SURFING FOR HOTELS

In addition to **Travelocity, Expedia, Orbitz, Priceline,** and **Hotwire** (see above), the following websites will help you with booking hotel rooms online:

- www.hotels.com
- www.quickbook.com
- www.travelaxe.net
- www.travelweb.com
- www.tripadvisor.com

It's a good idea to **get a confirmation number** and **make a printout** of any online booking transaction.

SURFING FOR RENTAL CARS

For booking rental cars online, the best deals are usually found at rental-car company websites, although all the major online travel agencies also offer rental-car reservations services. Priceline and Hotwire work well for rental cars, too; the only "mystery" is which major rental company you get, and for most travelers the difference between Hertz, Avis, and Budget is negligible.

Frommers.com: The Complete Travel Resource

For an excellent travel-planning resource, we highly recommend **Frommers.com** (www.frommers.com), voted Best Travel Site by *PC Magazine*. We're a little biased, of course, but we guarantee that you'll find the travel tips, reviews, monthly vacation giveaways, bookstore, and online-booking capabilities to be thoroughly indispensable. Special features include our popular **Destinations** section, where you can access expert travel tips, hotel and dining recommendations, and advice on the sights to see in more than 3,500 destinations around the globe; the **Frommers.com Newsletter,** with the latest deals, travel trends, and money-saving secrets; and our **Travel Talk** area featuring **Message Boards,** where Frommer's readers post queries and share advice, and where our authors sometimes show up to answer questions. Once you finish your research, the **Book a Trip** area can lead you to Frommer's preferred online partners' websites, where you can book your vacation at affordable prices.

TRAVEL BLOGS & TRAVELOGUES

To read a few blogs about Rome, try

- www.gridskipper.com
- www.salon.com/wanderlust
- www.travelblog.com
- www.travelblog.org
- www.worldhum.com
- www.writtenroad.com

9 Getting There

BY PLANE

High season on most airlines' routes to Rome is usually June to the beginning of September. This is the most expensive and crowded time to travel. **Shoulder season** is April and May, early September to October, and December 15 to 24. **Low season** is November 1 to December 14 and December 25 to March 31.

FROM NORTH AMERICA   Fares to Italy are constantly changing, but you can expect to pay somewhere in the range of $550 to $1,580 for a direct round-trip ticket from New York to Rome in coach class.

Flying time to Rome from New York, Newark, and Boston is 8 hours; from Chicago, 10 hours; and from Los Angeles, 12½ hours. Flying time to Milan from New York, Newark, and Boston is 8 hours; from Chicago, 9¼ hours; and from Los Angeles, 11½ hours.

American Airlines (© 800/433-7300; www.aa.com) offers daily nonstop flights to Rome from Chicago's O'Hare, with flights from all parts of American's vast network making connections into Chicago. **Delta** (© 800/221-1212; www.delta.com) flies from New York's JFK to Milan, Venice, and Rome, and from Atlanta to Rome and Milan. **America-West/US Airways** (© 800/428-4322; www.usairways.com) offers one flight daily to Rome out of Philadelphia (you can connect through Philly from most major U.S. cities). And **Continental** (© 800/525-0280; www.continental.com) flies five times a week to Rome and Milan from its hub in Newark.

Air Canada (© 888/247-2262; www.aircanada.ca) flies daily from Toronto to Rome. Two of the flights are nonstop; the others touch down en route in Montréal, depending on the schedule.

British Airways (© 800/AIRWAYS; www.british-airways.com), **Virgin Atlantic Airways** (© 800/821-5438; www.virgin-atlantic.com), **Air France** (© 800/237-2747; www.airfrance.com), **Northwest/KLM** (© 800/225-2525; www.nwa.com), and **Lufthansa** (© 800/645-3880; www.lufthansa-usa.com) offer some attractive deals for anyone interested in combining a trip to Italy with a stopover in, say, Britain, Paris, Amsterdam, or Germany.

Alitalia (© 800/223-5730; www.alitalia.com) is the Italian national airline, with nonstop flights to Rome from different North American cities, including New York (JFK), Newark, Boston, Chicago, Miami, Washington, and Toronto. Nonstop flights into Milan are from New York (JFK) and Newark. From Milan or Rome, Alitalia can easily book connecting domestic flights if your final destination is elsewhere in Italy. Alitalia participates in the frequent-flier programs of other airlines, including Continental and US Airways.

FROM THE UNITED KINGDOM Operated by the European Travel Network, **www.discount-tickets.com** is a great online source for regular and discounted airfares to destinations around the world. You can also use this site to compare rates and book accommodations, car rentals, and tours. Click on "Special Offers" for the latest package deals.

British newspapers are always full of classified ads touting slashed fares to Italy. One good source is *Time Out.* London's *Evening Standard* has a daily travel section, and the Sunday editions of almost any newspaper run many ads. Although competition is fierce, one well-recommended company that consolidates bulk ticket purchases and then passes the savings on to its consumers is **Trailfinders** (℗ **0845/058-5858;** www.trailfinder.com). It offers access to tickets on such carriers as SAS, British Airways, and KLM.

Both **British Airways** (℗ **0870/850-9850** in the U.K.; www.britishairways.co.uk) and **Alitalia** (℗ **0870/544-8259;** www.alitalia.it) have frequent flights from London's Heathrow to Rome. British Airways also has one direct flight a day from Manchester to Rome. Bargain fares are offered by smaller carriers flying from the British Isles to Italy. **Easyjet** (℗ **08712/442366;** www.easyjet.com) flies into Rome from London, as does **Ryanair** (℗ **0818/303030;** www.ryanair.com).

GETTING THROUGH THE AIRPORT

With the federalization of airport security, security procedures at U.S. airports are more stable and consistent than ever. Generally, you'll be fine if you arrive at the airport **1 hour** before a domestic flight and **2 hours** before an international flight; if you show up late, tell an airline employee so you can be whisked to the front of the line.

You'll need a current passport for international flights. Keep your ID at the ready to show at check-in, the security checkpoint, and sometimes even the gate. (Children under 18 do not need government-issued photo IDs for domestic flights, but they do for international flights to most countries.)

E-tickets have made paper tickets nearly obsolete. Passengers with e-tickets can still beat the ticket-counter lines by using airport **electronic kiosks** or even **online check-in** from your home computer. Online check-in involves logging on to your airlines' website, accessing your reservation, and printing out your boarding pass—and the airline may even offer you bonus miles to do so. If you're using a kiosk at the airport, bring the credit card you used to book the ticket or your frequent-flier card. Print out your boarding pass from the kiosk and simply proceed to the security checkpoint with your pass and a photo ID. If you're checking bags or looking to snag an exit-row seat, you will be able to do so using most airlines' kiosks. Even the smaller airlines are employing the kiosk system, but always call your airline to make sure these alternatives are available. **Curbside check-in** is also a good way to avoid lines, although a few airlines still ban curbside check-in; call before you go.

Security checkpoint lines are getting shorter, but some doozies remain. If you have trouble standing for long periods of time, tell an airline employee; the airline will provide a wheelchair. Speed up security by **not wearing metal objects** such as big belt buckles or carrying banned liquids (see below). If you've got metallic body parts, a note from your doctor can prevent a long chat with the security screeners. Keep in mind that only **ticketed passengers** are allowed past security, except for folks escorting children or passengers with disabilities.

Federalization has stabilized **what you can carry on** and **what you can't.** The general rule is that sharp things are out, nail clippers are okay, and many foods and beverages are banned. Bring food in your carry-on rather than checking it, as explosive-detection machines used on checked luggage have been known to mistake food (especially chocolate, for some reason) for bombs. Travelers in the U.S. are allowed one carry-on bag, plus a "personal item" such as a purse, briefcase, or laptop bag. Carry-on hoarders can

Tips   Don't Stow It—Ship It

If ease of travel is your main concern and money is no object, you can ship your luggage with one of the growing number of luggage-service companies that pick up, track, and deliver your luggage (often through couriers such as Federal Express) with minimum hassle for you. Traveling luggage-free may be ultra-convenient, but it's not cheap: One-way overnight shipping can cost from $100 to $200, depending on what you're sending. Still, for some people, especially the elderly or the infirm, it's a sensible solution to lugging heavy baggage. Specialists in door-to-door luggage delivery are **Virtual Bellhop** (www.virtualbellhop.com), **SkyCap International** (www.skycapinternational.com), **Luggage Express** (www.usxpluggageexpress.com), and **Sports Express** (www.sportsexpress.com).

stuff all sorts of things into a laptop bag; as long as it has a laptop in it, it's still considered a personal item. The Transportation Security Administration (TSA) has issued a list of restricted items; check its website (www.tsa.gov) for details.

Airport screeners may decide that your checked luggage needs to be searched by hand. You can now purchase luggage locks that allow screeners to open and relock a checked bag if hand searching is necessary. Look for Travel Sentry certified locks at luggage or travel shops and Brookstone stores (you can buy them online at www.brookstone.com). These locks, approved by the TSA, can be opened by luggage inspectors with a special code or key. For more information on the locks, visit www.travelsentry.org. If you use something other than TSA-approved locks, your lock will be cut off your suitcase if a TSA agent needs to hand-search your luggage.

FLYING FOR LESS: TIPS FOR GETTING THE BEST AIRFARE

Passengers sharing the same airplane cabin rarely pay the same fare. Travelers who need to purchase tickets at the last minute, change their itinerary at a moment's notice, or fly one-way often get stuck paying the premium rate. Here are some ways to keep your airfare costs down.

- Passengers who can book their ticket either **long in advance or at the last minute,** or who **fly midweek** or **at less-trafficked hours,** may pay a fraction of the full fare. If your schedule is flexible, say so, and ask if you can secure a cheaper fare by changing your flight plans.
- Search **the Internet** for cheap fares (see "Planning Your Trip Online").
- Keep an eye on local newspapers for **promotional specials** or **fare wars,** when airlines lower prices on their most popular routes. You rarely see fare wars offered for peak travel times, including the summer months, but if you can travel in the off-months, you may snag a bargain.
- **Consolidators,** also known as bucket shops, are great sources for international tickets, although they usually can't beat Internet fares within North America. Start by looking in Sunday newspaper travel sections; U.S. travelers should focus on the *New York Times, Los Angeles Times,* and *Miami Herald.* U.K. travelers should search in the *Independent, The Guardian,* or *The Observer.* For less-developed destinations, small travel agents who cater to immigrant communities in large cities often have the best deals. *Beware:* Bucket shop tickets are usually nonrefundable or rigged with stiff cancellation penalties, often as high as 50% to 75% of the ticket

---

Tips **Leave Your Cigarette Lighter at Home**

You cannot travel with a cigarette lighter on your person, in your carry-on, or even in your checked luggage. You may carry on up to four packs of matches. If you don't want to lose that sentimental lighter you've had for years, leave it at home and buy a disposable one when you get to your destination.

---

price, and some put you on charter airlines, which may leave at inconvenient times and experience delays. Several reliable consolidators are worldwide and available on the Internet. **STA Travel** (*©* **800/781-4040;** www.sta.com) is the world's lead consolidator for students, but their fares are competitive for travelers of all ages. **ELTExpress** (**Flights.com;** *©* **201/541-3836** or 312/332-0090; www.eltexpress.com) has excellent fares worldwide, particularly to Europe. They also have "local" websites in 12 countries. **Air Tickets Direct** (*©* **888/858-8884;** www.air ticketsdirect.com) is based in Montreal and leverages the currently weak Canadian dollar for low fares; they also book trips to places that U.S. travel agents won't touch, such as Cuba.

- Join **frequent-flier clubs.** Frequent-flier membership doesn't cost a cent, but it does entitle you to better seats, faster response to phone inquiries, and prompter service if your luggage is stolen or your flight is canceled or delayed, or if you want to change your seat. And you don't have to fly to earn points; **frequent-flier credit cards** can earn you thousands of miles for doing your everyday shopping. With more than 70 mileage awards programs on the market, consumers have never had more options. Investigate the program details of your favorite airlines before you sink points into any one. Consider which airlines have hubs in the airport nearest you,

and, of those carriers, which have the most advantageous alliances, given your most common routes. To play the frequent-flier game to your best advantage, consult Randy Petersen's **Inside Flyer** (www.insideflyer.com). Petersen and friends review all the programs in detail and post regular updates on changes in policies and trends.

BY TRAIN

If you plan to travel heavily on the European rails, you'll do well to secure the latest copy of the *Thomas Cook European Timetable of Railroads.* It's available online at www.thomascooktimetables.com.

Electric trains have made travel between France and Italy faster and more comfortable than ever. **France's TGVs** travel at speeds of up to 298km (185 miles) per hour and have cut travel time between Paris and Turin from 7 to 5½ hours, and between Paris and Milan from 7½ to 6¾ hours. **Italy's ETRs** travel at speeds of up to 233km (145 miles) per hour and currently run between Milan and Lyon (5 hr.), with a stop in Turin. From Milan, a train leaves for Rome every hour, taking 4½ hours.

ITALIAN RAIL PASSES If you'll be traveling beyond Rome by rail, you'll need to know a bit about the Italian train system. As a rule of thumb, second-class travel usually costs about two-thirds the price of an equivalent first-class trip. A couchette (a private fold-down bed in a communal cabin) requires a supplement above the price of first-class travel. Children ages 4 to 11 receive a discount of

50% off the adult fare, and children 3 and under travel free with their parents.

The **Trenitalia Pass** (www.trenitalia.it) offers 3 days of rail travel in 2 months, costing $219 in first class or $175 in second class, with additional rail days going for $28 and $23, respectively. Travel days may be used consecutively or nonconsecutively.

There are two other versions of this pass offered, including the **Trenitalia Pass Saver,** costing $187 in first class or $149 in second class and valid for 3 days of travel in 2 months, with additional days going for $24 and $19, respectively. This pass requires a minimum of two persons traveling together at all times.

Trenitalia Pass Youth, costing $147 in second class (3 days in 2 months), is the

way to go for ...
Additional rail da...

The **Italy Rail 'n ...**
any 4 days of unlimited ...
days in a Hertz car rental ...
mileage. You get a choice of t...
gories with manual transmission ...
category with automatic transmiss...
this deal, two adults in first class pay $...
for a compact car or $564 in second class.

With each of the special passes, a supplement must be paid to ride on certain rapid trains, designated **ETR-450** or **Pendolino trains.** The rail systems of Sardinia are administered by a separate entity and aren't included in the Railpass or any of the other passes.

10 Packages for the Independent Traveler

Before you start your search for the lowest airfare, you may want to consider booking your flight as part of a travel package such as an escorted tour or a package tour. What you lose in adventure, you'll gain in time and money saved when you book accommodations, and maybe even food and entertainment, along with your flight.

Package tours are not the same thing as escorted tours. With a package tour, you travel independently but pay a group rate. Packages usually include airfare, a choice of hotels, and car rentals, and packagers often offer several options at different prices. In many cases, a package that includes airfare, hotel, and transportation to and from the airport will cost you less than just the hotel alone would have, had you booked it yourself. That's because packages are sold in bulk to tour operators—who resell them to the public at a cost that drastically undercuts standard rates.

One good source of package deals is the airlines themselves. Most major airlines offer air/land packages, including **American Airlines Vacations** (© 800/321-

2121; www.aavacations.com), **Delta Vacations** (© 800/221-6666; www.delta vacations.com), **US Airways Vacations** (© 800/455-0123 or 800/422-3861; www.usairwaysvacations.com), **Continental Airlines Vacations** (© 800/301-3800; www.covacations.com), and **United Vacations** (© 888/854-3899; www.united vacations.com). Another contender is **Italiatour,** a company of the Alitalia Group (© 800/845-3365 or 212/903-3520; www.italiatour.com), offering a wide variety of tours through all parts of Italy. It specializes in packages for independent travelers (not tour groups) who ride from one destination to another by train or rental car. In most cases, the company sells pre-reserved accommodations, which are usually less expensive than if you had reserved them yourself. Because of the company's close link with Alitalia, the prices quoted for air passage are sometimes among the most reasonable on the retail market.

Vacation Together (© 800/839-9851; www.vacationtogether.com) allows you to search for and book packages offered by a number of tour operators and airlines. The

those under 26 years old.
...ys cost $19 on this pass.
Drive pass is good for
... train travel and 2
... with unlimited
... ree car cate-
... or one car
... on. In
...676

271-1584; www.libertytravel.com), one of
the biggest packagers in the Northeast,
often runs full-page ads in Sunday papers.
Or check ads in the national travel magazines such as *Arthur Frommer's Budget Travel
Magazine, Travel + Leisure, National Geographic Traveler,* and *Condé Nast Traveler.*

Tours

hotels, meals, tours, admission costs, and
local transportation.

The biggest operator of escorted tours
to Italy is **Perillo Tours** (© 800/431-
1515; www.perillotours.com), family
operated for three generations. Since it was
founded in 1945, it has sent more than a
million travelers to Italy on guided tours.
Perillo's tours cost much less than you'd
spend if you arranged a comparable trip
yourself. Accommodations are in first-class
hotels, and guides tend to be well qualified
and well informed.

Trafalgar Tours (© 866/544-4434;
www.trafalgartours.com) is one of Europe's
largest tour operators, offering affordable

guided tours with lodgings in unpretentious hotels. Check with your travel agent
for more information on these tours
(Trafalgar takes calls only from agents).

One of Trafalgar's leading competitors
is **Globus+Cosmos Tours** (© 800/338-
7092; www.globusandcosmos.com).
Globus has first-class escorted coach
tours of various regions lasting from 8 to
16 days. Cosmos, a budget branch of
Globus, sells escorted tours of about the
same length. Tours must be booked
through a travel agent, but you can call
the 800 number for brochures. Another
competitor is **Insight Vacations** (© 800/
582-8380; www.insightvacations.com),
which books superior first-class, fully
escorted motor-coach tours lasting from
1 week to a 36-day grand tour.

12 Recommended Books

GENERAL INTEREST & HISTORY

Presenting a "warts and all" view of the
Italian character, Luigi Barzini's *The Italians* should almost be required reading
for anyone contemplating a trip to Rome.
It's lively, fun, and not at all academic.

Edward Gibbon's 1776 *The History of
the Decline and Fall of the Roman
Empire* is published in six volumes, but
Penguin issues a manageable abridge-
ment. This work has been hailed as one of
the greatest histories ever written. No one
has ever captured the saga of the glory
that was Rome the way Gibbon did.

One of the best books on the long
history of the papacy—detailing its

excesses, triumphs, defeats, and most
vivid characters—is Michael Walsh's *An
Illustrated History of the Popes: Saint
Peter to John Paul II.*

In the 20th century, the most fascinating period in Italian history was the rise
and fall of fascism, as detailed in countless works. One of the best biographies of
Il Duce is Denis M. Smith's *Mussolini: A
Biography.* Another subject that's always
engrossing is the Mafia, which is detailed,
godfathers and all, in Pino Arlacchi's
*Mafia Business: The Mafia Ethic and
the Spirit of Capitalism.*

William Murray's *The Last Italian:
Portrait of a People* is his second volume

of essays on his favorite subject—Italy, its warm people, and its astonishing civilization. The *New York Times* called it "a lover's keen, observant diary of his affair."

Once Upon a Time in Italy: The Vita Italiana of an American Journalist, by Jack Casserly, is the entertaining and affectionate memoir of a former bureau chief in Rome from 1957 to 1964. He captures the spirit of *Italia sparita* (bygone Italy) with such celebrity cameos as Maria Callas and the American expatriate singer Bricktop.

ART & ARCHITECTURE

From the Colosseum to Michelangelo, T. W. Potter provides one of the best accounts of the art and architecture of Rome in *Roman Italy,* which is also illustrated. Another good book on the same subject is *Roman Art and Architecture,* by Mortimer Wheeler.

The Sistine Chapel: A Glorious Restoration, by Michael Hirst and others, uses nearly 300 color photographs to illustrate the lengthy and painstaking restoration of Michelangelo's 16th-century frescoes in the Vatican.

Giorgio Vasari's *Lives of the Artists Vols. I and II* is a collection of biographies of the great artists from Cimabue up to Vasari's 16th-century contemporaries. It's an interesting read, full of anecdotes and Vasari's theories on art practice. For a more modern art history take, the indispensable tome is Frederick Hartt's *History of Italian Renaissance Art.* For an easier and more colorful introduction, get Michael Levey's *Early Renaissance* and *High Renaissance.*

FICTION & BIOGRAPHY

No one does it better than John Hersey in his Pulitzer Prize–winning *A Bell for Adano,* a frequently reprinted classic. It's a well-written and disturbing story of the American invasion of Italy.

One of the best-known Italian writers published in England is Alberto Moravia, born in 1907. His neorealistic novels are immensely entertaining and are read around the world. Notable works include *Roman Tales, The Woman of Rome,* and *The Conformist.*

For the wildly entertaining books on ancient Rome, detailing its most flamboyant personalities and excesses, read *I, Claudius* and *Claudius the God,* both by Robert Graves. Borrowing from the histories of Tacitus and Suetonius, the series begins at the end of the Emperor Augustus's reign and ends with the death of Claudius in the 1st century A.D. In 1998, the Modern Library placed *I, Claudius* at no. 14 on its list of the 100 finest English-language novels published this century.

Colleen McCullough's "Masters of Rome" series is rich, fascinating, and historically detailed, bringing to vivid life such greats as Gaius Marius *(The First Man in Rome),* Lucius Cornelius Sulla *(The Grass Crown),* and Julius Caesar *(Fortune's Favorites* and *Caesar's Women).*

Michelangelo, a Biography, by George Bull, is a well-written scholarly take on the life of the artist, penned by a Renaissance expert and one of the most respected translators of Italian classic literature.

Irving Stone's *The Agony and the Ecstasy,* filmed with Charlton Heston playing Michelangelo, is the easiest to read and the most pop version of the life of this great artist. Heston views it as his greatest role and still tries to keep Michelangelo from coming out of the closet.

Many other writers have tried to capture the peculiar nature of Italy. Notable works include Italo Calvino's *The Baron in the Trees,* Umberto Eco's *The Name of the Rose,* E. M. Forster's *Where Angels Fear to Tread* and *A Room with a View,*

Henry James's *The Aspern Papers,* Giuseppe di Lampedusa's *The Leopard,* Carlo Levi's *Christ Stopped at Eboli,* Susan Sontag's *The Volcano Lover,* and Mark Helprin's underappreciated masterwork, *A Soldier of the Great War.*

In conclusion, try reading the novel, the *Da Vinci Code,* Dan Brown's controversial bestseller. Attacked by critics for his lack of writing style, Brown managed to infuriate the Vatican while getting rich in the process.

Suggested Itineraries

For visitors on the run, who are forced by their tight schedules to see Rome in anywhere from 1 to 3 days, we've devised a trio of self-guided tours, presented as three 1-day itineraries. With these ready-made itineraries, you can have a complete, unforgettable trip, even though the clock is ticking away.

"It's not possible!" a Roman might warn you. If such an idea, especially Rome in 1 day, were presented to the Pope, he might say, "I'll pray for you, dear child. Godspeed will be needed."

Actually, seeing Rome in 1 to 3 days is possible, but it calls for some discipline and fast moving on your part.

It's only fair to warn you that as we present these itineraries for "conquering" Rome in a nutshell, you'll actually need a month to develop a passing acquaintance with Rome. Save that for another trip when, perhaps, you'll have more time.

Start your voyage of discovery right outside your hotel door. We offer bus and Metro routes from place to place, but you'll find that many of the major sites in Rome are a short walk from one another.

1 The Best of Rome in 1 Day

Since time is wasting, arise early and begin your day with some "live theater" by walking the streets of The Eternal City around your hotel, as Rome awakens to another day. Deliveries are being made; Romans with early calls are reporting to work, and the famous cats of the city are out looking for a fish head. This walk can acclimatize you faster than anything else to the sights, sounds, and smells of this ancient capital, once the seat of one of the world's most powerful kingdoms, with many reminders of its heyday. This walk will get you centered before you catch a taxi, hop a bus, or board the Metro for a ride to the first attraction on our tour.

But, first, we suggest that you duck into a Roman cafe for breakfast. It doesn't matter which one. On virtually every street of Rome, you'll find one. If it's your desire, begin your day with a cup of coffee, a glass of blood-red orange juice, and one of those delicious Italian pastries.

Sit back and people-watch as patrons go through the same ritual as you, fortifying themselves for another day.

A lot of the museums, piazzas, and other attractions will have to wait for another day, if you have one. The "Rome in 1 Day" crowd will want to concentrate on the "greatest hits" itinerary by taking in the (barely) still standing monuments that made Imperial Rome feared throughout the known world.

If you have just 1 day, many visitors reject Imperial Rome (as hard as this is to do) and opt instead to explore St. Peter's and the Vatican. The choice is yours. We'll lead off with Day 1 with Imperial Rome, saving Day 2 for the Vatican and St. Peter's. But, if it's your wish, you can reverse these itineraries, of course.

Rome in 1 Day

National Gallery of Modern Art

Galleria Borghese

Viale Giulia
Viale di
Vle. dell'Aranciera
Vle. d. Magnolie
Viale P. Canonica
Viale dell'Uccelliera
Viale dei Cavalli Marini
Piazza di Siena

VILLA BORGHESE/ PARIOLI

Viale del Muro Torto

Via Po
Via Piciana
Via Savoia
Via Tevere
Via Isonzo

Via Salaria
Vle Regina Margherita

Corso D'Italia

Via Campania
Via Sardegna
Via Sicilia
Via Boncompagni

Via Nomentana

Piazzale di Porta Pia

Policlinico Ⓜ

Spagna Ⓜ **Spanish Steps**
Piazza di Spagna

Via di Porta Pinciana
Via Vittorio Veneto
Via Ludovisi

VIA VENETO

Via Plave

Viale Castro Pretorio

Castro Pretorio ⓘ

Via Sistina
Via Fr. Crispi

Barberini Ⓜ

Lgo. di S. Susanna

Via XX Settembre

ⓘ **National Roman Museum**

Piazza Indipendenza

PIAZZA BARBERINI

Via Barberini
Via Tritone

Lg. de Tritone

Palazzo del Quirinale

Via del Quirinale
Via delle Quattro Fontane

Piazza Repubblica

Repubblica Ⓜ

Piazza Cinque-cento

Termini Station ⓘ

Viale Pretoriano

ⓘ
Piazza Colonna
Trevi Fountain ⑨

Via del Corso

Piazza d. Quirinale

Via Nazionale

Via Milano

Piazza dell'Esquilino

Via Principe Amedeo

Termini Ⓜ

Via Marsala

Via Giovanni Giolitti

Via Marsala

SAN LORENZO

Palazzo Doria Pamphilj
Palazzo Colonna

Via XXIV Maggio
Via IV Nov.
Via d. Plebiscito

Teatro dell'Opera

Santa Maria Maggiore
V. Carlo Alberto

Via Cavour

Via Leopardi

Palazzo Venezia
Vittorio Emanuele Monument
Capitoline Museums ①

② Via Cavour

Via Dei Fori Imperiali

San Pietro in Vincoli

Ⓜ **Via Cavour**

Via Merulana

Vittorio Emanuele Ⓜ

Piazza Vittorio Eman. II

Via Manzoni

Via di Marcello
di Teatro

ANCIENT ROME
Roman Forum

⑤

④ ③

ⓘ **Colosseo** Ⓜ

Golden House of Nero

Colosseum

Piazza d. Colosseo
Viale d. Domus Aurea
Via Labicana

Manzoni Ⓜ

Vle. Manzoni

Via di S. Gregorio

Via d. S. Giovanni in Laterano

Vle. Manzoni

Piazza Bocca d. Verità

PALATINE HILL

Via Claudia

Circus Maximus
Via del Circo Massimo

AVENTINE HILL

Via di S. Anselmo

Piazza Albania

Circo Massimo Ⓜ
Piazza di Pta.Capena

Vle Aventino
Viale Aventino

Via Antonina

Via dela Navicella

Piazza di Pla. Metronia

Via Druso

Baths of Caracalla

Piramide Ⓜ

① Piazza del Campidoglio & Senatorium
② Fori Imperiali (Imperial Forums)
③ Colosseum
④ Arch of Constantine
⑤ Forum Romano & Palatino
⑥ The Pantheon
⑦ Scala di Spagna (Spanish Steps)
⑧ Piazza Navona
⑨ Fontana dei Trevi (Trevi Fountain)

One day is far too brief—after all, Rome wasn't built in a day, and you can't see it in one—but you can make the most of your limited time.

If you're in Rome for at least 3 days, stop by or call the ticket office of Galleria Borghese (p. 168) and secure a reservation for a visit on Day 2.

Start: Take bus 30, 40, 62, 64, 70, 87, 95, 170, 492, or 628 to Piazza dell'Ara Coeli and climb the stairs to Piazza del Campidoglio.

---

❶ Piazza del Campidoglio ★★

The Campidoglio stands on the summit of Capitoline Hill, the most sacred of ancient Rome, where the Temples of Jupiter and Juno once stood. This was the spiritual heart of ancient Rome, where triumphant generals made sacrifices to the gods for giving them victories. On the way up the graceful steps leading to the Campidoglio, take a look in the shrubs to the left of the stairway. Deep in the bushes is a large cage. In it are wolves perpetuating the memory of the she-wolf who suckled the infants Romulus and Remus.

At the top of the stairs is the fabled equestrian statue of the emperor Marcus Aurelius. Actually, it's a copy; the original is in the Capitoline Museum on your left. Across the piazza is the Palace of the Conservatori based on an architectural plan of Michelangelo. Save these museums for a future visit.

Walk around the corner (as you face it) of the Senatorium (Town Council) for a panoramic view of the Roman Forum, which we'll visit later. In the distance you can see the Colosseum, also coming up later in our itinerary. The decaying columns and crumbling temples of Imperial Rome rank as one of the grandest man-made views you'll see in Europe. Allow at least 30 minutes or more to walk up and down the steps leading to Capitoline Hill taking in the view.

After Capitoline Hill, head east following our map for a walk along Via dei Fori Imperiali, taking in:

❷ Fori Imperiali (Imperial Forums) ★★

From the railing that skirts Via dei Fori Imperiali, you can take in the view of the famous forums of Imperial Rome in about 30 minutes. Arm yourself with a trusty map so you'll know which ruins you're viewing. Right off Piazza Venezia stands **Trajan's Column,** with its intricate bas-relief sculpture depicting Trajan's victorious campaign against Dacia at the dawn of the 2nd century. Immediately east of the column is **Basilica Ulpia,** whose gray marble columns rise roofless into the sky. Moving east you come to the **Forum of Julius Caesar,** the first of the forums and the site of the ancient Roman stock exchange and the Temple of Venus. Next you'll pass on your left the **Forum of Augustus,** built before the birth of Christ and once home to a mammoth statue of Augustus. On your right is the **Forum of Nerva,** honoring an emperor with a 2-year reign (A.D. 96–98). Directly east of Nerva is the **Forum of Vespasian** begun by the emperor after the capture of Jerusalem in A.D. 71. Immediately following that is the **Temple of Venus and Roma,** or what little is left of it.

At this point you'll be at the doorway to the Colosseum.

❸ Colosseum ★★★

Construction on this amphitheater began in A.D. 72, and it was a marvel of engineering since its enormous weight rested in a swamp (Nero's former lake) on artificial supports. The completed stadium was dedicated by Titus in A.D. 80. Covered with marble, it could hold 80,000 spectators who watched games that nearly rendered extinct many species of animals from the Roman Empire. Allow at least 1½ hours to explore it; for more information, see p. 144.

Caffé Sant'Eustachio

For a break, head nearby to this cafe which Romans claim serves the most superior coffee in Rome. What's the secret? The pure water used in the brew is funneled into the city by an aqueduct built in 19 B.C. See p. 229 in chapter 11. Piazza Sant'Eustachio 82 (© **06-97618552**).

Next to the Colosseum is the:

④ Arch of Constantine ✿✿

This spectacular arch was erected in honor of Constantine's defeat of the pagan Maxentius in A.D. 306. Physically, it's beautiful, but marred by the hectic traffic zooming around it at all hours. You can gaze in awe at this remarkable arch with its intricate carving for at least 15 minutes before pressing on. Before tackling the Roman Forum and the Palatine Hill, we suggest a luncheon break in the area of the Colosseum. If you don't want to waste precious time, you can avail yourself of food on the run at a street vendor, or else patronize one of the trattorie in the vicinity, if you're seeking a sit-down meal.

Within a short walk of the Colosseum you can take in the glories of:

⑤ Forum Romano (Roman Forum), Palatino (Palatine Hill), and Museo Palatino (Palatine Museum) ✿✿✿

The Roman Forum was the literal heart of ancient Rome, a center for trade, religion, and politics. The entrance is off Via dei Fori Imperiali, right at the intersection with Via Cavour. For more detailed information, refer to chapter 8 (p. 147). There is also a walking tour of the area (p. 180) in chapter 9 if you need more guidance.

After you view the Roman Forum, you can explore Palatine Hill, which was once covered with the palaces of patrician families and early emperors. Today it's a tree-shaded hilltop of gardens and fragments of ancient villas. Allow at least 3 hours to take in these attractions and the Palatine Museum.

To reach our next attraction, pick up bus 46, 62, 64, 170, or 492 at Arco di Costantino to Largo di Torre, or Metro to Barberini.

⑥ The Pantheon ✿✿✿

This fabulous ancient monument was built and rebuilt several times, first by Agrippa who began it in 27 B.C. The present structure is the result of an early 2nd century A.D. reconstruction by the Emperor Hadrian. The Pantheon stands on Piazza della Rotonda, which is complete with obelisk and baroque fountain.. It is in an astonishing state of preservation, considering nearly 2 millennia of vandalism. Allow 45 minutes for a visit. For more information refer to p. 157 in chapter 8.

Take the Metro to Spagna for our next stop.

⑦ Scala di Spagna (Spanish Steps) ✿✿

Rising over the Piazza di Spagna in the very heart of Rome is a monumental baroque staircase—best viewed in spring when the flowers are in full bloom. It was the work of Francesco de Sanctis in the 18th century. The stairs lead to the Trinitá dei Monti Church. At no. 26 on the piazza is the Keats-Shelley House where Keats died of tuberculosis at the age of 25.

It's a rare visitor who hasn't sat for a while on one of the landings—there's one every 12 steps—perhaps to download an e-mail from home on a laptop or observe the other sitters, most often young. The fountain at the foot of the steps was designed by Bernini's father at the end of the 16th century, and it's reputed to have the sweetest water in Rome. Allow at least 30 minutes for a visit. For more information, see p. 162 in chapter 8.

After perhaps a shower and rest at your hotel, take bus 30, 40, 62, 64, 70, 87, 116, or 492 to reach the:

❽ Piazza Navona ✦✦✦

The most beautiful square in all of Rome—and best seen at night—is like an ochre-colored gem, unspoiled by new buildings, or even by traffic. The shape stems from the Stadium of Domitian, whose ruins lie underneath. Great chariot races were once held here. In the center is Bernini's Fountain of the Four Rivers, floodlit at night. During summer evenings there are outdoor art shows. Some of the oldest streets in Rome surround Piazza Navona. There is no more romantic place to dine in all the city; our selections of restaurants begins on p. 115, chapter 7.

For your arrivederci to Roma, take bus 62, 95, 95, 175, or 492.

❾ Fontana dei Trevi (Trevi Fountain) ✦✦

This is an 18th-century extravaganza of baroque stonework ruled over by a large statue of Neptune. Visitors come here at night for 20 minutes or so to toss a coin into the fountain, which is said to ensure that you will some day return to Rome.

2 The Best of Rome in 2 Days

If you thought Day 1 was hectic, wait until you sample our agenda for Day 2. Fortify yourself with a good breakfast and wear a pair of sturdy walking shoes. The great challenge of **St. Peter's Basilica** followed by the dazzling treasures of the **Vatican Museums** await you on this day. And, if you're lucky, you can also take in some of the wonder of the **Castel Sant'Angelo,** that mausoleum-turned-fortress, and even the best of the masterpieces of the **Galleria Borghese** if you can get in. Since it opens early (8am), get an early jump on the day by heading first for the **Basilica di San Pietro** (St. Peter's Basilica). *Start:* Metro to Ottaviano–San Pietro. See map on p. 52.

❶ Piazza San Pietro ✦✦✦

You can even arrive here early—perhaps 7:30am—for a 30-minute walk around before the basilica opens. This is one of the world's most famous squares, designed by Bernini in the 1630s. It is the gateway to the largest church in the world (see below). For more on this square, see p. 133 in chapter 8.

❷ Basilica di San Pietro (St. Peter's Basilica) ✦✦✦

When the church doors open, rush in. Once here, it's hard to do anything but gasp at the size and the magnificence. The cupola was designed by Michelangelo, and the artist also created the most famous *Pietà* in the world. There is so much to see here that you should allow at least 1½ hours. See p. 136 in chapter 8 for more details on the best of its treasures.

With what time remains in the morning, explore the:

❸ Musei Vaticani (the Vatican Museums) & the Cappella Sistina (Sistine Chapel) ✦✦✦

These museums are the richest in the world, and will take up the better part of your day—allow at least 3 hours for a cursory visit. They are well worth your valuable time. There are so many museums here in addition to Michelangelo's Sistine Chapel, plus several papal apartments. A full day is actually needed, but you can cut your visit to a fraction of that by previewing the attractions on p. 138 in chapter 8 and deciding in advance what you want to see. If you took our advice and had a large breakfast, you can hold out for a late lunch. For a list of restaurants in the area, see our selections on p. 125 in chapter 7.

After lunch, take bus 40, 62, or 74 to Castel Sant'Angelo/Piazza Pia.

❹ Castel Sant'Angelo ✦

Built in A.D. 135, this imposing fortress was originally constructed as a mausoleum for the Emperor Hadrian and his family. The entrance is across from the Ponte Sant Angelo, the bridge across the Tiber. Inside, you can visit the Popes' Apartments and from the terraces enjoy one of the great panoramic views in all of Rome. Allow at least 30 minutes (more if you can spare it) to look around.

❺ Galleria Borghese ✦✦✦

Only if you can fit it into your busy schedule, and have gone through the red tape of making a reservation, should you even attempt to see one of Italy's greatest art museums. See chapter 8 (p. 168) for more details. Sculptures by Canova and Bernini and paintings by Raphael, Correggio, Titian, and Caravaggio are awaiting your viewing pleasure. Take bus 116 or 910 to reach this museum of masterpieces, and allow at least an hour. After you leave, you can stroll in the **Villa Borghese** ✦✦ gardens, one of the most beautiful in all of Italy. See p. 168 in chapter 8 for more information.

After all this touring, wind down at the Piazza del Popolo (Metro: Flaminia).

❻ Piazza del Popolo ✦✦

With its Egyptian obelisk from the 13th century B.C. and lovely Santa Maria del Popolo church, this is our favorite place to head to for a drink in the late afternoon as the sun begins its descent over Rome. The square is also one of the great places in all of Rome for people-watching. Our two favorite cafes here are **Café Rosati** (p. 231) and **Canova Café** (p. 231), both in chapter 11.

After refreshing yourself, head back to your hotel for a rest and a shower before setting out for another night in Rome. Take bus 23, 30, 40, 62, 64, 70, 87, 116, or 492 to:

❼ Campo de' Fiori ✦

This is not only the geographic center of Rome but a cultural center as well and the site of an open-air food market. After the vendors have left for the day, the cafes and the square come alive. It's our favorite place in Rome for an evening *apertivo* at one of the piazza's cafes and wine bars. Try for a table at **Grappolo d'Oro Zampanò** at Piazza della Concalleria (✆ 06-6897080), which has 200 types of wine. It's found between V. Emanuele II and the Campo.

To cap a long day of sightseeing, hop on bus 56, 60, or 97 and pick a restaurant in:

❽ Trastevere ✦✦✦

We always like to end our final night in Rome by a visit to one of the characteristic trattorie of Trastevere, where locals tell you that you can experience the "real" Rome (as opposed to tourist Rome). Our selection of restaurants begins on p. 127 in chapter 7.

The district is separated from the heart of ancient Rome by the River Tiber. It still has much of the look of medieval Rome and remains the city's most "authentic" neighborhood. In one of its bustling restaurants, you can have a good and perhaps affordable meal to end a full day—unless you plan to hang with us for yet another busy day of touring.

3 The Best of Rome in 3 Days

On your final day, head outside of Rome to explore the attractions of the Appian Way, the hill town of Tivoli, the ruins of Hadrian's Villa, and the Villa d'Este gardens.

Start: Take bus 118 or a taxi to the Catacombe di San Callisto on the Appian Way. The entrance is 3.2km (2 miles) south of Porta San Sebastiano Gate.

Rome in 2 Days

National Gallery
of Modern Art

Galleria
Borghese
5

Piazza
di Siena

**VILLA
BORGHESE/
PARIOLI**

Corso D'Italia

Via Salaria

Vle. Regina Margherita

Via Savoia

Via Po

Via Isonzo

Via Pinciana

Via Tevere

Via Nomentana

Piazzale di
Porta Pia

Policlinico

Via Campania
Via Sardegna
Via Sicilia
Via Boncompagni

Via Piave

Spagna **Spanish
Steps**

Piazza
di Spagna

VIA VENETO

Viale Castro Pretorio

Castro Pretorio

Barberini

Lgo. di
S. Susanna

Via XX Settembre

Viale Pretoriano

**PIAZZA
BARBERINI**

National Roman
Museum

Piazza
Indipendenza

(i)

(i)

Lg. de
Tritone

Palazzo del
Quirinale

Piazza
Colonna

Piazza
Repubblica

Piazza
Cinque-
cento

Termini
Station

Repubblica

Via del Quirinale

Via Nazionale

**Trevi
Fountain**

Piazza d.
Quirinale

Teatro
dell'Opera

Termini

**SAN
LORENZO**

Palazzo
Doria
Pamphilj

Palazzo
Colonna

Piazza
dell'Esquilino
**Santa Maria
Maggiore**

Via Principe Amedeo

Via Giovanni Giolitti

**Palazzo
Venezia**

**Vittorio Emanuele
Monument**

Via Cavour

San Pietro
in Vincoli

Vittorio Emanuele

Piazza
Vittorio
Eman. II

**Capitoline
Museums**

ANCIENT ROME

**Roman
Forum**

(i)

Colosseo

Golden House
of Nero

Viale d. Domus Aurea

Manzoni

Colosseum

Piazza d.
Colosseo

*Via d. S. Giovanni
in Laterano*

Via Labicana

Vle. Manzoni

Piazza
Bocca
d. Verità

**PALATINE
HILL**

Circus Maximus

**AVENTINE
HILL**

Circo Massimo

Piazza di
Pta. Capena

Piazza di
Pla. Metronia

Piazza
Albania

Piramide

**Baths of
Caracalla**

Information *(i)*

City Walls

Metro **A**

Metro **B**

Railway

1 Piazza San Peitro

2 Basilica di San Pietro
  (St. Peter's Basilica)

3 Musei Vaticani & Sistine Chapel

4 Castel Sant'Angelo

5 Galleria Borghese

6 Piazza del Popolo

7 Campo de' Fiori

8 Trastevere

Rome in 3 Days

Inset

0   1/2 mi
0   1/2 km

- Colosseum
- Circus Maximus

TESTACCIO ❺

Via Gallia

Via d. Sette Chiese

Tiber

Via Ostiense

Via C. Colombo

Via Ardeatina

Via d. Sette Chiese

Via Appia Antica

❶

❷

Via

❸

3

4

4

Monterotondo

Mentana

○ Poggio Mirteto

A1

Tiber

4

ITALY

Rome ★

E80

○ Cerveteri

A12

ROME

see inset

Tivoli ❸ ■

A24

❹ ■ Villa d'Este

Palestrina

Fregene ○

Tiber

7

Frascati

○ Castelli Romani

✈ Marino

Fiumicino ○

■ Ostia Antica

Castel Gandolfo ○

Albano ○

Ariccia ○

Genzano ○

Lido di Ostia

Pomezia ○

601

148

○ Nemi

Rocca di Papa ○

A1

Velletri ○

Tyrrhenian Sea

207

Ardea ○

Aprília ○

Cisterna di Latina

7

Airport ✈

❶ Catacombe di San Callisto
❷ Catacombe di San Domitilla
❸ Hadrian's Villa (Villa Adriana)
❹ Villa d'Este
❺ Opera at the Baths of Caracalla

Nettuno ○

Anzio ○

0   5 mi
0   5 km

N

❶ Catacombe di San Callisto ✦✦

Perhaps no one has ever explored all 19km (12 miles) of these catacombs, where some half a million Christians were buried from the 1st to the 4th centuries. The catacombs are webbed with 9m (30-foot) tunnels containing these impressive tombs. After about an hour, you'll get the picture of what it's about. See p. 170 of chapter 8 for more information.

Before leaving the Appian Way, we'd recommend a visit to another important catacomb:

❷ Catacombe di San Domitilla ✦✦✦

Also reached by bus 218, and entered at Via d. Sette Chiese 282, this is the oldest of the catacombs, containing a 3rd century portrait of Christ and the Apostles. You enter through a sunken 4th century church. Allow 45 minutes for a visit. For more information, see p. 172 in chapter 8.

For our next attraction, we leave the city of Rome altogether, heading for the hill town of Tivoli, 32km (20 miles) east of Rome. For bus directions, see "Tivoli & the Villas" in chapter 12. We recommend a luncheon stopover here, preferably at a restaurant with a view over the countryside.

After lunch, head for the town's major attraction:

❸ Hadrian's Villa (Villa Adriana) ❀❀❀

The ancient ruins of the Villa of Hadrian (A.D. 135) are among the most impressive in Italy, lying some 6.5km (4 miles) from the center of Tivoli and reached by bus 4 or 4X from Tivoli. Allow at least 1½ hours to take in the major attractions here, including the Teatro Marittimo, a circular maritime theater. Hadrian was an amateur architect, and much of the villa was designed by him. For more details about the highlights to see, refer to p. 233 in chapter 12.

With the time remaining, return to the center of Tivoli and for a call on the spectacular:

❹ Villa d'Este ❀❀

The villa, built by a cardinal in the mid-16th century, is an afterthought to the hillside gardens, among the most beautiful in Greater Rome. The gardens appear like a fairytale of the Renaissance, using water as a medium of sculpture. There are fountains in every imaginable shape and size, the pathways lined with some 100 fountains, the stairs flanked with cascades on either side. Allow at least an hour for exploration; see p. 234 in chapter 12 for more information.

Return to Rome for the evening. If you made reservations in advance and it's summer, you can attend an:

❺ Opera at the Baths of Caracalla

You can head out for an opera at these ancient baths, entered along Villa della Terme di Caracalla. See p. 223, chapter 11, for more details. Take the Metro to Circo Massimo.

5

Getting to Know Rome

In this chapter, you'll find all the details to help you settle into Rome, from arriving at the airport to getting around. There's a quick breakdown of neighborhoods to help you figure out where you'll want to base yourself and that will help organize and orient all the hotels, restaurants, and sights in the following chapters. We round it off with a list of "Fast Facts"—everything from cybercafes and embassies to where to find English-speaking doctors and how to make a phone call.

1 Essentials

ARRIVING

BY PLANE Chances are, you'll arrive at Rome's **Leonardo da Vinci International Airport** (© 06-65951), popularly known as **Fiumicino**, 30km (18½ miles) from the city center. (If you're flying by charter, you might land at Ciampino Airport, discussed below.)

After you leave Passport Control, you'll see two **information desks** (one for Rome, one for Italy; © 06-65954471). At the Rome desk, you can pick up a general map and some pamphlets daily from 8:15am to 7pm; the staff can also help you find a hotel room if you haven't reserved ahead. A *cambio* (money exchange) operates daily from 7:30am to 11pm, offering surprisingly good rates.

There's a **train station** in the airport. To get into the city, follow the signs marked TRENI for the 30-minute shuttle to Rome's main station, **Stazione Termini** (arriving on Track 22). The shuttle runs from 6:37am to 11:37pm for 9.50€ ($11.40) one-way. On the way, you'll pass a machine dispensing tickets, or you can buy them in person near the tracks if you don't have small bills on you. When you arrive at Termini, quickly get out of the train, and grab a baggage cart. (It's a long schlep from the track to the exit or to the other train connections, and baggage carts can be scarce.)

A **taxi** from da Vinci airport to the city costs 45€ ($54) and up for the 1-hour trip, depending on traffic. The expense might be worth it if you have a lot of luggage or just don't want to bother taking a train. Call © **06-6645,** 06-3570, or 06-4994 for information.

If you arrive on a charter flight at **Ciampino Airport** (© 06-65951), you can take a CoTral bus (© **800-150008** within Italy), which departs every 30 minutes or so for the Anagnina stop of Metropolitana (subway) Line A. Take Line A to Stazione Termini, where you can make your final connections. Trip time is about 45 minutes and costs 1€ ($1.20). A **taxi** from this airport to Rome costs the same as the one from the da Vinci Airport (see above), but the trip is shorter (about 40 min.).

BY TRAIN OR BUS Trains and buses (including trains from the airport) arrive in the center of old Rome at the silver **Stazione Termini,** Piazza dei Cinquecento

---

Tips **A Few Train Station Warnings**

In Stazione Termini, you'll almost certainly be approached by touts claiming to work for a tourist organization. They really work for individual hotels (not always the nicest) and will say almost anything to sell you a room. Unless you know something about Rome's layout and are savvy, it's best to ignore them.

Be aware of all your belongings at all times, and keep your wallet and purse away from professionally experienced fingers. Never ever leave your bags unattended for even a second, and while making phone calls or waiting in line, make sure that your attention doesn't wander from any bags you've set by your side or on the ground. Be aware if someone asks you for directions or information—it's likely meant to distract you and easily will.

Ignore the taxi drivers soliciting passengers right outside the terminal; they can charge as much as triple the normal amount. Instead, line up in the official taxi stand in Piazza dei Cinquecento.

(© **800-431785**); this is the train, bus, and subway transportation hub for all of Rome and is surrounded by many hotels (especially cheaper ones).

If you're taking the **Metropolitana** (subway), follow the illuminated red-and-white M signs. To catch a bus, go straight through the outer hall and enter the sprawling bus lot of Piazza dei Cinquecento. You'll also find **taxis** there.

The station is filled with services. At a branch of the Banca San Paolo IMI (at tracks 1 and 24), you can exchange money. **Informazioni Ferroviarie** (in the outer hall) dispenses information on rail travel to other parts of Italy. There's also a **tourist information booth** here, along with baggage services, newsstands, and snack bars.

BY CAR   From the north, the main access route is the **Autostrada del Sole (A1)**, which cuts through Milan and Florence, or you can take the coastal route, **SS1 Aurelia,** from Genoa. If you're driving north from Naples, you take the southern lap of the **Autostrada del Sole (A2).** All the autostrade join with the **Grande Raccordo Anulare,** a ring road encircling Rome, channeling traffic into the congested city. Long before you reach this road, you should carefully study a map to see what part of Rome you plan to enter and mark your route accordingly. Route markings along the ring road tend to be confusing.

Important advice: Return your rental car immediately, or at least get yourself to a hotel, park your car, and leave it there until you leave Rome. Don't even try to drive in Rome—the traffic and parking are just too nightmarish. Many hotels do not have their own parking lots, and the closest paid parking garage may be blocks away.

VISITOR INFORMATION

Information is available at three locations maintained by the Azienda di Promozione Turistica di Roma (APT): a kiosk at **Leonardo da Vinci International Airport** (© 06-65954471), and a kiosk and administrative headquarters at **Via Parigi 5** (© 06-488991). The headquarters are open Monday to Saturday from 9am to 7pm. The office at the airport is open daily 8:15am to 7pm.

More helpful, and stocking maps and brochures, are the offices maintained by the **Comune di Roma** at various sites around the city, with red-and-orange or yellow-and-black signs saying COMUNE DI ROMA—PUNTI DI INFORMAZIONE TURISTICA. The

Comune di Roma has a Call Center for tourist information (© **06-36004399**). They're staffed daily from 9am to 6pm, except the one at Termini (daily 8am–9pm). Here are the addresses and phone numbers: in Stazione Termini (no phone); on Piazza Cinque Lune near Piazza Navona (© **06-68809240**); at Via Minghetti Marco near the Quirinale (© **06-6782988**); on Piazza Sonnino in Trastevere (© **06-58333457**); at Via della Stamperia, near the Trevi Fountain (© **06-6796540**); at Via Marsala, outside Termini (© **06-4740031**); at Via del Tempio della Pace, near the Colosseum (© **06-69924307**), and at Piazza del Campidoglio (© **06-6798921**).

Enjoy Rome, Via Marghera 88, near the train station (© **06-4451843;** www.enjoy rome.com), was begun by an English-speaking couple, Fulvia and Pierluigi. They dispense information about almost everything in Rome and are far more pleasant and organized than the Board of Tourism. They'll also help you find a hotel room, with no service charge (in anything from a hostel to a three-star hotel). Summer hours are Monday to Friday 8:30am to 7pm, and Saturday 8:30am to 2pm; winter hours are Monday to Friday 9am to 6pm, and Saturday 9am to 2pm.

CITY LAYOUT

Arm yourself with a detailed street map, not the general overview handed out free at tourist offices. Most hotels provide a pretty good version at their front desks.

The bulk of ancient, Renaissance, and baroque Rome (as well as the train station) lies on the east side of the **Tiber River (Fiume Tevere),** which meanders through town. However, several important landmarks are on the other side: **St. Peter's Basilica** and the **Vatican,** the **Castel Sant'Angelo,** and the colorful **Trastevere** neighborhood.

The city's various quarters are linked by large boulevards (large, at least, in some places) that have mostly been laid out since the late 19th century. Starting from the **Vittorio Emanuele Monument,** a controversial pile of snow-white Brescian marble that's often compared to a wedding cake, there's a street running practically due north to **Piazza del Popolo** and the city wall. This is **Via del Corso,** one of the main streets of Rome—noisy, congested, always crowded with buses and shoppers, and called simply "Il Corso." To its left (west) lie the Pantheon, Piazza Navona, Campo de' Fiori, and the Tiber. To its right (east) you'll find the Spanish Steps, the Trevi Fountain, the Borghese Gardens, and Via Veneto.

Back at the Vittorio Emanuele Monument, the major artery going west (and ultimately across the Tiber to St. Peter's) is **Corso Vittorio Emanuele.** Behind you to your right, heading toward the Colosseum, is **Via del Fori Imperiali,** laid out in the 1930s by Mussolini to show off the ruins of the Imperial Forums he had excavated, which line it on either side. Yet another central conduit is **Via Nazionale,** running from **Piazza Venezia** (just in front of the Vittorio Emanuele Monument) east to **Piazza della Repubblica** (near Stazione Termini). The final lap of Via Nazionale is called **Via Quattro Novembre.**

Finding an address in Rome can be a problem because of the narrow streets of old Rome and the little, sometimes hidden *piazze* (squares). Numbers usually run consecutively, with odd numbers on one side of the street and even numbers on the other. However, in the old districts, the numbers will sometimes run consecutively up one side of the street to the end, and then back in the opposite direction on the other side. Therefore, no. 50 could be opposite no. 308.

THE NEIGHBORHOODS IN BRIEF

This section will give you some idea of where you might want to stay and where the major attractions are located.

Near Stazione Termini The main train station, **Stazione Termini,** adjoins **Piazza della Repubblica,** and most likely this will be your introduction to Rome. Much of the area is seedy and filled with gas fumes from all the buses and cars, but it has been improving. If you stay here, you might not get a lot of atmosphere, but you'll have a lot of affordable options and a very convenient location, near the transportation hub of the city and not too far from ancient Rome. There's a lot to see here, including the **Basilica di Santa Maria Maggiore** and the **Baths of Diocletian.** Some high-class hotels are sprinkled in the area, including the **Grand,** but many are long past their heyday.

The neighborhoods on either side of Termini have been improving greatly, and some streets are now attractive. The best-looking area is ahead and to your right as you exit the station on the Via Marsala side. Most budget hotels here occupy a floor or more of a palazzo; many of their entryways are drab, although upstairs they're often charming or at least clean and livable. In the area to the left of the station as you exit, the streets are wider, the traffic is heavier, and the noise level is higher. This area off Via Giolitti is being redeveloped, and most streets are in good condition. A few still need improving; be careful at night.

Via Veneto & Piazza Barberini In the 1950s and early 1960s, **Via Veneto** was the swinging place to be, as the likes of King Farouk, Frank Sinatra, and Swedish actress Anita Ekberg paraded up and down the boulevard to the delight of the paparazzi. The street is still here and is still the site of luxury hotels and elegant cafes and restaurants, although it's no longer a hot spot. It's lined with restaurants catering to those visitors who've heard of this famous boulevard from decades past, but the restaurants are mostly overpriced and overcrowded tourist traps. Rome city authorities have tried to restore this legendary street to some of its former glory by banning vehicular traffic on the top half. It makes for a pleasant stroll, in any case.

To the south, Via Veneto comes to an end at **Piazza Barberini,** dominated by the 1642 **Triton Fountain** (Fontana del Tritone), a baroque celebration with four dolphins holding up an open scallop shell in which a triton sits blowing into a conch. Overlooking the square is the **Palazzo Barberini.** In 1623, when Cardinal Maffeo Barberini became Pope Urban VIII, he ordered Carlo Maderno to build a palace here; it was later completed by Bernini and Borromini.

Ancient Rome Most visitors explore this area first, taking in the **Colosseum, Palatine Hill, Roman Forum, Imperial Forums,** and **Circus Maximus.** The area forms part of the *centro storico* (historic district), along with **Campo de' Fiori** and **Piazza Navona** and the **Pantheon,** which are described below (we've considered them separately for the purposes of helping you locate hotels and restaurants). Because of its ancient streets, airy piazzas, classical atmosphere, and heartland location, this is a good place to stay. If you base yourself here, you can walk to the monuments and avoid the hassle of Rome's inadequate public transportation.

This area offers only a few hotels—most of them inexpensive to moderate in price—and not a lot of great restaurants. Many restaurant owners have

Rome Orientation

their eyes on the cash register and the tour bus crowd, whose passengers are often hustled in and out of these restaurants so fast that they don't know whether the food is any good.

Campo de' Fiori & the Jewish Ghetto South of Corso Vittorio Emanuele and centered on **Piazza Farnese** and the market square of **Campo de' Fiori,** this area includes many buildings that were constructed in Renaissance times as private homes. Stroll along **Via Giulia**—Rome's most fashionable street in the 16th century—with its antiques stores, interesting hotels, and modern art galleries.

West of Via Arenula lies one of the city's most intriguing districts, the old **Jewish Ghetto,** where restaurants far outnumber hotels. In 1556, Pope Paul IV ordered the Jews, about 8,000 at the time, to move into this area. The walls weren't torn down until 1849. Although ancient and medieval Rome has a lot more atmosphere, this working-class neighborhood is close to many attractions. You're more likely to want to dine here than to stay here.

Piazza Navona & the Pantheon One of the most desirable areas of Rome, this district is a maze of narrow streets and alleys dating from the Middle Ages. It is filled with churches and palaces built during the Renaissance and baroque eras, often with rare marble and other materials stripped from ancient Rome. The only way to explore it is on foot. Its heart is **Piazza Navona,** built over Emperor Domitian's stadium and bustling with sidewalk cafes, palazzi, street artists, musicians, and pickpockets. There are several hotels in the area and plenty of trattorie.

Rivaling Piazza Navona—in general activity, the cafe scene, and nightlife—is the area around the **Pantheon,** which remains from ancient Roman

times and is surrounded by a district built much later (this "pagan" temple was turned into a church and rescued, but the buildings that once surrounded it are long gone).

Piazza del Popolo & the Spanish Steps Piazza del Popolo was laid out by Giuseppe Valadier and is one of Rome's largest squares. It's characterized by an obelisk brought from Heliopolis in lower Egypt during the reign of Augustus. At the end of the square is the **Porta del Popolo,** the gateway in the 3rd-century Aurelian wall. In the mid–16th century, this was one of the major gateways into the old city. If you enter the piazza along Via del Corso from the south, you'll see twin churches, **Santa Maria del Miracoli** and **Santa Maria di Montesanto,** flanking the street. But the square's major church is **Santa Maria del Popolo** (1442–47), one of the best examples of a Renaissance church in Rome.

Since the 17th century, the **Spanish Steps** (the former site of the Spanish ambassador's residence) have been a meeting place for visitors. Some of Rome's most upscale shopping streets, including **Via Condotti,** fan out from here. The elegant **Hassler,** one of Rome's grandest hotels, lies at the top of the steps. This is Rome at its most upscale, full of $500-a-night hotels, designer boutiques, and high-end restaurants.

Around Vatican City Across the Tiber, **Vatican City** is a small city-state whose influence extends around the world. The **Vatican Museums, St. Peter's,** and the **Vatican Gardens** take up most of the land area, and the popes have lived here for 6 centuries. The neighborhood around the Vatican—called the "Borgo"—contains some good hotels (and several bad ones), but it's removed from the more happening

Tips **Handy Tip**

Rome has *four* daily rush hours: to work (8–9am), to home for lunch (1pm), back to work (3:30pm), and to home in the evening (6–7pm).

scene of ancient and Renaissance Rome, and getting to and from it can be time-consuming. The area is rather dull at night and contains few, if any, of Rome's finest restaurants. For the average visitor, Vatican City and its surrounding area are best for exploring during the day. Nonetheless, the area is very popular for those whose sightseeing or even business interests center on the Vatican.

Trastevere In Roman dialect, *Trastevere* means "across the Tiber." For visitors arriving in Rome decades ago, it might as well have meant Siberia. All that has changed now: This once medieval working-class district has been gentrified and overrun with visitors from all over the world. It started to change in the 1970s when expats and others discovered its rough charm. Since then, Trastevere has been filling up with tour buses, dance clubs, offbeat shops, sidewalk vendors, pubs, and little trattorie with menus printed in English. There are even places to stay here, but as of yet, it hasn't burgeoned into a major hotel district. There are some excellent restaurants here as well.

The original people of the district, and there are still some of them left, are of mixed ancestry—mainly Jewish, Roman, and Greek. For decades they were known for speaking their own dialect in a language rougher than that spoken in central Rome. Even their cuisine was spicier.

The area still centers on the ancient churches of **Santa Cecelia** and **Santa Maria** in Trastevere. Trastevere remains one of Rome's most colorful quarters, even if it is a bit overrun. Known as a "city within a city," it is at least a village within a city.

Testaccio & the Aventine In A.D. 55, Nero ordered that Rome's thousands of broken amphorae and terra-cotta roof tiles be stacked in a carefully designated pile to the east of the Tiber, just west of Pyramide and today's Ostia Railway Station. Over the centuries, the mound grew to a height of around 200 feet and then was compacted to form the centerpiece for one of the city's most unusual working-class neighborhoods, **Testaccio.** Eventually, houses were built on the terra-cotta mound and caves were dug into its mass to store wine and foodstuffs. Once home to the slaughterhouses of Rome and its former port on the Tiber, *Testaccio* means "ugly head" in Roman dialect. Bordered by the Protestant cemetery, Testaccio is known for its authentic Roman restaurants. Chefs here still cook traditionally, satisfying local—not tourist—palates. Change is on the way, however, and this is a neighborhood on its way up. Nightclubs have sprung up in the old warehouses, although they come and go rather quickly.

Another offbeat section of Rome is **Aventine Hill,** south of the Palatine and close to the Tiber. In 186 B.C., thousands of residents of the area were executed for joining in "midnight rituals of Dionysos and Bacchus." These bloody orgies are a thing of the past today, and the Aventine area is now a leafy and rather posh residential quarter.

The Appian Way Via Appia Antica is a 2,300-year-old road that has witnessed much of the history of the ancient world. By 190 B.C., it extended from Rome to Brindisi on the southeast coast. Its most famous sights today are the **catacombs,** the graveyards of patrician families (despite what it says in *Quo Vadis?*, they weren't used as a place for Christians to hide out while fleeing persecution). This is one of the most historically rich areas of Rome to explore, but it's not a viable place to stay. It does contain some restaurants, however, where you can order lunch on your visit to the catacombs.

Prati The little-known **Prati** district is a middle-class suburb north of the Vatican. It has been discovered by budget travelers because of its affordable *pensioni,* although it's not conveniently located for much of the sightseeing you'll want to do. The **Trionfale flower-and-food market** itself is worth the trip. The area also abounds in shopping streets less expensive than those found in central Rome, and street crime isn't much of a problem.

Parioli Rome's most elegant residential section, Parioli, is framed by the green spaces of the **Villa Borghese** to the south and the **Villa Glori** and **Villa Ada** to the north. It's a setting for some of the city's finest restaurants, hotels, and nightclubs. It's not exactly central, however, and it can be a hassle if you're dependent on public transportation. Parioli lies adjacent to Prati but across the Tiber to the east; like Prati, this is one of the safer districts. We'd call Parioli an area for connoisseurs, attracting those who shun the overrun Spanish Steps and the overly commercialized Via Veneto, and those who'd never admit to having been in the Termini area.

Monte Mario On the northwestern precincts of Rome, **Monte Mario** is the site of the deluxe **Cavalieri Hilton,** an excellent stop to take in a drink and the panorama of Rome. If you plan to spend a lot of time shopping and sightseeing in the heart of Rome, it's a difficult and often expensive commute. The area lies north of Prati, away from the hustle and bustle of central Rome. Bus no. 913 runs from Piazza Augusto Imperator near Piazza del Popolo to Monte Mario.

2 Getting Around

Rome is excellent for walking, with sites of interest often clustered together. Much of the inner core is traffic-free, so you'll need to walk whether you like it or not. However, in many parts of the city, it's hazardous and uncomfortable because of the crowds, heavy traffic, and narrow sidewalks. Sometimes sidewalks don't exist at all, and it becomes a sort of free-for-all with pedestrians competing for space against vehicular traffic (the traffic always seems to win). Always be on your guard. The hectic crush of urban Rome is considerably less during August, when many Romans leave town for vacation.

BY SUBWAY

The **Metropolitana,** or **Metro,** for short, is the fastest means of transportation, operating daily from 5:30am to 11:30pm. A big red M indicates the entrance to the subway.

Tickets are 1€ ($1.20) and are available from *tabacchi* (tobacco shops, most of which display a sign with a white T on a brown background), many newsstands, and vending machines at all stations. Some stations have managers, but they won't make

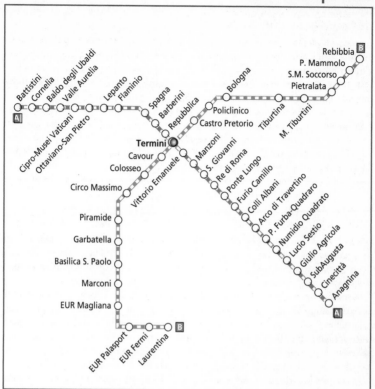

change. Booklets of tickets are available at tabacchi and in some terminals. You can also buy **passes** for 1 to 7 days (see "By Bus & Tram," below).

Building a subway system for Rome hasn't been easy because every time workers start digging, they discover an old temple or other archaeological treasure, and heavy earth-moving has to cease for a while.

BY BUS & TRAM

Roman buses and trams are operated by an organization known as **ATAC** (Azienda Tramvie e Autobus del Comune di Roma), Via Volturno 65 (© **800-431784** for information).

For 1€ ($1.20) you can ride to most parts of Rome, although it can be slow going in all that traffic, and the buses are often very crowded. Your ticket is valid for 75 minutes, and you can get on many buses and trams (and the subway) during that time by using the same ticket. Ask where to buy bus tickets, or buy them in tabacchi or bus terminals. You must have your ticket before boarding because there are no ticket-issuing machines on the vehicles.

At Stazione Termini, you can buy a **1-day ticket** *(biglietto giornaliero),* which costs 4€ ($4.80), or a **weekly ticket** *(biglietto settimanale "carta"),* which costs 16€ ($19.20). These passes allow you to ride the ATAC network without buying individual tickets. A **tourist pass** costs 11€ ($13.20) and is valid for 3 days. The tourist pass,

Tips **Two Bus Warnings**

Any map of the Roman bus system will likely be outdated before it's printed. Many buses listed on the "latest" map no longer exist; others are enjoying a much-needed rest, and new buses suddenly appear without warning. There's also talk of completely renumbering the whole system soon, so be aware that the route numbers we've listed might have changed by the time you travel.

Take extreme caution when riding Rome's overcrowded buses—pickpockets abound! This is particularly true on bus no. 64, a favorite of visitors because of its route through the historic districts and thus also a favorite of Rome's vast pickpocketing community. This bus has earned various nicknames, including the "Pickpocket Express" and "Wallet Eater."

the biglietto giornaliero, and the biglietto settimanale tickets are valid on buses, trams, and the subway—but never ride the trains when the Romans are going to or from work, or you'll be smashed flatter than fettuccine. On the first bus you board, you place your ticket in a small machine, which prints the day and hour you boarded, and then you withdraw it. You do the same on the last bus you take during the valid period of the ticket.

Buses and trams stop at areas marked FERMATA. At most of these, a yellow sign displays the numbers of the buses that stop there and a list of all the stops along each bus's route in order, so you can easily search out your destination. In general, they're in service daily from 6am to midnight. After that and until dawn, you can ride on special night buses (they have an N in front of their bus number), which run only on main routes. It's best to take a taxi in the wee hours—if you can find one.

At the **bus information booth** at Piazza dei Cinquecento, in front of the Stazione Termini, you can purchase a directory complete with maps summarizing the routes.

Although routes change often, a few reliable routes have remained valid for years, such as **no. 75** from Stazione Termini to the Colosseum, **H** from Stazione Termini to Trastevere, and **no. 40** from Stazione Termini to the Vatican. But if you're going somewhere and are dependent on the bus, be sure to carefully check where the bus stop is and exactly which bus goes there—don't assume that it'll be the same bus the next day.

BY TAXI

Don't count on hailing a taxi on the street or even getting one at a stand. If you're going out, have your hotel call one. At a restaurant, ask the waiter or cashier to dial for you. If you want to phone for yourself, try one of these numbers: © **06-6645,** 06-3570, or 06-4994.

The meter begins at 2.33€ ($2.80) for the first 3km (1¾ miles) and then rises .65€ ($.80) per kilometer. Every suitcase costs 1€ ($1.20), and on Sunday, a 3.36€ ($4.05) supplement is assessed. There's another 4.91€ ($5.90) supplement from 10pm to 7am. Avoid paying your fare with large bills—invariably, taxi drivers claim that they don't have change, hoping for a bigger tip (stick to your guns and give only about 10%).

BY CAR

All roads might lead to Rome, but you don't want to drive once you get here. Because the reception desks of most Roman hotels have at least one English-speaking person, call ahead to find out the best route into Rome from wherever you're starting out.

You're usually allowed to park in front of the hotel long enough to unload your luggage. You'll want to get rid of your rental car as soon as possible or park in a garage.

You might want to rent a car to explore the countryside around Rome or drive on to another city. You'll save the most money if you reserve before leaving home. But if you want to book a car here, **Hertz** is at Via Giovanni Giolitti 34 (✆ **06-4740389;** Metro: Termini) and **Avis** is at Stazione Termini (✆ **06-4814373;** Metro: Termini). **Maggiore,** an Italian company, has an office at Stazione Termini (✆ **06-4883715;** Metro: Termini). There are also branches of the major rental agencies at the airport.

FAST FACTS: Rome

American Express The Rome offices are at Piazza di Spagna 38 (✆ **06-67641;** Metro: Spagna). The travel service is open Monday to Friday 9am to 5:30pm and Saturday 9am to 12:30pm. Hours for the financial and mail services are Monday to Friday 9am to 5pm. The tour desk is also open Monday to Friday 9am to 5:30pm, and also Saturday 9am to 12:30pm (May–Oct).

Babysitters Most hotel desks in Rome will help you find a babysitter. Inquire as far in advance as possible. You can request an English-speaking sitter, but you may not always get one.

Banks In general, banks are open Monday to Friday 8:30am to 1:30pm and 3 to 4pm. Some banks keep afternoon hours from 2:45 to 3:45pm. There's a branch of **Citibank** at Via Abruzzi 2 (✆ **06-421561;** Metro: Barberini). The bank office is open Monday to Friday 8:30am to 1:30pm. Citibank does not provide currency exchange.

Currency Exchange There are exchange offices throughout the city, and they're also at all major rail and air terminals, including Stazione Termini, where the *cambio* (exchange booth) beside the rail information booth is open daily from 8am to 8pm. At some *cambi,* you'll have to pay commissions, often 1.5%. Likewise, banks often charge commissions.

Dentists For dental work, go to **American Dental Arts Rome,** Via del Governo Vecchio (✆ **06-6832613;** bus no. 41, 44, 46B), which uses all the latest technology, including laser denal techniques. There is also a 24-hour **G. Eastman Dental Hospital** at Viale Regina Elena 287B (✆ **06-844831;** Metro: Policlinico).

Doctors Call the U.S. Embassy at ✆ **06-46741** for a list of doctors who speak English. All big hospitals have a 24-hour first-aid service (go to the emergency room, *Pronto Soccorso*). You'll find English-speaking doctors at the privately run **Salvator Mundi International Hospital,** Viale delle Mura Gianicolensi 67 (✆ **06-588961;** bus no. 115). For medical assistance, the **International Medical Center** is on 24-hour duty at Via Firenze 47 (✆ **06-4882371;** Metro: Repubblica). You could also contact the **Rome American Hospital,** Via Emilio Longoni 69 (✆ **06-22551**), with English-speaking doctors on duty 24 hours. A more personalized service is provided 24 hours by **MEDI-CALL,** Studio Medico, Via Salaria 300, Palazzina C, interno 5 (✆ **06-8840113;** bus no. 53). It can arrange for qualified doctors to make a house call at your hotel or anywhere in Rome. In most cases, the doctor will be a general practitioner who can refer you to a specialist, if needed. Fees begin at around 100€ ($115) per visit and can go higher if a specialist or specialized treatments are necessary.

Drugstores A reliable pharmacy is **Farmacia Internazionale,** Piazza Barberini 49 (© **06-4825456;** Metro: Barberini), open day and night. Most pharmacies are open from 8:30am to 1pm and 4 to 7:30pm. In general, pharmacies follow a rotation system, so several are always open on Sunday.

Electricity It's generally 220 volts, 50 Hz AC, but you might find 125-volt outlets, with different plugs and sockets for each. Pick up a transformer either before leaving home or in any appliance shop in Rome if you plan to use electrical appliances. Check the exact local current at your hotel. You'll also need an adapter plug.

Embassies & Consulates In case of an emergency, embassies have a 24-hour referral service.

The **U.S. Embassy** is in Rome at Via Vittorio Veneto 119A (© **06-46741;** fax 06-46742356). **U.S. consulates** are in Florence at Lungarno Amerigo Vespucci 38 (© **055-266-951;** fax 055-284-088), in Milan at Via Principe Amedeo 2–10 (© **02-29-03-51;** fax 02-2900-1165), in Naples on Piazza della Repubblica 1 (© **081-583-8111;** fax 081-761-1869), and in Genoa at Via Dante 2 (© **010-58-44-92**). For consulate hours, see individual city listings.

The **Canadian Embassy** in Rome is at Via Salaria, 243 © 06-85-444-1.The **Canadian Consulate** and passport service is in Rome at Via Zara 30 (© **06-85-444-1;** fax 06-85-444-2912). (*Note:* Calls to the embassy or consulate offices are routed through the same number.) The Canadian Consulate in Milan is at V.V. Pisani 19 (© **02-67581**).

The **U.K. Embassy** is in Rome at Via XX Settembre 80A (© **06-42200001;** fax 06-42202334). The **U.K. Consulate** in Florence is at Lungarno Corsini 2 (© **055-284-133;** fax 055-219-112). The **Consulate General** in Naples is at Via Dei Mille 40 (© **081-4238-911;** fax 081-422-434). In Milan, contact the office at Via San Paolo 7 (© **02-723-001**).

The **Australian Embassy** is in Rome at Via Antonio Bosio 5 (© **06-852721;** fax 06-85272300). The **Australian Consulate** is in Rome at Corso Trieste 25 (© **06-852721**). The Australian Consulate in Milan is at Via Borgogna 2 (© 02-77-70-41).

The **New Zealand Embassy** is in Rome at Via Zara 28 (© **06-4417171;** fax 06-4402984). The **Irish Embassy** in Rome is at Piazza di Campitelli 3 (© **06-6979121;** fax 06-6792354). For consular queries, dial © **06-69791211.**

Emergencies Dial **113** for an ambulance or to call the police; to report a fire, call **115.**

Internet Access Try **The Net Gate,** Piazza Firenze 25 (© **06-6893445**) open daily 10:30am to 9pm, with 35 computers. There's also **Kokonet,** Vicolo D'Orfeo 13 (near the Vatican; © **06-66877264**), open daily 10:30am to 8:30pm.

Legal Aid The consulate of your country is the place to turn for legal aid, although offices can't interfere in the Italian legal process. They can, however, inform you of your rights and provide a list of attorneys. You'll have to pay for the attorney out of your pocket—there's no free legal assistance. If you're arrested for a drug offense, about all the consulate will do is notify a lawyer about your case and perhaps inform your family.

Liquor Laws Wine with meals has been a normal part of family life for hundreds of years in Italy. Children are exposed to wine at an early age, and consumption of alcohol isn't anything out of the ordinary. There's no legal drinking age for buying or ordering alcohol, and there's almost no restriction on what kinds of stores or what days of the week wine or liquor can be sold, as in the United States.

Luggage Storage/Lockers These are available at the Stazione Termini. Lockers, which are open daily from 6am to midnight, are on the underground floor of the Termini Wing accessible from the Forum Termini by means of the tapis-roulant, from via Giolitti, or platform 24. The charge is 3.80€ ($4.55) per piece of luggage per 5-hour period. Luggage storage is also available daily 7am to 11pm in the main arrivals building of the airport, costing 2€ ($2.40) per bag for up to 7 hours of storage, 3.50€ ($4.20) per bag between 7 and 24 hours, and 6€ ($7.20) for oversize luggage per day.

Mail Mail delivery in Italy is notoriously bad. Your family and friends back home might receive your postcards in 1 week, or it might take 2 weeks or more. Postcards, aerogrammes, and letters weighing up to 20 grams sent to the United States and Canada cost .80€ (95¢); to the United Kingdom and Ireland, .62€ (75¢); and to Australia and New Zealand, 1€ ($1.20). You can buy stamps at all post offices and at tabacchi, but it's easiest just to buy stamps and mail letters and postcards at your hotel's front desk. You can buy special stamps at the **Vatican City Post Office,** adjacent to the information office in St. Peter's Square; it's open Monday to Friday 8:30am to 7pm and Saturday from 8:30am to 6pm. Letters mailed at Vatican City reach North America far more quickly than mail sent from within Rome for the same cost.

Newspapers/Magazines You can get the *International Herald Tribune, USA Today, New York Times,* and *Time* and *Newsweek* magazines at most newsstands. The expatriate magazine (in English) *Wanted in Rome* comes out monthly and lists current events and shows. If you want to try your hand at reading Italian, the newspaper *La Repubblica* is full of cultural and entertainment listings.

Passports **For Residents of the United States:** Whether you're applying in person or by mail, you can download passport applications from the U.S. State Department website at **http://travel.state.gov.** For general information, call the **National Passport Agency** (☏ 202/647-0518). To find your regional passport office, either check the U.S. State Department website or call the **National Passport Information Center** (☏ 877/487-2778); the fee is 55¢ per minute for automated information and $1.50 per minute for operator-assisted calls.

For Residents of Canada: Passport applications are available at travel agencies throughout Canada or from the central **Passport Office,** Department of Foreign Affairs and International Trade, Ottawa, ON K1A 0G3 (☏ 800/567-6868; www.ppt.gc.ca).

For Residents of the United Kingdom: To pick up an application for a standard 10-year passport (5-year passport for children under 16), visit your nearest passport office, major post office, or travel agency, or contact the **United Kingdom Passport Service** at ☏ 0870/521-0410 or search its website at www.ukpa.gov.uk.

For Residents of Ireland: You can apply for a 10-year passport at the **Passport Office,** Setanta Centre, Molesworth Street, Dublin 2 (② **01/671-1633;** www.irl gov.ie/iveagh). Those under age 18 and over 65 must apply for a 12€ 3-year passport. You can also apply at 1A South Mall, Cork (② **021/494-4700**) or at most main post offices.

For Residents of Australia: You can pick up an application from your local post office or any branch of Passports Australia, but you must schedule an interview at the passport office to present your application materials. Call the **Australian Passport Information Service** at ② **131-232,** or visit the government website at www.passports.gov.au.

For Residents of New Zealand: You can pick up a passport application at any New Zealand Passports Office or download it from the website. Contact the **Passports Office** at ② **0800/225-050** in New Zealand or 04/474-8100, or log on to www.passports.govt.nz.

Police   Dial ② **113.**

Restrooms   Facilities are found near many of the major sights and often have attendants, as do those at bars, clubs, restaurants, cafes, and hotels, plus the airports and the rail station. (There are public restrooms near the Spanish Steps, or you can stop at the McDonald's there—it's one of the nicest branches of the Golden Arches you'll ever see!) You're expected to leave .10€ to .25€ (10¢–30¢) for the attendant. It's not a bad idea to carry some tissues in your pocket when you're out and about, either.

Safety   Pickpocketing is the most common problem. Men should keep their wallets in their front pocket or inside jacket pocket. Purse snatching is also commonplace, with young men on Vespas who ride past you and grab your purse. To avoid trouble, stay away from the curb, and keep your purse on the wall side of your body and place the strap across your chest. Don't lay anything valuable on tables or chairs, where it can be grabbed up. Children have long been a particular menace, although the problem isn't as severe as in years past. If they completely surround you, you'll often virtually have to fight them off. They might approach you with pieces of cardboard hiding their stealing hands. Just keep repeating a firm *no!*

Taxes   As a member of the European Union, Italy imposes a **value-added tax** (called **IVA** in Italy) on most goods and services. The tax that most affects visitors is the one imposed on hotel rates, which ranges from 9% in first- and second-class hotels to 20% in deluxe hotels.

Non-E.U. (European Union) citizens are entitled to a **refund of the IVA** if they spend more than 155€ ($186) at any one store, before tax. To claim your refund, request an invoice from the cashier at the store and take it to the Customs office *(dogana)* at the airport to have it stamped before you leave. *Note:* If you're going to another E.U. country before flying home, have it stamped at the airport Customs office of the last E.U. country you'll be in (for example, if you're flying home via Britain, have your Italian invoices stamped in London). Once back home, mail the stamped invoice (keep a photocopy for your records) back to the original vendor within 90 days of the purchase. The vendor will, sooner or later, send you a refund of the tax that you paid at the time of your original purchase. Reputable stores view this as a matter of ordinary paperwork and are businesslike about it. Less-honorable stores might lose your dossier. It pays to deal with established vendors on large purchases. You can also request that the refund be credited to the credit card with which you made the purchase; this is usually a faster procedure.

Many shops are now part of the **"Tax Free for Tourists"** network (look for the sticker in the window). Stores participating in this network issue a check along with your invoice at the time of purchase. After you have the invoice stamped at Customs, you can redeem the check for cash directly at the Tax Free booth in the airport (in Rome, it's past Customs; in Milan's airports, the booth is inside the Duty-Free shop) or mail it back in the envelope provided within 60 days.

Telephone To call Italy from the United States, dial the **international prefix, 011;** then Italy's **country code, 39;** and then the city code (for example, **06** for Rome or **055** for Florence), which is now built into every number. Then dial the actual **phone number.**

A **local phone call in Italy** costs around .10€ (10¢). **Public phones** accept coins, precharged phone cards (*scheda* or *carta telefonica*), or both. You can buy a *carta telefonica* at any tabacchi in increments of 1€ ($1.20), 2.50€ ($3), 3€ ($3.60), 5€ ($6), 7.50€ ($9) and 10€ ($12). To make a call, pick up the receiver and insert your card (break off the corner first). Most phones have a digital display that tells you how much money you've inserted (or how much is left on the card). Dial the number, and don't forget to take the card with you after you hang up.

To **call from one city code to another,** dial the city code, complete with the initial 0, and then dial the number. (Note that numbers in Italy range from 4 to 8 digits in length. Even when you're calling within the same city, you must dial that city's area code—including the 0. For example, when you call another Rome number from within Rome, you must dial 06 before the local number.)

To **dial direct internationally,** dial 00 and then the country code, the area code, and the number. **Country codes** are as follows: the United States and Canada, 1; the United Kingdom, 44; Ireland, 353; Australia, 61; New Zealand, 64. Make international calls from a public phone, if possible, because hotels almost invariably charge ridiculously inflated rates for direct dial—but bring plenty of *schede* (phone cards) to feed the phone. Calls dialed directly are billed on the basis of the call's duration only. A reduced rate is applied from 11pm to 8am Monday through Saturday and all day Sunday. Direct-dial calls from the United States to Italy are much cheaper, so arrange for whomever to call you at your hotel.

Telecom Italia, the biggest Italian phone company, offers an international phone card called **Time** for calling overseas. It comes in increments of 5€ ($6), 10€ ($12), and 25€ ($30), and it's usually available at any tabacchi. It costs (48¢) per minute to call the United States or Canada, and .45€ (5 to call Western Europe and Australia. You don't insert this card in merely dial © **4748** and then *2 (star 2) for instruction in prompted.

To call the **national telephone information** (in Italian) in Italy, dial ℂ **1254**. **International information** is available at ℂ **176** but costs .60€ (70¢) a shot. To make **collect or calling card calls,** drop in .10€ (10¢) or insert your card and dial one of the numbers given below; an American operator will come on shortly to assist you (because Italy has yet to discover the joys of the touch-tone phone, you'll have to wait for the operator). The following calling-card numbers work all over Italy: **AT&T** ℂ **800/172-444, MCI** ℂ **800/905-825,** and **Sprint** ℂ **800/172-405.** To make collect calls to a country besides the United States, dial ℂ **170,** and practice your Italian counting in order to relay the number to the Italian operator. Tell him or her that you want a *carico del destinatario. **Note:*** The 170 service is not free. The cost varies, depending on which country you are calling.

Don't count on all Italian phones having touch-tone service! You might not be able to access your voice mail or answering machine if you call home from Italy.

Time   In terms of standard time zones, Italy is 6 hours ahead of Eastern Standard Time in the United States. Daylight saving time goes into effect in Italy each year from the end of March to the end of September.

Tipping   This custom is practiced with flair in Italy—many people depend on tips for their livelihoods. In **hotels,** the service charge of 15% to 19% is already added to a bill. In addition, it's customary to tip the chambermaid .50€ (60¢) per day, the doorman (for calling a cab) .50€ (60¢), and the bellhop or porter 1.50€ to 2.50€ ($1.80–$3) for carrying your bags to your room. A concierge expects about 15% of his or her bill, as well as tips for extra services performed, which could include help with long-distance calls. In expensive hotels, these amounts are often doubled.

In **restaurants and cafes,** 15% is usually added to your bill to cover most charges. If you're not sure whether this has been done, ask, "*È incluso il servizio?*" (ay een-*cloo*-soh eel sair-*vee*-tsoh?). An additional tip isn't expected, but it's nice to leave the equivalent of an extra couple of dollars if you've been pleased with the service. Checkroom attendants expect .75€ (90¢), and washroom attendants should get .35€ (40¢). Restaurants are required by law to give customers official receipts.

Taxi drivers expect at least 10% of the fare.

Water   Most Italians take mineral water with their meals; however, tap water is safe everywhere, as are public drinking fountains. Unsafe sources will be marked ACQUA NON POTABILE. If tap water comes out cloudy, it's only the calcium or other minerals inherent in a water supply that often comes untreated from fresh springs.

6

Where to Stay in Rome

The good news is that Rome's hotels are in better shape than they've ever been. Dozens upon dozens of properties have undergone major renovations.

The bad news is that Rome has experienced a huge surge in tourism in recent years, and finding a hotel room at any time of the year is harder than ever. *Make your reservations as far ahead as possible.* If you like to gamble and arrive without a reservation, head quickly to the **airport information desk** or, once you get into town, to the offices of **Enjoy Rome** (p. 58)—their staff can help reserve you a room, if any are available.

Rome's high-end hotels are among the most luxurious in Europe. In addition to reviewing the best of the upscale hotels, we've tried to give you a good selection of moderately priced hotels, where you'll find comfortable, charming lodgings with private bathrooms. Even our inexpensive choices are clean and cheerful, and they offer more in services and facilities than you might expect from the prices. In the less expensive categories, you'll find a few *pensioni,* the Roman equivalent of a boardinghouse.

The Italian government controls the prices of its hotels, designating a minimum and a maximum rate. The difference between the two might depend on the season, the location of the room, and even its size. The government also classifies hotels with star ratings that indicate their category of comfort: five stars for deluxe, four for first class, three for second class, two for third class, and one for fourth class. Most former *pensioni* are now rated as one- or two-star hotels.

The distinction between a *pensione* hotel (where some degree of board was once required along with the room) and a regular hotel is no longer officially made, although many smaller, family-run establishments still call themselves *pensioni.* Government ratings don't depend on sensitivity of decoration or frescoed ceilings, but they're based on facilities, such as elevators and the like. Many of the finest hotels in Rome have a lower rating because they serve only breakfast.

Almost all the hotels listed serve breakfast (often a buffet with coffee, fruit, rolls, and cheese), but you can't take for granted that it's included in the room rate. That used to be universal, but it's not anymore, so check the listing carefully and ask the hotel to confirm what's included.

Nearly all hotels are heated in the cooler months, but not all are air-conditioned in summer, which can be vitally important during a stifling July or August. The deluxe and first-class ones are, but after that, it's a toss-up. Be sure to check the listing carefully before you book a stay in the dog days of summer!

All Italian hotels impose an **IVA (Imposta sul Valore Aggiunto),** or value-added tax. This tax is in effect throughout the European Union countries. It replaces some 20 other taxes and is an effort to streamline the tax structure. What does this mean for you? A higher hotel bill. Deluxe hotels will slap you with a whopping 13% tax, whereas first-class, second-class, and other hotels will impose a mere 9%. Most hotels quote a rate inclusive of this tax, but others prefer to add it on when you go to pay the bill. To avoid unpleasant surprises, ask to be quoted an all-inclusive rate—that is, with service, even a continental breakfast (which is often obligatory)—when you check in.

See "Best Hotel Bets," in chapter 1, for a quick-reference list of our favorite hotels in a variety of categories. See also "The Neighborhoods in Brief," in chapter 5, for a quick summary of each area that will help you decide if you'd like to stay there.

1 Near Stazione Termini

Despite a handful of pricey choices, this area is most notable for its concentration of cheap hotels. It's not the most picturesque location, and parts of the neighborhood are still transitional and edgy, but it's certainly convenient in terms of transportation and easy access to many of Rome's top sights.

VERY EXPENSIVE

Es. Hotel Rome ✦✦ *Finds*   If you want 19th-century Rome, check in elsewhere: If you prefer a hyper-modern atmosphere, the Es. Hotel is for you. This hotel is so dramatic, innovative, and high-tech that its opening sparked a bit of environmental recovery in the old but decaying Esquilino quarter on the fringe of the Termini. A government-rated five-star *luxe* hotel, it is posh and severe, yet comfortably modern. It's got everything from a Turkish bath to a business center.

Don't judge the hotel by its rather dull seven-story exterior, which resembles an office building. Inside, the lobby showcases the ruins of a 2nd-century A.D. Roman road. The midsize to spacious bedrooms emphasize minimalist Japanese designs, with wool rugs, glass desks, and plastic chairs in either orange or pea green. Tubs and showers are installed directly behind wooden beds and are separated by low screens. Rooms are soundproofed; some open onto balconies with city views.

In summer, a sun deck and pool are available. Especially alluring is the top-floor fitness center and the on-site spa. The top-floor restaurant provides a modern Italian cuisine.

Via Turati 171, 00185 Roma. ✆ 06-444841. Fax 06-44341396. www.eshotel.it. 235 units. 260€–296€ ($312–$355) double; from 275€–410€ ($330–$492) suite. AE, DC, MC, V. Parking 12€ ($14). Metro: Vittoria. Bus: 70 or 71. **Amenities:** 2 restaurants; bar; outdoor pool; fitness center; spa; room service (7am–midnight); babysitting; laundry service; dry cleaning; nonsmoking rooms. *In room:* A/C, TV, dataport, minibar, hair dryer, safe.

Hotel Artemide ✦✦   This boutique hotel, situated near the train station, combines stylish simplicity with modern comforts against a backdrop of Art Nouveau motifs. The original stained-glass skylight dome was retained in the lobby. The midsize to spacious guest rooms are furnished in natural colors and have tasteful furnishings, including elegantly comfortable beds, and spacious marble bathrooms with a tub/shower combination. For those who want to pay more, a series of deluxe rooms offers extras such as VCRs, battery chargers for cellular phones, and more deluxe bedding.

Via Nazionale 22, 00184 Roma. ✆ 06-489911. Fax 06-48991700. www.hotelartemide.it. 85 units. 345€ ($414) double; 390€ ($468) suite. Rates include buffet breakfast. AE, DC, MC, V. Parking 25€–30€ ($30–$36). Metro: Piazza Repubblica. **Amenities:** 2 restaurants; bar; room service (7am–midnight); laundry service; dry cleaning; nonsmoking rooms; 1 room for those w/limited mobility. *In room:* A/C, TV, dataport, minibar, hair dryer, safe, trouser press (in some).

Mecenate Palace Hotel ✦✦ *Finds*   A real gem, this little charmer lies 5 blocks south of the Termini. It's even more intimate and more professionally run than its closest competitor, the Artemide (although it's also pricier). Its downside is a location

Boscolo Hotel Aleph **2**	Hotel des Artistes **13**	La Residenza **4**
Empire Palace Hotel **11**	Hotel Donatello **23**	Mecenate Palace Hotel **24**
Es. Rome Hotel **21**	Hotel Eden **5**	Residenza Cellini **30**
Exedra **27**	Hotel Fiamma **12**	Rome Marriott Grand Hotel Flora **8**
Hotel Alexandra **1**	Hotel Giuliana **19**	Royal Court **15**
Hotel Aphrodite **17**	Hotel Italia **29**	St. Regis Grand **3**
Hotel Artemide **28**	Hotel Morgana **18**	Scott House Hotel **20**
Hotel Columbia **26**	Hotel Oxford **10**	Victoria Roma **9**
Hotel Contilia **25**	Hotel Regno **7**	Villa delle Rose **14**
Hotel Corot **16**	Kennedy Hotel **22**	Westin Excelsior **6**

that's inconvenient for those wanting to spend a lot of time visiting the Vatican or classical Rome.

The hotel is composed of two adjacent buildings. One of them was designed by Rinaldi in 1887; the second one (on Via Carlo Alberto) was designed a few years later. The guest rooms, where traces of the original detailing mix with contemporary furnishings, overlook the city rooftops or Santa Maria Maggiore. They range from small to medium but boast high ceilings and extras such as luxury mattresses. The spacious marble bathrooms are sumptuous, with makeup mirrors and deluxe toiletries. Three suites offer superior comfort, authentic 19th-century antiques, and a fireplace.

Via Carlo Alberto 3, 00185 Roma. © 06-44702024. Fax 06-4461354. www.mecenatepalace.com. 62 units. 430€ ($516) double; 750€ ($900) suite. Rates include buffet breakfast. AE, DC, MC, V. Parking 24€ ($29). Metro: Termini or Vittorio Emanuele. **Amenities:** Restaurant; cafe; bar; room service (7am–midnight); babysitting; laundry service; dry cleaning; nonsmoking rooms; rooms for those w/limited mobility. *In room:* A/C, TV, dataport, minibar, hair dryer, safe.

St. Regis Grand ★★★   This restored landmark is more plush and upscale than any hotel in the area—not even the comparable Excelsior or the Eden across town can match its sheer opulence. Its drawback is its location at the dreary Stazione Termini, but once you're inside its splendid shell, all thoughts of railway stations vanish.

When Ceásar Ritz founded this outrageously expensive hotel in 1894, it was the first to offer a private bathroom and two electric lights in every room. Today it is a magnificent Roman palazzo, combining Italian and French styles in decoration and furnishings. The lobby is decked out with Murano chandeliers, columns, marble busts, and cherubs. You'll also find Murano chandeliers in many of the guest rooms, which for the most part are exceedingly spacious and luxuriously furnished. Hand-painted frescoes are installed above each headboard, and the large bathrooms are done in fabulous marble. For the best rooms and the finest service, ask to be booked on the St. Regis floor.

Via Vittorio Emanuele Orlando 3, 00185 Roma. © **06-47091.** Fax 06-4747307. www.stregis.com/grandrome. 161 units. 720€–990€ ($864–$1,188) double; from 1,425€ ($1,710) suite. AE, DC, MC, V. Parking 20€–30€ ($24–$36). Metro: Repubblica. **Amenities:** Restaurant; bar; sauna; fitness center; 24-hr. room service; massage; babysitting; laundry service; dry cleaning; nonsmoking rooms; rooms for those w/limited mobility. *In room:* A/C, TV, dataport, minibar, coffeemaker, hair dryer, iron, safe.

EXPENSIVE

Empire Palace Hotel ★★   This hotel combines a historic core (in this case, a palazzo built around 1870) with modern luxuries; together these elements create a very comfortable and appealing ambience. The original builders, an aristocratic Venetian family, installed ceiling frescoes showing the heavens in azure blue on some of the ceilings. Some of the striking combinations of the original core with unusual modern paintings are showstoppers. Opened as a hotel in 1999, the Empire Palace is classified four stars by the Italian government. Most bedrooms are quite large. All have marble bathrooms and conservative cherry-wood furnishings.

The building's courtyard is outfitted with a splashing fountain and a verdant garden. Immediately adjacent, with tables spilling into the courtyard during fine weather, is the **Aureliano Restaurant,** outfitted with Murano chandeliers.

Via Aureliana 39, 00187 Roma. © 06-421281. Fax 06-42128400. www.empirepalacehotel.com. 113 units. 210€–360€ ($252–$432) double; 550€ ($660) suite. Rates include breakfast. AE, DC, MC, V. Parking 25€ ($30). Metro: Repubblica or Termini. **Amenities:** Restaurant; bar; fitness center; room service (6:30am–midnight); babysitting; laundry service; dry cleaning; nonsmoking rooms; rooms for those w/limited mobility. *In room:* A/C, TV, dataport, minibar, hair dryer, safe, Jacuzzi in suites.

Exedra ★★   This neoclassical palace overlooking the Piazza della Repubblica at the rail terminal also fronts the Baths of Diocletian and Michelangelo's Basilica degli Angeli. One of Rome's latest government-rated five-star luxury hotels, the Exedra is a study in modern elegance combined with the romance of the past. It's luxury living on a grand scale from the spacious standard double rooms to a variety of suites. Our favorite rooms are the top-floor accommodations in the Clementino Wing, each with bare brick walls and the original ceiling beams. You'll find creamy marble, lush carpeting, discreet lighting, and high ceilings throughout the building, while rooms feature such decorative notes as printed leather headboards and whorled silk wall coverings.

The marble bathrooms are luxurious, with tub/shower combinations. You can take morning coffee on the rooftop garden terrace overlooking the Fountain of the Naiads. Later you can retreat to one of Rome's best hotel spas. The spa is linked to the rooftop swimming pool by a glass elevator.

The restaurants celebrate Rome in the 1950s and 1960s—for example, La Frustra was inspired by Fellini's Oscar-winning film *8½*, and Tazio is a reverential tongue-in-cheek celebration of Tazio Secchiaroli, daddy of the dreaded paparazzi. For a taste of those heady days of *La Dolce Vita*, head for the Champagnerie.

Piazza della Repubblica 47, 00185 Roma. ℂ **06-489381.** Fax 06-48938000. www.boscolohotels.com. 240 units. 190€–530€ ($228–$636) double; from 500€ ($600) suite. AE, DC, MC, V. Parking 30€ ($36). Metro: Repubblica. **Amenities:** 3 restaurants; 2 bars; rooftop pool; spa; Jacuzzi; sauna; car-rental desk; business center; 24-hr. room service; babysitting; laundry service; dry cleaning; nonsmoking rooms; rooms for those w/limited mobility; rooftop garden terrace; solarium. *In room:* A/C, TV, dataport, minibar, hair dryer, safe.

Hotel Columbia ★★   This is one of the best hotels in the neighborhood, with a hardworking multilingual staff. A government-rated three-star choice, originally built around 1900, it underwent a well-done radical renovation in 1997. The interior contains Murano chandeliers and conservatively modern furniture. The compact, cozy guest rooms compare well with the accommodations in the best hotels nearby. Each contains a medium-size tiled bathroom with adequate shelf space and a tub/shower combination. The appealing rooftop garden has a view of the surrounding rooftops.

Via del Viminale 15, 00184 Roma. ℂ **06-4744289** or 06-4883509. Fax 06-4740209. www.hotelcolumbia.com. 45 units. 230€ ($276) double; 310€ ($372) triple. Rates include buffet breakfast. AE, DC, MC, V. Parking nearby 20€ ($24). Metro: Repubblica. **Amenities:** Breakfast room; bar; room service (7am–11pm); laundry service; nonsmoking rooms. *In room:* A/C, TV, dataport, minibar, hair dryer, safe.

MODERATE

Hotel Donatello   Named for the fabled painter, this small hotel is for those who prefer quiet streets. It lies about equidistant to the Stazione Termini and the Colosseum. With its inviting Roman hospitality, it is somewhat like a B&B. The surrounding area is a bit scruffy but reasonably safe. The hotel is spread across a three-floor terraced building, with basic but clean rooms, each well maintained. The best accommodations open onto small balconies. Bathrooms are midsize, and five have Majolica tiles; the rest are tiled with marble. The Prette family is welcoming and provides guests with much help and useful suggestions, such as how not to get ripped off in Rome.

Via di Portamaggiore 83, 00185 Roma. ℂ **06-7010833.** Fax 06-7011656. www.hoteldonatelloroma.com. 20 units. 75€–186€ ($90–$223) double; 85€–211€ ($102–$253) triple. Rates include breakfast. AE, DC, MC, V. Parking 15€ ($18). Metro: Manzoni. **Amenities:** Restaurant; bar; concierge; room service (breakfast only); laundry service; dry cleaning. *In room:* A/C, TV, minibar, hair dryer, safe.

Hotel Fiamma   Near the Baths of Diocletian, the Fiamma is in a renovated building, with five floors of bedrooms and a ground floor faced with marble and plate-glass windows. It's an old favorite, if a bit past its prime. The lobby is long and bright, filled with a varied collection of furnishings, including overstuffed chairs and blue enamel railings. On the same floor is an austere marble breakfast room. The comfortably furnished guest rooms range from small to medium. The small shower-only bathrooms are tiled, with adequate shelf space.

Via Gaeta 61, 00185 Roma. ℂ **06-4818436.** Fax 06-4883511. www.leonardihotels.com. 79 units (shower only). 154€ ($185) double; 196€ ($235) triple. Rates include buffet breakfast. AE, DC, MC, V. Parking 20€ ($24). Metro: Termini. **Amenities:** Breakfast room; room service (breakfast only). *In room:* A/C, TV, minibar, hair dryer.

Hotel Morgana   Between Santa Maria Maggiore and Stazione Termini, this hotel was last renovated in 2001 and is completely up-to-date. Bedrooms are comfortable and furnished in a vaguely English-style decor. The English-speaking staff is pleasant and will help guide you to some of the city's most important attractions, many of which lay only a short walk from the hotel. Because this hotel lies in a noisy area, all of the bedrooms are soundproofed. The hotel offers pick-up and transfer services to and from the airport. Bathrooms come in a range of sizes and have tub/shower combos.

Via F. Turati 33–37, 00185 Roma. © **06-4467230**. Fax 06-4469142. www.hotelmorgana.com. 106 units. 165€ ($198) double; 220€ ($264) suite. Rates include buffet breakfast. AE, DC, MC, V. Parking 12€ ($14.40). Metro: Termini. **Amenities:** Bar; 24-hr. room service; babysitting; laundry service; dry cleaning; nonsmoking rooms; rooms for those w/limited mobility. *In room:* A/C, TV, dataport (in some), minibar, hair dryer, safe.

Kennedy Hotel   A 5-minute walk from the Termini Station, this completely restored hotel is one of the best bets for those who want to stay in the rail station area. The hotel, launched in 1963 when President Kennedy died, was named to honor his memory. The building itself is from the late 19th century, although it has been much restored and modernized over the years. The hotel is within an easy walk of many of the historical monuments of Rome, including the Basilica of S. Maria Maggiore, the Opera House, the Colosseum, and the Roman Forum. Bedrooms are renovated, with tasteful furnishings and double-glass soundproofing. The bathrooms come with either tub or shower; many rooms open to views of the antique Roman wall of Servio Tullio.

Via Filippo Turati 62–64, 00185 Roma. © **06-4465373**. Fax 06-4465417. www.hotelkennedy.net. 52 units. 95€–160€ ($114–$192) double; 140€–260€ ($168–$312) suite. Rates include breakfast. AE, DC, MC, V. Bus: 71. **Amenities:** Bar; fitness center; scooter rentals; room service (breakfast only); nonsmoking rooms. *In room:* A/C, TV, hair dryer.

Residenza Cellini ⭐ *Finds*   This small hotel is run by the English-speaking De Palais family, who welcome guests with warm hospitality. In the heart of Rome, Cellini lies near the Termini rail station. Gaetano and Barbara De Palais have lavished attention on their small number of bedrooms, and the results are comfortable and stylish. Rooms are midsize and traditionally furnished, with polished wood pieces and Oriental carpets on the hardwood floors. The king-size beds have antiallergic orthopedic mattresses, and the bathrooms come with hydrojet showers or Jacuzzi.

Via Modena 5, 00184 Roma. © **06-47825204**. Fax 06-47881806. www.residenzacellini.it. 6 units. 165€–210€ ($198–$252) double; 185€–230€ ($222–$276) junior suite. Rates include buffet breakfast. AE, DC, MC, V. Parking 20€–25€ ($24–$30). Metro: Repubblica. **Amenities:** Bar; 24-hr. room service; laundry service; dry cleaning. *In room:* A/C, TV, dataport, minibar, hair dryer, safe.

Royal Court ⭐ *Finds*   This winner lies in a recently restored Liberty-style palace a short walk from the Termini. The hotel evokes a tranquil, elegantly decorated private town house. Some of the superior rooms offer Jacuzzis in their bathrooms, but all units feature well-maintained and designed bathrooms with tub/shower combinations. The superior rooms also come with small balconies opening onto cityscapes. Even the standard doubles are comfortable, but if you're willing to pay the price, you can stay in the deluxe doubles, which are like junior suites in most Rome hotels. Some of the bedrooms are large enough to sleep three or four guests comfortably.

Via Marghera 51, 00185 Roma. © **06-44340364**. Fax 06-4469121. www.morganaroyalcourt.com. 24 units. 130€–250€ ($156–$300) double. Rates include buffet breakfast. AE, DC, MC, V. Parking 24€ ($29). Metro: Termini. **Amenities:** Bar; breakfast room; car-rental desk; room service (7am–11pm); babysitting; laundry service; dry cleaning; nonsmoking rooms; 1 room for those w/limited mobility. *In room:* A/C, TV, dataport, minibar, beverage maker, hair dryer, safe, trouser press (in some).

Villa delle Rose _Kids_   Located less than 2 blocks north of the rail station, this hotel is an acceptable, if unexciting, choice. In the late 1800s, it was a villa with a dignified cut-stone facade inspired by the Renaissance. Despite many renovations, the ornate trappings of the original are still visible, including the lobby's Corinthian-capped marble columns and the flagstone-covered terrace that is part of the verdant back garden. The look is still one of faded grandeur. Much of the interior has been recently redecorated and upgraded with traditional wall coverings, new carpets, new mattresses, and tiled bathrooms, 80% of which have a shower only. Breakfasts in the garden do a lot to add country flavor to an otherwise very urban setting. Families often book here asking for one of the three rooms with lofts that can sleep up to five.

Via Vicenza 5, 00185 Roma. (✆ 06-4451788. Fax 06-4451639. www.villadellerose.it. 38 units (some w/shower only). 104€–180€ ($125–$216) double. Rates include buffet breakfast. AE, DC, MC, V. Free parking (only 4 cars). Metro: Termini or Castro Pretorio. _In room:_ A/C (30 rooms), TV, dataport, minibar (in some), hair dryer, safe.

INEXPENSIVE

Hotel Aphrodite _Value_   Completely renovated, this new government-rated three-star hotel in the heart of Rome is a good deal. Directly next to Stazione Termini, this four-story hotel is a reliable and well-run choice, although the surrounding area is a little seedy at night. For rail passengers who want quick check-ins and fast getaways, it's the most convenient choice there is. Bedrooms are attractively and comfortably furnished with modern pieces and parquet floors. The marble bathrooms come with showers and mosaic tiles. Ask at the desk about walking tours through the historic districts. A special feature here is the sunny rooftop terrace.

Via Marsala 90, 00185 Roma. (✆ 06-491096. Fax 06-491579. www.accommodationinrome.com. 50 units. 90€–120€ ($108–$144) double; 110€–150€ ($132–$180) triple. Rates include continental breakfast. AE, DC, MC, V. Parking 10€ ($13). Metro: Termini. **Amenities:** Gym; nonsmoking rooms; rooms for those w/limited mobility. _In room:_ A/C, TV, dataport, minibar, hair dryer, safe.

Hotel Contilia _Value_   As the automatic doors part to reveal a stylish marble lobby with Persian rugs and antiques, you might step back to double-check the address. The former Pensione Tony Contilia has taken over this building's other small hotels and become one of the neighborhood's best choices. The guest rooms have firm beds and built-in units. Rooms overlooking the cobblestone courtyard are the most tranquil. The smallish contemporary bathrooms have tub/shower combinations.

Via Principe Amadeo 81, 00185 Roma. (✆ 06-4466942. Fax 06-4466904. www.hotelcontilia.com. 42 units. 75€–165€ ($90–$198) double, 100€–225€ ($120–$270) triple. Rates include buffet breakfast. AE, DC, MC, V. Parking 25€ ($30); free on street. Metro: Termini. **Amenities:** Breakfast room; bar; room service (6am–midnight); nonsmoking rooms; 1 room for those w/limited mobility. _In room:_ A/C, TV, dataport, hair dryer, safe.

Hotel Corot   North of the train station, this simple, safe haven occupies the second and third floors of an early 1900s building that contains a handful of apartments and another inferior hotel. Each high-ceilinged guest room is soundproofed and has simple but traditional furniture, including a good bed, and a modern shower-only bathroom. Superior rooms have a bathtub Jacuzzi.

Via Marghera 15–17, 00185 Roma. (✆ 06-44700900. Fax 06-44700905. www.hotelcorot.it. 28 units. 110€–150€ ($132–$180) double; 135€–170€ ($162–$204) triple; 160€–195€ ($192–$234) quad. Rates include breakfast. AE, DC, MC, V. Parking 22€ ($26) for 1st night; 15€ ($18) for the 2nd. Metro: Termini. **Amenities:** Bar; lounge; room service (7am–11pm); nonsmoking rooms; 1 room for those w/limited mobility. _In room:_ A/C, TV, dataport, minibar, hair dryer, safe.

Hotel des Artistes _Value_   This modest choice lies a few steps from Stazione Termini and offers good-quality accommodations at a moderate price. One part of the hotel is a hostel with dormitory-style rooms, bathrooms in the corridors, and a TV in each room; rates for those accommodations range from 95€ to 165€ ($114–$198) for a triple. Regular rooms range from small to medium, some of them decorated with Oriental rugs. The furniture is simple but classic, and the maid service is excellent. The hotel's rooms have shower-only private bathrooms, small but neat and just renovated. Breakfast is the only meal served. The rooftop garden, open 24 hours, is an ideal place for socializing. The hotel is entirely nonsmoking.

Via Villafranca 20, 00185 Roma. ⓒ 06-4454365. Fax 06-4462368. www.hoteldesartistes.com. 45 units (shower only). 69€–155€ ($83–$186) double. Rates include buffet breakfast. AE, DC, MC, V. Parking nearby 13€–18€ ($16–$22). Metro: Castro Pretorio. Bus: 310. **Amenities:** Bar; babysitting. *In room:* A/C, TV, dataport, hair dryer, safe.

Hotel Giuliana   Close to the landmark Opera House deep in the heart of Rome, this is a well-maintained, neat little family-run hotel facing the Basilica Santa Maria Maggiore. Personal service is a hallmark. Although not grandly stylish, bedrooms are exceedingly comfortable and of good size, with up-to-date bathrooms. All rooms are nonsmoking. A generous breakfast is served every morning in a cozy room.

Via Agostino Depretis 70, 00184 Roma. ⓒ 06-4880795. Fax 06-4824287. www.hotelgiuliana.com. 11 units. 90€–180€ ($108–$216) double; 100€–240€ ($120–$288) triple. Rates include breakfast. AE, DC, MC, V. Metro: Repubblica. **Amenities:** Breakfast room; bar; 24-hr. room service. *In room:* A/C (some units), TV, hair dryer, safe.

Hotel Italia   This is a turn-of-the-20th-century building with an eight-room annex across the street. It's been a hotel for 20 years, but it has never been as well managed as it is now under the stewardship of the Valentini family. Both buildings employ a night porter/security guard, and both offer their guests a breakfast buffet that's one of the most appealing in the neighborhood. Midsize bedrooms are well maintained and conservatively decorated with comfortable yet simple furniture. Most units have parquet floors, and all rooms have private bathrooms, although the facilities for room no. 6 are across the hallway. The hotel is completely nonsmoking.

Via Venezia 18, 00184 Roma. ⓒ 06-4828355. Fax 06-4745550. www.hotelitaliaroma.com. 31 units. 70€–130€ ($84–$156) double; 110€–155€ ($132–$186) suite. Rates include buffet breakfast. AE, DC, MC, V. Parking nearby 15€–20€ ($18–$24). Metro: Repubblica. Bus: 64. **Amenities:** Bar; babysitting. *In room:* A/C, TV, hair dryer, safe.

Scott House Hotel   Simple but adequate for low-maintenance travelers on tight budgets, this hotel occupies the fourth and fifth floors of a building originally constructed in the 18th century. Bedrooms are high-ceilinged, freshly painted, and compact; most have comfortable beds and at least one upholstered armchair. Each was completely renovated in 1999.

Via Gioberti 30, 00185 Roma. ⓒ 06-4465392. Fax 06-4464986. www.scotthouse.com. 36 units (w/shower only). 63€–98€ ($76–$118) double. Rate includes breakfast. AE, DC, MC, V. Metro: Termini. **Amenities:** Bar; lounge. *In room:* A/C, TV, safe.

2 Near Via Veneto & Piazza Barberini

If you stay in this area, you definitely won't be on the wrong side of the tracks. Unlike the area around the dreary rail station, this is a beautiful and upscale commercial section, near some of Rome's best shopping.

To locate the hotels listed below, see the "Accommodations near Stazione Termini, Via Veneto & Piazza Barberini" map on p. 75.

VERY EXPENSIVE

Hotel Eden ✦✦✦ It's not as grand architecturally as the Westin Excelsior, it doesn't have the views of the Hassler, and it's certainly not a stunner like the Hilton. However, the Eden is Rome's top choice for discerning travelers who like their comforts striking but not ostentatious.

For several generations after its 1889 opening, this hotel, about a 10-minute walk east of the Spanish Steps, reigned over one of the world's most stylish shopping neighborhoods. Hemingway, Callas, Ingrid Bergman, Fellini—all checked in during its heyday, and the hotel still retains its former grandeur, coupled with the new amenities that its government-rated five-star status calls for. The Eden's hilltop position guarantees a panoramic city view from most guest rooms; all are spacious and elegantly appointed with a decor harking back to the late 19th century, plus marble-sheathed bathrooms with deluxe toiletries and makeup mirrors. Try to get one of the front rooms with a balcony boasting views over Rome. The hotel's restaurant, **La Terrazza,** is one of Rome's best (see chapter 7).

Via Ludovisi 49, 00187 Roma. ✆ 06-478121. Fax 06-4821584. www.hotel-eden.it. 121 units. 680€–780€ ($816–$936) double; from 1,900€ ($2,280) suite. AE, DC, DISC, MC, V. Parking 52€ ($62). Metro: Piazza Barberini. **Amenities:** Restaurant (La Terrazza; see chapter 7); bar; health club; car-rental desk; 24-hr. room service; babysitting; laundry service; dry cleaning; nonsmoking rooms. In room: A/C, TV, dataport, minibar, hair dryer, safe.

Rome Marriott Grand Hotel Flora ✦✦ This long-standing monument at the top of the Via Veneto has been restored for its new life in the 21st century. One of the grand stopovers in the heyday of *La Dolce Vita,* the hotel offers spacious, beautifully furnished bedrooms overlooking the Villa Borghese gardens. Its only drawback, as we see it, is that the individual visitor to Rome might get lost in a sea of businesspeople and tour groups. The bedrooms are supremely comfortable, although they evoke those found in a large American city more than the typical offerings in the Eternal City. Bathrooms are spacious, tiled, and well lit, with tub/shower combinations. TVs and minibars are hidden in elegant armoires. The suites are some of the grandest in Rome. The seventh-floor **Ailanto** restaurant has a terrific view over Rome.

Via Vittorio Veneto 191, 00187. ✆ **800/228-9290** in the U.S., or 06-489929. Fax 06-4820359. www.marriott.com. 155 units. 313€–530€ ($376–$636) double; from 700€ ($840) suite. AE, DC, MC, V. Parking 25€ ($30). Metro: Barberini. **Amenities:** Restaurant; bar; room service (6:30am–11:30pm); babysitting; laundry service; dry cleaning; nonsmoking rooms; rooms for those w/limited mobility. In room: A/C, TV, dataport, minibar, hair dryer, safe.

Westin Excelsior ✦ If money is no object, here's a good place to spend it. The Excelsior is more grandiose architecturally than either the Eden or the Hassler, but it is not as up-to-date or as beautifully renovated as the Eden or the St. Regis Grand. For our money, we prefer the newer Hotel de Russie, but the Excelsior remains a favorite, especially among seniors who remember it from decades past and don't mind that it has never really moved into the 21st century. Everything looks just a tad dowdy today, but the Excelsior endures, in no small part because of the hospitable staff. The baroque corner tower of this limestone palace, overlooking the U.S. Embassy, is a landmark in Rome. A string of cavernous reception rooms is adorned with thick rugs, marble floors, gilded garlands decorating the walls, and Empire furniture.

The guest rooms come in two varieties: new (the result of a major renovation) and traditional. The older ones are a bit worn, while the newer ones have more imaginative color schemes and plush carpeting. All are spacious and elegantly furnished, with deluxe mattresses and often with antiques and silk curtains. Most rooms are unique;

many have sumptuous Hollywood-style marble bathrooms with bidets. Ask for one of the larger doubles with spacious sitting areas; they're practically suites.

Via Vittorio Veneto 125, 00187 Roma. ⓒ **800/325-3589** in the U.S., or 06-47081. Fax 06-4826205. www. westin.com/excelsiorrome. 316 units. 780€ ($936) double; from 2,340€ ($2,808) suite. AE, DC, DISC, MC, V. Parking (public outdoor or private indoor) 16€–42€ ($19–$50). Metro: Barberini. **Amenities:** Restaurant; bar; indoor heated pool; health club; Jacuzzi; sauna; steam room; salon; 24-hr. room service; babysitting; laundry service; dry cleaning; rooms for those w/limited mobility. *In room:* A/C, TV, dataport, minibar, hair dryer, safe.

EXPENSIVE

Boscolo Hotel Aleph 🌟🌟 Called "sexy and decadent" by some hotel critics when it opened, this winning choice leads the pack among "new wave" Italian hotels. A luxury hotel in the center of Rome, Aleph was designed by Adam Tihany, who said he wanted to "humanize the rooms with indulgent details." Only a minute's walk from the Via Veneto, the hotel offers spacious guest rooms adorned with elegant Italian fabrics, a tasteful decor, and all the latest technology.

Murano chandeliers, window blinds made of strings of metal beads, a dramatic roof terrace overlooking the heart of Rome, and an indoor swimming pool are just some of the features of this hotel. Bathrooms are luxurious, with tub/shower combinations. The all-blue Paradise Spa evokes Roman decadence.

Tihany wanted something eccentric and intriguing, exclusive yet provocative—and his creation is all that and vastly comfortable as well, with its 1930s- and 1940s-inspired style. Large black-and-white blow-ups by New York street photographer (and father of the designer) Bram Tihany adorn the walls. Sublime Italian food is served in the *luxe* restaurant, which is totally dominated by the color of red. There's even a wine bar dedicated to Dionysus.

Via San Basilio 15, 00187 Roma. ⓒ **06-422901.** Fax 06-42290000. www.boscolohotels.com. 96 units. 250€–430€ ($300–$516) double; from 600€ ($720) suite. AE, DC, MC, V. Parking 35€ ($42). Metro: Barberini. **Amenities:** Restaurant; 2 bars; indoor heated pool; fitness center; spa; Jacuzzi; sauna; car-rental desk; business center; 24-hr. room service; massage; babysitting; laundry service; dry cleaning; nonsmoking rooms; rooms for those w/limited mobility. *In room:* A/C, TV, dataport, minibar, hair dryer, safe, CD player.

Hotel Alexandra 🌟 *(Finds)*   This is one of the few places you can stay on Via Veneto without going broke (although it's not exactly cheap). Set behind the dignified stone facade of what was a 19th-century mansion, the Alexandra offers immaculate guest rooms. Those facing the front are exposed to roaring traffic and street noise; those in back are quieter but have lesser views. The rooms range from rather cramped to medium size, but each has been recently redecorated and filled with antiques or tasteful contemporary pieces. Among the extras are swing-mirror vanities and brass or wood bedsteads. The full bathrooms are small to medium, and the largest doubles have tubs. The breakfast room is especially appealing: Inspired by an Italian garden, it was designed by noted architect Paolo Portoghesi.

Via Vittorio Veneto 18, 00187 Roma. ⓒ **06-4881943.** Fax 06-4871804. www.hotelalexandraroma.com. 60 units (some w/shower only). 210€–260€ ($252–$312) double; 360€–800€ ($432–$960) suite. Rates include buffet breakfast. AE, DC, MC, V. Parking 26€–36€ ($31–$43). Metro: Piazza Barberini. **Amenities:** Room service (7am–10pm); laundry service; dry cleaning; nonsmoking rooms; rooms for those w/limited mobility. *In room:* A/C, TV, dataport (in some), minibar, hair dryer, safe.

Victoria Roma 🌟   The Victoria Roma's great location overlooking the Borghese Gardens remains one of its most desirable assets; you can sit in the rooftop garden drinking your cocktail amid palm trees and potted plants, imagining that you're in a country villa. The lounges and living rooms retain a country-house decor, with soft touches that include high-backed chairs, large oil paintings, bowls of freshly cut flowers, provincial tables, and Oriental rugs. You don't get opulence, but you do get a sort of dowdy charm and good maintenance. Rooms range from standard to spacious; each is comfortably equipped with good beds, and most units were renovated during the late 1990s. Furnishings such as Oriental carpets are common, and the bathrooms are generally large, with dual basins, phones, tub/shower combinations, and scales. Some of the tubs are extra-long. Floor no. 5 has the best views of the Villa Borghese.

Via Campania 41, 00187 Roma. 🕜 06-473931. Fax 06-4871890. www.hotelvictoriaroma.com. 108 units. 250€–300€ ($300–$360) double; 300€–350€ ($360–$420) triple. Rates include breakfast. AE, DC, MC, V. Parking 26€ ($31). Metro: Barberini. Bus: 95 or 116. **Amenities:** Restaurant; bar; room service (6am–midnight); babysitting; laundry service; dry cleaning; nonsmoking rooms. *In room:* A/C, TV, dataport, minibar, hair dryer, safe.

MODERATE

Hotel Oxford   The Oxford is a solid, if not spectacular, choice adjacent to the Borghese Gardens. Recently renovated, it's now centrally heated and fully carpeted throughout. The midsize guest rooms, which contain modern furnishings, have large bathrooms with tub/shower combinations and adequate shelf space.

Via Boncompagni 89, 00187 Roma. 🕜 06-4203601. Fax 06-42815349. www.hoteloxford.com. 59 units. 150€–240€ ($180–$288) double; 260€–300€ ($312–$360) suite. Rates include buffet breakfast. AE, DC, MC, V. Parking 20€–25€ ($24–$30). Metro: Barberini. Bus: 53 or 63. **Amenities:** Restaurant; pleasant bar serving snacks; room service (7am–11pm); babysitting; laundry service; dry cleaning. *In room:* A/C, TV, minibar, hair dryer, safe.

Hotel Regno   Set in a great shopping area, this six-story hotel stands behind a severe stone facade. It was originally a library in the 1600s. In the 1960s, it was transformed into a simple hotel, and in 1999, it was upgraded into a well-managed, government-rated three-star hotel. Bedrooms are relatively small but comfortably appointed with nondescript modern furniture. All units contain neatly kept bathrooms. Some have showers, some tubs, and some both. The staff is friendly and hardworking. The hotel has a simple breakfast room, plus a sun deck on the building's roof.

Via del Corso 330, 00186 Roma. 🕜 06-6976361. Fax 06-6789239. www.hotelregno.com. 62 units. 160€–250€ ($192–$300) double; 260€–300€ ($312–$360) suite. Rates include buffet breakfast. AE, DC, MC, V. Parking: 26€ ($31). Metro: Spagna. **Amenities:** Breakfast room; bar; room service (breakfast only); babysitting; laundry service; dry cleaning. *In room:* A/C, TV, dataport, minibar, hair dryer, safe.

La Residenza 👁👁   In a superb but congested location, this converted villa successfully combines intimacy and elegance. A bit old-fashioned and homelike, this little hotel has an ivy-covered courtyard and a series of upholstered public rooms with Empire divans, oil portraits, and rattan chairs. Terraces are scattered throughout. The guest rooms are generally spacious, containing bentwood chairs and built-in furniture. The dozen or so junior suites boast balconies. The bathrooms have robes and even come equipped with ice machines.

Via Emilia 22–24, 00187 Roma. 🕜 06-4880789. Fax 06-485721. www.hotel-la-residenza.com. 29 units. 185€–199€ ($222–$239) double; 214€–228€ ($257–$274) suite. Rates include buffet breakfast. AE, MC, V. Parking (limited) 7€ ($8.40). Metro: Piazza Barberini. **Amenities:** Bar; room service (7am–10pm); babysitting; laundry service; dry cleaning. *In room:* A/C, TV, minibar, hair dryer, safe.

3 Near Ancient Rome

To locate the hotels in this section, refer to the "Accommodations Near Piazza del Popolo & the Spanish Steps" map on p. 91.

EXPENSIVE

Capo d'Africa ⊛ *Finds*   Installed within a beautiful 19th-century building with a strong colonial look, this hotel lies in the heart of Imperial Rome between the Forum and the Domus Aurea in the Celio district of Rome, a few steps from the Colosseum. Endowed with a "contemporary classic" look, it attracts visitors with its sophisticated interior design, works of art, high-tech facilities, and impeccable service. Best of all is a splendid rooftop terrace with a panoramic view over some of the dusty ruins of the world's most famous monuments. The hotel takes its name from an image known as *Caput Africae* that stood nearby in ancient times. Rooms are midsize and furnished with good taste; they are spread across three floors. The furnishings are stylized, including tall headboards of beech wood, red leather upholstery, and green marble wash basins.

Via Capo d'Africa 54, 00137 Roma. ☎ **06-772801**. Fax 06-77280801. www.hotelcapodafrica.com. 65 units. 240€–320€ ($288–$384) double; 425€–500€ ($510–$600) suite. Rates include breakfast. AE, DC, MC, V. Parking 25€ ($30). Metro: Colosseo. **Amenities:** Restaurant; bar; fitness center; 24-hr. room service; babysitting; nonsmoking rooms; rooms for those w/limited mobility; valet. *In room:* A/C, TV, dataport, minibar, hair dryer, safe.

Hotel Forum ⊛   Once a convent, this graceful, atmospheric building is a longtime favorite. Built around a medieval bell tower off the Fori Imperiali, the Hotel Forum offers old-fashioned elegance and accommodations that range from tasteful to opulent. The midsize rooms, which look out on the sights of the ancient city, are well appointed with antiques, mirrors, and Oriental rugs. About half the bathrooms have tubs; the others have showers. The hotel's lounges are conservative, with paneled walls and furnishings that combine Italian and French provincial styles. Dining is an event in the rooftop-garden restaurant; reserve well in advance.

Via di Tor de Conti 25–30, 00184 Roma. ☎ **06-6792446**. Fax 06-6786479. www.hotelforumrome.com. 80 units. 160€–340€ ($192–$408) double; 250€–550€ ($300–$660) suite. Rates include buffet breakfast. AE, DC, MC, V. Parking 25€ ($30). Metro: Colosseo. Bus: 40, 75, 85, 87, or 117. **Amenities:** Rooftop restaurant; 2 bars; 24-hr. room service; babysitting; laundry service; dry cleaning; nonsmoking rooms. *In room:* A/C, TV, dataport, hair dryer, safe.

MODERATE

Hotel Nerva   Some of the Nerva's walls and foundations date from the 1500s (others from a century later), but the modern amenities date only from 1997. The setting, above and a few steps from the Roman Forum, will appeal to any student of archaeology and literature, and the warm welcome from the Cirulli brothers will appeal to all. The decor is accented with wood panels and terra-cotta tiles; some guest rooms even retain the original ceiling beams. The furniture is contemporary and comfortable, with tiled bathrooms (mainly with showers) and adequate shelf space. All rooms are soundproofed.

Via Tor di Conti 3, 00184 Roma. ☎ **06-6781835**. Fax 06-69922204. www.hotelnerva.com. 19 units. 130€–220€ ($156–$264) double; 225€–350€ ($270–$420) suite. Rates include breakfast. AE, MC, V. Metro: Colosseo. **Amenities:** Bar; 24-hr. room service; babysitting; laundry service; nonsmoking rooms; 1 room for those w/limited mobility. *In room:* A/C, TV, minibar, hair dryer, safe, trouser press.

INEXPENSIVE

Colosseum Hotel   Two short blocks southwest of Santa Maria Maggiore, this hotel offers affordable and small but comfortable rooms. Someone with flair and pots of money designed the public areas and upper halls, which hint at baronial grandeur. The drawing room, with its long refectory table, white walls, red tiles, and provincial armchairs, invites lingering. The guest rooms are furnished with well-chosen antique reproductions (beds of heavy carved wood, dark-paneled wardrobes, and leatherwood chairs); all have stark white walls, and some have old-fashioned plumbing in the bathrooms.

Via Sforza 10, 00184 Roma. ✆ **06-4827228**. Fax 06-4827285. www.hotelcolosseum.com. 50 units (tub/shower). 125€–161€ ($150–$193) double; 150€–212€ ($180–$254) triple. Rates include buffet breakfast. AE, DC, MC, V. Parking 30€ ($36). Metro: Cavour. **Amenities:** Lounge; bar; room service (7am–8pm); babysitting; laundry service; dry cleaning. *In room:* A/C, TV, dataport, hair dryer, safe.

Hotel Duca d'Alba   A bargain near the Roman Forum and the Colosseum, this hotel lies in the Suburra neighborhood, which was once pretty seedy but is being gentrified. Completely renovated, the Duca d'Alba retains an old-fashioned air (it was built in the 19th c.). The guest rooms have elegant Roman styling, with soothing colors, light wood pieces, luxurious beds and bedding, and bathrooms, mainly with showers. The most desirable rooms are the four with private balconies. All rooms are soundproofed. *Warning:* Some of the rooms are just too cramped, even for Tiny Tim, and not all have safes.

Via Leonina 14, 00184 Roma. ✆ **06-484471**. Fax 06-4884840. www.hotelducadalba.com. 30 units (most w/shower only). 80€–260€ ($96–$312) double; 100€–290€ ($120–$348) suite. Rates include buffet breakfast. AE, DC, MC, V. Parking 26€ ($31). Metro: Cavour. **Amenities:** Dining area; bar; room service (7am–10pm); babysitting; laundry service; dry cleaning; nonsmoking rooms. *In room:* A/C, TV, dataport, minibar, hair dryer, safe.

Hotel Grifo *(Kids)*   In the historical center of Rome, this hotel opened in 1975, a small, cozy, and well-appointed choice that doesn't advertise for its business but depends on word of mouth from satisfied customers. The helpful English-speaking staff will ease you into the Eternal City. An unpretentious family-run hotel, it offers bedrooms that, while comfortably furnished, are in a sober, rather functional style. The hotel's most notable feature is a rooftop garden opening onto a panoramic view. Surprisingly for a hotel of this size, its bar is open 24 hours a day. Some three- and four-bedded rooms are available, making them suitable for small families.

Via del Boschetto 144, 00184 Roma. ✆ **06-4871395**. Fax 06-4742323. 21 units. 95€–157€ ($114–$188) double; 123€–205€ ($148–$246) triple; 134€–235€ ($161–$282) quad. Rates include buffet breakfast. AE, DC, MC, V. Parking in nearby garage 30€ ($36). Metro: Cavour. **Amenities:** Bar; concierge; 24-hr. room service; nonsmoking rooms. *In room:* A/C, TV, dataport, minibar.

4 Near Campo de' Fiori

EXPENSIVE

Hotel Ponte Sisto *✦ (Kids)*   Occupying prime real estate, this restored Renaissance palazzo lies on an ancient and narrow Roman street leading from the Campo dei Fiori to the Tiber. It is one of Rome's choice small inns. For lovers of landmarks and monuments, the location is idyllic, only a 10-minute stroll from the Piazza Navona. In neutral colors, the small to midsize bedrooms are handsomely furnished, often in cherry wood, and each comes with a moderate-size private bathroom lined with Siena marble and containing a tub/shower combination. Ten units have whirlpool tubs. If you've got the cash, go for one of the suites on the fourth floor with private terraces overlooking the rooftop of Old Rome. These have separate living rooms with sofas that can be converted for sleeping, which make them great for families.

Via dei Pettinari 64, 00186 Roma. ✆ **06-6863100**. Fax 06-68301712. www.hotelpontesisto.it. 103 units. 310€ ($372) double; 420€ ($504) suite. Rates include buffet breakfast. AE, DC, MC, V. Parking: 26€ ($31). Tram 8. **Amenities:** Restaurant for guests only; room service (6am–midnight); laundry service; dry cleaning; nonsmoking rooms; rooms for those w/limited mobility; garden. *In room:* A/C, TV, dataport, minibar, safe.

Residenza Farnese *✦ (Value)*   Among the "boutique hotels" springing up around Campo de' Fiori, the spanking new Farnese in a 15th-century mansion emerges near the top. Opt for one of the front rooms overlooking Palazzo Farnese, with Michelangelo's Renaissance cornice bathed in sunlight. Bedrooms are fresh and modernized, ranging in size from small to generous, each with a freshly restored private bathroom with a shower. The location in the heart of ancient Rome puts you within walking distance of many of the major sights, particularly the Roman Forum or even St. Peter's. The owner, Signora Zema, is a gracious host who can provide much helpful advice. She has placed contemporary art throughout as a grace note, and she believes in a generous breakfast to fortify you for the day.

Via del Mascherone 59, 00186 Roma. ⓒ **06-68891388.** Fax 06-68210980. www.residenzafarneseroma.it. 31 units. 250€–300€ ($300–$360) double; 350€–500€ ($420–$600) junior suite. Rates include buffet breakfast. MC, V. Bus: 64. **Amenities:** Bar; room service (7am–5pm); laundry service; dry cleaning; nonsmoking rooms; 1 room for those w/limited mobility. *In room:* A/C, TV, dataport (in 2 units), minibar, hair dryer, safe.

MODERATE

Casa di Santa Brigida 🔍 *Value*   Across from the Michelangelo-designed Palazzo Farnese on a quiet square a block from Campo de' Fiori, Rome's best and most comfortable convent hotel is run by the friendly sisters of St. Bridget in the house where that Swedish saint died in 1373. Basically, there isn't much difference between this place and many other little pensioni, except that it's run by sisters (it's not a great place for carousing, let's put it that way). Rooms where Santa Brigida lived and died are on the first floor. The library is quite large. This convent hotel accepts people of every age and creed. The comfy and roomy old-world guest rooms with antiques or reproductions on parquet (lower level) or carpeted (upstairs) floors justify the rates. The bathrooms are a little old. It has a rooftop terrace, a library, and a church.

Via Monserato 54 (off Piazza Farnese). Postal address: Piazza Farnese 96, 00186 Roma. ⓒ **06-68892596.** Fax 06-68891573. www.brigidine.org. 20 units. 180€ ($216) double. Rates include breakfast. MC, V. Bus: 46, 62, or 64. **Amenities:** Restaurant; library. *In room:* A/C, hair dryer.

Hotel Teatro di Pompeo 🔍🔍 *Finds*   Built atop the ruins of the Theater of Pompey, this small charmer lies near the spot where Julius Caesar met his end on the Ides of March. Intimate and refined, it's on a quiet piazzetta near the Palazzo Farnese and Campo de' Fiori. The rooms are decorated in an old-fashioned Italian style with hand-painted tiles, and the beamed ceilings date from the days of Michelangelo. The guest rooms range from small to medium, each with a tidy but cramped shower-only bathroom.

Largo del Pallaro 8, 00186 Roma. ⓒ **06-68300170.** Fax 06-68805531. www.hotelteatrodipompeo.it. 13 units (shower only). 170€–190€ ($204–$228) double; 200€–220€ ($240–$264) triple. Rates include buffet breakfast. AE, DC, MC, V. Bus: 46, 62, or 64. **Amenities:** Bar; room service (breakfast only); babysitting; laundry service; dry cleaning; nonsmoking rooms. *In room:* A/C, TV, dataport, minibar, hair dryer, safe.

INEXPENSIVE

Hotel Arenula 🔍 *Finds*   At last a hotel in Rome's old Jewish ghetto, and not only is it quite affordable, but a winner. It takes its name from Via Arenula, a time-worn street linking Largo Argentina to Ponte Garibaldi and the Trastevere area. The Patta family converted and restored a 19th-century building into a comfortable inn. Close at hand are the Pantheon, the Colosseum, and the Piazza Navona. Rooms are furnished in a tasteful, traditional way, and they are inviting and comfortable, with palewood pieces and immaculate bathrooms, each with a shower. There's no elevator, so be prepared to climb some stairs.

Via Santa Maria de' Calderari 47, 00186 Roma. ⓒ **06-6879454.** Fax 06-6896188. www.hotelarenula.com. 50 units. 125€ ($150) double. Rates include breakfast. AE, DC, MC, V. Metro: Colosseo. Bus: 40. **Amenities:** Breakfast lounge; room service (breakfast only). *In room:* A/C, TV, hair dryer.

Accommodations near Campo de' Fiori & Piazza Navona

Albergo Cesàri **9**
Albergo del Sole
    al Pantheon **7**
Albergo Santa Chiara **10**
Casa di Santa Brigida **3**
Hotel Coronet **11**

Hotel Navona **5**
Hotel Ponte Sisto **1**
Hotel Raphael **6**
Hotel Teatro di Pompeo **4**
Nazionale **8**
Residenza Farnese **2**

5 Near Piazza Navona & the Pantheon

Travelers who want to immerse themselves in the atmosphere of ancient Rome, or those looking for romance, will prefer staying in this area to the more commercial Via Veneto area. Transportation isn't the greatest and you'll do a lot of walking, but that's the reason many visitors come here in the first place—to wander and discover the glory that was Rome. You're within walking distance of the Vatican and classical ruins, as well as many bars and cafes.

VERY EXPENSIVE

Hotel Raphael ★★   With a glorious location adjacent to Piazza Navona, the Raphael is often the top choice of Italian politicos in town for the opening of Parliament. The ivy-covered facade invites you to enter the lobby, which is decorated with antiques that rival the cache in local museums (there's even a Picasso ceramics collection). The guest rooms (some quite small) were recently refurbished with a Florentine touch. Some of the suites have private terraces. We love its rooftop restaurant with views of all the major landmarks of Old Rome.

Largo Febo 2, 00186 Roma. ✆ **06-682831.** Fax 06-6878993. www.raphaelhotel.com. 65 units. 302€–570€ ($362–$684) double; 530€–1,000€ ($636–$1,200) suite. AE, DC, MC, V. Parking 25€–35€ ($30–$42). Bus: 70, 81,

87, or 115. **Amenities:** Restaurant; bar; fitness room; sauna; room service (7am–11pm); babysitting; laundry service; nonsmoking rooms; rooms for those w/limited mobility. *In room:* A/C, TV, dataport, minibar, hair dryer, safe.

EXPENSIVE

Albergo Del Sole al Pantheon ⊙★ You (and the likes of recent guest Patti Smith) are obviously paying for the million-dollar view at this government-rated four-star hotel, but one look at the Pantheon at sunrise and you might find that it's worth it. This building was constructed in 1450 as a home, and the first records of it as a hostelry appeared in 1467, making it one of the world's oldest hotels. The layout is amazingly eccentric—prepare to walk up and down a lot of three- or four-step staircases. The guest rooms vary greatly in decor, much of it hit or miss, with compact, tiled full bathrooms. The rooms opening onto the piazza still tend to be noisy at all hours. The quieter rooms overlook the quiet courtyard, but we always prefer to put up with the noise just to enjoy one of the world's greatest views. For the grandest view of the Pantheon, ask for room no. 106 or 108.

Piazza della Rotonda 63, 00186 Roma. ⓒ 06-6780441. Fax 06-69940689. www.hotelsolealpantheon.com. 30 units. 325€ ($390) double; 425€ ($510) junior suite. Rates include buffet breakfast. AE, DC, MC, V. Bus: 64. **Amenities:** Breakfast room; bar; Jacuzzi; room service (7am–11pm); babysitting; laundry service; dry cleaning. *In room:* A/C, TV, dataport, minibar, hair dryer, safe.

Nazionale ⊙★ The Nazionale faces the Piazza Colonna, with its Column of Marcus Aurelius, the Palazzo di Montecitorio, and the Palazzo Chigi. Because it's next to the Parliament buildings, the Albergo is often full of government officials and diplomatic staff. The lobbies are wood-paneled, with many antiques throughout. The guest rooms are high-ceilinged, comfortably proportioned, and individually decorated in a late-19th-century style. They have either carpet or marble floors, and some offer interesting views over the ancient square outside.

Piazza Montecitorio 131, 00186 Roma. ⓒ 06-695001. Fax 06-6786677. www.nazionaleroma.it. 221€–460€ ($265–$552) double. Rates include breakfast. AE, DC, MC, V. Parking 35€–50€ ($42–$60), depending on the size of the car. Bus: 52, 53, 58, 85, or 95. **Amenities:** Restaurant; bar; room service (7am–midnight); babysitting; laundry service; dry cleaning; nonsmoking rooms. *In room:* A/C, TV, dataport, minibar, hair dryer, safe.

MODERATE

Albergo Cesàri ⊙★★ If you want to lose yourself on an ancient street in Old Rome, head here. Since 1787, this inn has stood in an offbeat location between the Pantheon and the Trevi Fountain, two of Rome's most enduring landmarks. Its well-preserved exterior harmonizes with the Temple of Neptune and many little antiques shops nearby. The guest rooms have mostly functional modern pieces but contain a few traditional trappings to maintain character. Sixteen of the units come with tub/shower combinations.

Via di Pietra 89A, 00186 Roma. ⓒ 06-6749701. Fax 06-67497030. www.albergocesari.it. 47 units (most w/shower only). 160€–220€ ($192–$264) double; 195€–265€ ($234–$318) triple. Rates include buffet breakfast. AE, DC, MC, V. Parking 25€ ($30). Bus: 175 or 492 from Stazione Termini. **Amenities:** Bar; room service (7am–10pm); babysitting; laundry service; nonsmoking rooms; 1 room for those w/limited mobility. *In room:* A/C, TV, dataport, minibar, hair dryer, safe.

Albergo Santa Chiara This is a family-run hotel near the Pantheon in the very inner core of historic Rome. Since 1938, the Corteggiani family has been welcoming sightseers to classic Rome. The hotel's white walls and marble columns speak of former elegance, although the rooms today are simply furnished, functional, yet comfortable. The size? Rooms range from a broom closet to a suite large enough to be classified as a small Roman apartment. We go for those units facing the Piazza della Minerva, although you'll often have to listen to late-night revelers who don't know when to go home. Half the bedrooms come with complete tub/shower bathrooms.

Via Santa Chiara 21, 00186 Roma. ℂ 06-6872979. Fax 06-6873144. www.albergosantachiara.com. 98 units (half w/shower only). 190€–240€ ($228–$288) double; 365€–450€ ($438–$540) suite. Rates include breakfast. AE, DC, MC, V. Metro: Spagna. **Amenities:** Bar; room service (breakfast only); babysitting; laundry service; dry cleaning; rooms for those w/limited mobility. *In room:* A/C, TV, dataport, minibar, hair dryer, safe.

Hotel Adriano   This hotel is housed within the original walls of a 15th-century palazzo. It's been skillfully converted into a well-run and government-rated three-star hotel that houses guests comfortably. The location is close to some of Rome's major landmarks, including Piazza di Spagna, Piazza Navona, and the Pantheon. You can find a well-upholstered armchair waiting for you under the vaulted ceilings of the public rooms, perhaps with a view of a Titian nude reproduction. Bedrooms are simply furnished but tasteful, with excellent beds usually resting on hardwood floors. Bathrooms are small, simple, and clean. You can enjoy breakfast on the hotel's roof terrace.

Via di Pallacorda 2, 00186 Roma. ℂ 06-68802451. Fax 06-68803926. www.hoteladriano.com. 82 units. 150€–200€ ($180–$240) double; 350€–500€ ($420–$600) suite. Rates include breakfast. AE, DC, MC, V. Parking 26€ ($31). Bus: 95 or 175. **Amenities:** Bar; 24-hr. room service; laundry service; dry cleaning; babysitting. *In room:* A/C, TV, minibar, safe.

INEXPENSIVE

Hotel Coronet   Experience the charm of a bygone era at this modest hotel, impressively sited in a 17th-century palace linked to the aristocratic Doria Pamphili family and located near the Piazza Navona and the Parthenon. You'll step back into another era, yes, but don't expect grandeur. Bedrooms are high-ceilinged and spacious, but modestly furnished with a medley of antiques and plainly functional pieces. Most of the rooms have a modest bathroom with a shower; three have hallway bathrooms only. The best units (nos. 34, 35, and 45) come with sitting areas. The square in front is rarely noisy, but for total tranquillity, ask for an accommodation in the rear that opens onto a private garden.

Piazza Grazioli 5, 00186, Roma. ℂ 06-6790692. Fax 06-69922705. www.hotelcoronet.com. 13 units, 10 w/private bathroom. 80€–140€ ($96–$168) double w/shared bathroom; 120€–170€ ($144–$204) double w/private bathroom. Rates include breakfast. MC, V. Parking 15€–18€ ($18–$22). Bus: 46, 56, 60, 62, 64, 70, or 115. **Amenities:** Breakfast room; room service (breakfast only); nonsmoking rooms. *In room:* A/C, hair dryer.

Hotel Navona   This pensione is on a small street radiating from Piazza Navona's southeastern tip. The rooms aren't as grand as the exterior, but the Navona offers decent accommodations, some of which open to views of the central courtyard. Run by an Australian-born family of Italian descent, it boasts ceilings high enough to help relieve the midsummer heat, as well as an array of architectural oddities—the legacy of the continual construction that this palace has undergone since 1360. The beds, most often twins or doubles, have fine linens. Each is equipped with a cramped shower-only bathroom. You can get an air-conditioned room by request for 15€ ($17) extra per night (only in the doubles with bathrooms).

Via dei Sediari 8, 00186 Roma. ℂ 06-6864203. Fax 06-68803802. www.hotelnavona.com. 35 units (all w/bathroom and shower). 125€–140€ ($150–$168) double; 160€–185€ ($192–$222) triple. Rates include breakfast. MC, V. Bus: 64. **Amenities:** Restaurant; nonsmoking rooms. *In room:* A/C, hair dryer.

6 Near Piazza del Popolo & the Spanish Steps

This is a great place to stay if you're a serious shopper, but expect to part with a lot of extra dough for the privilege. This is a more elegant area than the Via Veneto—think Fifth Avenue all the way.

VERY EXPENSIVE

The Hassler 👍👍   The Westin Excelsior is a grander palace, and the Eden and the de Russie are more up-to-date, but The Hassler has something that no other hotel can boast—a coveted location at the top of the Spanish Steps, which ensures glorious views and easy access to upscale designer shopping. The Hassler, rebuilt in 1944 to replace the 1885 original, is not quite what it used to be, but because it's such a classic, and because of that incredible location, it gets away with charging astronomical rates. The lounges and the guest rooms, with their "Italian Park Avenue" trappings, still strike a glamorous, if faded, 1930s note. There's also a solarium for guests to enjoy.

The guest rooms range from small singles to some of the most spacious suites in town. High ceilings make them appear larger than they are, and many of them open onto private balconies or terraces. Only medium in size, the bathrooms are classy, complete with a range of deluxe body and hair products. The front rooms, dramatically overlooking the Spanish Steps, are often noisy at night, but the views are worth it. For panoramas of the Roman rooftops, ask for a room on the top floor. Although some of the accommodations remain a bit dowdy, those on the fourth floor have been recently and elegantly renovated and are the most desirable. Most requested is the famous corner room no. 403: For Rome's most spectacular hotel room with a view, we nominate this one.

Piazza Trinità dei Monti 6, 00187 Roma. (C) **800/223-6800** in the U.S., or 06-699340. Fax 06-6789991. www.hotel hasslerroma.com. 100 units. 500€–790€ ($600–$948) double; from 1,600€ ($1,920) suite. AE, DC, MC, V. Parking 30€ ($36). Metro: Spagna. **Amenities:** 2 restaurants; bar; tennis court; health club; sauna; free use of bicycles; salon; room service (6:30am–midnight); massage; babysitting; laundry service; dry cleaning; nonsmoking rooms; rooms for those w/limited mobility; solarium. *In room:* A/C, TV, minibar, hair dryer, dataport, safe.

Hotel de la Ville Inter-Continental Roma 👍👍   We prefer this place, designed in 1924 by the Hungarian architect Jozef Vago, to the overpriced glory of The Hassler next door. The hotel looks deluxe (although it's officially rated first class) from the minute you walk through the revolving door, where a smartly uniformed doorman greets you. Once inside this palace, built in the 19th century on the site of the ancient Gardens of Lucullus, you'll find Oriental rugs, marble tables, brocade furniture, and an English-speaking staff. Endless corridors lead to a maze of ornamental lounges. Some of the public rooms have a sort of 1930s elegance, and others are strictly baroque; in the middle of it all is an open courtyard.

The guest rooms and public areas are decorated in a beautifully classic and yet up-to-date way. The higher rooms with balconies have panoramic views of Rome, and everyone's welcome to use the rooftop terrace with the same view. Most units are small but boast chintz-covered fabrics and fine beds. The spacious bathrooms have deluxe toiletries and generous shelf space.

Via Sistina 67–69, 00187 Roma. (C) **800/327-0200** in the U.S. and Canada, or 06-67331. Fax 06-6784213. www. interconti.com. 192 units. 400€–500€ ($480–$600) double; from 750€ ($900) suite. Rates include continental breakfast. AE, DC, MC, V. Parking 32€ ($38). Metro: Spagna or Barberini. **Amenities:** Restaurant; bar; room service (7am–10pm); babysitting; laundry service; dry cleaning; nonsmoking rooms. *In room:* A/C, TV, dataport, minibar, hair dryer, safe.

Accommodations near Piazza del Popolo & the Spanish Steps

Capo d'Africa **27**
Casa Banzo **22**
Casa Howard **9**
Colosseum Hotel **26**
Fontanella Borghese **19**
Grand Hotel Plaza **18**
The Hassler **6**
Hotel Adriano **20**
Hotel Adrenula **21**
Hotel Condotti **11**
Hotel d'Inghilterra **14**
Hotel de la Ville Inter-
  Continental Roma **7**
Hotel de Russie **2**
Hotel Duca d'Alba **25**
Hotel Forum **25**
Hotel Grifo **23**
Hotel Locarno **1**
Hotel Madrid **16**
Hotel Manfredi **5**
Hotel Margutta **4**
Hotel Nerva **24**
Hotel Parlamento **17**
Hotel Piazza
  di Spagna **15**
Hotel Scalinata
  di Spagna **10**
The Inn at the Spanish
  Steps **12**
La Lumiére di Piazza
  Spagna **13**
Modigliani **8**
Piranesi **3**

City Walls
Metro A M
Post Office

Hotel de Russie ★★★ This government-rated five-star hotel has raised the bar for every other hotel in the city. For service, style, and modern luxuries, it beats out the Eden, the Westin Excelsior, and the St. Regis Grand. The multilingual staff works hard to make your stay comfortable.

Just off the Piazza del Popolo, it opened in the spring of 2000 to rave reviews of its opulent furnishings and choice location. In its previous reincarnation, it was a favorite of Russian dignitaries (hence its name), and it also has hosted Jean Cocteau, Stravinsky, and Picasso. In World War II, it was used by the Italian government as a secret military center for spy secrets.

Public areas are glossy and contemporary. About 30% of the bedrooms are conservative, with traditional furniture, while the remaining 70% are more minimalist, with a stark, striking style. Each is equipped with every conceivable high-tech amenity and offers lots of deeply upholstered comforts and views over a verdant garden.

The signature feature is the extensive terraced gardens, which can be seen from many of the bedrooms. Nothing is finer on a summer evening than sipping a cocktail in the **Stravinskij Bar,** which opens to the fragrant blooming gardens, and then enjoying an alfresco meal in **Le Jardin du Russie.**

Via del Babuino 9, 00187 Roma. ⓒ 800/323-7500 in North America, or 06-328881. Fax 06-3288888. www.roccoforte hotels.com. 125 units. 615€–840€ ($738–$1,008) double; from 1,155€ ($1,386) suite. AE, DC, MC, V. Metro: Flaminia. **Amenities:** Restaurant; bar; health club; spa; Jacuzzi; sauna; children's programs; salon; 24-hr. room service; babysitting; nonsmoking rooms; rooms for those w/limited mobility. *In room:* A/C, TV, dataport, minibar, hair dryer, safe.

Hotel d'Inghilterra ★★   Rome's most fashionable small hotel holds on to its traditions and heritage, even though it has been renovated. It's comparable to The Hassler and Inter–Continental. Situated between Via Condotti and Via Borgogna, this hotel in the 17th century was the guesthouse of the Torlonia princes. The rooms have mostly old pieces (gilt and lots of marble, mahogany chests, and glittery mirrors) complemented by modern conveniences. Some, however, are just too cramped. The preferred rooms are higher up, opening onto a tile terrace, with a balustrade and a railing covered with flowering vines and plants. The bathrooms have been refurbished and offer deluxe toiletries.

Via Bocca di Leone 14, 00187 Roma. ⓒ 06-69981. Fax 06-69922243. www.hoteldinghilterraroma.it. 98 units. 315€–511€ ($378–$613) double; from 724€ ($869) suite. AE, DC, MC, V. Parking 25€ ($30). Metro: Spagna. **Amenities:** 2 restaurants; bar; 24-hr. room service; babysitting; laundry service; dry cleaning; nonsmoking rooms. *In room:* A/C, TV, dataport, minibar, hair dryer, safe.

The Inn at the Spanish Steps ★★★ (Finds)   This intimate, upscale inn is the first new hotel to open in this location in years. The people who run Rome's most famous cafe, Caffè Greco, created it where Hans Christian Andersen once lived. Andersen praised the balcony roses and violets, and so, probably, will you. Every room is furnished in an authentic period decor, featuring antiques, elegant draperies, and parquet floors. The superior units come with a fireplace, a frescoed or beamed ceiling, and a balcony. The hotel is completely modern, with generous wardrobe space. Each marble-paneled bathroom comes with a full tub, and others offer a Jacuzzi as well. Designer boutiques galore lie nearby.

Via dei Condotti 85, 00187 Roma. ⓒ 06-69925657. Fax 06-6786470. www.atspanishsteps.com. 24 units. 314€–682€ ($379–$818) double; 539€–825€ ($649–$990) suite. Rates include buffet breakfast. Metro: Spagna. **Amenities:** Bar; 24-hr. room service; babysitting; laundry service; dry cleaning; nonsmoking rooms. *In room:* A/C, TV, dataport, minibar, hair dryer, safe.

EXPENSIVE

Grand Hotel Plaza ★   This grand old favorite is experiencing a renaissance. Pietro Mascagni composed his *Nerone* in one of the guest rooms here, and Vincent Price stayed here while making what he called, "all those bad movies." When you see the very grand decor, you'll understand why. This hotel's public rooms are vintage 19th century and contain stained-glass skylights, massive crystal chandeliers, potted palms, inlaid marble floors, and a life-size stone lion guarding the ornate stairway. The theatrical grandeur of the lobby carries over into the suites, where the furnishings mimic the gilded-age splendor of the public rooms on a smaller scale. But the standard guest rooms are just that—standard. They're contemporary, midsize, and streamlined, with efficient but comfortable furniture, and large marble bathrooms with tub/shower combinations.

Via del Corso 126, 00186 Roma. ⓒ 06-69921111. Fax 06-69941575. www.grandhotelplaza.com. 220 units. 265€–428€ ($318–$514) double; 450€–1,420€ ($540–$1,704) suite. AE, DC, MC, V. Parking 42€ ($50). Metro: Spagna. **Amenities:** Restaurant; bar; room service (6am–midnight); babysitting; laundry service; dry cleaning; nonsmoking rooms; rooms for those w/limited mobility. *In room:* A/C, TV, dataport, minibar, hair dryer, safe.

Hotel Locarno *(Moments)*   If you'd like to experience Rome the way visitors such as Mary Pickford and Douglas Fairbanks did in the 1920s, head for this monument to Art Deco. In the heart of Rome, near Piazza del Popolo, this hotel first opened its doors in 1925, and it's been receiving visitors ever since. In fair weather, breakfast is served in the garden or on the rooftop garden. Bedrooms in the older section are a bit chintzy, but the newer wing has brighter, fresher accommodations. All of the original floors, doors, and bathroom fixtures in this newer section were recently refurbished. Bathrooms are a bit small but immaculately maintained, each with a shower. Rooms are reached by taking a birdcage elevator. Amazingly, after all these years, Locarno remains relatively unknown and rarely makes an appearance in a guidebook.

Via della Penna 25, 00186 Roma. ✆ 06-3610841. Fax 06-3215249. www.hotellocarno.com. 66 units. 200€–310€ ($240–$372) double; 450€–600€ ($540–$720) suite. Rates include breakfast. AE, DC, MC, V. Parking 30€–40€ ($36–$48). Metro: Flaminio. Bus: 116 or 117. **Amenities:** Lunch buffet; bar; 24-hr. room service; laundry service; dry cleaning; nonsmoking rooms; 1 room for those w/limited mobility. *In room:* A/C, TV, dataport, minibar, safe.

Hotel Scalinata di Spagna ♠♠♠   This is Rome's most famous little boutique hotel. The deluxe Hassler is across the street but far removed in price and grandeur from this intimate, upscale B&B at the top of the Spanish Steps. This delightful little building—only two floors are visible from the outside—is nestled between much larger structures, with four relief columns across the facade and window boxes with bright blossoms. The recently redecorated interior features small public rooms with bright print slipcovers, old clocks, and low ceilings.

The decor varies radically from one guest room to the next. Some have low, beamed ceilings and ancient-looking wood furniture; others have loftier ceilings and more run-of-the-mill furniture. The tiled bathrooms range from small to medium but offer state-of-the-art plumbing. Each has a tub. The best units are any overlooking the steps, but the best of the best are room nos. 10 and 12.

Piazza Trinità dei Monti 17, 00187 Roma. ✆ 06-6793006. Fax 06-69940598. www.hotelscalinata.com. 16 units (tubs only). 200€–370€ ($240–$444) double; 300€–400€ ($360–$480) triple. Rates include buffet breakfast. AE, MC, V. Parking 40€ ($48). Metro: Spagna. **Amenities:** Bar; room service (breakfast only); babysitting; laundry service; dry cleaning. *In room:* A/C, TV, dataport, minibar, hair dryer, safe.

La Lumière di Piazza di Spagna ♠ *(Finds)*   We never thought another little inn would open near the Spanish Steps simply because there was no more real estate available. Wrong. Along comes this charmer installed in a five-story 18th-century building with an elevator. Rooms are spacious and exquisitely furnished in a classic style, with a panoramic view of the Spanish Steps. All of them have adjoining bathrooms with Jacuzzi spa showers. While you enjoy your breakfast buffet on the panoramic terrace, the entire city of Rome is at your feet. Outside your door you'll find Rome's best and most exclusive shops.

Via Belsiana 72, 00187 Roma. ✆ 06-69380806. Fax 06-69294231. www.lalumieredipiazzadispagna.com. 10 units. 150€–500€ ($180–$600) double; 180€–700€ ($216–$840) triple. AE, DC, MC, V. Parking 30€ ($36). Metro: Spagna. **Amenities:** Breakfast terrace; 24-hr. room service; laundry service. *In room:* A/C, TV, dataport, minibar, hair dryer, safe.

Piranesi ♠♠ *(Finds)*   Right off the Piazza del Popolo is one of Rome's most select boutique hotels—it could easily become your favorite address in Rome. It's more affordable than the Hotel de Russie, which fronts it. The street on which Piranesi sits is the major artery for antiques and art galleries in Rome. If you stay here, you'll be following in the footsteps of Goethe, Salvator Rosa, Trilussa, Poussin, and Giuseppe Valadier, among other well-known poets, writers, and artists. All around the hotel are historical churches and monuments.

Bedrooms are tranquil and decorated in a somewhat minimalist style, evocative of the Directoire style of the 18th century. The bare pine floors are a graceful note, as are the cherry wood furniture and the immaculate bathrooms with new showers. The most dramatic aspect is the panoramic rooftop terrace, taking in views of the Villa Borghese, Piazza del Popolo, and Michelangelo's dome at St. Peter's.

Via del Babuino 196, 00187 Roma. © 06-328041. Fax 06-3610597. www.hotelpiranesi.com. 32 units. 255€–360€ ($306–$432) double; 320€–520€ ($384–$624) suite. Rates include buffet breakfast. AE, MC, V. Parking 35€ ($42). Metro: Flaminio. Bus: 117. **Amenities:** Bar; health club; sauna; room service (7am–11pm); laundry service; dry cleaning; nonsmoking rooms; 1 room for those w/limited mobility. *In room:* A/C, TV, dataport (in some), minibar, hair dryer.

MODERATE

Casa Howard ☆ *Finds*   It's rare to make a new discovery in the tourist-trodden Piazza di Spagna area, which is why Casa Howard comes as a pleasant surprise. The little B&B occupies about two-thirds of the second floor of a historic structure. The welcoming owners maintain beautifully furnished guest rooms, each with its own private bathroom with a tub/shower combination (although some bathrooms lie outside the bedrooms in the hallway). The Pink Room is the most spacious, and has an en suite bathroom. Cristy, at reception, can "arrange anything" in Rome for you and will also invite you to use the house's private Turkish sauna. The hotel is entirely nonsmoking.

Via Capo le Case 18, 00187 Roma. © 06-69924555. Fax 06-6794644. www.casahoward.com. 10 units. 160€–230€ ($192–$276) double. MC, V. Metro: Spagna. **Amenities:** Room service (breakfast only); babysitting; laundry service; dry cleaning. *In room:* A/C, TV, dataport, beverage maker, hair dryer.

Fontanella Borghese ☆ *Finds*   Close to the Spanish Steps in the exact heart of Rome, this hotel surprisingly remains relatively undiscovered. Much renovated and improved, it has been installed on the third and fourth floor of a palace dating from the end of the 18th century. The building once belonged to the princes of the Borghese family, and the little hotel looks out onto the Borghese Palace. It lies within walking distance of the Trevi Fountain, the Pantheon, and the Piazza Navona. The location is also close to Piazza Augusto and the Ara Pacis. In the midsize bedrooms, plain wooden furniture rests on parquet floors, and everything is in a classical tradition, comfortably modernized for today's travelers. Half of the bathrooms come with tubs, the rest with showers. The staff of the front desk is one of the most helpful in Central Rome.

Largo Fontanella Borghese 84, 00186 Roma. © 06-68809504. Fax 06-6861295. www.fontanellaborghese.com. 29 units. 175€–255€ ($210–$306) double; 235€–350€ ($282–$420) suite. AE, DC, MC, V. Parking nearby 25€ ($30). Metro: Spagna. **Amenities:** Breakfast room; room service (7:30am–8pm). *In room:* A/C, TV, minibar, hair dryer.

Hotel Condotti *Value*   The Condotti is small, choice, and terrific for shoppers intent on staying near the tony boutiques. Book here for an affordable price in a platinum-card neighborhood and a great location. Despite its name, this hotel actually lies 2 blocks to the north of Via Condotti. The staffmembers, nearly all of whom speak English, are cooperative and hardworking. The mostly modern rooms might not have much historic charm (they're furnished like nice motel units), but they're comfortable and soothing, each with a shower-only bathroom. Each room is decorated with traditional furnishings, including excellent beds (usually twins). Room no. 414 is often requested for its geranium-filled terrace.

Via Mario de' Fiori 37, 00187 Roma. © 06-6794661. Fax 06-6790457. www.hotelcondotti.com. 21 units (shower only). 175€–273€ ($210–$328) double; 209€–293€ ($251–$352) triple. Rates include buffet breakfast. AE, DC, MC, V. Metro: Spagna. **Amenities:** Breakfast room; car-rental desk; room service (breakfast only); babysitting; laundry service; dry cleaning. *In room:* A/C, TV, dataport, minibar, hair dryer.

Hotel Madrid   Despite modern touches in the comfortable, if minimalist, guest rooms, the interior of the Madrid manages to evoke late-19th-century Rome. Guests often take their breakfast amid ivy and blossoming plants on the rooftop terrace with a panoramic view of rooftops and the distant dome of St. Peter's. Some of the doubles are large, with scatter rugs, veneer armoires, and shuttered windows. Others are quite small, so make sure you know what you're getting before you check in. The shower-only bathrooms are small but functional.

Via Mario de' Fiori 93–95, 00187 Roma. ✆ 06-6991510. Fax 06-6791653. www.hotelmadridroma.com. 26 units. 235€ ($282) double; 285€–325€ ($342–$390) suite. Rates include breakfast. AE, DC, MC, V. Parking nearby 26€–30€ ($30–$35). Metro: Spagna. **Amenities:** Breakfast room; lounge; 24-hr. room service, babysitting; laundry service. In room: A/C, TV, dataport, minibar, hair dryer, safe.

Hotel Manfredi ⭐ (Finds)   This renovated hotel near the Spanish Steps lies in the art district of Rome. It's a government-rated three-star that enjoys a glamorous address and is housed in a fully renovated 16th-century former private residence. The sound-proof rooms are midsize and beautifully decorated in an 18th-century style, with tiled bathrooms with tub/shower combinations. Pastels of pink, green, and blue predominate in this stylish, classic atmosphere.

Via Margutta 61, 00187 Roma. ✆ 06-3207676. Fax 06-3207736. www.hotelmanfredi.it. 18 units. 205€–310€ ($246–$372) double; 315€–390€ ($378–$468) junior suite. AE, DC, MC, V. Rates include buffet breakfast. Parking 15€ ($18). Metro: Spagna. **Amenities:** Bar; room service (7am–midnight); laundry service; dry cleaning; nonsmoking rooms. In room: A/C, TV, dataport, minibar, hair dryer, safe.

Hotel Piazza di Spagna   About a block from the downhill side of the Spanish Steps, this hotel is small but classic, with an inviting atmosphere made more gracious by the helpful manager, Elisabetta Giocondi. The guest rooms boast a functional streamlined decor; some even have Jacuzzis in the tiled bathrooms. Only eight units come with complete tub/shower combinations. Accommodations are spread across three floors, and the very tidy bedrooms have high ceilings and cool terrazzo floors.

Via Mario de' Fiori 61, 00187 Roma. ✆ 06-6796412. Fax 06-6790654. www.hotelpiazzadispagna.it. 17 units (some w/shower only). 180€–270€ ($216–$324) double; 250€–300€ ($300–$360) triple. Rates include buffet breakfast. AE, MC, V. Parking nearby 18€ ($22). Metro: Spagna. Bus: 117. **Amenities:** Bar; room service (7:30am–midnight); laundry service; dry cleaning; nonsmoking rooms. In room: A/C, TV, dataport, minibar, hair dryer.

Modigliani ⭐ (Finds)   The owners, who are also artists, have created an attractive, inviting atmosphere—one of "elegance and sympathy," as they define it. They named their hotel, which is near the Spanish Steps and the Via Veneto, after their favorite artist: Modigliani (1884–1920). The superior rooms are on the top floor, with windows opening onto a panoramic view over historical Rome. The other bedrooms face the garden or a tranquil old street. Bedrooms are well furnished, each with a well-maintained private bathroom with a shower. Breakfast is served on a terrace with a view of St. Peter's. The hotel is entirely nonsmoking.

Via della Purificazione 42, 00187 Roma. ✆ 06-42815226. Fax 06-42814791. www.hotelmodigliani.com. 24 units. 155€–198€ ($186–$238) double; 185€–220€ ($222–$264) triple; 335€–405€ ($402–$486) 4-bed suite. AE, DC, MC, V. Rates include buffet breakfast. Metro: Spagna. **Amenities:** Bar; laundry service; dry cleaning. In room: A/C, TV, minibar, hair dryer, safe.

INEXPENSIVE

Casa Banzo ⭐⭐ (Finds)   To live like a Roman aristocrat, check into one of the city's most elegant and undiscovered B&Bs. The dramatic entrance hall, with its marble floor and terra-cotta urns, sets a high tone, as do the balconies enveloping an inner courtyard. Casa Banzo nestles in a small square in the heart of Renaissance Rome in a converted 16th-century palazzo that was originally built for the noble Alibrandi family. In the 18th century, substantial additions were made, and there have been several renovations over the centuries. For four generations, the family that owns Casa Banzo has offered both deluxe rooms and elegant, self-catering apartments. Antique furnishings and a tasteful decor are punctuated by modern amenities. Stained glass and vaulted frescoed ceilings evoke the past. Even the breakfast room is appropriately elegant.

Piazza del Monte di Pietà 30, 00187 Roma. (*) 06-6833909. Fax 06-6864575. 7 units (5 double rooms and 2 apts.). 120€ ($144) double; 250€ ($300) apt. for 2. Rates include breakfast (only for those who stay in double rooms). AE, DC, MC, V. Parking 22€ ($26). Metro: Spagna. *In room:* A/C (in some), TV (in some), kitchenette (in apts).

Hotel Margutta   The Margutta, on a cobblestone street near Piazza del Popolo, offers attractively decorated but tiny guest rooms, a helpful staff, and a simple breakfast room. You'll sacrifice space, but you'll get an affordable price and a chic location. The best rooms are the three on the top floor, offering a great view. Two of these three (nos. 50 and 52) share a terrace, and the larger room (no. 54) has a private terrace. (There's usually a 20%–35% supplement for these.) Each room comes with a comfortable bed plus a small, but tidy, shower-only bathroom.

Via Laurina 34, 00187 Roma. (*) 06-3223674. Fax 06-3200395. www.hotelmargutta.it. 24 units (shower only). 90€–160€ ($108–$192). Rates include breakfast. AE, DC, MC, V. Metro: Flaminio. **Amenities:** Breakfast room; room service (breakfast only). *In room:* A/C, TV, hair dryer.

Hotel Parlamento   This three-story hotel has a four-star government rating at two-star prices. Expect a friendly pensione-style reception. The furnishings are antiques or reproduction, and the firm beds are backed by carved-wood or wrought-iron headboards. Fifteen rooms are air-conditioned, and the bathrooms have heated towel racks, phones, and (in a few) marble sinks. Only three come with a complete tub/shower combination. Rooms differ in style; the nicest are no. 82, with its original 1800s furniture; and nos. 104, 106, and 107, which open onto the rooftop garden. You can enjoy the chandeliered and tromp l'oeil breakfast room, or carry your cappuccino up to the small rooftop terrace with its view of San Silvestro's bell tower.

Via delle Convertite 5 (at the intersection w/Via del Corso), 00187 Roma. (*)/fax 06-69921000. www.hotel parlamento.it. 23 units. 80€–158€ ($96–$190) double; 105€–195€ ($126–$234) triple. Rates include breakfast. AE, DC, MC, V. Parking 20€ ($24). Metro: Spagna. **Amenities:** Bar; room service (breakfast only); rooftop terrace. *In room:* A/C, TV, hair dryer, safe.

7 Near the Vatican

For most visitors, this is a rather dull area in which to base yourself—it's well removed from the ancient sites, and it's not a great restaurant neighborhood. But if the main purpose of your visit centers on the Vatican, you'll be fine here, and you'll be joined by thousands of other pilgrims, nuns, and priests.

EXPENSIVE

Hotel dei Consoli ✶ (*Finds*)   In the neighborhood of the Vatican, this refined, rather elegant hotel in the Prati district is newly constructed, lying just a short stroll from the Vatican Museums. The hotel occupies three floors in a building that was painstakingly restored in the imperial style with cornices and columns. Stained glass and fine art create an inviting ambience. All the bedrooms are handsomely furnished and decorated, but units judged deluxe are outfitted with whirlpool baths, as are the junior suites.

Accommodations & Dining near the Vatican

DINING ◆
Cesare **9**
Hostaria dei Bastioni **2**
Insalata Ricca **3**
Les Etoiles **10**
Ristorante Giardinaccio **14**
Ristorante Il Matriciano **4**

ACCOMMODATIONS ■
Bramante **11**
Hotel Alimandi **1**
Hotel Columbus **12**
Hotel dei Consoli **5**
Hotel dei Mellini **7**

Hotel Sant'Angelo **8**
Residence Guiggioli **6**
Residenza Paolo VI **13**
Starhotel
  Michelangelo **15**

Draperies and bedding are in elegant silks, the bathrooms adorned with the finest porcelain. There's also a rooftop terrace with panoramic views.

Via Varrone 2 D, 00193 Roma. ✆ **06-68892972.** Fax 06-68212274. www.hoteldeiconsoli.com. 28 units. 265€–290€ ($318–$348) double; 340€–455€ ($408–$546) suite. Rates include breakfast. AE, DC, MC, V. Parking 28€–33€ ($34–$40). Metro: Ottaviano–San Pietro. **Amenities:** Bar; room service (7am–10pm); laundry service; dry cleaning; nonsmoking rooms; rooms for those w/limited mobility. *In room:* A/C, TV, dataport, minibar, safe.

Hotel dei Mellini ✰   This neoclassical hotel is a choice place for Vatican pilgrims. It dates from the early 1900s, when it was a town house. In 1995, after years of neglect, it was turned into a first-class hotel with a certain charm and luxury. It consists of two interconnected buildings, one with four floors and one with six; the top is graced with a terrace overlooking the baroque cupolas of at least three churches. A small staff maintains the lovely guest rooms, whose decor includes Art Deco touches, Italian marble, and mahogany furniture. Accommodations with room numbers ending in "16" come with large sitting areas. The tiled full bathrooms have adequate shelf space.

Via Muzio Clementi 81, 00193 Roma. ✆ **06-324771.** Fax 06-32477801. www.hotelmellini.com. 80 units. 280€–340€ ($336–$408) double; 490€–550€ ($588–$660) suite. Rates include buffet breakfast. AE, DC, MC, V. Parking 25€ ($30). Metro: Lepanto. **Amenities:** Restaurant; bar; room service (6:30am–midnight); laundry service; dry cleaning; nonsmoking rooms; rooms for those w/limited mobility. *In room:* A/C, TV, dataport, minibar, hair dryer, safe.

Residenza Paolo VI *★★ Finds*   Established on the premises of a former monastery, this hotel opened in 2000. Its marvelous views of St. Peter's Square rank among the greatest sights in Rome. One reader wrote, "I felt I was at the gates of heaven sitting on the most beautiful square in the Western world." In addition to its incomparable location, the hotel is filled with beautifully decorated and comfortable bedrooms, with modern bathrooms. In spite of its reasonable prices, this inn is like a small luxury hotel. The hotel is nonsmoking.

Via Paolo VI 29, 00193 Roma. ⓒ **06-68134108**. Fax 06-68677428. www.residenzapaolovi.com. 29 units. 249€–310€ ($299–$372) double; 430€–475€ ($516–$570) junior suite. Rates include American buffet breakfast. AE, DC, MC, V. Metro: Ottaviano–San Pietro. Bus: 64, 91, or 916. **Amenities:** Bar; room service (7am–4pm); babysitting; laundry service; dry cleaning. *In room:* A/C, TV, minibar, hair dryer, safe.

Starhotel Michelangelo *★*   How appropriate that this hotel took the name of the great Michelangelo, because it lies only a few minutes' walk from St. Peter's Square, where Michelangelo immortalized himself architecturally. Not only that, but many of its well-furnished and midsize bedrooms open onto a view of Michelangelo's dome at St. Peter's. The five-story hotel opened back in the glorious heyday of Rome in the '50s when it was a sought-after address for a *Roman Holiday* (shades of the Audrey Hepburn film). After a slumber, it's back again and better than ever after substantial improvements. The decor of the rooms has been glamorized with rich carpeting, swag draperies, and tasteful furnishings. The best bedrooms here are classified as "executive," and they are more spacious and better accessorized. Naturally, they are booked first. Most of the bathrooms have bathtubs, although some contain showers instead. The bar is a good watering hole near the Vatican (yes, priests can often be seen here, but drinking only wine). The elegant restaurant has a rich, varied menu of local and international specialties.

Via della Stazione di S. Pietro 14, 00165 Roma. ⓒ **06-398739**. Fax 06-632359. www.starhotels.com. 179 units. 270€ ($324) double; 295€ ($354) suite. AE, DC, MC, V. Parking 20€ ($24). Bus: 64. **Amenities:** Restaurant; bar; room service (7:30am–10pm); babysitting; laundry service; dry cleaning; nonsmoking rooms; 2 rooms for those w/limited mobility. *In room:* A/C, TV, dataport, minibar, hair dryer, safe.

MODERATE

Bramante   Lying just 100m (328 ft.) from St. Peter's Basilica, this hotel is ideal for those who want to spend a lot of time at the Vatican Museums. The location is in what was once the medieval burg of "Borgo Pio" close to the Passetto, the wall that separated the Vatican from Castel San Angelo. In 1574, the present hotel became the home of the famous architect Domenico Fontana, who was Pope Sixtus V's chief architect and whose masterpiece was the Palazzao Lateranense. All the bedrooms have been recently restored, and many rest under beamed ceilings. The owners call them "cozy"; you might find them cramped. But each is modernized and comfortable, with a small shower-only bathroom. The Bramante has some style, much comfort, and a location with few other hotels. Extra services include a private limo taking passengers to and from the airport.

Vicolo delle Palline 24, 00193 Roma. ⓒ **06-68806426**. Fax 06-68133339. www.hotelbramante.com. 16 units. 150€–235€ ($180–$282) double. Rates include American buffet breakfast. AE, DC, MC, V. Bus: 40. Metro: Ottaviano–San Pietro. **Amenities:** Breakfast room; babysitting; laundry service; dry cleaning. *In room:* A/C, TV, minibar, hair dryer, safe.

Hotel Alimandi   Named after the three brothers who run it (Luigi, Enrico, and Paolo), this friendly guesthouse was built as an apartment house in 1908 in a bland residential neighborhood. The guest rooms are comfortable, albeit a bit small, with

---

Then&Now **Hotel Columbus**

A starred property today (p. 99), and a popular choice 50 years ago when Arthur Frommer wrote: "If you want a hotel in a lovely area, go to the Via della Conciliazione, the wide boulevard which leads to the Vatican. The **Hotel Columbus** (at number 33) is quiet and clean, has Second Class prices, and rooms with a view of St. Peter's, the square and the fountains within. . . ."

---

unremarkable contemporary furniture and cramped but modern-looking bathrooms. Each of the three upper floors is serviced by two elevators leading down to a simple lobby. The social center and most appealing spot is the rooftop garden, with potted plants and views of St. Peter's dome.

Via Tunisi 8, 00192 Roma. ℂ 06-39723948. Fax 06-39723943. 35 units. 130€–155€ ($156–$186) double; 150€–180€ ($180–$216) triple. AE, DC, MC, V. Parking 10€ ($12). Metro: Ottaviano-San Pietro. **Amenities:** Bar; fitness room; rooftop garden. *In room:* A/C, TV, hair dryer, safe.

Hotel Columbus ⚹   This is an impressive 15th-century palace. The Columbus was once the home of the cardinal who became Pope Julius II, the man who tormented Michelangelo into painting the Sistine Chapel. It looks much as it must have centuries ago: a severe time-stained facade, small windows, and heavy wooden doors leading from the street to the colonnades and arches of the inner courtyard. The cobbled entranceway leads to a reception hall and a series of baronial public rooms. Note the main salon with its walk-in fireplace, oil portraits, battle scenes, and Oriental rugs.

The guest rooms are considerably simpler than the salons and are furnished with comfortable modern pieces. All are spacious, but a few are enormous and still have such original details as decorated wood ceilings and frescoed walls. The best and quietest rooms front the garden. The bathrooms are medium in size and offer all the standards, including up-to-date plumbing and fine toiletries.

Via della Conciliazione 33, 00193 Roma. ℂ 06-6865435. Fax 06-6864874. www.hotelcolumbus.net. 92 units. 160€–320€ ($192–$384) double; 220€–400€ ($264–$480) suite. Rates include buffet breakfast. AE, DC, MC, V. Free parking. Bus: 40. **Amenities:** Restaurant; bar; room service (7am–11pm); babysitting; laundry service; dry cleaning; nonsmoking rooms. *In room:* A/C, TV, dataport, minibar, hair dryer, safe.

Hotel Sant'Angelo   This hotel, right off Piazza Cavour (northeast of the Castel Sant'Angelo) and a 10-minute walk from St. Peter's, is in a relatively untouristy area. Maintained and operated by the Torre family, it occupies the second and third floors of an imposing 200-year-old building. The rooms are simple, modern, and clean, with wooden furniture and views of either the street or a rather bleak but quiet courtyard. Rooms are small but not cramped, each with a comfortable bed and a tiled, shower-only bathroom.

Via Mariana Dionigi 16, 00193 Roma. ℂ 06-3242000. Fax 06-320758. www.hotelsantangelo.net. 31 units (shower only). 95€–250€ ($114–$300) double; 125€–270€ ($150–$324) triple. Rates include breakfast. AE, DC, MC, V. Parking 25€–30€ ($30–$36). Metro: Spagna. **Amenities:** Breakfast room; bar; room service (breakfast only); babysitting; nonsmoking rooms; rooms for those w/limited mobility. *In room:* A/C, TV, dataport, hair dryer.

INEXPENSIVE

Residence Giuggioli ⚹   This family-run guesthouse was founded in the 1940s but was recently renovated, adding private bathrooms to each guestroom. It occupies most of the second floor of a five-story 1870s apartment house, with high-ceilinged rooms that were originally much grander but whose noble proportions are still obvious. Three of the five rooms have balconies overlooking the street. The Giuggioli is always crowded, partly because the rooms are larger than expected and have a scattering of antiques and reproductions (although the mattresses could use replacing).

If this place is full, walk a few flights up to the similar **Pensione Lady** (℡ **06-3242112**), where up to seven rooms might be available at about the same rates.

Via Germanico 198, 00192 Roma. ℡ **06-3242113**. 19 units. 85€–185€ ($102–$222) double; 115€–205€ ($138–$246) triple. Rates include breakfast. AE, DC, MC, V. Parking in nearby garage 20€ ($24). Metro: Ottaviano. **Amenities:** Lounge; breakfast room; 24-hr. room service; laundry service; dry cleaning; nonsmoking rooms. *In room:* A/C, TV, minibar, safe.

8 In Trastevere

Once upon a time, tourists avoided Trastevere, but today, although it's off the beaten track, it's becoming more popular as an up-and-coming neighborhood where you can experience a true slice of Roman life.

Trastevere Manara ⭐ *(Value)* Manara opened its restored doors in 1998 to meet the demand for accommodations in Trastevere. This little gem has fresh, bright bedrooms with immaculate tiles. All of the bathrooms have also been renovated and contain showers, although they're small. The price is hard to beat for those who want to stay in one of the most atmospheric sections of Rome. Most of the rooms open onto the lively Piazza San Cosimato, and all of them have comfortable, albeit functional, furnishings. Breakfast is the only meal served, but many good restaurants lie just minutes away.

Via L. Manara 24–25, 00153 Roma. ℡ **06-5814713**. Fax 06-5881016. 18 units. 103€–105€ ($124–$126) double. Rates include buffet breakfast. AE, DC, MC, V. Bus: H. Tram: 8. **Amenities:** Breakfast room. *In room:* TV, dataport.

9 In Parioli

Hotel degli Aranci This former villa is on a tree-lined street, surrounded by similar villas that are the homes of consulates and diplomats. Most of the accommodations have tall windows opening onto city views and are filled with provincial furnishings or English-style reproductions and good beds. The tiled, shower-only bathrooms have adequate shelf space. Scattered about the public rooms are medallions of soldiers in profile, old engravings of ruins, and classical vases. From the glass-walled breakfast room, you can see the tops of orange trees.

Via Barnaba Oriani 11, 00197 Roma. ℡ **06-8070202**. Fax 06-8070704. www.hoteldegliaranci.com. 58 units. 200€ ($240) double; from 250€ ($300) suite. Rates include breakfast. AE, DC, MC, V. Free parking. Bus: 3 or 53. **Amenities:** Restaurant; bar; room service (breakfast, lunch, and dinner but not 24 hr.); laundry service; dry cleaning; nonsmoking rooms. *In room:* A/C, TV, dataport, minibar, hair dryer, safe.

Hotel delle Muse ⭐ *(Value)* This little hotel, .5km (⅓ mile) north of the Villa Borghese, is a winning but undiscovered choice run by the efficient, English-speaking Giorgio Lazar. Most rooms have been renovated but remain rather minimalist, with modern furnishings. Nonetheless, you'll be reasonably comfortable and there is a tidy shower-only bathroom in each unit.

Via Tommaso Salvini 18, 00197 Roma. ℡ **06-8088333**. Fax 06-8085749. www.hoteldellemuse.com. 61 units. 75€–180€ ($90–$216) double; 95€–245€ ($114–$294) triple. Rates include buffet breakfast. AE, DC, MC, V. Parking 16€ ($19). Bus: 360. **Amenities:** Garden restaurant; bar; 24-hr. room service; babysitting; laundry service; dry cleaning; writing room. *In room:* TV, dataport, hair dryer, safe.

Hotel Lord Byron ★★★ Lots of sophisticated travelers are choosing this chic boutique hotel over old landmarks like the St. Regis Grand. In an Art Deco villa set on a residential hilltop in Parioli, an area of embassies and exclusive town houses at the edge of the Villa Borghese, the Lord Byron exemplifies modern Rome. From the curving entrance steps off the staffed parking lot in front, you'll notice striking design touches. Flowers are everywhere, the lighting is discreet, and everything is on an intimate scale. Each guest room is unique, but most have lots of mirrors, upholstered walls, sumptuous beds, spacious bathrooms with gray marble accessories, and big dressing rooms/closets. Ask for room no. 503, 602, or 603 for great views. Bathrooms are medium size. The hotel's restaurant, **Sapori del Lord Byron,** is one of Rome's top restaurants; see the full review on p. 131.

Via G. de Notaris 5, 00197 Roma. (✆ **06-3220404.** Fax 06-3220405. www.lordbyronhotel.com. 36 units. 305€–480€ ($366–$576) double; 720€–950€ ($864–$1,140) suite. Rates include buffet breakfast. AE, DC, MC, V. Parking 30€ ($36). Metro: Flaminio. Bus: 52. **Amenities:** Restaurant; bar; 24-hr. room service; babysitting; laundry service; dry cleaning; nonsmoking rooms; currency exchange. *In room:* A/C, TV, dataport, minibar, hair dryer, iron/ironing board, safe.

10 At the Airport
VERY EXPENSIVE

Hotel Hilton Rome Airport At long last, Rome has a first-class airport hotel for late-night arrivals and early morning departures. Only 200m (656 ft.) from the air terminal, this hotel is approached via a skywalk. The Hilton doesn't pretend to be more than it is—a bedroom factory at the airport. Follow the broad hallways to one of the midsize to spacious "crash pads," each with deep carpeting, generous storage space, and large, full bathrooms. The best units are the executive suites, with luxuries such as separate check-in, trouser press, dataports, and voice mail.

Via Arturo Ferrarin 2, 00050 Fiumicino. (✆ **800/445-8667** in the U.S. and Canada, or 06-65258. Fax 06-65256525. www.hilton.com. 517 units. 365€–380€ ($438–$456) double; 430€–455€ ($516–$546) suite. AE, DC, MC, V. Parking 23€ ($28). Metro: Fiumicino Aeroporto. **Amenities:** 2 restaurants; bar; coffee shop; indoor pool (heated in winter); tennis courts; health club; sauna; car-rental desk; 24-hr. room service; babysitting; laundry service; dry cleaning; nonsmoking rooms; rooms for those w/limited mobility. *In room:* A/C, TV, dataport, minibar, coffeemaker (in some), hair dryer, safe.

MODERATE

Hotel Cancelli Rossi If you're nervous about making your flight, you could book into this very simple motel-style place, located 2.5km (1½ miles) from the airport. Two floors are served by an elevator, and the decor is minimal. Rooms range from small to medium and are functionally furnished but reasonably comfortable, with good beds, and clean tiled bathrooms with shower stalls. The atmosphere is a bit antiseptic, but this place is geared more for business travelers than vacationers. A restaurant in an annex nearby serves Italian and international food. The hotel is entirely nonsmoking.

Via Portuense 2467, 00054 Fiumicino. (✆ **06-6507221.** Fax 06-65049168. www.cancellirossi.it. 50 units. 113€–150€ ($136–$180) double. Rates include breakfast. Free parking. Metro: Fiumicino, and then Bus 5 to hotel. Bus shuttle costing 6€ ($7.20) from/to the Leonardo da Vinci airport Mon–Sat 7–9:45am and 5:15–8:55pm every 20 min. **Amenities:** Restaurant; bar; room service (breakfast, lunch, and dinner but not 24 hrs.); babysitting; laundry service; dry cleaning; rooms for those w/limited mobility. *In room:* A/C, TV, dataport, minibar, hair dryer, safe.

7

Where to Dine in Rome

Rome remains one of the world's great capitals for dining, with more diversity today than ever. Although most of the trattorie haven't changed their menus in a quarter of a century (except to raise prices), there's an increasing number of chic, upscale spots with chefs willing to experiment, as well as a growing handful of ethnic spots for those days when you just can't face another plate of pasta. The great thing about Rome is that you don't have to spend a fortune to eat really well.

Most Italian restaurants are either called a *trattoria* or a *ristorante*. In theory, there's a difference, but in reality, it's difficult to discern. Traditionally, trattorie are smaller and less formal, but sometimes, in a kind of reverse snobbism, the management will call an elegant place a trattoria. A ristorante is supposed to be more substantial, but often the opposite is true.

It's difficult to compile a list of the best restaurants in a city such as Rome. Everybody—locals, expatriates, even those who have chalked up only one visit—has

personal favorites and finds. What follows is not a comprehensive list of all the best restaurants of Rome, but simply a running commentary on a number of our favorites. For the most part, we've chosen not to review every deluxe spot known to all big spenders. We've chosen a handful of splurge restaurants where you'll really get what you pay for, and then we've reviewed a large selection of moderately priced and affordable restaurants that will give you a wonderful meal, authentic cuisine, and a lovely experience without breaking the bank.

Roman meals customarily include at least three separate courses: pasta, a main course (usually a meat dish with vegetables or salad), and dessert. Meats, though tasty, are definitely secondary to the pasta dishes, which are generous and filling. The wine is so excellent (especially the white Frascati wine from the nearby Castelli Romani) and affordable that you might want to do as the Romans do and have it with both lunch and dinner.

PRACTICAL TIPS

For a quick bite, go to a **bar.** Although bars in Italy do serve alcohol, they function mainly as cafes. Prices have a split personality: *Al banco* is standing at the bar, while *à tavola* means sitting at a table, where you'll be waited on and charged two to four times as much. In bars you can find *panini* sandwiches on various rolls and *tramezzini* (giant triangles of white-bread sandwiches with the crusts cut off). These run 1.50€ to 3.10€ ($1.80–$3.70) and are traditionally put in a kind of tiny press to flatten and toast them so the crust is crispy and the filling is hot and gooey; unfortunately, microwaves have invaded and are everywhere, turning panini into something resembling a hot, soggy tissue.

Pizza a taglio or *pizza rustica* indicates a place where you can order pizza by the slice. *Pizzerie* are casual sit-down restaurants that cook large, round pizzas with very thin crusts in wood-burning ovens. A *tavola calda* (literally "hot table") serves ready-made hot foods that you can take away or eat at one of the few small tables often available. The food is usually very good. A *rosticceria* is the same type of place, and you'll see chickens roasting on a spit in the window.

A full-fledged restaurant will go by the name *osteria, trattoria,* or *ristorante.* Once upon a time, these terms meant something—osterie were basic places where you could get a plate of spaghetti and a glass of wine; trattorie were casual places serving full meals of filling peasant fare; and ristoranti were fancier places, with waiters in bow ties, printed menus, wine lists, and hefty prices. Nowadays, fancy restaurants often go by the name of *trattoria* to cash in on the associated charm factor; trendy spots use *osteria* to show they're hip; and simple, inexpensive places sometimes tack on *ristorante* to ennoble themselves.

The *pane e coperto* (bread and cover) is a 1€ to 5.50€ ($1.20–$6.60) cover charge that you must pay at most restaurants for the mere privilege of sitting at the table. Most Italians eat a leisurely full meal—appetizer and first and second courses—at lunch and dinner and will expect you to do the same, or at least a first and second course. To request the bill, ask *"Il conto, per favore"* (eel *con*-toh, pehr fah-*vohr*-ay). A tip of 15% is usually included in the bill these days, but if you're unsure, ask *"È incluso il servizio?"* (ay een-*cloo*-soh eel sair-*vee*-tsoh?).

You'll find at many restaurants, especially larger ones and in cities, a *menu turistico* (tourist's menu), sometimes called *menu del giorno* (menu of the day). This set-price menu usually covers all meal incidentals—including table wine, cover charge, and 15% service charge—along with a first course *(primo)* and second course *(secondo),* but it almost always offers an abbreviated selection of pretty bland dishes: spaghetti in tomato sauce and slices of pork. Sometimes a better choice is a *menu à prezzo fisso* (fixed-price menu). It usually doesn't include wine, but it sometimes covers the service and *coperto,* and often offers a wider selection of better dishes, occasionally house specialties, and local foods. Ordering a la carte, however, offers you the best chance for a memorable meal. Even better, forego the menu entirely and put yourself in the hands of your waiter.

The *enoteca* wine bar is a growing, popular marriage of a wine bar and an osteria, where you can sit and order from a host of local and regional wines by the glass (usually 1.55€–4.50€/$1.85–$5.40) while snacking on finger foods (and usually a number of simple first-course possibilities) that reflect the region's fare. Relaxed and full of ambience and good wine, these are great spots for light and inexpensive lunches—perfect to educate your palate and recharge your batteries.

Restaurants generally serve lunch between 1 and 3pm, and dinner between about 8 and 10:30pm; at all other times, restaurants are closed. Dinner is taken late in Rome,

Then&Now The Breakfast of Champions

Breakfast doesn't have to break your vacation budget, especially if you follow Arthur Frommer's advice, still savvy after 50 years: "Never go to a restaurant for breakfast in Europe. You'll find the same small continental breakfast available elsewhere (bars and cafés) at one-fifth the price. . . . On my own trips to Italy, I usually take the continental breakfast in a bar or café, then stroll over to a market place for fruit and cheese."

so although a restaurant might open at 7:30pm, even if you get there at 8pm, you'll often be the only one in the place. A heavier meal is typically eaten at midday, and a lighter one is eaten in the evening. We recommend that you leave a few hours free for dinner and go to a restaurant in a different part of town each night. It's a great way to get a real taste of Rome. Romans think of meals as leisurely affairs, so allow enough time to relax—do as the Romans do.

ROMAN CUISINE

Many visitors from North America erroneously think of Italian cuisine as one-dimensional. Of course, everybody's heard of minestrone, spaghetti, chicken cacciatore, and spumoni ice cream. But chefs hardly confine themselves to such a limited repertoire.

Rome's cooking isn't subtle, but its kitchens rival anything that the chefs of Florence or Venice can turn out. The city's chefs borrow—and sometimes improve on—the cuisine of other regions. Throughout your Roman holiday you'll encounter such savory treats as *zuppa di pesce* (a soup or stew of various fish, cooked in white wine and herbs), *cannelloni* (tube-shape pasta baked with any number of stuffings), *riso col gamberi* (rice with shrimp, peas, and mushrooms, flavored with white wine and garlic), *scampi alla griglia* (grilled prawns, one of the best-tasting and most expensive dishes in the city), *quaglie con risotto e tartufi* (quail with rice and truffles), *lepre alla cacciatore* (hare flavored with tomato sauce and herbs), *zabaglione* (a cream made with sugar, egg yolks, and Marsala), *gnocchi alla romana* (potato-flour dumplings with a sauce made with meat and covered with grated cheese), *stracciatella* (chicken broth with eggs and grated cheese), *abbacchio* (baby spring lamb, often roasted over an open fire), *saltimbocca alla romana* (literally "jump-in-your-mouth"—thin slices of veal with cheese, ham, and sage), *fritta alla romana* (a mixed fry that's likely to include everything from brains to artichokes), *carciofi alla romana* (tender artichokes cooked with mint and garlic, and flavored with white wine), *fettuccine all'uovo* (egg noodles served with butter and cheese), *zuppa di cozze o vongole* (a hearty bowl of mussels or clams cooked in broth), *fritta di scampi e calamaretti* (baby squid and prawns fast-fried), *fragoline* (wild strawberries, in this case from the Alban Hills), and *finocchio* (or fennel, a celery-like raw vegetable, the flavor of anisette, often eaten as a dessert and in salads).

Incidentally, except in the south, Italians don't use as much garlic in their food as most visitors seem to believe. Most northern Italian dishes are butter based. Virgin olive oil is preferred in the south. Spaghetti and meatballs is not an Italian dish, although certain restaurants throughout the country have taken to serving it for homesick Americans.

WINES & OTHER DRINKS

Italy is the largest wine-producing country in the world; as far back as 800 B.C., the Etruscans were vintners. It's said that more soil is used in Italy for the cultivation of grapes than for growing food. Many Italian farmers produce wine just for their own consumption or for their relatives. It wasn't until 1965, however, that laws were enacted to guarantee regular consistency in wine making. Wines regulated by the government are labeled DOC *(Denominazione di Origine Controllata)*. If you see DOCG on a label (the G means *garantita*), it means even better quality control.

Lazio (Rome's region) is a major wine-producing region of Italy. Many of the local wines come from the Castelli Romani, the hill towns around Rome. Horace and Juvenal sang the praises of Latium wines even in imperial times. These wines, experts agree, are best drunk when they are young, and they are most often white, mellow, and dry (or else demi-sec). There are seven different types, including *Falerno* (yellowish straw in color) and *Cecubo* (often served with roast meat). Try also *Colli Albani* (straw-yellow with amber tints and served with both fish and meat). The golden-yellow wines of **Frascati** are famous, produced in both a demi-sec and a sweet variety, the latter served with dessert.

Romans drink other libations as well. Their most famous drink is **Campari,** bright red in color and herb flavored, with a quinine-like bitterness to it. It's customary to serve it with ice cubes and soda.

Beer is also made in Italy and, in general, is lighter than German beer. If you order beer in a Roman bar or restaurant, chances are good that it will be imported unless you specify otherwise, and you'll be charged accordingly. Some famous names in European beer-making now operate plants in Italy, where the brew has been "adjusted" to Italian taste.

High-proof **grappa** is made from the leftovers after the grapes have been pressed. Many Romans drink this before or after dinner (some put it into their coffee). To an untrained foreign palate, it often seems rough and harsh; some say it's an acquired taste.

Other popular drinks include several **liqueurs.** Try herb-flavored Strega, or perhaps an almond-flavored Amaretto. One of the best known is Maraschino, taking its name from a type of cherry used in its preparation. Galliano is also herb flavored, and Sambuca (anisette) is made of aniseed and is often served with a "fly" (coffee bean) in it. On a hot day, the true Roman orders a vermouth, Cinzano, with a twist of lemon, ice cubes, and a squirt of soda water.

1 Near Stazione Termini

VERY EXPENSIVE

Agata e Romeo ✿✿ NEW ROMAN   One of the most charming places near the Vittorio Emanuele Monument is this striking duplex restaurant done up in turn-of-the-20th-century Liberty style. You'll enjoy the creative cuisine of Romeo Caraccio (who manages the dining room) and his wife, Agata Parisella (who prepares her own version of sophisticated Roman food). Look for pasta garnished with broccoli and cauliflower and served in skate broth, as well as risotto with saffron, taleggio cheese, rabbit croquettes, and thyme. Other dishes we've enjoyed here include medallions of tuna coated with sesame seeds and served in a sweet and sour sauce, and breaded sole with crisply baked vegetables. For dessert, consider Agata's *millefoglie,* puff pastry stuffed with almonds and sweetened cream. There's a charming wine cellar with a wide choice of international and domestic wines.

Via Carlo Alberto 45. ✆ **06-4466115.** Reservations recommended. All pastas 20€ ($24); meat and fish 30€ ($36). AE, DC, MC, V. Mon 8–10:30pm; Tues–Fri 1–2:30pm and 8–10:30pm. Closed Aug 13–Sept 11. Metro: Vittorio Emanuele.

MODERATE

Il Quadrifoglio NEAPOLITAN   Situated in a grandiose palace, this well-managed restaurant lets you sample the flavors and herbs of Naples and southern Italy. You'll find a tempting selection of antipasti, such as anchovies, peppers, capers, onions, and breaded and fried eggplant, all garnished with fresh herbs and virgin olive oil. The pastas are made daily, usually with tomato- or oil-based sauces and always with herbs and aged cheeses. Try a zesty rice dish (one of the best is *sartù di riso,* studded with vegetables,

Take a Gelato Break

If you're craving luscious gelato, our top choice is **Giolitti** ⟨*⟩⟨*⟩, Via Uffici del Vicario 40 (ⓒ **06-6991243**; www.giolitti.it), the city's oldest ice-cream shop, open daily from 7am to 2am. You'll find the usual *vaniglia* (vanilla), *cioccolato* (chocolate), *fragola* (strawberry), and *caffé* (coffee), but you'll also find great combinations like *gianduia* (chocolate hazelnut), plus such treats as *cassata alla siciliana* (orange-flavored sponge cake with canola cream), *zabaglione* (light custard flavored with marsala-sweet wine), *mascarpone* (crème fraiche, double cream, and buttermilk) and *maron glace* (chestnuts in a vanilla and butter glaze). The preposterously oversize showpiece sundaes have names such as Coppa Olimpica (made with sponge cake, zabaione, nougat, chocolate, and a touch of liquor flavoring). Other ice-cream flavors include Stracciatella, Ricotta, Champagne, Yogurt, Coconut, Peach, Apricot, Grape, Mandarin, and Blackberries.

Another favorite is the **Palazzo del Freddo Giovanni,** Via Principe Eugenio 65–67 (ⓒ **06-4464740**). More than 100 years old, this ice-cream outlet (part of a gelato factory) turns out yummy concoctions and specializes in rice ice cream. It's open Tuesday through Sunday from noon to 12:30am.

If you're fond of frothy *frullati* frappes, head to **Pascucci,** Via Torre Argentina 20 (ⓒ **06-6864816**), where blenders work all day grinding fresh fruit into delectable drinks. It's open Monday through Saturday from noon to 1am.

Prices at these shops range from 1.75€ to 8€ ($2.10–$9.60).

---

herbs, and meats), followed by sautéed grouper fish rolls or a simple but savory *granatine* (meatballs, usually of veal, bound together with mozzarella). Dessert anyone? A longtime favorite is *torta caprese,* with hazelnuts and chocolate.

Via del Boschetto 19. ⓒ **06-4826096**. Reservations recommended. Main courses 10€–16€ ($12–$19). AE, DC, MC, V. Mon–Fri 12:30–3pm and 7pm–midnight; Sat 7pm–midnight. Closed Aug 5–25. Metro: Cavour.

INEXPENSIVE

Monte Arci ROMAN/SARDINIAN   On a cobblestone street near Piazza Indipendenza, this restaurant is set behind a sienna facade. It features cheap Roman and Sardinian specialties (you'll spend even less for pizza) such as *nialoreddus* (a regional form of gnocchetti); pasta with clams, lobster, or the musky-earthy notes of porcini mushrooms; green and white spaghetti with bacon, spinach, cream, and cheese; and delicious lamb sausage flavored with herbs and pecorino cheese. It's all home cooking, hearty but not particularly creative.

Via Castelfirdardo 33. ⓒ **06-4941220**. Reservations recommended. Main courses 7€–14€ ($8–$17); fixed-price menu 25€ ($30). AE, DC, V. Mon–Fri noon–3pm and 7–11:30pm; Sat 7–11:30pm. Closed Aug. Metro: Stazione Termini.

Trimani Wine Bar ⟨*⟩ CONTINENTAL/WINE BAR   Opened as a tasting center for French and Italian wines, spumantis, and liqueurs, this is an elegant wine bar with a lovely decor (stylish but informal) and comfortable seating. More than 30 wines are available by the glass. To accompany them, you can choose from a bistro-style menu, with dishes such as salade niçoise, vegetarian pastas, herb-laden *fagiole* (bean soup), quiche, and

Dining near Stazione Termini, Via Veneto & Piazza Barberini

Agata e Romeo **8**	Il Dito e La Luna **10**
Arancia Blu **9**	Il Quadrifoglio **7**
Aurora 10 da	La Terrazza **3**
Pino il Sommelier **2**	Monte Arci **4**
Césarina **1**	Trimani
Colline Emiliane **6**	Wine Bar **5**

Hungarian goulash. Also available is a wider menu, including meat and fish courses. The specialty is the large choice of little *bruschette* with cheese and prosciutto—the chef orders every kind of prosciutti and cheese, from all over Italy. The dishes are matched with the appropriate wines. The dessert specialty is *Verduzzo di Ronco di Viere* (chestnut mousse served with a sauce of white wine), covered by whipped cream and meringue.

Trimani maintains a well-stocked **Italian wine shop** about 37m (120 ft.) from its wine bar, at V. Goito 20 (✆ **06-4469661**), where an astonishing array of wines is for sale. The shop is open from Monday to Friday 8:30am to 1:30pm and 3:30 to 8pm.

Via Cernaia 37B. ✆ **06-4469630.** Reservations recommended. Main courses 7.50€–16€ ($9–$19); glass of wine (depending on vintage) 2€–14€ ($2.40–$17). AE, DC, MC, V. Mon–Sat 11:30am–3pm and 6pm–12:30am (in Dec open also on Sun). Closed 2 weeks in Aug. Metro: Repubblica or Castro Pretorio.

2 In San Lorenzo

To locate the restaurants reviewed below, see the "Dining near Stazione Termini, Via Veneto & Piazza Barberini" map above.

INEXPENSIVE

Arancia Blu ★★ (Finds) VEGETARIAN/ITALIAN   Fabio Bassan and Enrico Bartolucci serve Rome's best vegetarian cuisine. Under soft lighting and wood ceilings, surrounded by wine racks and university intellectuals, the friendly waiters will help you compile a menu to fit any dietary need. The dishes at this trendy spot are inspired by peasant cuisines from across Italy and beyond. The appetizers range from hummus and tabbouleh to zucchini-and-saffron quiche and salad with apples, gorgonzola, and balsamic vinegar. The main courses change seasonally and might include lasagna with red onions, mushrooms, zucchini, and ginger; couscous *con verdure* (vegetable couscous); or *ravioli ripieni di patate e menta* (ravioli stuffed with potatoes and mint served under fresh tomatoes and Sardinian sheep's cheese). The restaurant offers 250 wines and inventive desserts, such as dark-chocolate cake with warm orange sauce.

Via dei Latini 55–65 (at Via Arunci). © 06-4454105. Reservations highly recommended. Main courses 8€–12€ ($9.60–$14). No credit cards. Daily 8pm–midnight (Sept–July Sun noon–3:30pm). Bus: 71.

Il Dito e La Luna ⚘ SICILIAN/ITALIAN   This charming, unpretentious bistro has counters and service areas accented with lovely displays of fresh fruits and vegetables. The menu—divided between traditional Sicilian and creative contemporary dishes—includes orange-infused anchovies served on orange segments, a creamy flan of mild onions and mountain cheese, and seafood couscous loaded with shellfish. The pastas are excellent, particularly the *tonnarelli* (square-cut spaghetti) with mussels, bacon, tomatoes, and exotic mushrooms. The specialty of the house is *caponata di melanzane,* chopped eggplant stewed in tomato sauce with onions and potatoes.

Via dei Sabelli 49–51, San Lorenzo. © 06-4940726. Reservations recommended. Main courses 11€–15€ ($13–$18). No credit cards. Mon–Sat 8pm–midnight. Metro: Vittorio Emanuele.

3 Near Via Veneto & Piazza Barberini

To locate the restaurants in this section, refer to the "Where to Dine near Stazione Termini, Via Veneto & Piazza Barberini" map on p. 107.

VERY EXPENSIVE

La Terrazza ⚘⚘⚘ INTERNATIONAL/ITALIAN   La Terrazza and Sapori del Lord Byron (p. 131) serve the city's finest cuisine, but here you get the added bonus of a sweeping view over St. Peter's. The service is formal and flawless, yet not intimidating. The new chef, Adriano Cavagnini, is brilliant, creative, and dynamic, and he learned how to cook from his ancestors who founded a restaurant on Lake Garda in 1885. He's cooked around the world and for such names as Tony Blair. You might start with zucchini blossoms stuffed with ricotta and black olives, or lobster medallions with apple purée and black truffles. Main courses might include red tortelli (whose coloring comes from tomato mousse) stuffed with mascarpone cheese and drizzled with lemon, or a sea bass baked in a crust of black olives and salt with oregano and potatoes.

In the Hotel Eden, Via Ludovisi 49. © 06-478121. Reservations recommended. Main courses 26€–59€ ($31–$71); fixed-price menu 100€ ($120). AE, DC, MC, V. Daily 12:30–2:30pm and 7:30–10:30pm. Metro: Barberini.

MODERATE

Aurora 10 da Pino il Sommelier ITALIAN   Skip the tourist traps along Via Veneto and walk another block or two for much better food and a crowd of regulars from the chic neighborhood. The waitstaff is welcoming to foreigners, although the service can be erratic. The place is noted for its array of more than 250 wines, representing every province. The *rigatoni alla siciliana* with eggplant, black olives, and tomato sauce is better than anything Carmela Soprano could whip up. The mixed seafood appetizer is one of the best in Rome, a great bowlful of delights from the sea.

The fish is fresh every day, and the chefs grill it to perfection. The .
dishes include grilled strips of filet with seasonal vegetables. Among the .
table desserts are crème brûlée and Neapolitan babba, filled with liqueur.

Via Aurora 10. ✆ 06-4742779. Reservations recommended. Main courses 12€–22€ ($14–$26). AE, DC,
Tues–Sun noon–3pm and 7–11pm. Metro: Barberini.

Césarina *(Kids* BOLOGNESE/EMILIANA-ROMAGNOLA/ROMAN Specializing in the cuisines of Rome and the region around Bologna, this place is named for
Césarina Masi, who opened it in 1960 (many old-timers fondly remember her strict
supervision of the kitchen and how she lectured regulars who didn't finish their *tagliatelle*). Although Césarina died in the mid-1980s, her traditions are kept going by her
family. This has long been a favorite of Roman families. The polite staff rolls a trolley
from table to table laden with an excellent *bollito misto* (an array of well-seasoned
boiled meats) and often follows with misto Césarina—four kinds of creamy, handmade pasta, each with a different sauce. Equally appealing are the *saltimbocca* (veal
with ham) and the *cotoletta alla bolognese* (tender veal cutlet baked with ham and
cheese). A dessert specialty is *semifreddo* Césarina with hot chocolate, so meltingly
good that it's worth the 5 pounds you'll gain.

Via Piemonte 109. ✆ 06-4880828. Reservations recommended. Main courses 7€–20€ ($8.40–$24). AE, DC, MC,
V. Mon–Sat 12:30–3pm and 7:30–11pm. Metro: Barberini. Bus: 910.

Colline Emiliane *(Kids* *(Finds* BOLOGNESE/EMILIANA-ROMAGNOLA Serving
the *classica cucina bolognese,* Colline Emiliane is a small, family-run place—the owner
is the cook, and his wife makes the pasta (about the best you'll find in Rome). The
house specialty is an inspired *tortellini alla panna* (with cream sauce and truffles), but
the less expensive pastas, including *maccheroni al funghetto* and *tagliatelle alla bolognese,* are excellent, too. As an opener, we suggest *culatello di Zibello,* a delicacy from
a small town near Parma that's known for having the world's finest prosciutto. Main
courses include *braciola di maiale* (boneless rolled pork cutlets stuffed with ham and
cheese, breaded, and sautéed) and an impressive *giambonnetto* (roast veal Emilian-style
with roast potatoes).

Via Avignonesi 22 (off Piazza Barberini). ✆ 06-4817538. Reservations highly recommended. Main courses
14€–18€ ($17–$22). MC, V. Tues–Sun 12:45–2:45pm; Tues–Sat 7:45–10:45pm. Closed Aug. Metro: Barberini.

4 Near Ancient Rome

To locate the restaurants in this section, refer to the "Dining near the Spanish Steps
& Ancient Rome" map on p. 123.

EXPENSIVE

Crab *(Kids* SEAFOOD Eating at this trattoria is ideal after a visit to the nearby Basilica
of San Giovanni. As you enter, you are greeted with a display of freshly harvested crustaceans and mollusks. The signature dish is king crab legs, but you might want to skip
the accompanying orange sauce; we thought it overpowered the delicate crab. Look for
fish from around the world, including oysters from France, lobster from the Mediterranean and the Atlantic, and some catches from the Adriatic. If you've had only Atlantic
lobster up to now, try the Mediterranean variety. It is more rare but of superior quality
(and, naturally, more expensive). The antipasti is practically a meal in itself. Our party
devoured a savory sauté of mussels and clams, an octopus salad, and scallops gratin,
which was followed by succulent lobster ravioli in *salsa vergine* (a lobster-based sauce).

vongole (fresh clams) is the best in all of Rome. For dessert, ...ment of sliced tropical fruit that evoked the campy hat worn ...l those late-night movies. Most of the main courses, except ...ellfish and lobster platters, are closer to the lower end of the

636. Reservations required. Main courses 10€–85€ ($12–$102). AE, DC, MC, V. 30pm and 8–11:30pm. Closed Aug. Metro: Colosseo. Tram: 3.

(Finds ROMAN   At last there's a good place to eat in the former gastronomic wasteland near the Roman Forum and Palatine Hill. The helpful staff welcomes you to a shady terrace or a dimly lit dining room resting under a vaulted brick ceiling and arched alcoves. The chef handles seafood exceedingly well (try the mini baby squid sautéed with Roman artichokes). His signature dish is seafood carpaccio made with tuna, turbot, or sea bass. Succulent meats, such as medallions of veal in a nutmeg-enhanced cream sauce, round out the menu at this family-friendly place. All the pastas are homemade.

Via dei Fienili 49–51. © 06-6780933. Reservations recommended. Main courses 13€–30€ ($16–$36). MC, V. Mon–Sat 12:30–3:30pm and 7:30pm–midnight. Closed 2 weeks at Christmas. Metro: Circo Massimo.

MODERATE

See also the listing for **Il Quadrifoglio** on p. 105; it's located about midway between Stazione Termini and Ancient Rome.

Scoglio di Frisio NEAPOLITAN/PIZZA   This trattoria, a longtime favorite, offers a great introduction to the Neapolitan kitchen. Here you can taste a genuine plate-size Neapolitan pizza (crunchy, oozy, and excellent) with clams and mussels. Or, you can start with a medley of savory stuffed vegetables and antipasti before moving on to chicken cacciatore or well-flavored tender veal scaloppini. Scoglio di Frisio also makes for an inexpensive night of hokey but still charming entertainment, as cornball "O Sole Mio" renditions and other Neapolitan songs issue forth from a guitar, mandolin, and strolling tenor. The nautical decor (in honor of the top-notch fish dishes) is complete with a high-ceiling grotto of fishing nets, crustaceans, and a miniature three-masted schooner.

Via Merulana 256. © 06-4872765. Reservations recommended. Main courses 10€–22€ ($12–$26). AE, DC, MC, V. Daily 4:30–11:30pm. Metro: Vittorio Emanuele. Bus: 714 or 16.

Tram Tram PUGLIA/ROMAN/SICILIAN   Around the Basilica of San Lorenzo, this is a Roman dining oddity, an address rarely frequented by visitors but beloved by locals. Its name comes from the seats and other artifacts that the owner salvaged from some of Rome's old trams. The crowded, often hysterically busy dining rooms showcase Signora di Vittorio's robust, hearty, and flavor-filled cuisine that combines the best of Lazio and Puglia.

Don't expect professional, or even good, service. But do expect good food and fair prices. We want to rush back soon for some more of the *orecchiette alla Norman,* with Sicilian eggplant, tomato sauce, and *ricotta salata* cheese. Another dish we're definitely reordering is the veal scallops rolled around a filling of prosciutto, breadcrumbs, and cheese. Other recommendations are the *pappardella Tram Tram,* broad noodles in a regional tomato sauce riddled with strips of lamb and roasted sweet peppers, and the stuffed Savoy cabbage filled with an herb-flavored ground meat in a spicy tomato sauce.

Via dei Reti 44–46. © 06-490416. Reservations recommended. Main courses 9€–16€ ($11–$19). AE, DC, MC, V. Tues–Sun 12:30–3:30pm and 7:30–11:30pm. Metro: San Giovanni. Bus: 71 or 492. Tram: 3.

Quick Bites

At **Dar Filettaro a Santa Barbara,** just off the southeast corner of Campo de' Fiori at Largo dei Librari 88 (© **06-6864018**), you can join the line of people threading their way to the back of the bare room to order a filet of baccalà (salt cod), fried golden brown and served *da portar via* (wrapped in paper to eat as you take a *passeggiata,* or stroll). It costs 3€ to 9€ ($3.60–$11) for to-go service only; the place is closed Sunday.

Lunchtime offers you the perfect opportunity to savor Roman fast food: **pizza rustica,** by the slice (often called *pizza à taglio*), half wrapped in waxed paper for easy carrying. Just point to the bubbling, steaming sheet with your preferred toppings behind the counter; 2€ ($2.40) buys a healthy portion of "plain" tomato sauce: basil-and-cheese *pizza margherita. Pizza rossa* (just sauce) and *pizza con patate* (with cheese and potatoes) cost even less, as does the exquisitely simple *pizza bianca* (plain dough brushed with olive oil and sprinkled with salt and sometimes rosemary).

A **rosticceria** is a *pizza à taglio* with spits of chickens roasting in the window and a few pasta dishes kept warm in long trays. You can also sit down for a quick pasta or prepared meat dish steaming behind the glass counters at a **tavola calda** (literally "hot table") for about half the price of a *trattoria.* A Roman **bar,** though it does indeed serve liquor, is what we'd call a cafe, a place to grab a cheap *panino* (flat roll stuffed with meat, cheese, or vegetables) or *tramezzino* (large triangular sandwiches on white bread with the crusts cut off, like giant tea sandwiches).

INEXPENSIVE

Abruzzi *(value* ABRUZZESE/ROMAN   Abruzzi, which takes its name from the region east of Rome, is at one side of Piazza S. S. Apostoli, just a short walk from Piazza Venezia. The good food and reasonable prices make it a big draw for students. The chef offers a satisfying assortment of cold antipasti. With your starter, we suggest a liter of garnet-red wine; we once had one whose bouquet was suggestive of Abruzzi's wildflowers. If you'd like soup as well, you'll find a good *stracciatella* (egg-and-Parmesan soup). A typical main dish is *vitella tonnata con capperi* (veal in tuna sauce with capers). But the menu ranges far wider than that; it's a virtual textbook of classical Italian dishes, everything from a creamy baked eggplant with mozzarella to meltingly tender veal cutlets in the Milanese style (fried with potatoes). No one in Italy does roast lamb better than the Romans, and the selection here is good—tender, grilled to perfection, seasoned with virgin olive oil and fresh herbs, and dished up with roast potatoes.

Via del Vaccaro 1. © **06-6793897.** Reservations recommended. Main courses 7.50€–15€ ($9–$18). AE, DC, MC, V. Sun–Fri 12:30–3pm and 7–11pm. Closed 3 weeks in Aug. Bus: 44 or 46.

Hostaria Nerone *(* ITALIAN/ROMAN   Built atop the ruins of the Golden House of Nero, this trattoria is run by the energetic de Santis family, who cook, serve, and handle the large crowds of hungry locals and visitors. Opened in 1929 at the edge of the Colle Oppio Park, it contains two compact dining rooms, plus a shrub-lined terrace with views of the Colosseum and the Baths of Trajan. The copious antipasti buffet represents the bounty of Italy's fields and seas. The pastas include savory spaghetti with clams and, our favorite, *pasta fagioli* (with beans). There's also grilled crayfish and swordfish, and Italian sausages with polenta. Roman-style tripe is a local favorite, but maybe you'd prefer the *osso buco* (braised veal shanks) with mashed potatoes and seasonal mushrooms. The broad list of some of the best Italian wines is reasonably priced.

Via Terme di Tito 96. (© 06-4817952. Reservations recommended. Main courses 7.50€–13€ ($9–$16). AE, DC, MC, V. Mon–Sat noon–3pm and 7–11pm. Metro: Colosseo. Bus: 75, 85, 87, 117, or 175.

5 Near Campo de' Fiori & the Jewish Ghetto
VERY EXPENSIVE

Camponeschi ✦✦ ROMAN/SEAFOOD The fish dishes served here are legendary, and so is the front-row view of the Piazza Farnese. The restaurant is elegance itself, with a 2:1 staff/diner ratio. The cuisine is creative, refined, and prepared with only the freshest of ingredients, with a superb wine list guaranteed to appeal to even the most demanding oenophiles. The chefs work hard to make their reputation anew every night, and they succeed admirably with such dishes as lobster with black truffles and raspberry vinegar for an appetizer, or foie gras with port and sultana. We love their generous use of truffles, particularly in a masterpiece of a dish, tagliolini soufflé flavored with white truffles. Among the more succulent pastas is one made with a roe deer sauce. If the pope ever dined here, he would assuredly bestow papal blessings on such main courses as the rack of venison marinated with blueberries or a heavenly partridge in a brandy sauce with fresh mushrooms. As fine as the meat dishes are, we always enjoy the seafood, too, especially the shrimp with vermouth served with rice pilaf or the filet of turbot with grapes.

Piazza Farnese 50. (© 06-6874927. Reservations required. Main courses 25€–50€ ($30–$60). MC, V. Mon–Sat 7:30pm–midnight. Closed 2 weeks in Aug. Metro: Piazza Argentina.

Il Sanpietrino ROMAN This Jewish Ghetto restaurant, with three formal dining rooms, is stylish but affordable, with a sophisticated selection of both traditional and modern dishes. Chef Luca Bonapace uses market-fresh ingredients to prepare a seasonal cuisine that's varied and inventive at any time of the year. His combinations are often a surprise but generally delightful; for example, cream of *fagioli* (bean) soup comes not only with the traditional ingredients, but also with mussels and even octopus. The medley of fish antipasti, some of it smoked, is so tempting that you might want to make a meal of it, enjoying items such as savory fresh anchovies baked between layers of well-seasoned eggplant. Also look for asparagus-flavored tortellini with cheese, spaghetti with fresh anchovies and tomatoes, and a delectable version of cream of monkfish soup. Crème brûlée always makes a tempting dessert.

Piazza Costaguti 15. (© 06-68806471. Reservations recommended. Main courses 27€–35€ ($32–$42). AE, DC, MC, V. Mon–Sat 7:30–10:30pm. Metro: Colosseo or Circo Massimo.

EXPENSIVE

Il Drappo ✦ SARDINIAN A favorite of the local artsy crowd, Il Drappo lies on a narrow street near the Tiber and is run by a woman known to regulars only as "Valentina." You have your choice of two tastefully decorated dining rooms festooned with patterned cotton draped from the ceiling. Flowers and candles are everywhere. Fixed-price dinners reflecting diverse choices might begin with wafer-thin *carte di musica* (literally, "sheet-music paper"), a flat, layered bread topped with tomatoes,

Dining near Campo de' Fiori, the Jewish Ghetto & Piazza Navona

Al Bric **22**	Il Miraggio **17**	Osteria del Gallo **6**
Alfredo alla Scrofa **1**	Il Sanpietrino **30**	Osteria dell'Ingegno **15**
Boccondivino **14**	Insalata Ricca **27**	Passetto **7**
Bramante **4**	Insalata Ricca 2 **19**	Piperno **28**
Café Riccioli **10**	L'Eau Vive **18**	Pizzeria Baffetto **20**
Camponeschi **24**	La Rosetta **12**	Quinzi & Gabrieli **11**
Hosteria dei Pesce **23**	L'Orso 80 **2**	Quirino **16**
Il Bacaro **8**	Macheroni **13**	Ristorante da Pancrazio **25**
Il Convivio **3**	Myosotis **9**	Ristorante der Pallaro **26**
Il Drappo **21**	Osteria dell'Antiquario **5**	Vecchia Roma **29**

green peppers, parsley, and olive oil, and then followed with fresh spring lamb in season or fish stew made with tuna caviar. For dessert, try the *seadas* (cheese-stuffed fried cake in special dark honey). Valentina's cuisine is a marvelous change of pace from the typical Roman diet, with an inventiveness that keeps us coming back.

Vicolo del Malpasso 9. ⓒ **06-6877365**. Reservations required. Main courses 10€–24€ ($12–$29); fixed-price menu 38€ ($46). AE, DC, MC, V. Mon–Sat 1–3pm and 7pm–midnight. Closed Aug 12–31. Bus: 46, 62, or 64.

Piperno ⋆ JEWISH/ROMAN   This longtime favorite, opened in 1856 and now run by the Mazzarella and Boni families, celebrates the Jerusalem artichoke (which is not really an artichoke at all, by the way) by incorporating it into a number of recipes. The advice and suggestions put forth by the uniformed crew of hardworking waiters are worth considering. You might begin with aromatic *fritto misto vegetariano* (artichokes, cheese-and-rice croquettes, mozzarella, and stuffed squash blossoms) before moving on to a fish filet, veal, succulent beans, or a pasta creation. Many of the foods are fried or deep-fried but emerge flaky and dry, not at all greasy.

Via Monte de' Cenci 9. © **06-68806629.** Reservations recommended. Main courses 18€–20€ ($22–$24). AE, DC, MC, V. Tues–Sat 1–2:30pm and 8–10:30pm; Sun 1–2:30pm. Closed Aug. Bus: 23.

MODERATE

Hosteria dei Pesce ⭐⭐ SEAFOOD   The "House of Fish" is one of Rome's finest seafood restaurants. The owners are justifiably proud of the freshness of the offerings, and the staff lays out the catch of the day in bins at the entrance for you to inspect what you're about to consume. After the selection is made, each offering is delectably prepared by a skilled staff, including superb sea bass, baby squid, freshly harvested clams, and fat prawns. The seafood-studded pastas are some of the best in town. We're especially fond of the gnocchi sautéed with shrimp, cherry tomatoes, and pecorino cheese. Also delicious is the homemade pasta, paccheri, served with calamari. Some fish dishes are baked whole in a salt crust to retain the juices. Lobster alla Catalana with tomatoes and onions is another specialty.

The location is close to the Piazza Campo de' Fiori. Via di Monserrato 32. © **06-6865617.** Reservations required. Main courses 10€–25€ ($12–$30). MC, V. Mon–Sat 8pm–midnight. Closed Aug 7–30. Bus: 116.

Ristorante da Pancrazio ROMAN   This place is popular as much for its archaeological heritage as for its food. One of its two dining rooms is gracefully decorated in the style of an 18th-century tavern; the other occupies the premises of Pompey's ancient theater and is lined with carved capitals and bas-reliefs. In this historic setting, you can enjoy time-tested Roman food. Once a simple fishermen's dish, flavorful *risotto alla pescatora* (with seafood) enjoys a certain chic today, and the scampi is grilled to perfection. Two particular classics are prepared with great skill: saltimbocca and tender roast lamb with potatoes. For a superb pasta dish, opt for the ravioli stuffed with artichoke hearts.

Piazza del Biscione 92. © **06-6861246.** Reservations recommended. Main courses 10€–20€ ($12–$24), fixed-price menu 30€ ($36). AE, DC, MC, V. Thurs–Tues noon–3pm and 7:30–11:15pm. Closed 2 weeks in Aug (dates vary). Bus: 46, 62, or 64.

Ristorante del Pallaro ⭐⭐ *Value* ROMAN   The stern woman in white who emerges in clouds of steam from the bustling kitchen is owner Paola Fazi, who runs two simple dining rooms where value-conscious Romans go for good food at bargain prices. (She also claims—although others dispute it—that Julius Caesar was assassinated on this very site.) The fixed-price menu is the only choice and has made the place famous. Ms. Fazi prepares everything as if she were feeding her extended family. As you sit down, your antipasto, the first of eight courses, appears. Then comes the pasta of the day, followed by roast veal, white meatballs, or (on Fri) dried cod, along with potatoes and eggplant. For your final courses, you're served mozzarella, cake with custard, and fruit in season. The meal also includes bread, mineral water, and half a liter of the house wine. If you're faint-of-heart and not used to Roman rudeness, seek another address for dining.

Largo del Pallaro 15. © **06-68801488.** Reservations recommended. Fixed-price menu 22€ ($26). No credit cards. Tues–Sun noon–3:30pm and 7pm–12:30am. Closed Aug 12–25. Bus: 40, 46, 60, 62, or 64.

Vecchia Roma ITALIAN/ROMAN   Vecchia Roma is a charming, moderately priced trattoria in the heart of the Ghetto. Movie stars have frequented the place, sitting at the crowded tables in one of the four small dining rooms (the back room is the most popular). The owners are known for their *frutti de mare* (fruits of the sea), a selection of briny fresh seafood. The minestrone is made with fresh vegetables, and an interesting selection of antipasti, including salmon or vegetables, is always available. The pastas and risottos are savory, including linguine alla marinara with calamari and risotto with red cabbage and "fruits of the sea." The chef's specialties are lamb and *spigola* (a type of white fish).

Via della Tribuna di Campitelli 18. ✆ 06-6864604. Reservations recommended. Main courses 12€–18€ ($14–$22). AE, DC. Thurs–Tues 1–3:30pm and 8–11pm. Closed 10 days in Aug. Bus: 46, 64, 84, or 916. Metro: Colosseo.

INEXPENSIVE

Vegetarians looking for monstrous salads (or anyone who just wants a break from heavy meats and starches) can find great food at the neighborhood branch of **Insalata Ricca,** Largo dei Chiavari 85 (✆ **06-39730387**).

6 Near Piazza Navona & the Pantheon

To locate these restaurants, see the "Dining near Campo de' Fiori, the Jewish Ghetto & Piazza Navona" map on p. 113.

VERY EXPENSIVE

La Rosetta ✿✿ SEAFOOD   You won't find any red meat on the menu at this sophisticated choice near Piazza Navona, where the Riccioli family has been directing operations since the mid-1960s. This is one of Rome's best seafood restaurants. Only Quinzi & Gabrieli (see below) does it better. An excellent start is insalata di frutti di mare, studded with squid, lobster, octopus, and shrimp. Menu items include just about every fish native to the Mediterranean, as well as a few from the Atlantic coast of France. There's even a sampling of lobster imported from Maine, which can be boiled with drawn butter or served Catalan style with tomatoes, red onions, and wine sauce. Hake, monkfish, and sole can be grilled or roasted in rock salt and served with potatoes. Everyone at our table agreed that the homemade spaghetti garnished with shrimp, pumpkin blossoms, and pecorino cheese, with a drizzling of olive oil and herbs adding a savory zing, was tops.

Via della Rosetta 8–9. ✆ 06-6861002. Reservations recommended. Set-price menu 40€–55€ ($48–$66). AE, DC, MC, V. Mon–Fri 12:45–2:45pm and 7:30–11pm. Bus: 70. Metro: Spagna.

Quinzi & Gabrieli ✿✿✿ SEAFOOD   We've never found better or fresher seafood than what's served in this 15th-century building. Don't be put off by the rough-and-ready service; just enjoy the great food. (And be prepared to pay for the privilege because fresh seafood is extremely expensive in Rome.) Alberto Quinzi and Anna Gabrieli have earned their reputation on their simply cooked and presented fresh fish, such as sea urchin, octopus, sole, and red mullet. They're also known for their raw seafood, including a delicate carpaccio of swordfish, sea bass, and deep-sea shrimp. The house specialty is spaghetti with lobster. Sometimes the headwaiters will prepare wriggling crab or scampi on the grill right before you. In summer, French doors lead to a small dining terrace.

Via delle Coppelle 5–6, 00185 Roma. ✆ 06-6879389. Reservations required as far in advance as possible. Main courses 25€–40€ ($30–$48). AE, DC, MC, V. Mon–Sat 7:30–11:30pm. Closed Aug. Bus: 44, 46, 55, 60, 61, 62, 64, or 65.

EXPENSIVE

Il Convivio ✿ INTERNATIONAL/ROMAN   This is one of the most acclaimed restaurants in Rome—and one of the very few to have a coveted Michelin star. Its

16th-century building is a classic setting in pristine white with accents of wood. The Troiano brothers turn out an inspired cuisine based on the best and freshest ingredients at the market. Their menu is seasonally adjusted to take advantage of what's good during any month. Start with caramelized tuna fish with chestnut honey, ginger, green pepper, rosemary, and green apple purée. Other tantalizing menu items include *tagliatelle* with a white pork ragout, wild asparagus, and ginger; or stuffed sole with Roman-style artichokes, Sevruga caviar, shallots, clams, and cream. Salt cod is prepared according to an old Roman recipe with tomato confit, olives, and Jerusalem artichokes.

Vicolo dei Soldati 31. ℂ 06-6869432. Reservations required. Main courses 25€–35€ ($30–$42). AE, DC, MC, V. Tues–Sat 8–11pm. Bus: 40 or 64. Metro: Spagna.

MODERATE

Alfredo alla Scrofa INTERNATIONAL/ROMAN   Yes, folks, this is one of two places in Rome claiming to have created fettuccine Alfredo, which almost seems as well known in America today as it is in Italy. Douglas Fairbanks and Mary Pickford liked this dish so much they presented a golden spoon and fork to the owners when they parted with the recipe. Thus, a culinary legend was born. Although the fettuccine is the star of the menu, you can also try a pasta dish that's a little lighter and healthier, like *tagliolini allo scoglio,* served with fresh tomatoes and shellfish. We always enjoy the filet mignons; one is offered with a delicious sauce made from Barolo wine, another with a sauce of wine and Gorgonzola. Another filet mignon dish, named after Casanova, is prepared with wine sauce, freshly ground pepper, and foie gras. A final offering is the sautéed breast of turkey covered with thin slices of white truffles from Italy's Piedmont district, a truly wonderful dish.

Via della Scrofa 104. ℂ 06-68806163. Reservations recommended. Main courses 11€–22€ ($13–$26). AE, DC, MC, V. Daily 12:30–3pm and 6–11:30pm. Bus: 87, 492, or 680. Metro: Spagna.

Boccondivino 🔆 ITALIAN   Part of the fun of this restaurant involves wandering through historic Rome to reach it. Inside you'll find delicious food and an engaging mix of Italian Renaissance and imperial and ancient Rome, thanks to recycled columns salvaged from ancient monuments by 16th-century builders. Modern art and a hip staff dressed in black and white serve as a tip-off, though, that the menu is completely up-to-date. Dishes vary with the seasons, but you might find fettuccine with shellfish and parsley; carpaccio of beef; various risottos, including a version with black truffles; and grilled steaks and veal. Especially intriguing is whipped codfish resting on spikes of polenta, or grilled ravioli stuffed with scorpion fish and served with pumpkin flower sauce. If you're a seafood lover, look for either the marinated and grilled salmon or a particularly subtle blend of roasted turbot stuffed with foie gras. Desserts feature the fresh fruits of the season, perhaps marinated pineapple or fruit-studded house-made ice creams. The restaurant's name, incidentally, translates as "divine mouthful."

Piazza in Campo Marzio 6. ℂ 06-68308626. Reservations required. Main courses 12€–15€ ($14–$18); fixed-price lunch 20€ ($24). AE, DC, MC, V. Mon–Sat 12:30–3pm and 7:30–11pm. Bus: 87 or 175.

Bramante ROMAN   Set in an exquisite 18th-century structure on a cobblestone street behind Piazza Navona, this cafe-restaurant opens onto a delightful small square of vine-draped taverns. Behind the ivy-covered facade, the interior is completely hand painted; white candles illuminate the marble bar, making for a cozy, inviting atmosphere. The owner, Mr. Giuseppe, tries to make visitors appreciate Italian food and traditions, and he succeeds admirably. Almost all his dishes are handmade, and the cooks use only the freshest ingredients, such as *Parmigiano,* fresh vegetables, and extra-virgin olive oil. Recipes are simple but rich in Mediterranean flavor. Try wonderful pastas made with fresh tomato sauce, garlic, and pasta, or opt for something heavier, such as braised beef or tender grilled steak flavored with herbs and served with potatoes.

Via della Pace 25. ⓒ **06-68803916.** Reservations recommended. Main courses 10€–18€ ($12–$22). AE, DC, MC, V. Mon–Sat 5:30pm–2am; Sun noon–2am. Closed Dec 24. Bus: 44, 46, 55, 60, 61, 62, 64, or 65.

Café Riccioli ⭐ ITALIAN/JAPANESE   Stylish and hip, this restaurant builds its reputation on its sashimi-style raw fish, plus a menu of sophisticated and upscale Italian cuisine. The setting is a trio of artfully minimalist dining rooms painted in bright primary colors; after lunch and dinner, this place becomes a buzzing late-night cafe. No one will mind if you order just a light meal (we've often spotted models here doing just that). Dishes include platters of sashimi, priced at around 30€ ($36); salads of raw marinated hake with Italian herbs; and more substantial fare such as roast beef with green apples; sea bass with mango sauce; and richly textured chocolate tortes laced with Marsala wine.

Piazza delle Coppelle 10A. ⓒ **06-68210313.** Reservations recommended. Main courses 8€–30€ ($10–$36). AE, DC, MC, V. Mon–Sat noon–1am. Closed Aug 6–20. Metro: Spagna. Bus: 64 or 492. Tram 8.

Il Bacaro ⭐ ITALIAN   Unpretentious and very accommodating to foreigners, this restaurant contains only about a half-dozen tables and operates from an ivy-edged hideaway alley near Piazza di Spagna. The restaurant is well known for its fresh and tasty cheese. This was a palazzo in the 1600s, and some vestiges of the building's former grandeur remain, despite an impossibly cramped kitchen where the efforts of the staff to keep the show moving are nothing short of heroic. The offerings are time-tested and flavorful: homemade ravioli stuffed with *Parmigiano* and mushrooms (in season), grilled beef filet with roasted potatoes, and an unusual version of warm carpaccio of beef. What dish do we prefer year after year? Radicchio stuffed with Gorgonzola, delicious but, admittedly, an acquired taste. The pastas come with unusual and often exquisite combinations, such as *tagliatelle* with fresh zucchini and pumpkin in a saffron sauce. A marvelous dessert is Millefoglie's crumbs, which comes with freshly made vanilla custard.

Via degli Spagnoli 27, near Piazza delle Coppelle. ⓒ **06-6864110.** Reservations recommended. Main courses 10€–18€ ($12–$22). DC, MC, V. Mon–Sat 8pm–midnight. Metro: Spagna.

L'Eau Vive ⭐ *Finds* FRENCH/INTERNATIONAL   Here you'll find an elegant dining experience with unique food and atmosphere. Fine French cuisine and a daily exotic dish are prepared and served by a lay sisterhood of missionary Christians from five continents who dress in traditional costumes. Nonsmokers can skip the plain stuccoed vaulting downstairs and head to the 16th-century Palazzo Lantante della Rovere, where the high ceilings are gorgeously frescoed. Pope John Paul II dined here when he was archbishop of Krakow. You never know until you arrive what will be on the menu. We've enjoyed beef filet flambé with cognac, toasted goat cheese coated with mustard and almond slivers, and duck filet in Grand Marnier sauce with puff-fried potatoes. The homemade pâtés are always flavorful. At 10pm, when most customers are finished with dinner, the recorded classical music is interrupted so that the sisters can sing the "Ave Maria of Lourdes," and some evenings, they interpret a short Bible story in ballet.

Via Monterone 85. © **06-68801095.** Reservations recommended. Main courses 7.50€–19€ ($9–$23); fixed-price menus 14€–30€ ($17–$36). AE, MC, V. Mon–Sat 12:30–2:30pm and 7:30–10:30pm. Closed Aug. Bus: 64, 70, 81, 87, or 115.

Myosotis ⊛ ITALIAN   Midway between Piazza Navona, the Pantheon, and the Italian Parliament, the building that contains Myosotis is relatively modern and nondescript, but as the name promises (translated from Latin, it means "forget-me-not"), you're likely to remember the food for a long time. Menu items include a cornucopia of fresh-baked bread; *tagliatelle* with an old-fashioned country recipe that uses sautéed bread crumbs instead of beef; grilled buffalo steak; grilled, very fresh prawns served as simply as possible, with virgin olive oil and herbs; and baked swordfish stuffed with cheese, bread crumbs, and capers. There's also a *frittura mista* (mixed fish fry) that some diners claim is one of the best dishes served here, and a flavorful filet of pork with a sauce of carefully aged pecorino cheese. Available fresh fish includes sea bass, gilthead, and the ever-present calamari.

Vicolo della Vaccarella 3–5. © **06-6865554.** Reservations recommended. Main courses 8€–21€ ($10–$25). AE, DC, MC, V. Mon–Sat 7:30–11:30pm. Closed 2 weeks in Aug. Metro: Spagna. Bus: 70, 87, 186, or 492.

Osteria dell'Antiquario ⊛ *Finds* INTERNATIONAL/ROMAN   This virtually undiscovered osteria enjoys a good location a few blocks down the Via dei Coronari as you leave the Piazza Navona and head toward St. Peter's. In a stone-built stable from the 1500s, Osteria dell'Antiquario has three dining rooms used in winter. In nice weather, try to get an outdoor table on the terrace; shaded by umbrellas, they face a view of the Palazzo Lancillotti. We like to begin with the sautéed shellfish (usually mussels and clams), or you could opt for the risotto with porcini mushrooms. For a main course, try the filet of ostrich covered by a slice of ham and grated Parmesan, or shellfish flavored with saffron. The fish soup with fried bread is excellent, as is an array of freshly made soups and pastas.

Piazzetta di S. Simeone 26–27, Via dei Coronari. © **06-6879694.** Reservations recommended. Main courses 12€–24€ ($14–$29). AE, DC, MC, V. Mon–Sat 7:30–11pm. Closed 15 days in mid-Aug, Christmas, and Jan 1–10. Bus: 70, 87, or 90.

Osteria dell'Ingegno ROMAN   This is another offbeat trattoria in the vicinity of the much-trodden Piazza Navona. The menu is simple but fairly innovative, and it's adjusted seasonally. The restaurant is decorated in a rather modern style and is warmly welcoming and inviting, its walls hung with paintings by local artists, many of whom live in the area and come here to dine. The chefs are experts in the use of aromatic herbs and spices, and their dishes are full of flavor. Among our favorite recent samplings are the walnut-filled ravioli in a sublime cheese sauce, followed by marinated salmon with three kinds of pepper, orange, and ginger spicing. A true favorite that made us want to return is the roast duck with a sweet and sour sauce flavored with wine and raisins. All the desserts are homemade.

Piazza di Pietra 45. © **06-6780662.** Reservation required. Main courses 8€–21€ ($10–$25). AE, DC, MC, V. Mon–Sat noon–3pm and 7pm–midnight. Closed 2 weeks in Aug (dates vary). Metro: Colosseo.

Passetto ⊛ ITALIAN/ROMAN   Passetto, dramatically positioned at the north end of Piazza Navona, is still drawing patrons after a century and a half with excellent food. The stylish interior consists of a trio of high-ceilinged dining rooms, each outfitted with antique furniture and elaborate chandeliers. In summer, however, you'll want to sit outside looking out on Piazza Sant'Apollinare. The pastas are exceptional, including *farfalle passetto* (pasta with shrimp, mushrooms, and fresh tomatoes).

Another specialty is *rombo passetto* (a fish similar to sole) cooked in cognac and pine nuts. An eternal Roman favorite is lamb in the style of Abruzzi (oven-roasted with potatoes). Fresh fish is often priced by its weight, so be careful—your bill can soar quickly. Fresh vegetables are abundant in summer, and for dessert it doesn't get much better than seasonal berries with fresh, thick cream.

Piazza San Apollinare 41. ℰ 06-68806569. Reservations recommended. Main courses 10€–25€ ($12–$30). AE, DC, MC, V. Daily noon–3:30pm and 7–11pm. Bus: 87.

Quirino ITALIAN/ROMAN/SICILIAN   Quirino is a good place to dine after you've tossed your coin into the Trevi. The atmosphere is typically Italian, with hanging Chianti bottles, a beamed ceiling, and muraled walls. We're fond of the mixed fry of tiny shrimp and squid rings, and the vegetarian pastas are prepared with market-fresh ingredients. The regular pasta dishes are fabulous; our favorite comes with baby clams and porcini mushrooms. A variety of perfectly grilled fresh and tasty fish is always available. For dessert, try the yummy chestnut ice cream with hot chocolate sauce or the homemade cannoli.

Via delle Muratte 84. ℰ 06-6794108. Reservations recommended. Main courses 10€–18€ ($12–$22); fish dishes 13€–15€ ($16–$18). AE, MC, V. Mon–Sat noon–11:30pm. Closed 3 weeks in Aug. Metro: Barberini or Spagna.

INEXPENSIVE

Al Bric *(Value)* ITALIAN   With four separate and artfully minimalist dining rooms in a 16th-century building close to Campo de' Fiori, this well-managed restaurant combines creative cooks with a polite and efficient waitstaff. Many of the dishes include dollops of goat or herbed cheese, or French Brie, flavors that seem to make the wines taste even better. Menu items are based on a combination of traditional and creative modern cuisine. Examples include house-made, ultrafresh swordfish stroganoff flavored with fresh thyme and squid sauce; *bucatini* flavored with fresh-ground black pepper and aged *caciocavallo* cheese; *tonnarelli* pasta with Sicilian broccoli and aged pecorino cheese; and orange-flavored duck with foie gras and black truffle.

Via del Pellegrino 51. ℰ 06-6879533. Reservations recommended. Main courses 7.80€–18€ ($9–$22). Tues–Sat 7:30–11:30pm; Sun 12:30–2:30pm and 7:30–11:30pm. Closed Aug. Bus: 64.

Il Miraggio ROMAN/SARDINIAN/SEAFOOD   You might want to escape the roar of traffic along Via del Corso by ducking into this informal spot on a crooked side street (about midway between Piazza Venezia and Piazza Colonna). It's a cozy neighborhood setting with rich and savory flavor in every dish. The risotto with scampi and the fettuccine with porcini mushrooms will have you begging for more. Some dishes are classic, such as roast lamb with potatoes, but others are more inventive, such as sliced stew beef with arugula. We love grilled scampi, or you might prefer a steaming kettle of mussels flavored with olive oil, lemon juice, and fresh parsley. We're also fond of the house specialty, *spaghetti alla bottarga* with roe sauce, especially if it's followed by *spigola alla vernaccia* (sea bass sautéed in butter and vernaccia wine from Tuscany). For dessert, try the typical Sardinian *seadas,* thin-rolled pastry filled with fresh cheese, fried, and served with honey.

Vicolo Sciarra 59. ℰ 06-6780226. Reservations recommended. Main courses 8€–16€ ($10–$19). AE, MC, V. Thurs–Tues 12:30–3:30pm and 7:30–11pm. Closed 15 days in Jan. Metro: Barberini. Bus: 62, 81, 85, 95, 117, 119, 160, 175, or 492.

Insalata Ricca 2 *(Value)* ITALIAN/VEGETARIAN   This choice fulfills a need for more vegetarian restaurants and lighter, low-fat fare in Rome. Most people call ahead for an outdoor table, although on summer days you might prefer the smoke-free, air-conditioned inside. The more popular of the oversize salads are the *baires* (lettuce, rughetta, celery, walnuts, apples, Gorgonzola) and *siciliana* (lettuce, rughetta, sun-dried tomatoes, green olives, corn, hard salted ricotta). Also on the menu are dishes such as *gnocchi verdi al gorgonzola* (spinach gnocchi with Gorgonzola sauce) and *pasta integrale* (whole-wheat pasta in tomato-and-basil sauce). For the true carnivore, a few meat dishes are also served. The branches near Campo de' Fiori and near the Vatican (mentioned under their respective neighborhoods) offer the same basic menu, which can be a refreshing relief after too many days of heavy meals and rich sauces.

Piazza Pasquino 72 (southwest of Piazza Navona). © 06-68307881. Reservations recommended. Main courses 5€–15€ ($6–$18). AE, DC, MC, V. Daily noon–4pm and 6:30pm–midnight. Bus: 40, 64, or 70.

L'Orso 80 (Finds) ROMAN/SEAFOOD (Finds) Fleeing the fancy-schmancy places opening onto Piazza Navona, we recently discovered this nugget on an unpretentious street north and a little west of the Piazza Navona. In-the-know locals have been recommending its fabulous array of tasty Roman dishes for years. Bright and bustling, the trattoria lies on a street known for its artisan workshops. The antipasti selection is absolutely delightful, and we quickly plowed into mushrooms with whole peppercorns, succulent little baby artichokes, cauliflower flavored with capers, freshly made mozzarella, fried zucchini fingers, and *fagioli* (beans) in tomato sauce. Terrific main courses include fresh grilled fish, pasta with porcini mushrooms, and our favorite, *abbacchio allo spiedo* (lamb on the spit). End your meal with ricotta cake, a real Roman specialty.

Via dell'Orso 33. © 06-6864904. Reservations recommended. Main courses 6.50€–16€ ($7.80–$19). AE, DC, MC, V. Tues–Sun 1–3:30pm and 7–11:30pm. Closed in Aug and Dec 24–26. Metro: Lepanto.

Macheroni ROMAN Here in the heart of Rome you can dine in a rustic tavern enjoying traditional Roman food more often found in the Latium countryside. The decor is informal, with wood-paneled walls and pop art, and on a good night the place seats 160 satisfied diners, both visitors and locals. Pasta is the house specialty, and it doesn't get better than the spaghetti with bacon and onion. Also recommended are *maccheroni matriciana* (a pasta that comes in a red version with tomatoes, bacon, and pecorino cheese; and a white version that skips the tomatoes.) Some very tender and juicy beefsteaks are also served. A well-chosen wine list includes a house Chianti.

Piazza della Copelle 44. © 06-68307895. Reservations recommended. Main courses 8€–15€ ($10–$18). AE, MC, V. Daily noon–3pm and 8pm–midnight. Metro: Spagna. Bus: 64, 70, 75, or 116.

Osteria del Gallo (Finds) ROMAN You can escape the tourist traps of the Piazza Navona by seeking out this place in a narrow little alley off the west/northwest side of the fabled square. It's tiny, with a lovely area for outdoor seating, and definitely off the beaten track. The chef/owner comes out to take your order personally and is justly proud of his homemade pastas. We opted for the ravioli stuffed with porcini mushrooms and were so glad we did. Menu items include a variety of fresh fish dishes roasted in a salt crust to retain their juice and flavor. Other favorites include filet of beef cooked with green pepper. The homemade desserts include one of the best tiramisus in the area and a traditional favorite, *panna cotta,* an Italian pudding made with cooked fresh cream.

Vicolo di Montevecchio 27. © 06-6873781. Reservations highly recommended. Main courses 4.50€–15€ ($5.40–$18). MC, V. Daily 12:30–3pm and 7–11pm. Closed Aug 8–25 (dates may vary). Metro: Spagna.

THE TRAVELOCITY GUARANTEE

...THAT SAYS EVERYTHING YOU BOOK WILL BE RIGHT, OR WE'LL WORK WITH OUR TRAVEL PARTNERS TO MAKE IT RIGHT, RIGHT AWAY.

*To drive home the point,
we're going to use the word "right" in every single sentence.*

Let's get right to it. Right to the meat! Only Travelocity guarantees everything about your booking will be right, or we'll work with our travel partners to make it right, right away. Right on!

Here's a picture taken smack dab right in the middle of Antigua, where the Guarantee also covers you.

The Guarantee covers all but one of the items pictured to the right.

For example, what if the ocean view you booked actually looks out at a downright ugly parking lot? You'd be right to call – we're there for you. And no one in their right mind would be pleased to learn the rental car place has closed and left them stranded. Call Travelocity and we'll help get you back on the right track.

Now, you may be thinking, "Yeah, right, I'm so sure." That's OK; you have the right to remain skeptical. That is until we mention help is always right around the corner. Call us right off the bat, knowing our customer service reps are there for you 24/7. Righting wrongs. Left and right.

Now if you're guessing there are some things we can't control, like the weather, well you're right. But we can help you with most things – to get all the details in righting,* visit travelocity.com/guarantee.

*Sorry, spelling things right is one of the few things not covered under the Guarantee.

I'd give my right arm for a guarantee like this, although I'm glad I don't have to.

travelocity

You'll never roam alone.

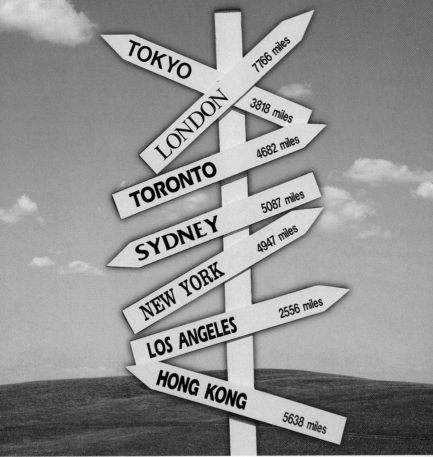

Frommers.com

So many places, so little time?

TOKYO 7766 miles

LONDON 3818 miles

TORONTO 4682 miles

SYDNEY 5087 miles

NEW YORK 4947 miles

LOS ANGELES 2556 miles

HONG KONG 5638 miles

Frommers.com makes the going fast and easy.

Find a destination. ✓ Buy a guidebook. ✓ Book a trip. ✓ Get hot travel deals.
Enter to win vacations. ✓ Check out the latest travel news.
Share trip photos and memories. ✓ Download podcasts. ✓ And much more.

Frommers.com

Rated #1 Travel Web Site by *PC Magazine*®

Pizzeria Baffetto ★ *Kids* PIZZA Our Roman friends always take out-of-towners here when they ask for the best pizza in Rome. Arguably, Pizzeria Baffetto fills the bill and has done so for the past 80 years. Pizzas are sold as *piccolo* (small), *media* (medium), or *grande* (large). Most pizza aficionados order the margherita, which is the simplest version, with mozzarella and tomato sauce, but a wide range of toppings is served. The chef is proud of his pizza Baffetto, the house specialty. It comes with a topping of tomato sauce, mozzarella, mushrooms, onions, sausages, roasted peppers, and eggs. The pizza crusts are delightfully thin, and the pies are served piping hot from the intense heat of the ancient ovens.

Via del Governo Vecchio 114. ℂ 06-6861617. Reservations not accepted. Pizza 4€–8€ ($4.80–$10). No credit cards. Daily 6:30pm–1am. Closed Aug 12–31. Bus: 46, 62, or 64.

7 Near Piazza del Popolo & the Spanish Steps

VERY EXPENSIVE

The Hassler Rooftop Restaurant ★★ INTERNATIONAL/ITALIAN Great food and a sweeping panorama of Ancient Rome lure patrons to the sixth floor of this deluxe hotel on the Spanish Steps. There's so much talk of the view that it is easy to overlook the superb traditional Italian cuisine. Chefs frequent the Roman markets early in the morning, securing the freshest products for their menu, which changes daily. Our last meal here, and we remember it well (as Maurice Chevalier used to sing), began with steamed king prawns served with Sicilian couscous and garnished with mozzarella and fresh basil. You might follow with savory Sorrento-style home-made pasta with seafood sauce and fresh zucchini flowers. For a main course, the roasted filet of sea bass with eggplant in a ginger sauce is delightful. The chef's dessert specialty is ricotta cheese baked with white chocolate and exotic fruits.

At night, romantic piano music is played. If, in *Casablanca*, Ingrid Bergman had gone back to Bogie, he could have taken her here to celebrate the end of the war. It's a fine atmosphere for lovers.

In the Hotel Hassler, Piazza della Trinità dei Monti 6. ℂ 06-699340. Reservations required. Jacket and tie for men at dinner. Main courses 28€–42€ ($34–$50). AE, DC, MC, V. Daily 12:30–2:30pm and 7:30–10:30pm. Metro: Spagna.

EXPENSIVE

El Toulà ★★ ROMAN/VENETIAN El Toulà, offering sophisticated haute cuisine, is the glamorous flagship of an upscale chain that has gone international. The setting is elegant, with vaulted ceilings, large archways, and a charming bar. The impressive menu has one section devoted to Venetian specialties, in honor of the restaurant's origins. Expect dishes created on the spur of the moment, as well as longtime customer favorites. We like to begin with a bowl of linguine with lobster, cherry tomatoes, and sweet red pepper, or a bowl of Venetian-style fish soup. Two of our favorite main courses are potato dumplings with basil-laced pesto and prawns, and scallops with fresh asparagus and black truffles. Finish off with a chocolate parfait with vanilla sauce and hazelnut ice cream, or one of the seasonal sorbets and sherbets; the cantaloupe and fresh strawberry are celestial, and you can request a mixed plate if you'd like to sample several. El Toulà usually isn't crowded at lunchtime. The wine list is extensive and varied, but hardly a bargain.

Via della Lupa 29B. ℂ 06-6873498. Reservations required for dinner. Main courses 15€–28€ ($18–$34); 5-course tasting menu 70€ ($84); 4-course tasting menu 62€ ($74). AE, DC, MC, V. Tues–Fri 12:30–3pm; Mon–Sat 7:30–11pm. Closed Aug. Bus: 70, 81, 87, 116, or 196.

Reef 🐾 *Finds* MEDITERRANEAN/SUSHI   Twins Marco and Gianluigi are called the Romulus and Remus of Rome's culinary circuit. To carry out the watery theme of their restaurant, the boat-shape wood floor is ringed with sand trapped under glass and the bar evokes a fish tank. And, of course, seafood dominates the menu. It's fresh, well prepared, and never dominated by finicky sauces. The sushi ranks among the best of any served in Rome, but if you prefer your fish cooked, the grilled seafood platter or one of the various filets of Mediterranean fish is the way to go. Some dishes, such as the sublime cod ravioli or the exotic sushi, incorporate Asian accents. If you don't want fish, try the veal loin with spring vegetables, lemon, and chili sauce. Only top-quality ingredients are used.

Piazza Augusto Imperatore 42–48. © 06-68301430. Reservations required. Main courses 16€–40€ ($19–$48); tasting menus 40€–60€ ($48–$72). AE, DC, MC, V. Mon–Sat 1–3:30pm and 8pm–midnight. Closed Dec 24–25 and 2 weeks in Aug (dates vary). Metro: Spagna.

MODERATE

Al Moro 🐾 ITALIAN   This 1929 trattoria is a difficult-to-locate place behind the Trevi Fountain. Franco, the son of founding father Moro, is in charge. You're not a true Roman until Franco has thrown you out of his joint at least once. In spite of his scowling, locals recommend that you persevere and get a table. Once you've overcome the initial hostility at the door, you're served some of the most authentic specialties in Rome, including crispy baby goat roasted dark golden and flavored with fresh rosemary. Roman-style milk-fed lamb is stewed with fresh tomatoes and cooked until it's so tender it falls from your fork. Our favorite vegetables are the crispy fried artichokes. As far as pasta goes, we love the light version of spaghetti carbonara served here. The chef likes to cook with salt, so be sure not to salt anything before you taste it. The wine list is one of the most unusual in the capital.

Vicolo delle Bollette 13. © 06-6783495. Reservations required. Main courses 13€–26€ ($16–$31). MC, V. Mon–Sat 1–3:30pm and 7:30–11:30pm. Closed Aug. Metro: Spagna. Bus: 60 or 62.

Cafe Romano 🐾 INTERNATIONAL   On Rome's most exclusive "fashion street," this stylish venue is neither restaurant nor brasserie. Annexed to the landmark Hotel d'Inghilterra, the cafe can feed you all day long, whether you're looking for breakfast or for a late post-theater dinner. The atmosphere is very cosmopolitan, and the menu eclectic and well chosen. You can taste dishes from around the world, from moussaka to fish couscous, from the Lebanese mezze (appetizers) to Chicago rib-eye steak, from the Thai-like green-curry chicken to the Japanese-inspired salmon teriyaki. From lobster to pear with Roquefort, the salads are among the finest in town. If you're dropping in for an afternoon visit, try one of the yummy desserts, such as apple strudel, New York cheesecake, or a creamy chocolate mousse. There are a few outside tables for people-watching.

In the Hotel d'Inghilterra, Via Borgognona 4. © 06-69981500. Main courses 10€–50€ ($12–$60). AE, MC, V. Daily noon–11pm. Metro: Spagna.

Dal Bolognese 🐾 BOLOGNESE/EMILIANA-ROMAGNOLA   This is one of those rare, chic dining spots with food that actually lives up to the scene. Young actors, shapely models, artists from nearby Via Margutta, and even corporate types on expense accounts show up, trying to land one of the few sidewalk tables. To begin, we suggest *misto di pasta:* four pastas, each with a different sauce, arranged on the same plate. Another good choice is thin slices of savory Parma ham or prosciutto and vine-ripened melon. For your main course, specialties that win hearts year after year are

Dining near the Spanish Steps & Ancient Rome

lasagne verde and *tagliatelle alla bolognese.* The chefs also turn out the town's best veal cutlets bolognese topped with cheese. They're not inventive, but they're simply superb.

You might want to cap your evening by dropping into the **Rosati** cafe next door (or its competitor, the **Canova,** across the street) to enjoy a tempting pastry.

Piazza del Popolo 1–2. (C) **06-3611426.** Reservations required. Main courses 10€–20€ ($12–$24). AE, DC, MC, V. Tues–Sun 1–3pm and 8:15pm–midnight. Closed 20 days in Aug. Metro: Flaminio.

Da Mario FLORENTINE/ROMAN   Da Mario is noted for its flavorful game specialties and excellent Florentine-style dishes (meats marinated in olive oil with fresh herbs and garlic and lightly grilled). The rich bounty of meats available during hunting season makes this a memorable choice, but even if you aren't feeling game (sorry), you'll find this a convivial and quintessentially Roman trattoria. A good beginning is the wide-noodle pappardelle, best when served with a *caccia* (game sauce) or with chunks of *coniglio* (rabbit), available only in winter. *Capretto* (kid), beefsteaks, and roast quail with polenta are other good choices. The wine cellar is well stocked with sturdy reds, the ideal accompaniment for the meat dishes. For dessert we heartily recommend the *gelato misto,* a selection of mixed velvety ice cream. You can dine in air-conditioned comfort at street level or descend to the cellars.

Via della Vite 55–56. (C) **06-6783818.** Reservations recommended. Main courses 8.50€–15€ ($10–$18). AE, DC, MC, V. Mon–Sat noon–3pm and 7–11pm. Closed Aug. Metro: Spagna.

Di Fronte a . . . ITALIAN   After a hard morning shopping in the Piazza di Spagna area, this is an ideal spot for a lunch break. Its name (which translates as "in front of ...") comes from the fact that the restaurant lies right in front of a stationery shop (owned by the father of the restaurant's proprietor). We prefer the dining room in the rear, with its changing exhibitions of pictures. The chef prepares tasty cuisine that is simple but good—nothing creative, but a fine boost of energy to hit the stores again. Salads are very large, as are the juicy half-pound burgers. You can also order more substantial food, such as succulent pastas and tender steaks. The pizza isn't bad, either. For dessert, try the pizza blanca, which is a pizza crust topped with chocolate cream or seasonal fruits.

Via della Croce 38. (C) **06-6780355.** Reservations recommended for dinner. Main courses 10€–15€ ($12–$18). AE, MC, DC, V. Tues–Sun noon–3:30pm and 7–11pm. Metro: Spagna.

Gusto 🌟 *(Finds* ITALIAN/PACIFIC RIM   This restaurant is made up of two separate parts. The simpler and more informal of the two is a street-level pizzeria, where at least a dozen kinds of homemade pastas and pizzas are offered along with freshly made salads and simple platters of such grilled specialties as veal, chicken, steak, and fish. More upscale, and somewhat calmer, is the upstairs restaurant, where big windows, high ceilings, floors of glowing hardwood, and lots of exposed brick create an appropriately minimalist setting for cutting-edge cuisine. Look for a fusion of Italian and Pacific Rim cuisine in such combinations as spaghetti stir-fried in a Chinese wok with fresh al dente vegetables, prawns and spring baby vegetables tempura style, buffalo mozzarella intriguingly entwined with tuna and arugula, Middle Eastern staples, and stir-fried scallops with Italian herbs.

Piazza Augusto Imperatore 9. (C) **06-3226273.** Reservations recommended. Main courses in street-level pizzeria 5€–10€ ($6–$12); main courses in upstairs restaurant 12€–22€ ($14–$26). AE, MC, V. Daily 1–3pm and 7:30pm–midnight. Metro: Flaminio.

INEXPENSIVE

Also consider the **Gusto** pizzeria, reviewed above under "Moderate."

Impressions

In Italy, the pleasure of eating is central to the pleasure of living. When you sit down to dinner with Italians, when you share their food, you are sharing their lives.

—Fred Plotkin, *Italy for the Gourmet Traveler,* 1996

Caffeterria Canova Tadolini *Finds* ROMAN   One of Rome's chicest cafes is part of a museum dedicated to Antonio Canova, the neoclassical sculptor, and his student, Adamo Tadolini. Lying only a few steps from the Piazza del Popolo, the museum cafe seats you at *ottocento-style tables* evocative of the famous 18th century designer Ortolan, beneath statues and plaster fragments.

It serves a wide selection of drinks, but also full meals, including succulent pastas. Typical Roman specialties include *spaghetti all'amatriciana* or *alla carbonara* (with bacon). *Alla pepe* is another good selection with lots of creamy cheese and pepper.

Via del Babuino 150 A–B. (06-32110702. Reservations recommended. Main courses 7€–15€ ($8.40–$18). AE, DC, MC, V. Mon–Sat 8am–8:30pm. Metro: Flaminio or Spagna.

Enoteca Corsi ROMAN   Here's a breath of unpretentious fresh air in a pricey neighborhood, an informal wine tavern open for lunch only. Both dining rooms are usually packed and full of festive diners, just as they've been since 1943. The wine list includes affordable choices from around Italy, to go perfectly with the platters of straightforward cuisine. It's nothing fancy, just hearty Italian home cooking like bean soup, gnocchi, Roman tripe, and roasted codfish with garlic and potatoes.

Via del Gesù 87–88. (06-6790821. Reservations not necessary. Main courses 9€ ($11) each; pastas 6€ ($7.20); vegetable side dishes 4€ ($4.80). AE, DC, MC, V. Mon–Sat noon–3:30pm. Closed Aug. Metro: Spagna.

Otello alla Concordia *Kids* ROMAN   On a side street amid the glamorous boutiques near the northern edge of the Spanish Steps, this is one of Rome's most consistently reliable restaurants. A stone corridor from the street leads into the dignified Palazzo Povero. Choose a table in the arbor-covered courtyard or the cramped but convivial dining rooms. Displays of Italian bounty decorate the interior, where you're likely to rub elbows with many of the shopkeepers from the fashion district. The *spaghetti alle vongole veraci* (with clams) is excellent, as are Roman-style saltimbocca (veal with ham), *abbacchio arrosto* (roast lamb), eggplant parmigiana, a selection of grilled or sautéed fish dishes (including swordfish), and several preparations of veal.

Via della Croce 81. (06-6791178. Reservations recommended. Main courses 6.50€–18€ ($7.80–$22); fixed-price menu 20€ ($24). AE, DC, MC, V. Mon–Sat 12:30–3pm and 7:30–11pm. Closed 2 weeks in Jan. Metro: Spagna.

8 Near the Vatican

To locate these restaurants, see the "Accommodations & Dining near the Vatican" map on p. 97.

VERY EXPENSIVE

Les Etoiles *Finds* MEDITERRANEAN   Les Etoiles (The Stars) is a garden in the sky where you'll have an open window over Rome's rooftops—a 360-degree view of landmarks, especially the floodlit dome of St. Peter's. A flower terrace contains a trio of little towers named Michelangelo, Campidoglio, and Ottavo Colle. In summer everyone wants a table outside, but in winter almost the same view is available near the picture windows. Savor the textures and aromas of sophisticated Mediterranean cuisine with perfectly balanced flavors, perhaps choosing quail in a casserole with mushrooms and herbs, artichokes stuffed with ricotta and pecorino cheeses, Venetian-style risotto with squid ink, or roast suckling lamb perfumed with mint. The creative chef is justifiably proud of his many regional dishes, and the service is refined, with an exciting French and Italian wine list.

In the Hotel Atlante Star, Via Vitelleschi 34. ⓒ **06-6873233**. Reservations required. Main courses 20€–40€ ($24–$48). AE, DC, MC, V. Daily 12:30–2:30pm and 7:30–10:30pm. Metro: Ottaviano-San Pietro.

MODERATE

Cesare ROMAN/TUSCAN   The area around the Vatican is not the place to go in search of great restaurants, but Cesare is a fine old-world spot known for its deft handling of fresh ingredients. You can select your fish from the refrigerated glass case at the entrance. We come here for the fresh and tender seafood salad, brimming with cuttlefish, shrimp, squid, mussels, and octopus, and dressed with olive oil, fresh parsley, and lemon. Our table was blessed with an order of *spaghetti all'amatriciana* in a spicy tomato sauce flavored with hot peppers and tiny bits of salt pork. The *saltimbocca alla romana,* that classic Roman dish, is masterful here—butter-tender veal slices topped with prosciutto and fresh sage and sautéed in white wine. Another specialty is smoked swordfish. Order fresh sardines and fresh anchovies if you want to go truly Roman.

Via Crescenzio 13, near Piazza Cavour. ⓒ **06-6861227**. Reservations recommended. Main courses 6€–28€ ($7.20–$34); fixed-price *Tuscan* menu 32€ ($38). AE, DC, MC, V. June 15–Aug 7 Mon–Sat 12:30–3pm and 7:30pm–midnight; off season Tues–Sat 12:30–3pm and 7:30–midnight, Sun 12:30–3pm. Closed 3 weeks Aug. Metro: Lepanto or Ottaviano-San Pietro. Bus: 23, 34, or 49.

Ristorante Giardinaccio ITALIAN/MOLISIAN/ROMAN   This popular restaurant, operated by Nicolino Mancini, is only a stone's throw from St. Peter's. Unusual for Rome, it offers Molisian specialties from southeastern Italy. This is robust peasant fare, a perfect introduction to the cuisine of a region rarely visited by Americans. It's rustically decorated in a country-tavern style with dark wood and exposed stone. Flaming grills turn out quail, goat, and other dishes, but try the mutton goulash if you want to be more adventurous. The many pasta dishes include homemade *taconelle* with lamb sauce. Vegetarians will like the large self-service selection of antipasti made from market-fresh ingredients.

Via Di Porta Cavallegeri 2. ⓒ **06-631367**. Reservations recommended, especially on weekends. Main courses 6€–15€ ($7.20–$18); fixed-price menus 20€–25€ ($24–$30). AE, DC, MC, V. Daily 12:15–3:15pm and 7:15–11:15pm. Metro: Stazione San Pietro. Bus: 34, 46, 49, 246, 247, 881, 889, or 905.

Ristorante Il Matriciano ★ (Kids) ROMAN   Il Matriciano is a family restaurant with a devoted following and a convenient location near St. Peter's. The food is good but mostly country fare. In summer, try to get one of the sidewalk tables behind a green hedge and under a shady canopy. For openers, you might enjoy a bracing *zuppa di verdura* (vegetable soup) or creamy ravioli di ricotta. From many dishes, we recommend *scaloppa alla valdostana* (chicken sautéed with ham and mushrooms in a cream sauce) or *abbacchio* (suckling lamb) *al forno,* each evocative of the region's bounty. The specialty, and our personal favorite, is *bucatini matriciana,* a variation on the favorite sauce in the Roman repertoire, *amatriciana,* richly flavored with bacon, tomatoes, and basil. Dining at the convivial tables, you're likely to see an array of Romans, including prelates and cardinals ducking out of the nearby Vatican for a meal.

Via dei Gracchi 55. ℭ 06-3212327. Reservations required. Main courses 9.50€–17€ ($11–$20). DC, MC, V. Daily 12:30–3pm and 8–11:30pm. Closed Aug 5–31; Wed in winter; Sat in summer. Metro: Ottaviano-San Pietro.

INEXPENSIVE

The no. 6 branch of **Insalata Ricca,** the popular chain of salad-and-light-meals restaurants, is across from the Vatican walls at Piazza del Risorgimento 5 (ℭ **06-39730387**).

Hostaria dei Bastioni ROMAN   This simple but well-managed restaurant is about a minute's walk from the entrance to the Vatican Museums and has been open since the 1960s. Although a warm-weather terrace doubles the size during summer, many diners prefer the inside room as an escape from the roaring traffic. The menu features the staples of Rome's culinary repertoire, including fisherman's *risotto* (a broth-simmered rice dish studded with fresh fish, usually shellfish), a vegetarian *fettuccine alla bastione* with orange-flavored creamy tomato sauce, an array of grilled fresh fish, and cutlets of tender beef with mushrooms. The food is first-rate—and a real bargain at these prices.

Via Leone IV 29. ℭ 06-39723034. Reservations recommended Fri–Sat. Main courses 6€–12€ ($7.20–$14). AE, DC, MC, V. Mon–Sat noon–3pm and 7–11:30pm. Closed July 15–Aug 1. Metro: Ottaviano-San Pietro.

9 In Trastevere

EXPENSIVE

Alberto Ciarla 🌶🌶 SEAFOOD   The Ciarla, in an 1890 building set in an obscure corner of an enormous square, is Trastevere's best restaurant and one of its most expensive. You'll be greeted cordially and with a lavish display of seafood on ice. A dramatically modern decor plays light against shadow for a Renaissance chiaroscuro effect. The specialties include a handful of ancient recipes subtly improved by Signor Ciarla (such as the pasta and bean soup with seafood). Original dishes include gilthead bream (a kind of fish) in orange sauce, savory spaghetti with clams, and a full array of delicious shellfish. The sea bass filet is prepared in at least three ways, including an award-winning version with almonds.

Piazza San Cosimato 40. ℭ 06-5818668. Reservations required. Main courses 15€–31€ ($18–$37); fixed-price menus 50€–84€ ($60–$101). AE, DC, MC, V. Mon–Sat 8:30pm–12:30am. Closed Jan 4–14 and 1 week in Aug. Bus: 44, 75, 170, 280, or 718.

Sabatini 🌶 ROMAN/SEAFOOD   This is a real neighborhood spot in a lively location. (You might have to wait for a table even if you have a reservation.) In summer, tables are placed on the charming piazza, and you can look across at the church's floodlit golden frescoes. The dining room sports beamed ceilings, stenciled walls, lots of paneling, and framed oil paintings. The spaghetti with seafood is excellent, and the fresh fish and shellfish, especially grilled scampi, are also very tempting. For a savory treat, try *pollo con peperoni,* chicken with red and green peppers. The large antipasti table is also excellent, as are the delicious pastas and the superb chicken and veal dishes. Wash it all down with the delightful white Frascati wine or the house Chianti. (Order carefully; your bill can skyrocket if you choose grilled fish or the Florentine steaks.)

Piazza Santa Maria in Trastevere 13. ℭ 06-5812026. Reservations recommended. Main courses 15€–30€ ($18–$36). AE, DC, MC, V. Daily 12:30–2:30pm and 7:45–11:30pm. Closed 2 weeks in Aug (dates vary). Bus: 45, 65, 170, 181, or 280.

MODERATE

Antico Arco 🌶 *Finds* ITALIAN   Named after one of the gates of early medieval Rome (Arco di San Pancrazio), which rises nearby, Antico Arco is on Janiculum Hill not far from Trastevere and the American Academy. It's a hip restaurant with a young, stylish clientele. It's run by three investors (a married couple, Maurizio and Patrizia, and their friend Domenico) who are often on-site, making sure that food and service flow smoothly. Carefully created dishes include herb-laden onion flan with Parmesan sauce, and a palate-awakening truffle and rabbit-meat salad with sliced Parmesan and honey sauce. A bitter orange sauce and sesame-flavored chutney are terrific foils for roasted duck. Macaroni carbonara, *tagliolini con bottarga* (a Sardinian dish composed of pasta flavored with fish roe), and spaghetti served with pecorino romano cheese, heavenly fried zucchini blossoms, and fresh-ground pepper are our favorite pastas here.

Piazzale Aurelio 7. ⓒ 06-5815274. Reservations recommended. Main courses 14€–26€ ($17–$31). AE, DC, MC, V. Mon–Sat 6pm–midnight. Bus: 44 or 870.

Asinocotto ITALIAN   Within a pair of cramped dining rooms (one on street level, the other upstairs), you'll be served by a cheerful staff that's well practiced in hauling steaming platters of food up the steep flight of stairs. This is Rome's newest gay-owned and gay-friendly restaurant. The simple white-painted walls accented by dark timbers and panels are a nice background to the flavorful dishes that stream from the busy kitchens of Giuliano Brenna. The menu is fairly sophisticated, thanks to the owner's stint as a chef at the Hotel Eden, one of Rome's more upscale hotels. Look for elaborate antipasti such as quail and watercress in a "Parmesan basket," or marinated salmon with fresh cucumbers and pistachio nuts. You might follow with handmade ravioli filled with sea bass, lettuce, and a sauvignon sauce, or a zesty oxtail soup with artichoke hearts au gratin. Other imaginative dishes that enthralled us were duck roasted with five spices and served in a maple syrup sauce, and the baked grouper with a shellfish-laced leek sauce flavored with fresh rosemary. The restaurant's name, incidentally, translates as "cooked donkey meat," but don't look for that on the menu anytime soon.

Via dei Vascellari 48. ⓒ 06-5898985. Reservations recommended. Main courses 12€–20€ ($14–$24). AE, DC, MC, V. Tues–Sun 8–11pm; Sun 12:30–2:30pm. Tram: 8.

Glass ⭐ *Finds* ROMAN/WINE BAR   When this chic restaurant and wine bar opened, management claimed it was an "attempt to give Trastevere back to the Romans." Pretend you're a native—not a tourist—and you should have a good time here on one of its two floors. Theatrical lighting and lots of glass (including the floors) give the place a modernist aura, rather rare for the district. Glass doubles as a wine bar. The cuisine is both innovative and traditional. Some of our favorite bite-downs include gnocchi made with red turnips and served with pecorino, crisp anchovies, and tuna. The *tagliolini* is homemade and sautéed with cherry tomatoes, duck, and fresh mushrooms. A sublime pigeon comes in a berry sauce encased in a chicory pie. You might also try the celestial fresh fish in an almond and lavender crust with a sweet wine sauce laced with cheese.

Vicolo del Cinque 58. ⓒ 06-58335903. Reservations recommended. Main courses 11€–18€ ($13–$22); fixed-price menus 35€–40€ ($42–$48). AE, DC, MC, V. Restaurant daily 8–11:30pm, wine bar daily 8pm–2am. Bus: 23.

La Cisterna ROMAN   If you like traditional home cooking based on the best regional ingredients, head here. La Cisterna, named for an ancient well from imperial times discovered in the cellar, lies deep in the heart of Trastevere. For more than 75 years, it has been run by the wonderful Simmi family. In good weather, you can dine at sidewalk tables. From the ovens emerge Roman-style suckling lamb that's amazingly tender and seasoned with fresh herbs and virgin olive oil. The spicy *rigatoni all'amatriciana* is served with red-hot peppers, and the delectable *papalini romana* consists of

Dining in Trastevere

Alberto Ciarla	**3**
Antico Arco	**2**
Asinocotto	**7**
Glass	**1**
La Cisterna	**4**
Paris	**5**
Sabatini	**6**

wide noodles flavored with prosciutto, cheese, and eggs. The shrimp is perfectly grilled, and an array of fresh fish includes flaky sea bass baked with fresh herbs.

Via della Cisterna 13. ℭ **06-5812543.** Reservations recommended. Main courses 7€–15€ ($8.40–$18). AE, DC, MC, V. Mon–Sat 7pm–1:30am. Bus: 44, 75, 170, 280, or 710.

Paris ROMAN   For about a century, there's been a restaurant here in this weathered stone building erected about 600 years ago in Trastevere. Over the years, this cramped but convivial place has turned out thousands of platters of authentic Roman cuisine, usually with an emphasis on seafood. This is old-fashioned cooking; don't look for the latest foodie trends. Despite that, you're likely to be very happy here, thanks to heaping portions of dishes such as fried filet of sole; turbot with mushrooms, olive oil, and herbs; several interpretations of scampi; Roman tripe; *coda alla vaccinara* (slow-baked rump steak in the Roman style); and succulent grilled baby lamb chops. Vegetarians will appreciate one of the house specialties—a beautifully presented platter of fried, very fresh vegetables that can be a main course for one diner or a shared antipasti for two or three. We especially love the deep-fried zucchini blossoms stuffed with mozzarella and anchovies, when they're available.

Piazza San Calisto 7A. ℭ **06-5815378.** Reservations recommended. Main courses 12€–20€ ($14–$24). AE, DC, MC, V. Tues–Sun noon–3pm; Tues–Sat 7:45am–11pm. Closed Aug. Bus: H, 44.

A Romantic Picnic in the Borghese Gardens

Our favorite place for a picnic in all of Rome is in the Borghese Gardens, followed by a reserved visit to the Galleria Borghese. **Gina,** 7A Via San Sebastianello (© **06-6780251**), has come up with a marvelous idea. This deli will provide you with a hamper complete with thermos, glasses, and linen for a picnic to be enjoyed in the fabled gardens. For 35€ ($42), two persons can enjoy panini (tomato, eggplant, and mozzarella on focaccia) along with a fresh fruit salad, dessert, and coffee.

10 In Villa Borghese

EXPENSIVE

Casina Valadier ✦ ROMAN   After a long hiatus, this chic restaurant has reopened, and once again the glitterati of Rome are flocking here for the to-die-for cocktails, the superb cuisine, and the panoramic views of Rome. In the heart of Villa Borghese, the terrace of the restaurant is the most evocative in the city. Placed on the site of the ancient Collis Hortulorum, the highest point of the Pincio district, the original building dates from 1816 and was the creation of the famous architect, Giuseppe Valadier. In its heyday, this restaurant was the most fashionable place in Rome, attracting people such as King Farouk of Egypt and Pirandello, Gandhi, and Strauss.

The best of the menu is a regionally based repertoire of savory dishes with imaginative, intelligent associations of flavors. Diners take delight in jazzed up Roman classics such as rigatoni with bacon, onions, peppers, and pecorino, or a cherry- and sesame-encrusted pork filet. Start, perhaps, with a duck breast carpaccio or a warm ricotta cheese round with an olive and pistachio pesto. For dessert, dare you try the fried zucchini flowers stuffed with rice and served with cinnamon ice cream?

Villa Borghese, Piazza Bucarest. © **06-69922090.** Reservations required. Main courses 12€–40€ ($15–$48). Tues–Sun 12:30–3pm; Tues–Sat 8–11pm. Bus: 53.

11 In Testaccio

MODERATE

Checchino dal 1887 ✦ ROMAN   During the 1800s, a wine shop flourished here, selling drinks to the butchers working in the nearby slaughterhouses. In 1887, the ancestors of the restaurant's present owners began serving food, too. Slaughterhouse workers in those days were paid part of their meager salaries with the *quinto quarto* (fifth quarter) of each day's slaughter (the tail, feet, intestines, and other parts not for the squeamish). Following centuries of Roman traditions, Ferminia, the wine shop's cook, somehow transformed these products into the tripe and oxtail dishes that form an integral part of the menu. Many Italian diners come here to relish the *rigatoni con pajata* (pasta with small intestines), *coda alla vaccinara* (oxtail stew), *fagioli e cotiche* (beans with intestinal fat), and other examples of *la cucina povera* (food of the poor). In winter, a succulent wild boar with dried prunes and red wine is served. Safer and possibly more appetizing is the array of salads, soups, pastas, steaks, cutlets, grills, and ice creams. The English-speaking staff is helpful, tactfully proposing alternatives if you're not ready for Roman soul food. The wine cellar stocks more than 600 kinds of wines from all over the world.

Via di Monte Testaccio 30. ℰ **06-5743816.** Reservations recommended. Main courses 10€–24€ ($12–$29); fixed-price menu 31€–60€ ($37–$72). AE, DC, MC, V. Tues–Sat 12:30–3pm and 8pm–midnight. Closed Aug and 1 week at Christmas. Bus: 75 from Termini Station.

12 In Parioli

VERY EXPENSIVE

Sapori del Lord Byron *✻✻✻* ITALIAN   This *luxe* restaurant is one of the best places to go for both traditional and creative cuisine. A chichi crowd with demanding palates packs it nightly. There are places in Rome with better views, but the setting here is far more elegant. Inside one of the capital's most exclusive small hotels, the light-hearted decor combines white latticework with bold colors and flowers. The service is impeccable. The creative menu features a variety of succulent regional dishes and one of the best hotel wine *cartes* in Rome. Tantalizing appetizers are likely to include zucchini carpaccio with pine nuts, fresh mint, and tomato, or a mild smoked salmon with sweet and sour red onion. Our favorite Roman specialties include homemade *tagliolini* pasta in an oxtail sauce, as well as fava beans with Roman pecorino cheese. For main course delights, try the fresh *pappardella* pasta with arugula, shrimp, saffron, and fresh orange. The sea bass steak is a treat, with its flavor of lemongrass. Veal medallions are enlivened with sun-dried tomatoes, fresh olives, and an eggplant confit.

In the Hotel Lord Byron, Via G. de Notaris 5. ℰ **06-3613041.** Reservations required. Main courses 25€–32€ ($30–$38). AE, DC, MC, V. Mon–Sat 12:30–2:30pm and 8–10:30pm. Closed Aug. Metro: Flaminio. Bus: 19 or 52.

MODERATE

Al Ceppo *✻* ROMAN   Because the place is somewhat hidden (although it's only 2 blocks from the Villa Borghese, near Piazza Ungheria), you're likely to rub elbows with more Romans here than tourists. It's a longtime favorite. "The Log" features an open wood-stoked fireplace on which the chef roasts lamb chops, liver, and bacon to perfection. Other intriguing items include fusilli pasta with bacon and artichokes, and a breaded, grilled fish of the day. A true delight is the tender beef filet with black truffles. To warm your soul, order the white chocolate and peach terrine with a fresh mint sauce.

Via Panama 2. ℰ **06-8419696.** Reservations recommended. Main courses 15€–23€ ($18–$28). AE, DC, MC, V. Tues–Sun 12:30–3pm and 8–11pm. Closed last 2 weeks of Aug. Bus: 56 or 310.

13 In Monte Mario

La Pergola *✻✻✻* MEDITERRANEAN   Many Roman food critics call this the best restaurant in the city. After a brief hesitation, we, too, cast our vote for the Cavalieri Hilton's spectacular panoramic restaurant high atop Monte Mario. Arrive early and enjoy the view and Rome's most elegant cocktail bar. In summer, there is alfresco dining on an adjacent terrace. The setting is as elegant as you would expect: trompe l'oeil ceilings, wood paneling, beautifully set tables with Flanders linen and silver, fine porcelain, flickering candles, and sliding glass walls. The staff functions so beautifully they've been compared to a Viennese orchestra.

Since 1994, a talented German chef, Heinz Beck, has been dazzling sophisticated Roman taste buds. Even though he's not a native, he has taken Italian haute cuisine to dizzying new heights, delighting critics and diners with an array of colors and aromas. The surprises go on and on, as you partake of one of the finest meals you are likely to be served in Italy. On a recent visit, we found balance, harmony, and unusual flavor combinations in such dishes as an appetizer of lobster with orange sauce and fresh basil; and a pasta *tagliolini* with shrimp, fresh lime, and zucchini flowers. Pigeon and duck liver came with a tantalizing mustard-seed sauce. Other recommendations include deep-fried zucchini flowers with shellfish and a saffron consommé, and lamb baked in puff pastry with fresh baby eggplant.

In the Cavalieri Hilton, Via Cadlolo 101. ✆ **06-35092152.** Reservations required. Main courses 35€–50€ ($42–$60); fixed-price menu 130€–150€ ($156–$180). AE, DC, MC, V. Tues–Sat 7:30pm–midnight. Closed Aug 8–23. Free shuttle bus to and from city center.

8

Exploring Rome

Where else but in Rome could you admire a 17th-century colonnade designed by Bernini while resting against an Egyptian obelisk carried off from Heliopolis while Jesus was still alive? Or stand amid the splendor of Renaissance frescoes in a papal palace built on top of the tomb of a Roman emperor? Where else, for that matter, are vestal virgins buried adjacent to the Ministry of Finance?

Rome went all out to spruce up for 2000 Jubilee, and when you visit in 2007, you'll benefit from all those improvements made at the end of the 20th century. For the Jubilee, decades' worth of grime from car exhaust and other pollution was scrubbed from the city's facades, revealing the original glory of the Eternal City (although Rome could still stand even more work on this front), and ancient treasures such as the Colosseum were shored up. Many of the most popular areas (such as the Trevi Fountain and Piazza Navona) are sparkling and inviting again.

Whether they're still time-blackened or newly gleaming, the city's ancient monuments are a constant reminder that Rome was one of the greatest centers of Western civilization. In the heyday of the empire, all roads led to Rome, and with good reason. It was one of the first cosmopolitan cities, importing slaves, gladiators, great art, and even citizens from the far corners of the world. Despite its carnage and corruption, Rome left a legacy of law, a heritage of great art, architecture, and engineering, and an uncanny lesson in how to conquer enemies by absorbing their cultures.

But ancient Rome is only part of the spectacle. The Vatican has had a tremendous influence on making the city a tourism center. Although Vatican architects stripped down much of the city's glory, looting ancient ruins for their precious marble, they created great Renaissance treasures and even occasionally incorporated the old into the new—as Michelangelo did when turning the Baths of Diocletian into a church. And in the years that followed, Bernini adorned the city with the wonders of the baroque, especially his glorious fountains.

1 St. Peter's & the Vatican

If you want to know more about the Vatican, check out its website at **www.vatican.va**.

IN VATICAN CITY

In 1929, the Lateran Treaty between Pope Pius XI and the Italian government created the **Vatican,** the world's second-smallest sovereign independent state. It has only a few hundred citizens and is protected (theoretically) by its own militia, the curiously uniformed (some say by Michelangelo) Swiss guards.

The only entrance to the Vatican for the casual visitor is through one of the glories of the Western world: Bernini's **St. Peter's Square (Piazza San Pietro).** As you stand

Rome Attractions

National Gallery
of Modern Art 25
Galleria
Borghese 26
Piazza
di Siena
VILLA
BORGHESE/
PARIOLI 27

Corso D'Italia
Piazzale di
Porta Pia
Policlinico

VIA VENETO

Spagna
Spanish
Steps 28
Piazza
di Spagna 29

Barberini
Lgo. di
S. Susanna

National Roman
Museum 33 34
Piazza
Indipendenza

Castro Pretorio

30

PIAZZA
BARBERINI 31
32
Piazza
Repubblica
Piazza
Cinque-
cento
Termini
Station
Repubblica
Termini

Trevi
Fountain
Palazzo del
Quirinale 36
Piazza d.
Quirinale

Palazzo
Doria
Pamphilj 37

Palazzo
Colonna

Teatro
dell'Opera
Piazza
dell'Esquilino 49
Santa Maria
Maggiore

SAN
LORENZO

Palazzo
Venezia 38
Vittorio Emanuele
Monument 39 40 41
42 46 47
Capitoline 43
Museums 44
45 48

Via Cavour
See "The Colosseuem,
The Forum & Ancient
Rome" map

Vittorio Emanuele
Piazza
Vittorio
Eman. II

San Pietro
in Vincoli 50

ANCIENT ROME
Roman
Forum

Golden House
of Nero 51
Colosseo
Manzoni

Colosseum 55
56 Piazza d.
Colosseo 57
52
54
San Giovanni
in Laterano 58
59
S. Giovanni

PALATINE
HILL 53

AVENTINE
HILL
Circo Massimo
Piazza di
Pta.Capena
Re di Roma

Piazza
Albania 61 62
Piramide
Baths of
60 Caracalla 63

Information
City Walls
Metro A
Metro B
Railway

0   1/4 mi
0   0.25 km

135

in the huge piazza, you'll be in the arms of an ellipse partly enclosed by a majestic **Doric-pillared colonnade.** Atop it stands a gesticulating crowd of some 140 saints. Straight ahead is the facade of **St. Peter's Basilica** (Sts. Peter and Paul are represented by statues in front, with Peter carrying the keys to the kingdom), and, to the right, above the colonnade, are the dark-brown buildings of the **papal apartments** and the **Vatican Museums.** In the center of the square is an **Egyptian obelisk,** brought from the ancient city of Heliopolis on the Nile delta. Flanking the obelisk are two 17th-century **fountains.** The one on the right (facing the basilica), by Carlo Maderno, who designed the facade of St. Peter's, was placed here by Bernini himself; the other is by Carlo Fontana.

On the left side of Piazza San Pietro is the **Vatican Tourist Office** (© **06-69881662**), open Monday through Saturday from 8:30am to 6:30pm. It sells maps and guides that'll help you make more sense of the riches you'll be seeing in the museums. It also accepts reservations for tours of the Vatican Gardens and tries to answer questions.

Basilica di San Pietro (St. Peter's Basilica) ✿✿✿

In ancient times, the Circus of Nero, where St. Peter is said to have been crucified, was slightly to the left of where the basilica is now located. Peter was allegedly buried here in A.D. 64 near the site of his execution, and in 324 Constantine commissioned a basilica to be built over Peter's tomb. That structure stood for more than 1,000 years until it verged on collapse. The present basilica, mostly completed in the 1500s and 1600s, is predominantly High Renaissance and baroque. Inside, the massive scale, which is almost too much to absorb, showcases some of Italy's greatest artists: Bramante, Raphael, Michelangelo, and Maderno. In a church of such grandeur—overwhelming in its detail of gilt, marble, and mosaic—you can't expect much subtlety. It's meant to be overpowering.

In the nave on the right (the first chapel) stands one of the Vatican's greatest treasures: Michelangelo's exquisite *Pietà* ✿✿✿, created while the master was still in his early 20s but clearly showing his genius for capturing the human form. (The sculpture has been kept behind reinforced glass since a madman's act of vandalism in the 1970s.) Note the incredibly lifelike folds of Mary's robes and her youthful features (although she would've been middle-aged at the time of the Crucifixion, Michelangelo portrayed her as a young woman to convey her purity).

Much farther on, in the right wing of the transept near the Chapel of St. Michael, rests Canova's neoclassic **sculpture of Pope Clement XIII** ✿✿. The truly devout stop to kiss the feet of the 13th-century **bronze of St. Peter** ✿, attributed to Arnolfo di Cambio (at the far reaches of the nave, against a corner pillar on the right). Under Michelangelo's dome is the celebrated twisty-columned **baldacchino** ✿✿ (1524), by

---

⌐Tips A St. Peter's Warning

St. Peter's has a strict dress code: no shorts, no skirts above the knee, and no bare shoulders. You will not be let in if you don't come dressed appropriately. In a pinch, men and women alike can buy a big, cheap scarf from a nearby souvenir stand and wrap it around their legs as a long skirt or throw it over their shoulders as a shawl. If you're still showing too much skin, a guard hands out blue paper capes similar to what you wear in a doctor's office. No photographs are allowed.

Bronze Door (Portone di Bronzo) **7**
Excavations Office (Ufficio Scavi) **11**
Grottoes Entrance **10**
Hall of Audiences **14**
House of Pius IV **5**
Michelangelo's *Pietà* **9**
Palace of the Governorship **4**

Sacristy & Treasury **12**
Sistine Chapel **6**
Statue of St. Peter **10**
Vatican Gardens **2**
Vatican Museum Entrance **1**
Vatican Post Office **8, 13**
Vatican Radio **3**

Bernini, resting over the papal altar. The 29m-high (96-ft.) ultrafancy canopy was created in part, so it's said, from bronze stripped from the Pantheon, although that's up for debate.

In addition, you can visit the **Treasury** ✿, which is filled with jewel-studded chalices, reliquaries, and copes. One robe worn by Pius XII strikes a simple note in these halls of elegance. The sacristy contains a **Historical Museum (Museo Storico)** ✿ displaying Vatican treasures, including the large 1400s bronze tomb of Pope Sixtus V by Antonio Pollaiuolo and several antique chalices.

You can also head downstairs to the **Vatican grottoes** ✿✿, with their tombs of the popes, both ancient and modern (Pope John XXIII gets the most adulation). Behind a wall of glass is what's assumed to be the tomb of St. Peter himself.

To go even farther down, to the **Vatican necropolis** ✿✿, the area around St. Peter's tomb, you must apply in advance at the Ufficio Scavi (✆ **06-69885318,** scavi@fsp.va), through the arch to the left of the stairs up the basilica. You specify your name, the number in your party, your language, and dates you'd like to visit. They'll notify you by phone or email of your admission date and time. For 10€ ($12), you'll take a guided tour of the tombs that were excavated in the 1940s, 23 feet beneath the church floor. For details, check **www.vatican.va**.

Impressions

As a whole St. Peter's is fit for nothing but a ballroom, and it is a little too gaudy even for that.

—John Ruskin, letter to the Rev. Thomas Dale, 1840

After you leave the grottoes, you'll find yourself in a courtyard and ticket line for the grandest sight: the climb to **Michelangelo's dome** 𝕲𝕲𝕲, about 113m (375 ft.) high. You can walk up all the steps or take the elevator as far as it goes. The elevator saves you 171 steps, and you'll *still* have 320 to go after getting off. After you've made it to the top, you'll have an astounding view over the rooftops of Rome and even the Vatican Gardens and papal apartments—a photo op, if ever there was one.

Piazza San Pietro. ℂ 06-69881662 (for information on celebrations). Basilica (including grottoes) free admission. Guided tour of excavations around St. Peter's tomb 10€ ($12); children younger than 15 are not admitted. Stairs to the dome 4€ ($4.80); elevator to the dome 5€ ($6); sacristy (w/Historical Museum) free. Basilica (including the sacristy and treasury) daily 9am–6pm. Grottoes daily 8am–5pm. Dome Oct–Mar daily 8am–5pm; Apr–Sept 8am–6pm. Metro: Ottaviano-San Pietro, and then a long stroll. Bus: 23, 49, or 492.

Vatican Museums (Musei Vaticani) & the Sistine Chapel (Cappella Sistina) 𝕲𝕲𝕲

The Vatican Museums boast one of the world's greatest art collections. They're a gigantic repository of treasures from antiquity and the Renaissance, all housed in a labyrinthine series of lavishly adorned palaces, apartments, and galleries leading you to the real gem: the Sistine Chapel. The Vatican Museums occupy a part of the papal palaces built from the 1200s onward. From the former papal private apartments, the museums were created over a period of time to display the vast treasure trove of art acquired by the Vatican.

To reach the ticket windows, you take an escalator, although you exit down a magnificent spiral ramp. Signs will direct you on your way to the highlights. Obviously, 1, 2, or even 20 trips will not be enough to see the wealth of the Vatican, much less to digest it. With that in mind, we've previewed only a representative sampling of the masterpieces on display (in alphabetical order).

Borgia Apartments 𝕲: Frescoed with biblical scenes by Pinturicchio of Umbria and his assistants, these rooms were designed for Pope Alexander VI (the infamous Borgia pope). They might be badly lit, but they boast great splendor and style. At the end of the Raphael Rooms (see below) is the Chapel of Nicholas V, an intimate room frescoed by the Dominican monk Fra Angelico, the most saintly of all Italian painters.

Chiaramonti Museum: Founded by Pope Pius VII, also known as Chiaramonti, the museum includes the *Corridoio* (Corridor), the Galleria Lapidaria, and the *Braccio Nuovo* (New Side). The Corridor hosts an exposition of more than 800 Greek and Roman works, including statues, reliefs, and sarcophagi. In the Galleria Lapidaria are about 5,000 Christian and pagan inscriptions. You'll find a dazzling array of Roman sculpture and copies of Greek originals in these galleries. In the Braccio Nuovo, built as an extension of the Chiaramonti, you can admire *The Nile* 𝕲, a magnificent reproduction of a long-lost Hellenistic original and one of the most remarkable pieces of sculpture from antiquity. The imposing statue of Augustus of Prima Porta presents him as a regal commander.

Collection of Modern Religious Art: This museum, opened in 1973, represents American artists' first invasion of the Vatican. Of the 55 rooms, at least 12 are devoted

The Vatican Museums

Entrance

Cortile della Pigna

Floor 1

Cortile della Pigna

Floor 2

Cortile del Belvedere

Cortile del Belvedere

Cortile di San Damaso

Cortile di San Damaso

- Ancient civilizations
- Greek/Roman period
- Early Christian art
- Medieval and modern art, history and geography
- Ethnology, contemporary history and art

Appartamento Borgia & Collezione
  d'Arte Religiosa Moderna **10**
Cappella di Nicholas V **17**
Cappella Sistina (Sistine Chapel) **11**
Galleria degli Arazzi **14**
Galleria del Candelabri **13**
Galleria delle Carte Geografiche **15**
Galleria Lapidaria **9**
Library **7**

Museo Chiaramonti **8**
Museo Gregoriano Egizio **6**
Museo Gregoriano Etrusco **12**
Museo Gregoriano Profano **1**
Museo Missionario Ethnologico **2**
Museo Pio-Clementino **5**
Museo Storico **4**
Pinacoteca **3**
Stanze di Raffaello **16**

Tips   **Buy the Book**

In the Vatican Museums you'll find many overpacked galleries and few labels on the works. At the Vatican Tourist Office (mentioned above), you can buy a detailed guide that'll help you make more sense of the incredible riches you'll be seeing here.

---

to American artists. All the works chosen were judged on their "spiritual and religious values." Among the American works is Leonard Baskin's 1.5m (5-ft.) bronze sculpture of *Isaac.* Modern Italian artists such as De Chirico and Manzù are also displayed, and there's a special room for the paintings of the Frenchman Georges Rouault. You'll also see works by Picasso, Gauguin, Gottuso, Chagall, Henry Moore, Kandinsky, and others.

Egyptian–Gregorian Museum: Experience the grandeur of the pharaohs by studying sarcophagi, mummies, statues of goddesses, vases, jewelry, sculptured pink-granite statues, and hieroglyphics.

Etruscan–Gregorian Museum *⚘*: This was founded by Gregory XIV in 1837 and then enriched year after year, becoming one of the most important and complete collections of Etruscan art. With sarcophagi, a chariot, bronzes, urns, jewelry, and terracotta vases, this gallery affords remarkable insights into an ancient civilization. One of the most acclaimed exhibits is the Regolini–Galassi tomb, unearthed in the 19th century at Cerveteri. It shares top honors with the *Mars of Todi,* a bronze sculpture probably dating from the 5th century B.C.

Ethnological Museum: This is an assemblage of works of art and objects of cultural significance from all over the world. The principal route is a .5km (⅓-mile) walk through 25 geographical sections, displaying thousands of objects covering 3,000 years of world history. The section devoted to China is especially interesting.

Historical Museum: This museum tells the history of the Vatican. It exhibits arms, uniforms, and armor, some dating from the early Renaissance. The carriages displayed are those used by the popes and cardinals in religious processions.

Pinacoteca (Picture Gallery) *⚘⚘⚘*: The Pinacoteca houses paintings and tapestries from the 11th to the 19th centuries. As you pass through room no. 1, note the oldest picture at the Vatican, a keyhole-shape wood panel of the *Last Judgment* from the 11th century. In room no. 2 is one of the finest pieces—the *Stefaneschi Triptych* (six panels), by Giotto and his assistants. Bernardo Daddi's masterpiece of early Italian Renaissance art, *Madonna del Magnificat,* is also here. And you'll see works by Fra Angelico, the 15th-century Dominican monk who distinguished himself as a miniaturist (his *Virgin with Child* is justly praised—check out the Madonna's microscopic eyes).

In the **Raphael salon** *⚘⚘⚘* (room no. 8), you can view three paintings by the Renaissance giant himself: the *Coronation of the Virgin,* the *Virgin of Foligno,* and the massive *Transfiguration* (completed shortly before his death). There are also eight tapestries made by Flemish weavers from cartoons by Raphael. In room no. 9, seek out Leonardo da Vinci's masterful but uncompleted **St. Jerome with the Lion** *⚘⚘*, as well as Giovanni Bellini's *Pietà* and one of Titian's greatest works, the *Virgin of Frari.* Finally, in room no. 10, feast your eyes on one of the masterpieces of the baroque, **Caravaggio's *Deposition from the Cross*** *⚘⚘*.

Pio Clementino Museum *⚘⚘⚘*: Here you'll find Greek and Roman sculptures, many of which are immediately recognizable. The rippling muscles of the ***Belvedere***

Torso ✦✦✦, a partially preserved Greek statue (1st century B.C.) much admired the artists of the Renaissance, especially Michelangelo, reveal an intricate knowledge of the human body. In the rotunda is a large gilded bronze of *Hercules* from the late 2nd century B.C. Other major sculptures are under porticoes opening onto the Belvedere courtyard. From the 1st century B.C., one sculpture shows **Laocoön** ✦✦✦ and his two sons locked in eternal struggle with the serpents. The incomparable **Apollo Belvedere** ✦✦✦ (a late Roman reproduction of an authentic Greek work from the 4th century B.C.) has become the symbol of classic male beauty, rivaling Michelangelo's *David*. Some members of the Vatican staff once discovered Michelangelo in front of the Belvedere Apollo "publicly aroused in defilement." He was caned and shamed accordingly and had to promise to "create something grand" to compensate for his "shocking" behavior.

Raphael Rooms ✦✦: While still a young man, Raphael was given one of the greatest assignments of his short life: to decorate a series of rooms in the apartments of Pope Julius II. Raphael and his workshop carried out the commission from 1508 to 1524. In these works, Raphael achieves the Renaissance aim of blending classic beauty with realism. In the first chamber, the Stanza dell'Incendio, you'll see much of the work of Raphael's pupils but little of the master—except in the fresco across from the window. The figure of the partially draped Aeneas rescuing his father (to the left of the fresco) is sometimes attributed to Raphael, as is the surprised woman with a jug balanced on her head to the right.

Raphael reigns supreme in the next and most important salon, the Stanza della Segnatura, the first room decorated by the artist, where you'll find the majestic **School of Athens** ✦✦✦, one of his best-known works, depicting such philosophers from the ages as Aristotle, Plato, and Socrates. Many of the figures are actually portraits of some of the greatest artists of the Renaissance, including Bramante (on the right as Euclid, bent over to draw on a chalkboard), Leonardo da Vinci (as Plato, the bearded man in the center pointing heavenward), and even Raphael himself (looking out at you from the lower-right corner). While he was painting this masterpiece, Raphael stopped work to walk down the hall for the unveiling of Michelangelo's newly finished Sistine Chapel ceiling. He was so impressed that he returned to his *School of Athens* and added to his design a sulking Michelangelo sitting on the steps. Another well-known masterpiece here is the *Disputa del Sacramento*.

The *Stanza d'Eliodoro,* also by the master, manages to flatter Raphael's papal patrons (Julius II and Leo X) without compromising his art (although one rather fanciful fresco depicts the pope driving Attila from Rome). Finally, there's the *Sala di Constantino,* which was completed by his students after Raphael's death. Raphael designed the loggia, which is frescoed with more than 50 scenes from the Bible, but his students did the actual work.

Sistine Chapel ✦✦✦: Michelangelo considered himself a sculptor, not a painter. While in his 30s, he was commanded by Julius II to stop work on the pope's own tomb and to devote his considerable talents to painting ceiling frescoes (an art form of which the Florentine master was contemptuous). Michelangelo labored for 4 years (1508–12) over this epic project, which was so physically taxing that it permanently damaged his eyesight. All during the task, he had to contend with the pope's incessant urgings to hurry up; at one point, Julius threatened to topple Michelangelo from the scaffolding—or so Vasari relates in his *Lives of the Artists.*

at a project undertaken against the artist's wishes would form his most
d. Glorifying the human body as only a sculptor could, Michelangelo
anels, taken from the pages of Genesis, and surrounded them with
ibyls. The most notable panels detail the expulsion of Adam and Eve
from the Garden of Eden and the creation of man. *Tip:* Bring along binoculars so you
can see the details better.

The Florentine master was in his 60s when he began the masterly *Last Judgment* ✹✹✹
on the altar wall. Again working against his wishes, Michelangelo presented a more
jaundiced view of people and their fate; God sits in judgment and sinners are plunged
into the mouth of hell. A master of ceremonies under Paul III, Monsignor Biagio da
Cesena, protested to the pope about the "shameless nudes" painted by Michelangelo.
Michelangelo showed that he wasn't above petty revenge by painting the prude with
the ears of a jackass in hell. When Biagio complained to the pope, Paul III maintained
that he had no jurisdiction in hell. However, Daniele de Volterra was summoned to
drape clothing over some of the bare figures, thus earning for himself a dubious distinction as a haberdasher.

On the side walls are frescoes by other Renaissance masters, such as Botticelli,
Perugino, Signorelli, Pinturicchio, Roselli, and Ghirlandaio. Unfortunately, because
they compete with Michelangelo's artistry, they're virtually ignored by visitors.

Papal Audiences

When the pope is in Rome, he gives a public audience every Wednesday
beginning at 10:30am (sometimes at 10am in summer). It takes place in the
Paul VI Hall of Audiences, although sometimes St. Peter's Basilica and St.
Peter's Square are used to accommodate a large attendance. Anyone is welcome, but you must first obtain a **free ticket** from the office of the Prefecture of the Papal Household, accessible from St. Peter's Square by the
Bronze Door, where the colonnade on the right (as you face the basilica)
begins. The office is open from Monday through Saturday from 9am to
1pm. Tickets are readily available on Monday and Tuesday; sometimes you
won't be able to get into the office on Wednesday morning. Occasionally, if
there's enough room, you can attend without a ticket.

You can also write ahead to the **Prefecture of the Papal Household,** 00120
Città del Vaticano (✆ **06-69883114**), indicating your language, the dates of
your visit, the number of people in your party, and (if possible) the hotel in
Rome to which the cards should be sent the afternoon before the audience.
American Catholics, armed with a letter of introduction from their parish
priest, should apply to the **North American College,** Via dell'Umiltà 30, 00187
Roma (✆ **06-690011**).

At noon on Sunday, the pope speaks briefly from his study window and
gives his blessing to the visitors and pilgrims gathered in St. Peter's Square.
From about mid-July to mid-September, the Angelus and blessing take place
at the summer residence at Castelgandolfo, some 26km (16 miles) out of
Rome and accessible by Metro and bus.

The twisting *ignudi* or male nudes that decorate the corners of the ceiling were terribly controversial when executed.

The restoration of the Sistine Chapel in the 1990s touched off a worldwide debate among art historians. The chapel was on the verge of collapse, from both its age and the weather, and restoration took years as restorers used advanced computer analyses in their painstaking and controversial work. They reattached the fresco and repaired the ceiling, ridding the frescoes of their dark and shadowy look. Critics claim that in addition to removing centuries of dirt and grime—and several of the added "modesty" drapes—the restorers removed a vital second layer of paint as well. Purists argue that many of the restored figures seem flat compared with the originals, which had more shadow and detail. Others have hailed the project for saving Michelangelo's masterpiece for future generations to appreciate and for revealing the vibrancy of his color palette.

Vatican Library ✿: The library is richly decorated, with frescos created by a team of Mannerist painters commissioned by Sixtus V. The library is open only to qualified researchers.

Vatican City, Viale Vaticano (a long walk around the Vatican walls from St. Peter's Square). ℂ 06-69883333. Admission 12€ ($14) adults, 8€ ($10) children under 14 years of age, free for children under 6. Nov–Feb Mon–Sat 8:45am–12:20pm; Mar–Oct Mon–Fri 8:45am–3:20pm, Sat 8:45am–12:20pm. Closed Jan 1 and 6, Easter, May 1 and 20, Nov 1, and Dec 8, 25, and 26. Metro: Cipro-Musei Vaticani.

Vatican Gardens ✿   Separating the Vatican from the secular world on the north and west are 23 hectares (58 acres) of lush gardens filled with winding paths, brilliantly colored flowers, groves of massive oaks, and ancient fountains and pools. In the midst of this pastoral setting is a small summer house, Villa Pia, built for Pope Pius IV in 1560 by Pirro Ligorio. The gardens contain medieval fortifications from the 9th century to the present. Water spouts profusely from a variety of fountains.

To make a reservation to visit the Vatican Gardens, send a fax to **06-69884676.** Once the reservation is accepted, you must go to the Vatican information office (at Piazza San Pietro, on the left side looking at the facade of St. Peter's) and pick up the tickets 2 or 3 days before your visit. Tours of the gardens are Tuesday, Thursday, and Friday at 10am; they last for 2 hours, and the first half-hour is by bus. The cost of the tour is 9€ ($11). For further information, contact the **Vatican Tourism Office** (ℂ **06-69881662**).

North and west of the Vatican. See previous paragraph for tour information.

NEAR VATICAN CITY

The trio of arches in the Tiber River's center has been basically unchanged since the **Ponte Sant'Angelo** was built around A.D. 135; the arches abutting the river's embankments were added late in the 19th century as part of a flood-control program. On December 19, 1450, so many pilgrims gathered on this bridge (which at the time was lined with wooden buildings) that about 200 of them were crushed to death.

Since the 1960s, the bridge has been reserved for pedestrians, who can stroll across and admire the statues designed by Bernini. On the southern end is **Piazza Sant'Angelo,** the site of one of the most famous executions of the Renaissance. In 1599, Beatrice Cenci and several members of her family were beheaded on orders of Pope Clement VIII. Their crime? Plotting the murder of their rich and brutal father. Their tale inspired a tragedy by Shelley and a novel by 19th-century Italian politician Francesco Guerrazzi.

Castel Sant'Angelo ✪ This overpowering castle on the Tiber was Rome's chief citadel and dungeon and has seen more blood, treachery, and turmoil than any other left in Rome. Even those on a rushed visit to Rome might want to spend some time here. It was built in the 2nd century as a tomb for Emperor Hadrian; it continued as an imperial mausoleum until the time of Caracalla. If it looks like a fortress, it should— that was its function in the Middle Ages. It was built over the Roman walls and linked to the Vatican by an underground passage that was much used by the fleeing papacy, who escaped from unwanted visitors such as Charles V during his 1527 sack of the city. In the 14th century, it became a papal residence, enjoying various connections with Boniface IX, Nicholas V, and Julius II, patron of Michelangelo and Raphael. However, its legend rests largely on its link with Pope Alexander VI, whose mistress bore him two children (those darlings of debauchery, Cesare and Lucrezia Borgia).

The highlight is a trip through the Renaissance apartments, with their coffered ceilings and lush decoration. Their walls have witnessed some of the most diabolical plots and intrigues of the High Renaissance. Later you can go through the dank cells that once echoed with the screams of Cesare's torture victims. The most famous figure imprisoned here was Benvenuto Cellini, the eminent sculptor/goldsmith, remembered chiefly for his candid *Autobiography.* Now an art museum, the castle halls display the history of the Roman mausoleum, along with a wide-ranging selection of ancient arms and armor. You can climb to the top terrace for another one of those dazzling views of the Eternal City. An audio guide is available to help you understand what you're seeing.

The bumper-to-bumper cars and buses that once roared around Castel Sant'Angelo are now gone. The area around the castle has been turned into a pedestrian zone. Visitors can now walk in peace through the landscaped section with a tree-lined avenue above the Tiber and a formal garden. In 2000, the moat under the ramparts was opened to the public for the first time. You can wander the footpaths and enjoy the new beeches providing shade in the sweltering summer.

Lungotevere Castello 50. ✆ **06-39967600**. Admission 7€ ($8.40). Tues–Sun 9am–7pm. Metro: Ottaviano-San Pietro, and then a long stroll. Bus: 40, 62, or 74.

2 The Colosseum, the Roman Forum & Highlights of Ancient Rome

THE TOP SIGHTS IN ANCIENT ROME

If you'd like more guidance as you explore this area, turn to "Walking Tour 1: Rome of the Caesars," on p. 145.

The Colosseum (Colosseo) ✪✪✪ Now a mere shell, the Colosseum still remains ancient Rome's greatest architectural legacy. Vespasian ordered the construction of the elliptical bowl, called the Amphitheatrum Flavium, in A.D. 72; it was inaugurated by Titus in A.D. 80 with a bloody combat between gladiators and wild beasts that lasted many long weeks. At its peak, under the cruel Domitian, the Colosseum could seat 50,000. The vestal virgins from the temple screamed for blood, as more exotic animals were shipped in from the far corners of the empire to satisfy jaded tastes (lion versus bear, two humans vs. hippopotamus). Not-so-mock naval battles were staged (the canopied Colosseum could be flooded), and the defeated combatants might have their lives spared if they put up a good fight. Many historians now believe that one of the most enduring legends about the Colosseum (that Christians were fed to the lions) is unfounded.

The Colosseum, the Forum & Ancient Rome Attractions

Antiquarium Comunale **43**
Arch of Constantine **33**
Arch of Septimius Severus **20**
Arch of Titus **35**
Basilica of Constantine &
  Maxentius **27**
Basilica de San Clemente **31**
Basilica de San Giovanni
  in Laterno **31**
Basilica Julia **18**
Baths of Caracalla **44**
Capitoline Museum **11**
Circus Maximus **42**
Colosseum **32**
Curia **21**
Farnese Gardens **38**
Forum of Augustus **7**

Forum of Julius Caesar **9**
Forum of Nerva **8**
Forum of Trajan **5**
Galleria Colonna **4**
Golden House of Nero **30**
Hippodrome **36**
House of Livia **37**
House of the Vestal Virgins **25**
National Museum of
  Palazzo Venezia **1**
Palatine Museum **34**
Palazzo dei Conservatori **12**
Palazzo Senatorio **15**
San Pietro in Vincoli **29**
Santa Maria d'Aracoeli **10**
Santa Maria in Cosmedin **41**
Tabularium **14**

Temple of Antoninus
  & Faustina **26**
Temple of the Dioscuri **23**
Temple of Fortuna Virile
  (Temple of the Portunus) **39**
Temple of Hercules **40**
Temple of Romulus **28**
Temple of Saturn **17**
Temple of Vespasian & Titus **16**
Temple of Vesta **24**
Theater of Pompey **13**
Trajan's Column **3**
Trajan's Market **6**
Umbilicus Urbus /
  Imperial Rostra **19**
Via Sacra **22**
Vittorio Emanuele Monument **2**

Hail to the Gladiator

Good news for fans of the Oscar-winning smash film *Gladiator:* You can get the same center-stage view of the Colosseum that the fighters had before they met a bloody death or glory in the ring. Renovations allow visitors to wander spaces under the Colosseum where elephants, lions, and wild animals from North Africa once waited to be hoisted up in cages to take on the gladiators.

Long after the Colosseum ceased to be an arena to amuse sadistic Romans, it was struck by an earthquake. Centuries later it was used as a quarry, its rich marble facing stripped away to build palaces and churches. On one side, part of the original four tiers remains; the first three levels were constructed in Doric, Ionic, and Corinthian styles, respectively, to lend variety. Inside, the seats are gone, as is the wooden floor.

On a user-friendly note, two elevators have been installed to allow visitors to reach the second tier without having to climb steps 10 inches high. The Colosseum has become the turnstile for Rome's largest traffic circle, around which thousands of cars whip daily, spewing exhaust over this venerable monument. You can explore on your own or rent an audio guide for 4€ ($4.80).

The **Arch of Constantine** 🏛🏛, the highly photogenic memorial next to the Colosseum, was erected by the Senate in A.D. 315 to honor Constantine's defeat of the pagan Maxentius (in 306). Many of the reliefs have nothing whatsoever to do with Constantine or his works, but they tell of the victories of earlier Antonine rulers (they were apparently lifted from other, long-forgotten memorials).

Historically, the arch marks a period of great change in the history of Rome and thus the history of the world. Converted to Christianity by a vision on the battlefield, Constantine ended the centuries-long persecution of the Christians (during which many devout followers of the new religion had been put to death gruesomely). While Constantine didn't ban paganism (which survived officially until the closing of the temples more than half a century later), he espoused Christianity himself and began the inevitable development that culminated in the conquest of Rome by the Christian religion.

After visiting the Colosseum, it's convenient to head over to the recently reopened **Domus Aurea (Golden House of Nero)** on the Esquiline Hill; it faces the Colosseum and is adjacent to the Forum (see below).

Piazzale del Colosseo, Via dei Fori Imperiali. (©) **06-39967600.** Admission 10€ ($12) all levels. Nov–Feb 15 daily 9am–4:30pm; Feb 16–Mar 15 daily 9am–5pm; Mar 16–Mar 27 daily 9am–5:30pm; Mar 28–Aug daily 9am–7:15pm; Sept daily 9am–7pm; Oct daily 9am–6pm. Guided tours in English with an archaeologist 7 times per day Mar 28–Oct 30 (9:30am, 10:15am, 11:15am, 12:30pm, 3pm, 4:15pm, and 5:15pm) 3.50€ ($4.20). **Note:** Admission to the Colosseum also includes a visit to Palatine Hill. Metro: Colosseo.

Golden House of Nero (Domus Aurea) 🏛

"Nero's Folly" finally reopened in 1999 after a 15-year restoration. After the disastrous fire of A.D. 64 swept over Rome (it has never been proven that Nero set the fire, much less fiddled while Rome burned), the emperor seized about three-quarters of the burned-out historic core (more than 80 hectares/200 acres) to create in just 4 years one of the most sumptuous palaces in history. Subsequent emperors destroyed much of the golden palace, but what remains is now on view.

The area that is the Colosseum today was a central ornamental lake reflecting the glitter of the Golden House. At the entrance Nero installed a 45m (150-ft.) statue of himself in the nude. In the words of Suetonius, "all parts of it were overlaid with gold and adorned with jewels and mother-of-pearl." During the Renaissance, painters such as Raphael chopped holes in the long-buried ceilings to gain admittance and were inspired by the frescoes. The word *grotto* comes from this palace because of the "grotesque" figures painted throughout. Remnants of these almost 2,000-year-old frescoes and fragments of mosaics remain. Out of the original 250 rooms, 30 are now open to the public. Some of the sculptures that survived are also on view.

However, the centuries have taken their toll. Expect a relic that gives only a hint of Nero's former abode. Since none of the rooms is labeled, you might prefer to take an audio or guided tour.

Of particular interest are the Hall of Hector and Andromache *(Sala di Ettore e Andromaca)*, once illustrated with scenes from Homer's *Iliad;* the Hall of Achilles *(Sala di Achille)*, with a gigantic shell decoration; the Hall of Ninfeo *(Sala di Ninfeo)*, which once had a waterfall; and the Hall of the Gilded Vault *(Sala della Volta Dorata)*, depicting satyrs raping nymphs, plus Cupid driving a chariot pulled by panthers. You'll be amazed by the beauty of the floral frescoes along the *cryptoportici* (long corridors); the longest is about 60m (200 ft.). The most spectacular sight is the Octagonal Hall, Nero's banqueting hall, where the menu included casseroles of flamingo tongues and other rare dishes. When Nero moved in, he shouted, "At last I can start living like a human being!"

Practical matters: When visiting the Domus Aurea, chances are you can purchase a ticket on site and return anywhere from 1 to 3 hours later for your tour. If you want more certainty of the date and time of your tour, make a reservation (by phone) at Pierreci, Via Tunisis 4 (bus no. 55N, 490, or 492; Mon–Sat 9am–1:30pm and 2:30–5pm). You may also book your visit before you leave home through Select Italy (© **847/853-1667** in the U.S.; www.selectitaly.com). Or, once you're in Rome, call © **06-39967600,** where a recorded message in both Italian and English will guide you through the reservation process. The tours (whether guided or audio) last about 1 hour. Visitors enter in groups of no more than 25. Guided tours cost 3.50€ ($4.20) and are offered daily January to May and October to December at 11:20am and 6pm, and daily June to September at 11am and 3:20pm. Audio tours cost 2€ ($2.40).

Via della Domus Aurea. © **06-39967700.** Admission 5€ ($6), plus 1.50€ ($1.80) for a reservation. Wed–Mon 9am–7:45pm. Last admission 1 hr. before closing. Metro: Colosseo.

Roman Forum (Foro Romano), Palatine Hill (Palatino), and Palatine Museum (Museo Palatino) *୧୧୧*   When it came to cremating Caesar, purchasing

---

Tips **No More Lines**

The endless lines outside Italian museums and attractions are a fact of life. But reservation services can help you avoid the wait, at least for some of the major museums. Select Italy allows you to reserve tickets for the Colosseum, the Palatine and Forum & Museum, Palazzo Altemps, the Domus Aurea, the Galleria Borghese, and more, plus many other museums in Florence and Venice. The cost varies from 17€ to 35€ ($20–$42), depending on the museum, and several combination passes are available. Contact Select Italy at (© **847/853-1667**), or buy your tickets online at **www.selectitaly.com**.

a harlot for the night, or sacrificing a naked victim, the Roman Forum was the place to be. Traversed by the **Via Sacra (Sacred Way)** ⊛, the Broadway of ancient Rome, the Forum was built in the marshy land between the Palatine and Capitoline hills, and it flourished as the center of Roman life in the days of the Republic before it gradually lost prestige to the Imperial Forums.

You'll see only ruins and fragments, an arch or two, and lots of overturned boulders, but with some imagination you can feel the rush of history here. That any semblance of the Forum remains today is miraculous because it was used for years (like the Colosseum) as a quarry. Eventually it reverted to what the Italians call a *campo vaccino* (cow pasture). But excavations in the 19th century began to bring to light one of the world's most historic spots.

By day, the columns of now-vanished temples and the stones from which long-forgotten orators spoke are mere shells. Bits of grass and weeds grow where a triumphant Caesar was once lionized. But at night, when the Forum is silent in the moonlight, it isn't difficult to imagine vestal virgins still guarding the sacred temple fire. The best view of the Roman Forum at night is from Campidoglio, or Capitoline Hill, Michelangelo's Renaissance piazza that overlooks the Forum.

You can spend at least a morning wandering alone through the ruins of the Forum. If you're content with just looking at the ruins, you can do so at your leisure. To imbue the stones with some meaning, buy a detailed plan at the gate (the temples are hard to locate otherwise).

Turn right at the bottom of the entrance slope to walk west along the old Via Sacra toward the arch. Just before it on your right is the large brick **Curia** ⊛⊛ built by Julius Caesar, the main seat of the Roman Senate (pop inside to see the 3rd-c. marble inlay floor).

The triumphal **Arch of Septimius Severus** ⊛⊛ (A.D. 203) displays time-bitten reliefs of the emperor's victories in what are today Iran and Iraq. During the Middle Ages, Rome became a provincial backwater, and frequent flooding of the nearby river helped to rapidly bury most of the Forum. This former center of the empire became a cow pasture. Some bits did still stick out above ground, including the top half of this arch, which was used to shelter a barbershop! It wasn't until the 19th century that people really became interested in excavating these ancient ruins to see what Rome in its glory must have been like.

Just to the left of the arch, you can make out the remains of a cylindrical lump of rock with some marble steps curving off it. That round stone was the **Umbilicus Urbus,** considered the center of Rome and of the entire Roman Empire; the curving steps are those of the **Imperial Rostra** ⊛, where great orators and legislators stood to speak, and the people gathered to listen. Nearby, the much-photographed trio of fluted columns with Corinthian capitals supporting a bit of architrave form the corner of the **Temple of Vespasian and Titus** ⊛⊛ (emperors were routinely turned into gods upon dying).

Start heading to your left toward the eight Ionic columns marking the front of the **Temple of Saturn** ⊛⊛ (rebuilt 42 B.C.), which housed the first treasury of Republican Rome. It was also the site of one of the Roman year's biggest annual blowout festivals, the December 17 feast of *Saturnalia,* which, after a bit of tweaking, is now celebrated as Christmas. Now turn left to start heading back east, past the worn steps and stumps of brick pillars outlining the enormous **Basilica Julia** ⊛⊛, built by Julius Caesar. Past it are the three Corinthian columns of the **Temple of the Dioscuri** ⊛⊛⊛,

Hollywood on the Tiber

The days of the '50s and '60s when all of Hollywood seemed to show up in Rome, and the paparazzi mobbed such Hollywood stars as Elizabeth Taylor and Ingrid Bergman along the Via Veneto, are but lovely memories. Even if you didn't see these major films previewed below at the time of their release, you can catch all of them on the late show. Movie buffs are fond of visiting the actual sites where these films were shot.

No street in Rome was more famous than the *Via Veneto* when Federico Fellini released his now classic *La Dolce Vita* in 1960. It's no longer chic, but there was a time you could see Shelley Winters and Vittorio Gassman battling each other here for the benefit of the paparazzi.

The stars of *La Dolce Vita,* Marcello Mastroianni and Anita Ekberg, also frolicked in the rococo *Fountain of Trevi.* Tourists still come here to toss coins in the fountain, as the actors did in the 1954 film *Three Coins in the Fountain,* which is said to ensure their return to The Eternal City.

It was on Via Margutta that Gregory Peck spent the night with his runaway princess, Audrey Hepburn, in *Roman Holiday* (1953). Fellini and his wife, Giulietta Masina, once lived on this street as well. In one of *Roman Holiday*'s most memorable scenes, the Bocca della Verità, at Santa Maria in Cosmedin, 18 Piazza della Verità, is still standing. This ancient stone face is said to bite those who dare to lie while sticking their hand in the "mouth of truth."

It was along Via Montecuccoli that Anna Magnani, playing Pina, was gunned down on her wedding day in one of the most unforgettable scenes from Roberto Rossellini's 1945 *Rome, Open City.*

More recent films include 1999's *The Talented Mr. Ripley,* starring Matt Damon as the Machiavellian Tom Ripley. Based on the Patricia Highsmith novel, this thriller features many gorgeous shots of Rome.

In 1996, scenes from Jane Campion's *Portrait of a Lady* were shot at the Palazzo dei Conservatori, at Piazza del Campodoglio. In the courtyard here, Isabel Archer (played by Nicole Kidman) faces the cruel fact that her marriage is as fragmented as the pieces of Constantine's statue stacked against the wall.

dedicated to the Gemini twins, Castor and Pollux. Forming one of the most celebrated sights of the Roman Forum, a trio of columns supports an architrave fragment. The founding of this temple dates from the 5th century B.C.

Beyond the bit of curving wall that marks the site of the little round **Temple of Vesta** (rebuilt several times after fires started by the sacred flame housed within), you'll find the partially reconstructed **House of the Vestal Virgins** ✯✯ (3rd–4th c. A.D.) against the south side of the grounds. This was the home of the consecrated young women who tended the sacred flame in the Temple of Vesta. Vestals were young girls chosen from patrician families to serve a 30-year-long priesthood. During their tenure, they were among Rome's most venerated citizens, with unique powers such as the ability to pardon condemned criminals. The cult was quite serious about the "virgin" part of the job description—if any of Vesta's earthly servants were found to have "misplaced" their virginity, the miscreant Vestal was summarily buried alive. (Her amorous accomplice was merely flogged to death.) The overgrown rectangle of their gardens has lilied goldfish ponds and is lined with broken, heavily worn statues of senior Vestals on pedestals (and, at any given time when the guards aren't looking, two to six tourists are posing as Vestal Virgins on the empty pedestals).

The path dovetails back to join Via Sacra at the entrance. Turn right and then left to enter the massive brick remains and coffered ceilings of the 4th-century **Basilica of Constantine and Maxentius** ✦✦. These were Rome's public law courts, and their architectural style was adopted by early Christians for their houses of worship (the reason so many ancient churches are called "basilicas").

Return to the path and continue toward the Colosseum, veering right to the second great surviving triumphal arch, the **Arch of Titus** ✦✦ (A.D. 81), on which one relief depicts the carrying off of treasures from Jerusalem's temple—look closely and you'll see a menorah among the booty. The war that this arch glorifies ended with the expulsion of Jews from the colonized Judea, signaling the beginning of the Jewish Diaspora throughout Europe. From here you can enter and climb the only part of the Forum's archaeological zone that still charges admission, the **Palatine Hill** ✦ (open the same hour as the Forum). Before you make the climb, look for a sign pointing to **Santa Maria Antigua,** the oldest Christian church in the Roman Forum, dating from the 16th century. It's been closed since the early 1980s for a major renovation and the restoration of interior frescoes.

The Palatine, tradition tells us, is the spot on which the first settlers built their huts, under the direction of Romulus. In later years, the hill became a patrician residential district that attracted such citizens as Cicero. In time, however, the area was gobbled up by imperial palaces and drew a famous and infamous roster of tenants, such as Livia (some of the frescoes in the House of Livia are in miraculous condition), Tiberius, Caligula (murdered here by members of his Praetorian Guard), Nero, and Domitian.

Only the ruins of its former grandeur remain today, and you really need to be an archaeologist to make sense of them because they're more difficult to understand than those in the Forum. But even if you're not interested in the past, it's worth the climb for the panoramic view of the Roman and Imperial Forums, as well as the Capitoline Hill and the Colosseum.

The **Palatine Museum (Museo Palatino)** ✦ displays a good collection of Roman sculpture from the ongoing digs in the Palatine villas. In summer you can take guided tours in English Monday through Sunday at noon for 3.50€ ($4.20); call in winter to see if they're still available. If you ask the museum's custodian, he might take you to one of the nearby locked villas and let you in for a peek at surviving frescoes and stuccoes. **Orti Farnesiani** ✦, or the Farnese Gardens, were ordered laid out by Cardinal Alessandro Fernese, Pope Paul III's nephew, in the 16th century. The designer was Gincomo de Vignola, the great Renaissance architect. Resplendent with wild flowers, spring-scented orange groves, and delightful walkways, the site is one of the world's first botanical gardens. It has pavilions, rose gardens, terraces, and **panoramic views** ✦✦ of the Forum over Ancient Rome. Certain sections are sometimes closed due to reconstruction work and ongoing excavations.

Largo Romolo e Remo. ✆ **06-39967700.** Forum free admission; Palatine Hill 10€ ($12; ticket to Palatine good for same-day admission to the Colosseum, and vice versa). Oct 30–Dec 31 and Jan 2–Feb 15 daily 8:30am–4:30pm; Feb

---

Tips **Before & After**

To appreciate the Colosseum, the Roman Forum, and other ruins more fully, buy a copy of the small red book *Rome Past and Present* (Vision Publications), sold in bookstores or by vendors near the Forum. Its plastic overleafs show you the way things looked 2,000 years ago.

16–Mar 15 daily 8:30am–5pm; Mar 16–26 daily 8:30am–5:30pm; Mar 27–Aug 31 daily 8:30am–7:15pm; Sept daily 8:30am–7pm; Oct 1–29 daily 8:30am–6:30pm. Last admission 1 hr. before closing. Guided tours of the Roman Forum in are given in English daily at 10:30am, 3.50€ ($4.55); guided tours of the Roman Forum in English daily at noon. Guided tours in English cost 3€ ($3.60), last 1 hour, and are given daily at 11am. Closed holidays. Metro: Colosseo. Bus: 60, 75, 85, 87, 95, or 175.

Imperial Forums (Fori Imperiali) 🐾🐾 It was Mussolini who issued the controversial orders to cut through centuries of debris and junky buildings to carve out Via dei Fori Imperiali, thereby linking the Colosseum to the grand 19th-century monuments of Piazza Venezia. Excavations under his fascist regime revealed many archaeological treasures.

Begun by Julius Caesar as an answer to the overcrowding of Rome's older forums, the Imperial Forums were, at the time of their construction, flashier, bolder, and more impressive than the buildings in the Roman Forum. This site conveyed the unquestioned authority of the emperors at the height of their absolute power. On the street's north side, you'll come to a large outdoor restaurant, where Via Cavour joins the boulevard. Just beyond the small park across Via Cavour are the remains of the **Forum of Nerva,** built by the emperor whose 2-year reign (A.D. 96–98) followed that of the paranoid Domitian. You'll be struck by just how much the ground level has risen in 19 centuries. The only really recognizable remnant is a wall of the Temple of Minerva with two fine Corinthian columns. This forum was once flanked by that of Vespasian, which is now gone. It's possible to enter the Forum of Nerva from the other side, but you can see it just as well from the railing.

The next forum you approach is the **Forum of Augustus** 🐾🐾, built before the birth of Christ to commemorate the emperor's victory over the assassins Cassius and Brutus in the Battle of Philippi (42 B.C.). Like the Forum of Nerva, you can enter this forum from the other side (cut across the tiny footbridge).

Continuing along the railing, you'll see the vast semicircle of **Trajan's Market** 🐾🐾, Via Quattro Novembre 144 (📞 **06-6790048,** see p. 187), whose teeming arcades stocked with merchandise from the far corners of the Roman world collapsed long ago, leaving only a few cats to watch after things. The shops once covered a multitude of levels, and you can still wander around many of them. In front of the perfectly proportioned facade (designed by Apollodorus of Damascus at the beginning of the 2nd c.) are the remains of a great library, and fragments of delicately colored marble floors still shine in the sun between stretches of rubble and tall grass. Trajan's Market is worth the descent below street level. To get there, follow the service road you're on until you reach the monumental Trajan's Column on your left; turn right and go up the steep flight of stairs leading to Via Nazionale. At the top, about half a block farther on the right, you'll see the entrance. It's open Monday through Saturday from 9am to 6pm. Admission is 5.10€ ($6.10).

Before you head down through the labyrinthine passages, you might like to climb the **Tower of the Milizie** ★, a 12th-century structure that was part of the medieval headquarters of the Knights of Rhodes. The view from the top (if it's open) is well worth the climb.

You can enter the **Forum of Trajan** ★★ on Via Quattro Novembre near the steps of Via Magnanapoli. Once through the tunnel, you'll emerge into the newest and most beautiful of the Imperial Forums, built between A.D. 107 and 113, and designed by Greek architect Apollodorus of Damascus (who laid out the adjoining market). There are many statue fragments and pedestals bearing still-legible inscriptions, but more interesting is the great Basilica Ulpia, whose gray marble columns rise roofless into the sky. This forum was once regarded as one of the architectural wonders of the world.

Beyond the Basilica Ulpia is **Trajan's Column** ★★★, in magnificent condition, with intricate bas-relief sculpture depicting Trajan's victorious campaign (though, from your vantage point, you'll be able to see only the earliest stages). The next stop is the **Forum of Julius Caesar** ★★, the first of the Imperial Forums. It lies on the opposite side of Via dei Fori Imperiali. This was the site of the Roman stock exchange as well as the Temple of Venus.

After you've seen the wonders of ancient Rome, you might continue up Via dei Fori Imperiali to **Piazza Venezia** ★★, where the white Brescian marble **Vittorio Emanuele Monument** dominates the scene. (You can't miss it.) Italy's most flamboyant landmark, it was built in the late 1800s to honor the first king of Italy. It has been compared to everything from a frosty wedding cake to a Victorian typewriter and has been ridiculed because of its harsh white color in a city of honey-gold tones. An eternal flame burns at the Tomb of the Unknown Soldier. The interior of the monument has been closed for many years, but you'll come to use it as a landmark as you figure your way around the city.

Via de Fori Imperiali. Free admission. Metro: Colosseo. Keep to the right side of the street.

Circus Maximus (Circo Massimo)

The Circus Maximus, with its elongated oval proportions and ruined tiers of benches, still evokes the setting of *Ben-Hur*. Today a formless ruin, the once-grand circus was pilfered repeatedly by medieval and Renaissance builders in search of marble and stone. At one time, 250,000 Romans could assemble on the marble seats while the emperor observed the games from his box high on the Palatine Hill. What the Romans called a "circus" was a large arena enclosed by tiers of seats on three or four sides, used especially for sports or spectacles.

The circus lies in a valley formed by the Palatine on the left and the Aventine on the right. Next to the Colosseum, it was the most impressive structure in ancient Rome, located in one of the most exclusive neighborhoods. For centuries, the pomp and ceremony of imperial chariot races filled this valley with the cheers of thousands.

When the dark days of the 5th and 6th centuries fell, the Circus Maximus seemed symbolic of Rome's complete ruin. The last games were held in A.D. 549 on the orders of Totila the Goth, who had seized Rome in 547 and established himself as emperor. He lived in the still-glittering ruins on the Palatine and apparently thought the chariot races in the Circus Maximus would lend credibility to his charade of an empire. It must've been a pretty miserable show because the decimated population numbered something like 500 when Totila recaptured the city. The Romans of these times were caught between Belisarius, the imperial general from Constantinople, and Totila the Goth, both of whom fought bloodily for control of Rome. After the travesty of 549, the Circus Maximus was never used again, and the demand for building materials reduced it, like so much of Rome, to a great dusty field.

Between Via dei Cerchi and Via del Circo Massimo. Metro: Circo Massimo. Bus: 30, 60, 75, 95, 118, 170, or 175.

Capitoline Museum (Museo Capitolino) and Palazzo dei Conservatori 𝄢𝄢

Of Rome's seven hills, the Capitoline (Campidoglio) is the most sacred—its origins stretch way back into antiquity (an Etruscan temple to Jupiter once stood on this spot). Climbing Michelangelo's long, sloping steps makes for a dramatic approach. At the top is a perfectly proportioned square, **Piazza del Campidoglio** 𝄢𝄢, also laid out by the Florentine artist. Michelangelo positioned the bronze equestrian statue of Marcus Aurelius in the center, but it has now been moved inside for protection from pollution (a copy was placed on the pedestal in 1997). The other steps adjoining Michelangelo's approach will take you to Santa Maria d'Aracoeli (see "Other Attractions near Ancient Rome," below).

One side of the piazza is open; the others are bounded by the **Senatorium (Town Council),** the statuary-filled **Palace of the Conservatori (Curators),** and the **Capitoline Museum.** These museums house some of the greatest pieces of classical sculpture in the world.

The **Capitoline Museum,** built in the 17th century, was based on an architectural sketch by Michelangelo. In the first room is *The Dying Gaul* 𝄢𝄢, a work of majestic skill that's a copy of a Greek original dating from the 3rd century B.C. In a special gallery all her own is the *Capitoline Venus* 𝄢𝄢, who demurely covers herself. This statue was the symbol of feminine beauty and charm down through the centuries (also a Roman copy of a 3rd-c. B.C. Greek original). *Amore* (Cupid) and *Psyche* are up to their old tricks near the window.

The famous **equestrian statue of Marcus Aurelius** 𝄢𝄢, whose years in the piazza made it a victim of pollution, has recently been restored and is now kept in the museum for protection. This is the only bronze equestrian statue to have survived from ancient Rome, mainly because it was thought for centuries that the statue was that of Constantine the Great, and papal Rome respected the memory of the first Christian emperor. The statue is housed in an impressive, newly-opened exhibition area, along with several other Capitoline treasures.

The **Palace of the Conservatori** 𝄢𝄢, across the way, was also based on a Michelangelo architectural plan and is rich in classical sculpture and paintings. One of the most notable bronzes, a Greek work of incomparable beauty dating from the 1st century B.C., is *Lo Spinario* 𝄢𝄢𝄢 (a little boy picking a thorn from his foot). In addition, you'll find *Lupa Capitolina (Capitoline Wolf)* 𝄢𝄢𝄢, a rare Etruscan bronze that could date from the 5th century B.C. (Romulus and Remus, the legendary twins who were suckled by the wolf, were added at a later date.) The palace also contains a *Pinacoteca*

⌒*Moments* A View to Remember

Standing on Piazza del Campidoglio, walk around the right side of the Palazzo Senatorio to a terrace overlooking the city's best panorama of the Roman Forum, with the Palatine Hill and the Colosseum as a backdrop. At night, the Forum is dramatically floodlit and the ruins look even more impressive and haunting.

(Picture Gallery)—mostly works from the 16th and 17th centuries. Notable canvases are Caravaggio's *Fortune-Teller* and his curious *John the Baptist; The Holy Family,* by Dosso Dossi; *Romulus and Remus,* by Rubens; and Titian's *Baptism of Christ.* The entrance courtyard is lined with the remains (head, hands, a foot, and a kneecap) of an ancient colossal statue of Constantine the Great.

Piazza del Campidoglio. © **06-67102071.** Admission (to both) 7.80€ ($9.35). Tues–Sun 9am–8pm. Bus: 30, 40, 62, 64, 70, 87, 95, 170, 492, or 628.

Baths of Caracalla (Terme di Caracalla) ℱ   Named for Emperor Caracalla, the baths were completed in the early 3rd century. The richness of decoration has faded, and the lushness can be judged only from the shell of brick ruins that remain. In their heyday, they sprawled across 11 hectares (27 acres) and could handle 1,600 bathers at one time. As such, these baths are the largest to survive from Rome's imperial era. The baths are in a bad state of disrepair. Because of decay, sections will sometimes close without notice. Most tours start with a visit to the *palestra* or gym, followed by a look at the *laconicum* or Turkish bath. You can also view the *caldarium* which was the "boiling pot" section of the baths. Sweaty bodies cooled down afterward with a soak in the lukewarm waters of the *tepidarium.* The session for the Romans ended at the *frigidarium* with a dip in cold waters. These hot immersions and cold dips were followed by massages and rubdowns by slave boys, many of whom were also recruited for their sexual services to their Roman masters. There remain the ruins of an open-air *natatio* or swimming pool.

Via delle Terme di Caracalla 52. © **06-39967700.** Admission 6€ ($7.20). Oct daily 9am–6pm; Nov and Dec daily 9am–4:30pm; Jan–Feb 15 daily 9am–4:30pm; Feb 16–Mar 15 daily 9am–5pm; Mar 16–27 daily 9am–5:30pm; Mar 28–Aug daily 9am–7:15pm; Sept daily 9am–7pm. Last admission 1 hr. before closing. Closed holidays. Bus: 30, 60, 75, 95, 118, or 170.

OTHER ATTRACTIONS NEAR ANCIENT ROME

Basilica di San Clemente ℱ   From the Colosseum, head up Via San Giovanni in Laterano to this basilica. It isn't just another Roman church—far from it. In this church-upon-a-church, centuries of history peel away. In the 4th century A.D., a church was built over a secular house from the 1st century, beside which stood a pagan temple dedicated to Mithras (god of the sun). Down in the eerie grottoes (which you can explore on your own), you'll discover well-preserved frescoes from the 9th to the 11th centuries. The Normans destroyed the lower church, and a new one was built in the 12th century. Its chief attraction is the bronze-orange mosaic (from that period) adorning the apse, as well as a chapel honoring St. Catherine of Alexandria with frescoes by Masolino.

Via San Giovanni in Laterano at Piazza San Clemente, Via Labicana 95. © **06-7740021.** Basilica free admission; excavations 3€ ($3.60). Mon–Sat 9am–noon and 3–6:30pm; Sun 10am–noon and 3–6:30pm. Metro: Colosseo. Bus: 85, 87, or 850.

Basilica di San Giovanni in Laterano ℱ   This church (not St. Peter's) is the cathedral of the diocese of Rome, where the pope comes to celebrate Mass on certain holidays. Built in A.D. 314 by Constantine, it has suffered the vicissitudes of Rome, forcing it to be rebuilt many times. Only fragmented parts of the original baptistry remain.

The present building is characterized by its 18th-century facade by Alessandro Galilei (statues of Christ and the Apostles ring the top). A 1993 terrorist bomb caused severe damage, especially to the facade. Borromini gets the credit (some say blame) for

---

Moments Rome from a Tiber Perspective

Battelli di Roma (*©* **06-69294147;** www.battellidiroma.it) runs tours aboard a "water bus" that passes under the bridges of Rome. You'll see such landmarks as St. Peter's Basilica (in the distance), Castel Sant'Angelo, and the little island in the Tiber, Isola Tiberina. If you want to use the bus as transportation, the cost of a one-way ticket is just 1€ ($1.20). For a 75-minute guided tour, you'll pay 12€ ($14). Children ages 6 to 12 pay 6.50€ ($7.80); under 6 ride for free. Tours start at Ponte Sant'Angelo near the Vatican and are conducted daily at 10am, 11:30am, 3:30pm, and 5pm. An evening tour that includes a four-course dinner departs nightly from Ponte Sant'Angelo at 8pm and lasts 2½ hours. The cost is 53€ ($64) for adults and 51€ ($61) for kids.

---

the interior, built for Innocent X. It's said that, in the misguided attempt to redecorate, frescoes by Giotto were destroyed (remains believed to have been painted by Giotto were discovered in 1952 and are now on display against a column near the entrance on the right inner pier). In addition, look for the unusual ceiling and the sumptuous transept, and explore the 13th-century cloisters with twisted double columns. Next door, **Palazzo Laterano** (not open to the public) was the original home of the popes before they became voluntary "Babylonian captives" in Avignon, France, in 1309.

Across the street is the **Santuario della Scala Santa (Palace of the Holy Steps),** Piazza San Giovanni in Laterano (*©* **06-7726641**). It's alleged that the 28 marble steps here (now covered with wood for preservation) were originally at Pontius Pilate's villa in Jerusalem and that Christ climbed them the day he was brought before Pilate. According to a medieval tradition, Constantine's mother, Helen, brought the steps from Jerusalem to Rome in 326, and they've been in this location since 1589. Today pilgrims from all over the world come here to climb the steps on their knees. This is one of the holiest sites in Christendom, although some historians say the stairs might date only to the 4th century. **Santuario della Scala Santa** is open daily 6:15am to noon and 3:30 to 6:30pm.

Piazza San Giovanni in Laterano 4. *©* **06-69886452.** Basilica free admission; cloisters 2€ ($2.40). Summer daily 7am–6:45pm (off season to 6pm). Metro: San Giovanni.

Galleria Colonna *☆ (Finds*   For those who saw the classic Audrey Hepburn film, *Roman Holiday,* this spectacular private *palazzo,* with its 17th-century *Sala Grande,* is already familiar to you. In it, Hepburn, playing a princess, held a press conference where she bid an elegant adieu to the handsome reporter she'd fallen in love with, Gregory Peck. Today the palace houses a celebrated art collection in its *Galeria Colonna,* which has extremely limited visiting times. The art collection is one of the most prestigious in Rome, all of it acquired after the Renaissance. The greatest art is from the 17th century, and the collection embraces many grand masters of Europe, including small paintings on copper by Jan Brueghel the Elder. Note also the series of eternally fresh temperas by Gaspard Dughet. There are also several magnificent paintings by Gasper van Wittel, among others. The beautiful, even lavishly decorated rooms of the palace compete with the art itself. Frescoes, for example, by the famous Bernardino di Betto (better known as "Pinturicchio"), decorate the ceiling of "the Room of the Fountain."

Piazza SS, Apostoli 66. ✆ **06-6794362.** www.galleriacolonna.it. Admission 7€ ($8.40) or 5.50€ ($6.60) for those under 10 and over 65. Sat only 9am–1pm. Metro: Colosseo.

National Museum of Palazzo Venezia (Museo Nazionale di Palazzo Venezia) ✦

The Palazzo Venezia, in the geographic heart of Rome near Piazza Venezia, served as the seat of the Austrian Embassy until the end of World War I. During the fascist regime (1928–43), it was the seat of the Italian government. The balcony from which Mussolini used to speak to the people was built in the 15th century. You can now visit the rooms and halls containing oil paintings, porcelain, tapestries, ivories, and ceramics. No one particular exhibit stands out—it's the sum total that adds up to a major attraction. The State Rooms occasionally open to host temporary exhibits.

Via del Plebiscito 118. ✆ **06-69994318.** Admission 4€ ($4.80). Tues–Sun 8:30am–7:30pm. Bus: 30, 40, 60, 62, 64, 70, 85, 87, or 492.

St. Peter in Chains (San Pietro in Vincoli) ✦

This church, which has undergone recent renovations, was founded in the 5th century to house the chains that bound St. Peter in Palestine (they're preserved under glass). But its drawing card is the tomb of Pope Julius II, with one of the world's most famous sculptures: **Michelangelo's *Moses* ✦✦✦**. Michelangelo was to have carved 44 magnificent figures for the tomb. That didn't happen, but the pope was given a great consolation prize—a figure intended to be "minor" that's now counted among Michelangelo's masterpieces. In the *Lives of the Artists,* Vasari wrote about the stern father symbol of Michelangelo's *Moses:* "No modern work will ever equal it in beauty, no, nor ancient either."

Piazza San Pietro in Vincoli 4A (off Via degli Annibaldi). ✆ **06-4882865.** Free admission. Spring/summer daily 7am–12:30pm and 3:30–7pm (fall/winter to 6pm). Metro: Colosseo or Cavour, and then cross the boulevard and walk up the flight of stairs. Turn right, and you'll head into the piazza; the church will be on your left.

Fun Fact Did You Know?

- Along with miles of headless statues and acres of paintings, Rome has 913 churches.
- Some Mongol khans and Turkish chieftains pushed westward to conquer the Roman Empire after it had ceased to exist.
- At the time of Julius Caesar and Augustus, Rome's population reached one million—it was the largest city in the Western world. Some historians claim that by the year A.D. 500, only 10,000 inhabitants were left.
- Pope Leo III snuck up on Charlemagne and set an imperial crown on his head, a surprise coronation that launched a precedent of Holy Roman Emperors being crowned by popes in Rome.
- More than 90% of Romans live in apartment buildings, some of which rise 10 floors and have no elevators.
- The Theater of Marcellus incorporated a gory realism in some of its stage plays: Condemned prisoners were often butchered before audiences as part of the plot.
- Christians might not have been fed to the lions at the Colosseum, but in 1 day 5,000 animals were slaughtered (about 1 every 10 sec.). North Africa's native lions and elephants were rendered extinct.

Santa Maria d'Aracoeli ✦   On the Capitoline Hill, [...] built for the Franciscans in the 13th century. According [...] ordered a temple erected on this spot, where a sibyl forecas [...] the interior are a coffered Renaissance ceiling and a mosaic [...] in the Byzantine style. If you poke around, you'll find a tom [...] Renaissance sculptor Donatello. The church is known for its [...] terpiece by Pinturicchio, who frescoed it with scenes illustra [...] St. Bernardino of Siena. He also depicted St. Francis recei [...] frescoes are a high point in early Renaissance Roman painti.... You have to climb a long flight of steep steps to reach the church, unless you're already on neighboring Piazza del Campidoglio, in which case you can cross the piazza and climb the steps on the far side of the Museo Capitolino (see above).

Piazza d'Aracoeli. ✆ **06-6798155.** Free admission. Daily 9am–12:30pm and 3:30–5:30pm. Bus: 30, 40, 62, 64, 70, 87, 95, 170, or 492.

Santa Maria in Cosmedin   This little church was begun in the 6th century but was subsequently rebuilt, and a Romanesque campanile was added at the end of the 11th century, although its origins go back to the 3rd century. The church was destroyed several times by earthquakes or by foreign invasions, but it has always been rebuilt.

People come not for great art treasures, but to see the **"Mouth of Truth,"** a large disk under the portico. As Gregory Peck demonstrated to Audrey Hepburn in the film *Roman Holiday,* the mouth is supposed to chomp down on the hands of liars who insert their paws. (According to local legend, a former priest used to keep a scorpion in back to bite the fingers of anyone he felt was lying.) The purpose of this disk (which is not of particular artistic interest) is unclear. One hypothesis says that it was used to collect the faithful's donations to God, which were introduced through the open mouth.

Piazza della Bocca della Verità 18. ✆ **06-6781419.** Free admission. Summer daily 9am–8pm; off-season daily 9am–5pm. Metro: Circo Massimo.

3 The Pantheon & Attractions near Piazza Navona & Campo de' Fiori

THE PANTHEON & NEARBY ATTRACTIONS

The Pantheon stands on **Piazza della Rotonda,** a lively square with cafes, vendors, and great people-watching.

The Pantheon ✦✦✦   Of all ancient Rome's great buildings, only the Pantheon (All the Gods) remains intact. It was built in 27 B.C. by Marcus Agrippa and was reconstructed by Hadrian in the early 2nd century A.D. This remarkable building, 43m (142 ft.) wide and 43m (142 ft.) high (a perfect sphere resting in a cylinder) and once ringed with white marble statues of Roman gods in its niches, is among the architectural wonders of the world because of its dome and its concept of space. Hadrian himself is credited with the basic plan, an architectural design that was unique for the time. The once-gilded dome is merely show. A real dome, a perfect hemisphere of cast concrete, rests on a solid ring wall, supporting this massive structure. Before the 20th century, this was the biggest pile of concrete ever constructed. The ribbed dome outside is a series of almost weightless cantilevered brick. Animals were sacrificed ar[...] burned in the center, and the smoke escaped through the only means of light, the [...] lus, an opening at the top 5.4m (18 ft.) in diameter. Michelangelo came here [...]

e designing the cupola of St. Peter's (whose dome is .6m/2 ft. smaller
theon's). The walls are 7.5m (25 ft.) thick, and the bronze doors leading
building weigh 20 tons each. About 125 years ago, Raphael's tomb was dis-
d here (fans still bring him flowers). Vittorio Emanuele II, king of Italy, and his
cessor, Umberto I, are interred here as well.

Piazza della Rotonda. © 06-68300230. Free admission. Mon–Sat 8:30am–7:30pm; Sun 9am–6pm. Bus: 46, 62,
64,170, or 492 to Largo di Torre.

Galleria Doria Pamphilj ✦   This museum offers a look at what it was like to live
in an 18th-century palace. It has been restored to its former splendor and expanded
to include four rooms long closed to the public. It's partly leased to tenants (on the
upper levels), and there are shops on the street level—but you'll overlook all this after
entering the grand apartments of the Doria Pamphilj family, which traces its lineage
to before the great 15th-century Genoese admiral Andrea Doria. The apartments surround the central court and gallery. The **ballroom, drawing rooms, dining rooms,**
and **family chapel** are full of gilded furniture, crystal chandeliers, Renaissance tapestries, and family portraits. The **Green Room** is especially rich, with a 15th-century
Tournay tapestry, paintings by Memling and Filippo Lippi, and a seminude portrait
of Andrea Doria by Sebastiano del Piombo. The **Andrea Doria Room,** dedicated to
the admiral and to the ship of the same name, contains a glass case with mementos of
the great 1950s maritime disaster.

   Skirting the central court is a **picture gallery** with a memorable collection of frescoes, paintings, and sculpture. Most important are the portrait of Innocent X, by
Velázquez; *Salome,* by Titian; works by Rubens and Caravaggio; the *Bay of Naples,* by
Pieter Brueghel the Elder; and a copy of Raphael's portrait of Principessa Giovanna
d'Aragona de Colonna (who looks remarkably like Leonardo's *Mona Lisa*). Most of the
sculpture came from the Doria country estates: marble busts of Roman emperors,
bucolic nymphs, and satyrs.

Piazza del Collegio Romano 2 (off Via del Corso). © 06-6797323. Admission 8€ ($10) adults, 5.70€ ($6.85) stu-
dents/seniors. Fri–Wed 10am–5pm. Closed on holidays. Private visits can be arranged. Metro: Barberini or Colosseo.

Santa Maria Sopra Minerva   Beginning in 1280, early Christian leaders ordained
that the foundation of an ancient temple dedicated to Minerva (goddess of wisdom)

⟨Moments **Where Emperors Ruled & Cats Now Reign**

At the site where it is believed that Julius Caesar was stabbed to death, right in
the heart of historic Rome, you can visit the city's vast feline population. The
Torre Argentina Cat Sanctuary, at Largo di Torre Argentina (© 06-6872133;
www.romancats.de), is at the intersection of via Arenula and via Florida, right
off Corso Vittorio Emanuele, a short walk from the Pantheon and Piazza
Navona. Where four Republican-era temples dating from 200 to 300 B.C. once
e 300 abandoned house cats are cared for by a group of vol-
ll shapes and sizes are everywhere, craving human attention.
d homes with visitors from around the world. The attraction
ly from noon to 6pm (until 8pm in summer). The cats will be

Campidoglio (Capitoline Hill) **20**
Campo de' Fiori **26**
Column of Marcus Aurelius **13**
Chiesa del Gesù **23**
Chiesa di San Giovanni dei Fiorentini **1**
Fountain of the Four Rivers **10**
Fountain of the Moor **11**
Fountain of Neptune **9**
Galleria Doria Pamphilj **16**
· Museo Nazionale del Palazzo di Venezia **17**
Palazzo Altemps **4**
Palazzo Farnese **27**
Palazzo Spada **28**
Pantheon **14**
Piazza Colonna **7**
Piazza di Montecitorio **6**
Piazza Navona **10**
Piazza Pasquino **12**
Ponte Sant'Angelo **2**
San Agostino **5**
San Luigi dei Francesi **8**
Santa Maria d'Aracoeli **19**

Santa Maria della Pace **3**
Santa Maria Sopra Minerva **15**
Sant'Andrea della Valle **25**
Sant'Ivo alla Sapienza **13**
Sinagoga Romana & Jewish Museum **21**
Toree Argentina Cat Sanctuary **24**
Turtle Fountain **22**
Vittorio Emanuele Monument **18**

be reused as the base for Rome's only Gothic church. Architectural changes and redecorations in the 1500s and 1900s stripped it of some of its magnificence, but it still includes an awe-inspiring collection of medieval and Renaissance tombs. You'll find a beautiful chapel frescoed by Fillipino Lippi and, to the left of the apse, a muscular *Risen Christ* carrying a rather small marble cross carved by Michelangelo (the bronze drapery covering Christ's nudity was added later). Under the altar lie the remains of St. Catherine of Siena. After St. Catherine died, her head was separated from her body, and now the head is in Siena, where she was born. In the passage to the left of the choir, surrounded by a small fence, is the floor tomb of the great monastic painter Fra Angelico. The amusing baby elephant carrying a small obelisk in the piazza outside was designed by Bernini.

Piazza della Minerva 42. © 06-6793926. Free admission. Daily 8am–7pm. Bus: 30, 40, 62, 64, 70, 87, 116, or 492.

PIAZZA NAVONA & NEARBY ATTRACTIONS

Piazza Navona ✹✹✹, one of the most beautifully baroque sites in all Rome, is an ocher-colored gem, unspoiled by new buildings or traffic. Its shape results from the ruins of the Stadium of Domitian, lying underneath. Great chariot races were once held here (some rather unusual, such as the one in which the head of the winning horse was lopped off as it crossed the finish line and was then carried by runners to be offered as a sacrifice by the Vestal Virgins atop the Capitoline). In medieval times, the popes used to flood the piazza to stage mock naval encounters. Today the piazza is packed with vendors and street performers, and lined with pricey cafes where you can enjoy a cappuccino or gelato and indulge in unparalleled people-watching.

In addition to the twin-towered facade of 17th-century Santa Agnes, the piazza boasts several baroque masterpieces. The best known, in the center, is Bernini's **Fountain of the Four Rivers (Fontana dei Quattro Fiumi)** ✹✹✹, whose four stone personifications symbolize the world's greatest rivers: the Ganges, Danube, della Plata, and Nile. It's fun to try to figure out which is which. (**Hint:** The figure with the shroud on its head is the Nile, so represented because the river's source was unknown at the time.) At the south end is the **Fountain of the Moor (Fontana del Moro),** also by Bernini. The **Fountain of Neptune (Fontana di Nettuno),** which balances that of the Moor, is a 19th-century addition; it was restored after a demented 1997 attack by two men broke the tail of one of its sea creatures. To get there, take bus no. 30, 40, 62, 64, 70, 87, 116, or 492.

Palazzo Altemps ✹   This branch of the National Roman Museum is housed in a 15th-century palace that was restored and opened to the public in 1997. It is home to the fabled Ludovisi Collection of Greek and Roman sculpture. Among the masterpieces of the Roman Renaissance, you'll find the *Ares Ludovisi,* a Roman copy of the original dated 330 B.C. and restored by Bernini during the 17th century. In the *Sala delle Storie di Mosè* is *Ludovisi's Throne,* representing the birth of Venus. The *Sala delle Feste* (the Celebrations' Hall) is dominated by a sarcophagus depicting the Romans fighting against the Ostrogoth Barbarians; this masterpiece, carved from a single block, dates back to the 2nd century A.D. and today is called *Grande Ludovisi* (Great Ludovisi). Other outstanding art from the collection includes a copy of Phidias's celebrated *Athena,* which once stood in the Parthenon in Athens. (The Roman copy here is from the 1st c. B.C. because the original *Athena* is lost to history.) The huge *Dionysus with Satyr* is from the 2nd century A.D.

Piazza San Apollinare 48, near the Piazza Navona. (€) **06-39967700**. Admission 7€ ($8.40). Tues–Sun 9am–7:45pm. Last admission 1 hr. before closing. Bus: 70, 81, 87, or 116.

San Luigi dei Francesi   This has been the national church of France in Rome since 1589, and a stone salamander (the symbol of the Renaissance French monarch François I) is subtly carved into its facade. Inside, in the last chapel on the left, is a noteworthy series of oil paintings on canvas by Caravaggio: the celebrated *Calling of St. Matthew* on the left, *St. Matthew and the Angel* in the center, and the *Martyrdom of St. Matthew* on the right. The "divine" Caravaggio's best painting is the *Calling of St. Matthew*, with his familiar motif—a beautiful young man with a slightly scornful leer.

Via Santa Giovanna d'Arco 5. (€) **06-688271**. Free admission. Fri–Wed 8am–12:30pm and 3:30–7pm; Thurs 8am–12:30pm. Bus: 70, 81, or 87.

Santa Maria della Pace   According to legend, blood flowed from a statue of the Virgin above the altar here after someone threw a pebble at it. This legend motivated Pope Sixtus to rebuild the church in the 1500s on the foundations of an even older sanctuary. For generations after that, its curved porticos, cupola atop an octagonal base, cloisters by Bramante, and frescoes by Raphael helped make it one of the most fashionable churches for aristocrats residing in the surrounding palazzos.

Vicolo del Arco della Pace 5 (off Piazza Navona). (€) **06-6861156**. Free admission. Mon–Sat 10am–noon and 4–6pm; Sun 10am–noon. Bus: 70 or 492.

CAMPO DE' FIORI & THE JEWISH GHETTO

During the 1500s, **Campo de' Fiori** ☆ was the geographic and cultural center of secular Rome, site of dozens of inns. From its center rises a statue of the severe-looking monk Giordano Bruno, whose presence is a reminder that religious heretics were occasionally burned at the stake here. Today, circled by venerable houses, the campo is the site of an **open-air food market** held Monday through Saturday from early in the morning until around noon (or whenever the food runs out). Take bus no. 30, 40, 62, 64, 70, 87, 116, 492, 571, or 628 to Corso Vittorio Emanuele.

Built from 1514 to 1589, the **Palazzo Farnese** ☆, on Piazza Farnese, was designed by Sangallo and Michelangelo, among others, and was an astronomically expensive project for the time. Its famous residents have included a 16th-century member of the Farnese family, plus Pope Paul III, Cardinal Richelieu, and the former Queen Christina of Sweden, who moved to Rome after abdicating. During the 1630s, when the heirs couldn't afford to maintain the palazzo, it became the site of the French Embassy, as it still is (it's closed to the public). For the best view of it, cut west from Via Giulia along any of the narrow streets (we recommend Via Mascherone or Via dei Farnesi).

Palazzo Spada ☆, Capo di Ferro 3 (€) **06-6861158**), built around 1550 for Cardinal Gerolamo Capo di Ferro and later inhabited by the descendants of several other cardinals, was sold to the Italian government in the 1920s. Its richly ornate facade, covered in high-relief stucco decorations in the Mannerist style, is the finest of any building from 16th-century Rome. The State Rooms are closed, but the richly decorated courtyard and a handful of galleries of paintings are open. Admission is 6€ ($7.20); it's open Tuesday through Saturday from 8:30am to 7:30pm. To get there, take bus no. 46, 56, 62, 64, 70, 87, or 492.

Also in this neighborhood stands the **Sinagoga Romana** (€) **06-6840061**), open only for services. Trying to avoid all resemblance to a Christian church, the building (1874–1904) evokes Babylonian and Persian details. The synagogue was attacked by

913 Churches, 1 Synagogue: Jews in the Capital of Christendom

Nestled midway between the Isola Tiberina and the monument to Vittorio Emanuele II, Rome's Jewish ghetto was designated during the administration of Pope Paul IV between 1555 and 1559. At the time, it enclosed several thousand people in a cramped 1-hectare (2½-acre) tract of walled-in, overcrowded real estate that did much to contribute to the oppression of the Jews during the Italian Renaissance.

Jews had played an important part in the life of Rome prior to that time. They migrated to the political center of the known world during the 1st century B.C., and within 200 years, their community had grown to a very noticeable minority. Most of it was based in Trastevere, a neighborhood that for many years was referred to as the *Contrada Iudaeorum* (Jewish Quarter). By 1309, ordinances were passed that forced Jews to indicate their religious and cultural backgrounds with special garments, and their ability to worship as they wished depended on the indulgence of the pope.

In 1363, additional ordinances were passed that limited Jewish cemeteries to an area adjacent to the Tiber, near the present-day Church of San Francesco a Ripa. During the 1400s, the Jewish population regrouped onto the opposite side of the Tiber, in an area around the square that's known today as Piazza Mattei.

In 1492, Queen Isabella and King Ferdinand of Spain killed, tortured, forcibly converted, or forced the emigration of thousands of Jews from Spain. Many came to Rome, swelling the ranks of the city. Pope Alexander VI (1492–1503), whose political sympathies lay firmly with the Spanish monarchs, grudgingly admitted the refugees into his city, on condition that each pay a hefty fee in gold. His papal bull, *Cum nimis absurdium,* defined the borders of the Jewish ghetto within the boundaries of the Sant'Angelo district and

terrorists in 1982 and since then has been heavily guarded by *carabinieri* (a division of the Italian army) armed with machine guns. It houses the **Jewish Museum** (© 06-6840061), open Saturday to Thursday 9am to 5pm, Friday 9am to 12pm. Admission is 7.50€ ($9). Many rare and even priceless treasures are here, including a Moroccan prayer book from the early 14th century and ceremonial objects from the 17th-century Jewish Ghetto.

4 The Spanish Steps, the Trevi Fountain & Attractions Nearby

ON OR AROUND PIAZZA DI SPAGNA

The Spanish Steps ☆☆ (Scalinata di Spagna; Metro: Spagna) are filled in spring with azaleas and other flowers, flower vendors, jewelry dealers, and photographers snapping pictures of visitors. The steps and the square (Piazza di Spagna) take their names from the Spanish Embassy, which used to be headquartered here. Designed by Italian architect Francesco de Sanctis and built from 1723 to 1725, they were funded almost entirely by the French as a preface to Trinità dei Monti at the top.

later enlarged them to include the muddy, frequently flooded banks of the Tiber. Water levels often reached the third floors of the houses of the poorest families, who were forced, by law and economics, to settle here. Piling humiliation on humiliation, the residents of the nearly uninhabitable riverbanks were forced to pay for the construction of the embankments that prevented the neighborhood from flooding. For centuries, no one could enter or leave the ghetto between sundown and sunrise.

In 1848, the walls that had defined and confined the ghetto were demolished under the auspices of the relatively lenient Pope Leo XII. In 1883, during the surge of nationalism that preceded the unification of Italy, the ghetto was abolished altogether.

Tragically, on October 16, 1943, the segregation of Rome's Jews was re-established when German Nazi soldiers rounded up most of the Jews from throughout Rome into a re-creation of the medieval ghetto and imposed a ridiculously high ransom on them. Amazingly, this fee—more than 100 pounds of gold per resident—was eventually collected. Having made the payment, the Jews were rounded up and deported to the death camps anyway, one of the most horrible episodes of Italy's participation in the war years.

Today the neighborhood, centered on Piazza Mattei and its elegant Renaissance fountain, lacks any coherent architectural unity; it's a colorful hodge-podge of narrow, twisting streets and occasionally derelict buildings. One of the most unusual streets is Via del Portico d'Ottavia, where medieval houses and pavements adjoin kosher food stores and simple trattorie that almost invariably feature *carciofi alla Giudeai* (deep-fried Jerusalem artichokes).

Although it bears the scars and honors of centuries of occupation by Jews, today this is a Jewish neighborhood mostly in name only. Its centerpiece is the synagogue on Via Catalana.

The steps and the piazza below are always packed with a crowd: strolling, reading in the sun, browsing the vendors' carts, and people-watching. Near the steps, you'll also find an American Express office, public restrooms (near the Metro stop), and the most sumptuous McDonald's we've ever seen (cause for uproar among the Romans when it first opened).

Keats–Shelley House   At the foot of the Spanish Steps is this 18th-century house where John Keats died of consumption on February 23, 1821, at age 25. Since 1909, when it was bought by well-intentioned English and American literary types, it has been a working library established in honor of Keats and Percy Bysshe Shelley, who drowned off the coast of Viareggio with a copy of Keats's poems in his pocket. Mementos range from the kitsch to the immortal. The apartment where Keats spent his last months, carefully tended by his close friend Joseph Severn, shelters a strange death mask of Keats, as well as the "deadly sweat" drawing by Severn.

Piazza di Spagna 26. (C) 06-6784235. Admission 3.50€ ($4.20). Mon–Fri 9am–1pm and 3–6pm; Sat 11am–2pm and 3–6pm. Guided tours by appointment. Metro: Spagna.

Finds Great Art in the Stables

Across from the Palazzo del Quirinale, the 18th-century Quirinal stables called the **Scuderie del Quirinale or Scuderie Papali,** Via XXIV Maggio 16 (*©* **06-39967500**), originally built for the pope's horses, have been transformed into an art gallery that hosts changing exhibitions. Check to see what's on. Recent exhibits have ranged from 100 masterpieces on loan from the Hermitage to Botticelli's drawings illustrating Dante's *Divine Comedy.* The stables were built on the site of the 3rd-century Temple of Serapis (some of the ruins can still be seen from the glass-enclosed stairs overlooking a private garden). The galleries are open Sunday to Thursday 10am to 8pm, Friday and Saturday 10am to 10:30pm. Admission is 9€ ($10.80).

Palazzo del Quirinale ★★   Until the end of World War II, this palace was the home of the king of Italy; before that, it was the residence of the pope. Despite its Renaissance origins (nearly every important architect in Italy worked on some aspect of its sprawling premises), it's rich in associations with ancient emperors and deities. The colossal statues of the twin heroes, or dioscuri Castor and Pollux, which now form part of the fountain in the piazza, were found in the nearby great Baths of Constantine; in 1793 Pius VI had the ancient Egyptian obelisk moved here from the Mausoleum of Augustus. The sweeping view of Rome from the piazza, which crowns the highest of the seven ancient hills of Rome, is itself worth the trip.

Piazza del Quirinale. Admission 5€ ($6). Sun 8:30am–noon. Metro: Barberini. **Note:** Palazzo del Quirinale remains closed July 3–Sept 11.

Trevi Fountain (Fontana dei Trevi) ★★   As you elbow your way through the summertime crowds around the Trevi Fountain, you'll find it hard to believe that this little piazza was nearly always deserted before the film *Three Coins in the Fountain* brought the stampede of tour buses. Today this newly restored gem is a must on everybody's itinerary.

Supplied by water from the Acqua Vergine aqueduct and a triumph of the baroque style, it was based on the design of Nicolo Salvi (who's said to have died of illness contracted during his supervision of the project) and was completed in 1762. The design centers on the triumphant figure of Neptunus Rex, standing on a shell chariot drawn by winged steeds and led by a pair of tritons. Two allegorical figures in the side niches represent good health and fertility.

On the southwestern corner of the piazza is a somber, not particularly spectacular-looking church, **SS. Vincenzo e Anastasio,** with a strange claim to fame. Within it survive the hearts and intestines of several centuries of popes. According to legend, the church was built on the site of a spring that burst from the earth after the beheading of St. Paul; the spring is one of the *three* sites where his head is said to have bounced off the ground.

Piazza di Trevi. Metro: Barberini. Bus: 62, 85, 95, 175, or 492.

AROUND VIA VENETO & PIAZZA BARBERINI

Piazza Barberini lies at the foot of several Roman streets, among them Via Barberini, Via Sistina, and Via Vittorio Veneto. It would be a far more pleasant spot were it not

Attractions near the Spanish Steps & Piazza del Popolo

City Walls ▬▬▬
Metro Ⓐ▬Ⓜ
Post Office ✉

for the heavy traffic swarming around its principal feature, Bernini's **Fountain of the Triton (Fontana del Tritone)** ✦. For more than 3 centuries, the strange figure sitting in a vast open clam has been blowing water from his triton. Off to one side of the piazza is the aristocratic side facade of the **Palazzo Barberini,** named for one of Rome's powerful families; inside is the **Galleria Nazionale d'Arte Antica** (see below). The Renaissance Barberini reached their peak when a son was elected pope as Urban VIII; he encouraged Bernini and gave him great patronage.

As you go up Via Vittorio Veneto, look for the small fountain on the right corner of Piazza Barberini—it's another Bernini, the small **Fountain of the Bees (Fontana delle Api).** At first they look more like flies, but they're the bees of the Barberini, the crest of that powerful family complete with the crossed keys of St. Peter above them (the keys were always added to a family crest when a son was elected pope).

To find these attractions, see the map titled "Attractions near Stazione Termini, Via Veneto & Piazza Barberini," on p. 171. Metro: Barberini.

National Gallery of Ancient Art (Galleria Nazionale d'Arte Antica) ✦✦
Palazzo Barberini, right off Piazza Barberini, is one of the most magnificent baroque palaces in Rome. It was begun by Carlo Maderno in 1627 and completed in 1633 by Bernini, whose lavishly decorated rococo apartments, the **Gallery of Decorative Art (Galleria d'Arte Decorativa),** are on view. This gallery is part of the National Gallery of Ancient Art.

The bedroom of Princess Cornelia Costanza Barberini and Prince Giulio Cesare Colonna di Sciarra stands just as it was on their wedding night, and many household objects are displayed in the decorative art gallery. In the chambers, which boast frescoes and hand-painted silk linings, you can see porcelain from Japan and Bavaria, canopied beds, and a wooden baby carriage.

On the first floor is a splendid array of paintings from the 13th to the 16th centuries, most notably *Mother and Child,* by Simone Martini, and works by Fillipino Lippi, Andrea Solario, and Francesco Francia. Il Sodoma has some brilliant pictures here, including *The Rape of the Sabines* and *The Marriage of St. Catherine.* One of the best-known paintings is Raphael's beloved *La Fornarina,* the baker's daughter who was his mistress and who posed for his Madonna portraits. Titian is represented by his *Venus and Adonis.* Also here are Tintorettos and El Grecos. Many visitors come just to see the magnificent Caravaggios, including *Narcissus.*

Via Barberini 18. ✆ 06-4824184. Admission 6€ ($7.20). Tues–Sun 9am–7pm. Metro: Barberini.

Monumental Cemetery of the Capuchin Brothers (Cimitero Monumentale dei Padri Cappuccini) One of the most horrifying sights in all Christendom, this is a series of chapels with hundreds of skulls and crossbones woven into mosaic "works

---

⌐ Then&Now **The Call of Rome, Then**

While an interest in history, art, or religion are the most quoted reasons why travelers visit Rome today, a romantic and carefree view of the city as seen in the cinema seems to have been the biggest draw 50 years ago. According to Arthur Frommer, "Rome needs no build up in this book. A vast percentage of Americans saw *Three Coins in a Fountain* and have been aching to get here ever since. They won't be disappointed."

Tips Seeing the Sights at Night

Some of Rome's most popular monuments, archaeological sites, and museums not only stay open until 8 or 10pm during summer, but are also part of a program called **Art and Monuments Under the Stars.** For these special summer schedules, they reopen one or more nights from around 8:30 to 11:30pm. Offerings include guided tours (often in English), concerts, or simply general admission to sights for night owls, with tours of some ancient areas usually closed to the public, such as the Tomb of Augustus and the Stadium of Domitian (under Piazza Navona). Check the events guides from mid-June to September.

---

of art." To make this allegorical dance of death, the bones of more than 4,000 Capuchin brothers were used. Some of the skeletons are intact, draped with Franciscan habits. The creator of this chamber of horrors? The tradition of the friars is that it was the work of a French Capuchin. Their literature suggests that you should visit the cemetery while keeping in mind the historical moment of its origins, when Christians had a rich and creative cult for their dead and great spiritual masters meditated and preached with a skull in hand. Those who've lived through the days of crematoriums and other such massacres might view the graveyard differently, but to many who pause to think, this sight has a message. It's not for the squeamish, however. The entrance is halfway up the first staircase on the right of the church.

Beside the Church of the Immaculate Conception, Via Vittorio Veneto 27. (*C*) **06-4871185.** Donation required. Fri–Wed 9am–1pm and 3–6pm. Metro: Barberini.

NEAR PIAZZA DEL POPOLO

The restored **Piazza del Popolo** 🎭🎭 is haunted with memories. According to legend, the ashes of Nero were enshrined here until 11th-century residents began complaining to the pope about his imperial ghost. The **Egyptian obelisk** dates from the 13th century B.C., removed from Heliopolis to Rome during Augustus's reign (it stood at the Circus Maximus). The piazza was designed in the early 19th century by Valadier, Napoleon's architect. The lovely **Santa Maria del Popolo** 🎭🎭, with two Caravaggios, is at its northern curve, and opposite are almost-twin baroque churches, overseeing the never-ending traffic. Take the Flaminio Metro.

Altar of Peace (Ara Pacis) 🎭   In an airy glass-and-concrete building beside the eastern banks of the Tiber rests a reconstructed treasure from the reign of Augustus. It was built by the Senate as a tribute to that emperor and the peace he brought to the Roman world. On the marble wall, you can see portraits of the imperial family—Augustus, Livia (his second wife), Tiberius (Livia's son from her first marriage and Augustus's successor), and even Julia (Augustus's unfortunate daughter, who divorced her first husband to marry Tiberius and then was exiled by her father for her sexual excesses). The altar was reconstructed from literally hundreds of fragments scattered in museums for centuries. A major portion came from the foundations of a Renaissance palace on the Corso. The reconstruction (quite an archaeologic story in itself) took place during the 1930s.

Lungotevere Augusta. (*C*) **06-82059127.** Admission 6.50€ ($7.80). Tues–Sun 9am–9pm. Bus: 70,

9a.

Augustus's Mausoleum (Mausoleo Augusteo) ⚔ This seemingly indestructible pile of bricks has been here for 2,000 years and will probably remain for another 2,000. Like the larger tomb of Hadrian across the river, this was once a circular marble-covered affair with tall cypresses, symmetrical groupings of Egyptian obelisks, and some of Europe's most spectacular ornamentation. Many of the 1st-century emperors had their ashes deposited in golden urns inside, and it was probably because of this crowding that Hadrian decided to construct an entirely new tomb (the Castel Sant'Angelo) for himself in another part of Rome. The imperial remains stayed intact here until the 5th century, when invading barbarians smashed the bronze gates and stole the golden urns, emptying the ashes on the ground outside. After periods when it functioned as a Renaissance fortress, a bullfighting ring, and a private garden, the tomb was restored in the 1930s by Mussolini, perhaps because he had an eye on it as a burial place for himself. You can't enter, but you can walk along the four streets encircling it.

Piazza Augusto Imperatore. ℂ 06-57250410. Metro: Spagna. Bus: 81, 115, or 590.

5 In the Villa Borghese

Villa Borghese ⚔⚔, in the heart of Rome, is 5.5km (3½ miles) in circumference. One of Europe's most elegant parks, it was created by Cardinal Scipione Borghese in the 1600s. Umberto I, king of Italy, acquired it in 1902 and presented it to the city of Rome. With lovely landscaped vistas, the greenbelt is crisscrossed by roads, but you can escape from the traffic and seek a shaded area under a pine or oak tree to enjoy a picnic or simply relax. On a sunny weekend afternoon, it's a pleasure to stroll here and see Romans at play, relaxing or in-line skating. There are a few casual cafes and some food vendors throughout; you can also rent bikes here. In the northeast of the park is a small zoo; the park is also home to a few outstanding museums.

Galleria Borghese ⚔⚔⚔ After a complete renovation, Galleria Borghese reopened in early 1997. This fabulous treasure trove includes such masterpieces as Bernini's *Apollo and Daphne,* Titian's *Sacred and Profane Love,* Raphael's *Deposition,* and Caravaggio's *Jerome.* The collection began with the gallery's founder, Scipione Borghese, who by the time of his death in 1633 had accumulated some of the greatest art of all time, even managing to acquire Bernini's early sculptures. Some paintings were spirited out of Vatican museums or even confiscated when their rightful owners were hauled off to prison until they became "reasonable" about turning over their art. The great collection suffered at the hands of Napoleon's notorious sister, Pauline, who married Prince Camillo Borghese in 1807 and sold most of the ancient collection (many works are now in the Louvre in Paris). One of the most popular pieces of sculpture in today's gallery, ironically, is Canova's life-size sculpture of Pauline in the pose of *Venus Victorious.* (When Pauline was asked whether she felt uncomfortable posing in the nude, she replied, "Why should I? The studio was heated.")

Important information: No more than 360 visitors at a time are allowed on the ground floor, and no more than 90 are allowed on the upper floor. Reservations are essential, so call ℂ **06-32810** (Mon–Fri 9am–6pm). However, the number always seems to be busy. If you'll be in Rome for a few days, try stopping by in person on your first day to reserve tickets for a later day. Better yet, before you leave home, contact **Select Italy** (ℂ **847/853-1661;** www.selectitaly.com).

Piazza Scipione Borghese 5 (off Via Pinciano). ℂ **06-32810** for information. Admission 8.50€ ($10). Tues–Sun –7pm. Bus: 116 or 910.

National Etruscan Museum (Museo Nazionale di Villa Giulia) ★★★ This 16th-century papal palace shelters a priceless collection of art and artifacts from the mysterious Etruscans, who predated the Romans. Known for their sophisticated art and design, they left a legacy of sarcophagi, bronze sculptures, terra-cotta vases, and jewelry, among other items. If you have time for only the masterpieces, head for room no. 7, with a remarkable 6th-century B.C. *Apollo from Veio* (clothed, for a change). The other two widely acclaimed statues here are *Dea con Bambino (Goddess with a Baby)* and a greatly mutilated but still powerful *Hercules* with a stag. In room no. 8, you'll see the lions' sarcophagus from the mid–6th century B.C., which was excavated at Cerveteri, north of Rome.

Finally, one of the world's most important Etruscan art treasures is the bride and bridegroom coffin from the 6th century B.C., also dug out of the tombs of Cerveteri (in room no. 9). Near the end of your tour, another masterpiece of Etruscan art awaits you in room no. 33: the Cista Ficoroni, a bronze urn with paw feet, mounted by three figures, dating from the 4th century B.C.

Piazzale di Villa Giulia 9. ℭ 06-3201951. Admission 4€ ($4.80). Tues–Sun 8:30am–7:30pm. Metro: Flaminio. Tram: 2, 3, or 19.

National Gallery of Modern Art (Galleria Nazionale d'Arte Moderna) ★ This gallery of modern art is a short walk from the Etruscan Museum (see above). With its neoclassic and Romantic paintings and sculpture, it makes a dramatic change from the glories of the Renaissance and ancient Rome. Its 75 rooms also house the largest collection in Italy of 19th- and 20th-century works by Balla, Boccioni, De Chirico, Morandi, Manzù, Burri, Capogrossi, and Fontana. Look for Modigliani's *La Signora dal Collaretto* and large *Nudo*. There are also many works of Italian optical and pop art and a good representation of foreign artists, including Degas, Cézanne, Monet, and van Gogh. Surrealism and expressionism are well represented by Klee, Ernst, Braque, Mirò, Kandinsky, Mondrian, and Pollock. You'll also find sculpture by Rodin. Several other important sculptures, including one by Canova, are on display in the museum's gardens. You can see the collection of graphics, the storage rooms, and the Department of Restoration by appointment Tuesday through Friday.

Viale delle Belle Arti 131. ℭ 06-322981. Admission 6.50€ ($7.80). Tues–Sun 8:30am–7:30pm. Bus: 19, 95, or 910.

6 The Appian Way & the Catacombs

Of all the roads that led to Rome, **Via Appia Antica** (built in 312 B.C.) was the most famous. It eventually stretched all the way from Rome to the seaport of Brindisi, through which trade with the colonies in Greece and the East was funneled. (According to Christian tradition, it was along the Appian Way that an escaping Peter encountered the vision of Christ, causing him to go back into the city to face subsequent martyrdom.) The road's initial stretch in Rome is lined with the great monuments and ancient tombs of patrician Roman families—burials were forbidden within the city walls as early as the 5th century B.C.—and, beneath the surface, miles of tunnels hewn out of soft tufa stone.

These tunnels, or catacombs, were where early Christians buried their dead and, during the worst times of persecution, held church services discreetly out of the public eye. A few of them are open to the public, so you can wander through mile after mile of musty-smelling tunnels whose soft walls are gouged out with tens of thousands of burial niches (long shelves made for 2–3 bodies each). In some dank, dark grottoes (never stray too far from your party or one of the exposed light bulbs), you can still discover the remains of early Christian art. The requisite guided tours, hosted by priests and monks, feature a smidgen of extremely biased history and a large helping of sermonizing.

The Appia Antica has been a popular Sunday lunch picnic site for Roman families (following the half-forgotten pagan tradition of dining in the presence of one's ancestors on holy days). This practice was rapidly dying out in the face of the traffic fumes that for the past few decades have choked the venerable road, but a 1990s initiative closed the Via Appia Antica to cars on Sundays, bringing back the picnickers and bicyclists—along with in-line skaters and a new Sunday-only bus route to get out here.

You can take **bus no. 218** from the San Giovanni Metro stop, which follows the Appia Antica for a bit and then veers right on Via Ardeatina at Domine Quo Vadis Church. After another long block, the bus stops at the square Largo M.F. Via d. Sette Chiese. From here, you can follow the signs to the San Domitilla catacombs; or, walk left down Via d. Sette Chiese to the San Sebastiano catacombs.

An alternative is to ride the **Metro** to the Colli Albani stop and catch **bus no. 660,** which wraps up the Appia Antica from the south, veering off it at the San Sebastiano catacombs (if you're visiting all three, you can take bus no. 218 to the first two, walk to San Sebastiano, and then catch bus no. 660 back to the Metro). On Sundays, the road is closed to traffic, but **bus no. 760** trundles from the Circo Massimo Metro stop down the Via Appia Antica, turning around after it passes the Tomb of Cecilia Metella.

Of the monuments on the Appian Way, the most impressive is the **Tomb of Cecilia Metella** ✸, within walking distance of the catacombs. The cylindrical tomb honors the wife of one of Julius Caesar's military commanders from the Republican era. Why such an elaborate tomb for such an unimportant person in history? Cecilia Metella happened to be singled out for enduring fame because her tomb has remained while others have decayed.

Catacombs of St. Callixtus (Catacombe di San Callisto) ✸✸ "The most venerable and most renowned of Rome," said Pope John XXIII of these funerary tunnels. The founder of Christian archaeology, Giovanni Battista de Rossi (1822–94), called them "catacombs par excellence." These catacombs are often packed with tour-bus groups, and their tour is perhaps the cheesiest, but the tunnels are simply phenomenal. They're the first cemetery of Rome's Christian community and burial place of 16 popes in the 3rd century. They bear the name of St. Callixtus, the deacon hired to run the catacombs by Pope St. Zephyrinus, who was later elected pope (A.D. 217–22) in his own right. The complex is a network of galleries stretching for nearly 19km (12 miles), structured in five levels and reaching a depth of about 20m (65 ft.). There are many sepulchral chambers and almost half a million tombs of early Christians. Paintings, sculptures, and epigraphs (with such symbols as the fish, anchor, and dove) provide invaluable material for the study of the life and customs of the ancient Christians and the story of their persecutions.

Entering the catacombs, you see at once the most important crypt, that of nine popes. Some of the original marble tablets of their tombs are still preserved. The next crypt is that of St. Cecilia, the patron of sacred music. This early Christian martyr received three ax strokes on her neck, the maximum allowed by Roman law, which failed to kill her outright. Farther on, you'll find the famous Cubicula of the Sacraments with its 3rd-century frescoes.

Finds Beneath It All: Touring Roma Sotteranea

Talk about the "underground," and a growing legion of Romans will excitedly take up the story, offering tidbits about where to go, whom to talk to, what's been seen, and what's allegedly awaiting discovery around the next bend in the sewer. The sewer? That's right. **Roma Sotteranea (Subterranean Rome)** is neither a subway nor a trendy arts movement, but the vast historic ruins of a city that has been occupied for nearly 3,000 years, the first 2 millennia of which are now largely buried by natural sediment and artificial landfills. Archaeologists estimate that these processes have left the streets of ancient Rome as much as 18.3m (60 ft.) beneath the surface.

Consider this: Each year, an inch of dust in the form of pollen, leaves, pollution, sand, and silt from disintegrating ruins settles over Rome. That silt has really taken a toll in its own right. Archaeologists estimate that the ruins of a one-story Roman house will produce debris 6 feet deep (1.8 meters) over its entire floor plan. When you multiply that by more than 40,000 apartment buildings, 1,800 palaces, and numerous giant public buildings, a real picture of the burial of the ancient city presents itself. You should also take note of the centuries-old Roman tradition of burying old buildings in landfills, which can raise the level of the earth up to several yards all at once. In fact, past builders have often filled up massive stone ruins with dirt or dug down through previous landfills to the columns and vaults of underlying structures, and then laid a foundation for a new layer of Roman architecture.

As a result, many buildings on the streets today actually provide direct access to Rome's inner world. Doorways lead down to hidden crypts and shrines—the existence of which are closely guarded secrets. Nondescript locked doors in churches and other public buildings often open on whole blocks of the ancient city, streets still intact. For example, take **San Clemente,** the 12th-century basilica east of the Colosseum, where a staircase in the sacristy leads down to the original 4th-century church. Not only that, but a staircase near the apse goes down to an earlier Roman apartment building and temple, which in turn leads down to a giant public building dating back to the Great Fire (A.D. 64). Another interesting doorway to the past is in the south exterior wall of **St. Peter's,** leading down to an intact necropolis. That crumbling brick entry in the gardens on the east side of Esquiline Hill carries you into the vast **Domus Aurea (Golden House),** Nero's residence, built on the ruins left by the Great Fire.

Don't expect a road map of this subterranean world; it's a meandering labyrinth beneath the streets. A guided tour can be useful, especially those focusing on Roman excavations and anything to do with church crypts. Several tour companies now offer selected subterranean views, lasting 90 to 120 minutes and costing 13€ to 25€ ($16–$30). The best are provided by **Itinera** (☎ 06-27800785) and **LUPA** (☎ 06-5741974), both run by trained archaeologists. **Città Nascosta** (☎ 06-3216059) offers offbeat tours to less-visited churches and monuments, and advertises the week's schedule via a recorded phone announcement that changes every week.

Via Appia Antica 110–126. ℭ **06-51301580**. Admission 5€ ($6) adults, 3€ ($3.60) children 6–15, free for children 5 and under. Apr–Oct Thurs–Tues 8:30am–noon and 2:30–5:30pm (to 5pm Nov–Mar). Closed Feb. Bus: 118.

Catacombs of St. Domitilla (Catacombe di San Domitilla) ✸✸✸   This oldest of the catacombs is also the hands-down winner for most enjoyable catacomb experience. Groups are small, most guides are genuinely entertaining and personable, and, depending on the mood of the group and your guide, the visit can last anywhere from 20 minutes to over an hour. You enter through a sunken 4th-century church. There are fewer "sights" than in the other catacombs—although the 2nd-century fresco of the Last Supper is impressive—but some of the guides actually hand you a few bones out of a tomb niche. (Incidentally, this is the only catacomb where you'll still see bones; the rest have emptied their tombs to rebury the remains in ossuaries on the inaccessible lower levels.)

Via d. Sette Chiese 283. ℭ **06-5110342**. Admission 5€ ($6) adults, 3€ ($3.60) children 6–14. Wed–Mon 8:30am–noon and 2:30–5pm. Closed Jan. Bus: 118.

Catacombs of St. Sebastian (Catacombe di San Sebastiano) ✸   Today the tomb of St. Sebastian is in the basilica, but his original resting place was in the catacombs underneath it. From the reign of Valerian to the reign of Constantine, the bodies of Sts. Peter and Paul were hidden in the catacombs, which were dug from tufa, a soft volcanic rock. The big church was built in the 4th century. The tunnels here, if stretched out, would reach a length of 11km (6⅔ miles). In the tunnels and mausoleums are mosaics and graffiti, along with many other pagan and Christian objects from centuries even before the time of Constantine. Though the catacombs themselves are fascinating, the tour here is one of the shortest and least satisfying of all the catacomb visits.

Via Appia Antica 136. ℭ **06-7850350**. Admission 5€ ($6) adults, 3€ ($3.60) children 6–15, free for children 5 and under. Mon–Sat 9am–noon and 2:30–5:30pm. Closed mid-Nov to mid-Dec. Bus: 118.

7 More Attractions

AROUND STAZIONE TERMINI

Basilica di Santa Maria Maggiore ✸   This great church, one of Rome's four major basilicas, was built by Pope Liberius in A.D. 358 and was rebuilt by Pope Sixtus III from 432 to 440. Its 14th-century **campanile** is the city's loftiest. Much doctored in the 18th century, the church's facade isn't an accurate reflection of the treasures inside. Restoration of the 1,600-year-old church was completed in 2000. The basilica is especially noted for the 5th-century Roman mosaics in its nave, as well as for its coffered ceiling, is said to have been gilded with gold brought from the New World. In the 16th century, Domenico Fontana built a now-restored "Sistine Chapel." In the following century, Flaminio Ponzo designed the **Pauline (Borghese) Chapel** in the baroque style. The church also contains the **tomb of Bernini,** Italy's most important baroque sculptor/architect. Ironically, the man who changed the face of Rome with his elaborate fountains is buried in a tomb so simple that it takes a sleuth to track it down (to the right near the altar).

Piazza di Santa Maria Maggiore. ℭ **06-4465836**. Free admission. Daily 7am–7pm. Metro: Termini.

MUSEO NAZIONALE ROMANO

Originally, this museum occupied only the Diocletian Baths. Today it is divided into four different sections: Palazzo Massimo alle Terme; the Terme di Diocleziano (Diocletian

Attractions near Stazione Termini, Via Veneto & Piazza Barberini

American Embassy **6**

Basilica di Santa
Maria Maggiore **1**

Cimitero Monumentale
dei Padri Cappucini
(Capuchin Crypt) **7**

Diocletian Baths (Terme
di Diocleziano) **12**

Fountain of the Bees
(Fontana dei Api) **8**

Museo Nazionale d'Arte
Antica (Palazzo
Borghese) **10**

Octagonal Hall
(Aula Ottagona) **12**

Palazzo del Quirinale **2**

Palazzo Massimo
alle Terme **13**

Quattro Fontane **11**

Santa Maria degli
Angeli **12**

Santa Maria della
Vittorio **15**

Spanish Steps **4**

Trevi Fountain
(Fontana de Trevi) **3**

Triton Fountain **9**

Via Veneto **6**

Villa Borghese Park **5**

Baths), with the annex Octagonal Hall; and Palazzo Altemps (which is near Piazza Navona; see p. 160 for a complete listing).

Diocletian Bath (Terme di Diocleziano) and the Octagonal Hall (Aula Otta-gona) Near Piazza dei Cinquecento, which fronts the rail station, this museum occupies part of the 3rd-century A.D. Baths of Diocletian and part of a convent that might have been designed by Michelangelo. The Diocletian Baths were the biggest thermal baths in the world. Nowadays they host a marvelous collection of funereal art works, such as sarcophagi, and decorations dating back to the Aurelian period. The Baths also have a section reserved for temporary exhibitions.

The **Octagonal Hall** occupies the southwest corner of the central building of the Diocletian Baths. Here you can see the *Lyceum Apollo*, a copy of the 2nd-century A.D. work inspired by the Prassitele. Also worthy of note is the *Aphrodite of Cyrene*, a copy dating back to the second half of the 2nd century A.D. and discovered in Cyrene, Libya.

Viale E. di Nicola 79. ℂ 06-39967700. Admission to the Baths 7€ ($8.40); Octagonal Hall free admission. The same ticket will admit you to Palazzo Massimo alle Terme. Tues–Sun 9am–7:45pm. Last admission 1 hr. before closing. Metro: Termini.

Palazzo Massimo alle Terme If you'd like to go wandering in a virtual garden of classical statues, head for this palazzo, built from 1883 to 1887 and opened as a museum in 1998. Much of the art here, including the frescoes; stuccoes; and mosaics, was discovered in excavations in the 1800s but has never been put on display before.

If you ever wanted to know what all those emperors from your history books looked like, this museum makes them live again, togas and all. In the central hall are works representing the political and social life of Rome at the time of Augustus Caesar. Note the statue of the emperor with a toga covering his head, symbolizing his role as the head priest of state. Other works include an altar from Ostia Antica, the ancient port of Rome, plus a statue of a wounded Niobid from 440 B.C. that is a masterwork of expression and character. Upstairs, stand in awe at all the traditional art from the 1st century B.C. to the Imperial Age. The most celebrated mosaic is of the *Four Chario-teers*. In the basement is a rare numismatic collection and an extensive collection of Roman jewelry.

Largo di Villa Peretti 67. ℂ 06-39967700. Admission 7€ ($8.40); the same ticket will admit you to the Diocletian Baths. Tues–Sun 9am–7:45pm. Last admission 1 hr. before closing. Metro: Termini.

IN THE TESTACCIO AREA, THE AVENTINE & SOUTH

Montemartini Museum (Museo Centrale Di Montemartini) *Finds*   Hike out to this old power plant if you want to see some of the finest sculptures in ancient Rome, including many items from the Capitoline Museum stockpile that haven't been exhibited in Rome since Mussolini was in power. They're displayed against a backdrop of Industrial Age machinery that once supplied electricity to the area. The prize here is the *Togato Barberini*, a berobed aristocrat from Rome of 90 B.C. He carries two heads, the symbol of an old custom in Republican Rome when patricians maintained hollow wax portrait busts of their former ancestors. They brought these busts out for special celebrations. By carrying the head, they were signifying that they were the stand-in for their illustrious progenitors.

You'll find everything from a Greek Aphrodite from the 5th century B.C. to an end-less array of marble busts and statues, many of which might have come from the area of the Imperial Forum. Many of the statues, especially those in the rooms upstairs, are superb Roman copies of Greek originals. The most stunning of these is a towering goddess statue from 100 B.C. that once graced the Temple of Fortuna in Largo di Teatro Argentina.

Via Ostiense 106. ✆ 06-5748030. Admission 4.50€ ($5.40) adults, free for ages 18 and under. Tues–Sun 9:30am–7pm. Metro: Piramide or Garbatella. Bus: 23 or 271.

Museum of Roman Civilization (Museo della Civiltà Romana)
Some 5.5km (3½ miles) south of the historic center of Rome is a more modern city conceived by the fascist-era dictator Mussolini. At the height of his power, he launched a complex of impersonal modern buildings, many of them in cold marble, to dazzle Europe with a scheduled world's fair in 1942 that never happened. Il Duce got strung up, and EUR—the neighborhood in question—got hamstrung. The new Italian government that followed inherited the unfinished project and turned it into a center of government and administration.

The most intriguing sight here is this Museum of Roman Civilization, in which are housed two fascinating scale models that reproduce Rome in two different epochs: the early Republican Rome and the city in its imperial heyday in the 4th century A.D. You'll see the then-impressive Circus Maximus, the intact Colosseum, the Baths of Diocletian—and lots more. You can also see examples of late imperial and paleochristian art, including more than a hundred casts of the reliefs that climb Trajan's Column in the Imperial Forum.

Piazza Giovanni Agnelli 10 (in EUR, south of the city center). ✆ 06-5926041. Admission 6.20€ ($7.45); free for children. Metro: EUR–Fermi.

Protestant Cemetery (Cimitero Protestante)
Near Porta San Paola, in the midst of cypress trees, lies the old cemetery where John Keats is buried. In a grave nearby, Joseph Severn, his "deathbed" companion, was interred beside him 6 decades later. Dejected and feeling that his reputation as a poet was being diminished by the rising vehemence of his critics, Keats asked that the following epitaph be written on his tombstone: "Here lies one whose name was writ in water." A great romantic poet Keats certainly was, but a prophet, thankfully not. Percy Bysshe Shelley, author of *Prometheus Unbound,* drowned off the Italian Riviera in 1822, before his 30th birthday, and his ashes rest beside those of Edward John Trelawny, a fellow romantic.

Via Caio Cestio 6. ✆ 06-5741900. Free admission (but a 1€–2€/$1.20–$2.40 offering is customary). Apr–Sept Tues–Sun 9am–6pm (Oct–Mar to 4:30pm). Metro: Piramide.

Pyramid of Caius Cestius ✦
From the 1st century B.C., the Pyramid of Caius Cestius, about 36m (120 ft.) high, looks as if it belongs to the Egyptian landscape. It was constructed during the "Cleopatra craze" in architecture that swept across Rome. You can't enter the pyramid, but it's a great photo op. And who was Caius Cestius? He was a rich magistrate in imperial Rome whose tomb is more impressive than his achievements. You can visit at any time.

Piazzale Ostiense. Metro: Piramide.

St. Paul Outside the Walls (Basilica di San Paolo Fuori le Mura) ✦
The Basilica of St. Paul, whose origins go back to the time of Constantine, is Rome's fourth great patriarchal church; it's believed to have been erected over the tomb of St. Paul. The basilica fell victim to fire in 1823 and was subsequently rebuilt. It is the second-largest church in Rome after St. Peter's. From the inside, its windows might appear to be stained glass, but they're actually translucent alabaster. With its forest of single-file columns and mosaic medallions (portraits of the various popes), this is one of the

most streamlined and elegantly decorated churches in Rome. Its most important treasure is a 12th-century candelabra by Vassalletto, who's also responsible for the remarkable cloisters, containing twisted pairs of columns enclosing a rose garden. Of particular interest is the *baldachino* (richly embroidered fabric of silk and gold, usually fixed or carried over an important person or sacred object) of Arnolf di Cambio, dated 1285, that miraculously wasn't damaged in the fire. The Benedictine monks and students sell a fine collection of souvenirs, rosaries, and bottles of Benedictine every day except Sunday and religious holidays.

Via Ostiense 184. ℂ 06-5410341. Free admission. Basilica daily 7am–6:30pm; cloisters daily 9am–1pm and 3–6pm. Metro: San Paolo Basilica.

Santa Sabina ⍟ *(Finds)*   A rarity, Santa Sabina is Rome's best remaining example of a paleochristian church. It dates from A.D. 422, and its original wooden doors from that time are still intact. The doors alone are worth the trek here. They are handsomely carved with Bible scenes, including one that depicts the crucifixion, one of the earliest examples of this in the art of the Western world. You'll find it carved on a door at the end of a "porch" from the 1400s. The porch itself contains ancient sarcophagi.

Santa Sabina was the site of the temple of Juno Regina, the patroness of Rome's Etruscan archrival, Veii, who was seduced into switching sides in 392 B.C. Sabina was martyred to the Christian cause. In 1936 much of the church was restored to its original appearance, and today it is one of Rome's most beautiful churches. The surviving 2 dozen Corinthian columns might have come from the Temple of Juno. The delicate windows were pieced together from 9th-century fragments. In the floor of the nave is Rome's only surviving mosaic tomb, dating to around 1300.

Piazza Pietro d'Iliria. ℂ 06-5743573. Free admission. Daily 6am–12:45pm and 3–7pm. Bus: 30, 60, 75, 95, 118, 170, or 175.

IN TRASTEVERE

Rome boasts many wonderful views, but one of the best spots for a memorable vista is the **Gianicolo (Janiculum Hill)** ⍟⍟, across the Tiber. It's not considered one of the "Seven Hills" of Rome, but it's certainly one of the most visited. Not even included within the original city walls (the area was built by Urban VII for defensive purposes), today most of Gianicolo is parkland. We like to come here at dawn and watch the sun rise over Rome. Here you can also look at the **Tempietto of Bramante,** the most evocative work of the High Renaissance in Rome.

Legend has it that Gianicolo was the site of the city founded by the god Janus. One of his kids, Tiber, lent his name to the river of Rome. For the best view, position yourself at the open space in front of the church, San Pietro in Montorio, which was constructed at the end of the 1400s during the reign of Sixtus IV. There is no grander panorama of Rome than the one you'll see here, extending from Monte Mario. Later you can follow the Passeggiata del Gianicolo or Janiculum Walk, which winds along the crest of the hill.

If you don't want to walk up the hill, you can catch bus no. 41 from the Ponte Sant'Angelo. But we prefer to walk along the medieval Via Garibaldi reached from Via della Scale in Trastevere. You'll reach the summit of the hill in about 15 minutes of steady climbing.

Galleria Nazionale di Palazzo Corsini   After you've seen Italy's National Gallery of Art at the Palazzo Barberini, head to Trastevere to view the other half of the collection. This collection is installed in what was the 18th-century mansion of Pope

Botanical Gardens **3**
Ex Instituto San
  Michele a Ripa **14**
Folklore Museum **8**
Galleria Nazionale di
  Palazzo Corsini **5**
Gianicolo (Janiculum Hill) **4**
Palazzo Corsini
  (Galleria Nazionale
  d'Arte/Antica) **2**
Piazza Piscinula/Casa
  dei Mattei **10**
Piazza di San Cosimato **16**
Porta Portese Market **17**
San Benedetto **11**
San Francesco a Ripa **15**
Santa Cecilia in
  Trastevere **12**
Santa Maria dell'Orto **13**
Santa Maria della Scala **6**
Santa Maria in Trastevere **9**
Santa Sabina **18**
Tempietto **7**
Villa Farnesina **1**

Clemente XII (whose real name was Lorenzo Corsini, of the famous banking family). Before it was damaged by French attacks in 1849, the palace was the grandest in Rome. Queen Christina died here in her bedroom (room no. 5) in 1689, and Napoleon's mother, Letizia, once lived here as well. The palace is still rich in neoclassical works of the Napoleonic era.

The gallery hosts a wide array of paintings from the 16th and 17th centuries, although they are bunched together and badly displayed. Nonetheless, this is an outstanding treasure trove of such European masters as Van Dyck, although Italian artists dominate. Seek out in particular Caravaggio's *St. John the Baptist* and also a rendition of the same subject by Guido Reni, who painted *Salome with the Head of St. John the Baptist.* Murillo's *Madonna and Bambino* is one of his less saccharine efforts, and some Rubens paintings are a bit overripe, notably a *St. Sebastian* and a *Madonna.* For sheer gore, Salvator Rosa's version of *Prometheus* tops them all.

Via della Lungara 10. (C) **06-68802323.** Admission 4€ ($4.80) adults, free for children 14 and under. Tues–Sat 9:30am–12:30pm; Sun 8:30am–7pm. Bus: 44, 60, 65, 23, or 280.

Santa Cecilia in Trastevere ✪
A cloistered and still-functioning convent with a fine garden, Santa Cecilia contains *The Last Judgment,* by Pietro Cavallini (ca. 1293), a masterpiece of Roman medieval painting. Another treasure is a late-13th-century

baldachino by Arnolfo di Cambio over the altar. The church is built on the reputed site of Cecilia's long-ago palace, and for a small fee you can descend under the church to inspect the ruins of some Roman houses as well as peer through a gate at the stuccoed grotto beneath the altar.

Piazza Santa Cecilia 2. ℭ **06-5899289.** Church free admission; Cavallini frescoes 2€ ($2.40); excavations 2.50€ ($3). Main church and excavations daily 9:30am–noon and 4–6:30pm; frescoes Tues–Thurs 10am–noon; Sun 11:30am–noon. Bus: 23, 271, 280, or 780.

Santa Maria in Trastevere ℛ   This Romanesque church at the colorful center of Trastevere was built around A.D. 350 and is one of the oldest in Rome. The body was added around 1100, and the portico was added in the early 1700s. The restored mosaics on the apse date from around 1140, and below them are the 1293 mosaic scenes depicting the life of Mary done by Pietro Cavallini. The faded mosaics on the facade are from the 12th or 13th centuries, and the octagonal fountain in the piazza is an ancient Roman original that was restored and added to in the 17th century by Carlo Fontana.

Piazza Santa Maria in Trastevere. ℭ **06-5814802.** Free admission. Daily 8:30am–9pm. Bus: 23, 280, or 780.

Villa Farnesina ℛℛ   Agostino "il Magnifico" Chigi (1465–1520), the richest man in Europe, once lived in this sumptuous villa built for him by the architect Baldassare Peruzzi between 1508 and 1511. Some of Rome's grandest feasts and parties, the likes of which were unknown since the days of imperial Rome, were staged here, often for popes, diplomats, artists, philosophers, and even high-priced courtesans. The Siennese banker would order his guests to toss their gold and silver plates into the Tiber after every course. Unknown to the guests, the savvy banker had placed nets under the water so that he could retrieve his treasures.

Even before this outrageous banker came to live here, the site was famous. Once it was the country villa of Julius Caesar, and Cleopatra stayed here in 44 B.C. with their illegitimate child, Caesarion.

Chigi was Raphael's most ardent patron and friend, and he called upon this great artist to help decorate part of his villa, along with such towering figures as Francesco Penni, Giulo Romano, Sebastian del Piombo, and "Il Sodoma" (so called because of his sexual practices). Together these artists created a series of paintings that stand as one of the treasures of the Renaissance, especially the *Loggia of Cupid and Psyche* ℛ.

Also stunning is the *Galatea* ℛℛ from 1511—Raphael painted Nereus's sea-maiden riding in a shell drawn by pug-nosed dolphins in a frolicking romp. Paintings depicting scenes from Ovid's *Metamorphoses* are by Sebastiano del Piombo; frescoes of the constellations on the ceiling are by Baldasarre Peruzzi.

Upstairs you can see Peruzzi's masterful *Salone delle Prospettive,* an early example of trompe l'oeil views of Rome and Il Sodoma's masterpiece *Scenes from the Life of Alexander the Great.*

Via d. Lungara 230. ℭ **06-68027268.** Admission 5€ ($6) adults, 4€ ($4.80) children and students. Mon–Sat 9am–1pm. Bus: 23.

8 The Gardens of Rome

The greatest garden of Rome is the **Villa Borghese,** which has already been previewed, as have the gardens of the Vatican. But there are other "secret gardens" of Rome where you can slip away from the hordes and the traffic.

Villa dei Medici Gardens, Viale Trinità dei Monti 2 (☎ **06-67611**), was called "the most enchanting place" in Rome by Henry James, who went on to write that the gardens were possessed with an "incredible, impossible charm."

Covering 17 sprawling acres on Pincio Hill above the Piazza di Spagna, they offer our favorite panoramic view of Rome. In the 1st century B.C., the site was covered by the Gardens of Lucullus. With their tree-lined avenues, statues, and fountains, these gardens were built around the severe, fortress-like facade of the Villa dei Medici in 1540. The Medici grand dukes acquired them in 1580. When Galileo was under house arrest by the Inquisition (1630–33), the dukes offered him shelter here.

In 1801, Napoleon purchased the villa to make it the seat of the French Academy. *Prix de Rome* scholars stay here, studying art, architecture, and archaeology. In front of the villa is a round fountain with a wide basin. Its spout was made from a cannon-ball shot from Castel Sant'Angelo.

The gardens—not the villa itself—can be visited only on Saturday and Sunday tours at 10:30am and again at 11:30am. The cost of a tour is 6.50€ ($7.80) per person (Metro: Spagna). It is open all year.

9 Organized Tours

Because of the sheer number of sights to see, some first-time visitors like to start out with an organized tour. While few things can really be covered in any depth on these overview tours, they're sometimes useful for getting your bearings.

One of the leading tour operators is **American Express,** Piazza di Spagna 38 (☎ **06-67641;** Metro: Spagna). A popular tour is their 4-hour orientation of Rome and the Vatican, which departs most mornings at 9:30am and costs 60€ ($72) per person. Another 4-hour tour, which focuses on the Rome of antiquity (including visits to the Colosseum, the Roman Forum, the ruins of the Imperial Palace, and San Pietro in Vincoli), costs 60€ ($72). From April to October, a good excursion outside Rome is a 5-hour bus tour to Tivoli, where tours are conducted of the Villa d'Este and its spectacular gardens and the ruins of the Villa Adriana, all for 50€ ($60) per person.

Through Eternity Tours, Via Sinuessa 8 (☎ **06-7009336;** mobile 347/336-5298), is staffed by a team of art historians, archaeologists, and experts on ancient Rome. Its guided tour of Vatican City is the best in Rome, a comprehensive 5-hour tour that brings life to the artifacts in this vast treasure trove. The cost is 40€ ($48) per person. Other tours include Rome at Twilight, a 2½-hour evening tour of the city's beautiful piazzas and fountains, costing 25€ ($30) per person; and a 2½-hour tour of the Ancient City costing 25€ ($30) per person.

Another option is **Scala Reale,** Via Varese 52 (☎ **888/467-1986** in the U.S., or 06-4820911), a cultural association founded by American architect Tom Rankin. He offers small group tours and excursions focusing on the architectural and artistic significance of Rome. Tours include visits to monuments, museums, and piazzas, as well as to neighborhood trattorie. Custom-designed tours are available. Prices begin at 20€ ($24). Children 12 and under are admitted free to walking tours. Tour discounts are available for a group of four.

9

Strolling Through Rome

Rome is a great city for walking—be sure to allow yourself enough time to just wander and let yourself get lost. Those of you who want more guidance in your exploration might enjoy the walking tours we've designed in this chapter. Visitors with very limited time might want to concentrate on Walking Tour 1, "Rome of the Caesars," and Walking Tour 2, "The Heart of Rome." Those with more time can try out "Renaissance Rome" and "Trastevere." Many of the major sights along these routes, especially on walking tours 2 to 4, are covered fully in chapter 7. These tours serve both to string the sights together and to reveal some lesser-known hidden gems along the way.

WALKING TOUR 1	ROME OF THE CAESARS

Start:	Via Sacra, in the Roman Forum
Finish:	Circus Maximus
Time:	5½ hours
Best Times:	Any sunny day
Worst Times:	After dark or midday, when the place is overrun with tour groups

This tour takes in the most central of the monuments and ruins that attest to the military and architectural grandeur of ancient Rome. As a whole, they make up the most famous and evocative ruins in the world, despite such drawbacks as roaring traffic that's the bane of the city's civic planners and a general dustiness and heat that can test even the hardiest amateur archaeologists.

After the collapse of Rome and during the Dark Ages, the forums and many of the other sites on this tour were lost to history, buried beneath layers of debris, their marble mined by medieval builders, until Benito Mussolini set out to restore the grandeur of Rome by reminding his compatriots of their glorious past.

THE ROMAN FORUM

The western entrance to the Roman Forum (there are two entrances) is at the corner of Via dei Fori Imperiali and Via Cavour, adjacent to Piazza Santa Maria Nova. The nearest Metro is the Colosseo stop. As you walk down into the Forum along a masonry ramp, you'll be heading Via Sacra, the ancient Roman road that ran through the Forum connecting the Capitoline Hill, to your right, with the Arch of Titus (1st c. A.D.), off to your left. The Roman Forum is the more dignified and austere of the two forums you'll visit on this walking tour. Although it consists mostly of artfully evocative ruins scattered confusingly around a sun-baked terrain, it represents almost 1,000

Walking Tour 1: Rome of the Caesars

1 Basilica Aemilia	**18** House of Livia
2 Curia	**19** Orti Farnesiani
3 Lapis Niger	(Farnese Gardens)
4 Arch of Septimius Severus	**20** The Colosseum
5 Rostra	☕ Bar Martini
6 Basilica Julia	**21** Via dei Fori Imperiali
7 Column of Phocas	**22** Forum of Nerva
8 Temple of Julius Caesar	**23** Forum of Augustus
9 Temple of the Castors	**24** Trajan's Market
10 Temple of Vesta	**25** Tower of the Milizie
11 Temple of Antoninus and Faustina	**26** Forum of Trajan
12 Temple of Romulus	**27** Trajan's Column
13 Basilica of Constantine	**28** Forum of Julius Caesar
14 Arch of Titus	**29** Vittorio Emanuele Monument
15 Flavian Palace	**30** Teatro di Marcello
16 Domus Augustana	**31** Temple of Fortuna Virile
17 Hippodrome	**32** Circus Maximus

years of Roman power during the severely disciplined period that preceded the legendary decadence of the later Roman emperors.

Arriving at Via Sacra, turn right. The random columns on the right as you head toward the Arch of Septimius Severus belong to the:

❶ Basilica Aemilia

This was once the site of great meeting halls and shops, all maintained for centuries by the noble Roman family who gave it its name. At the corner nearest the Forum entrance are some traces of melted bronze decoration that was fused to the marble floor during a great fire set by invading Goths in A.D. 410.

The next important building is the:

❷ Curia, or Senate House

It's the large brick building on the right that still has its roof. Romans had been meeting on this site for centuries before the first structure was erected, and that was still centuries before Jesus was born. The present building is the fifth (if you count all the reconstructions and substantial rehabilitations) to stand on the site. Legend has it that the original building was constructed by an ancient king with the curious name of Tullus Hostilius. The tradition he began was noble indeed, and our present legislative system owes much to the Romans who met in this hall. Unfortunately, the high ideals and inviolate morals that characterized the early republican senators gave way to the bootlicking of imperial times, when the Senate became little more than a rubber stamp. Caligula, who was only the third emperor, had his horse appointed to the Senate, which pretty much sums up the state of the Senate by the middle of the 1st century A.D.

The building was a church until 1937, when the fascist government tore out the baroque interior and revealed what we see today. The original floor of Egyptian marble and the tiers that held the seats of the senators have miraculously survived. In addition, at the far end of the great chamber we can see the stone on which rested the fabled golden statue of Victory. Originally installed by Augustus, it was disposed of in the 4th century by a fiercely divided Senate whose Christian members convinced the emperor that it was improper to have a pagan statue in such a revered place.

Outside, head down the Curia stairs to the:

❸ Lapis Niger

These are the remains of black marble blocks that reputedly mark the tomb of Romulus. Today they bask under a corrugated metal roof. Go downstairs for a look at the excavated tomb. There's a stone here with the oldest Latin inscription in existence, which, unfortunately, is nearly illegible. All that can be safely assumed is that it genuinely dates from the Rome of the kings, an era that ended in a revolution in 510 B.C.

Across from the Curia, you'll see the:

❹ Arch of Septimius Severus

The arch was dedicated at the dawn of the troubled 3rd century to the last decent emperor to govern Rome for some time. The friezes on the arch depict victories over Arabs and Parthians by the cold but upright Severus and his two dissolute sons, Geta and Caracalla. Severus died on a campaign to subdue the unruly natives of Scotland. At the end of the first decade of the 3rd century, Rome unhappily fell into the hands of the young Caracalla, chiefly remembered today for the baths he ordered built.

Walk around to the back of the Severus arch, face it, and look to your right. There amid the rubble can be discerned a semicircular stair that led to the famous:

❺ Rostra

This was the podium from which dictators and Caesars addressed the throngs on the Forum below. You can just imagine the emperor, shining in his white toga, surrounded by imperial guards and distinguished senators, gesticulating grandly like one of the statues on a Roman roofline. The motley crowd falls silent, the senators pause and listen, the merchants put down their measures, and even the harlots and unruly soldiers lower their voices in such an august presence. Later emperors didn't have much cause to use the Rostra; they made their policies known through edicts and assassinations instead.

Now, facing the colonnade of the Temple of Saturn, once the public treasury, and going to the left, you'll come to the ruins of the:

❻ Basilica Julia

Again, little more than a foundation remains. The basilica is named for Julius Caesar, who dedicated the first structure in 46 B.C. Like many buildings in the Forum, the basilica was burned and rebuilt several times, and the last structure dated from the shaky days after the Gothic invasion in A.D. 410. Throughout its history, it was used for the hearing of civil court cases, which were conducted in the pandemonium of the crowded Forum, open to anyone who happened to pass by. The building was also reputed to be particularly hot in the summer, and it was under these sweaty and unpromising circumstances that Roman justice, the standard of the world for a millennium, was meted out.

Walking back down the ruined stairs of the Basilica Julia and into the broad area whose far side is bounded by the Curia, you'll see the:

❼ Column of Phocas

Probably lifted from an early structure in the vicinity, this was the last monument to be erected in the Roman Forum, and it commemorates the Byzantine Emperor Phocas's generous donation of the Pantheon to the pope of Rome, who almost immediately transformed it into a church.

Now make your way down the middle of the Forum, nearly back to the ramp from which you entered. The pile of bricks with the semicircular indentation that stands in the middle of things was the:

❽ Temple of Julius Caesar

It was erected some time after the dictator was deified, and judging from the reconstruction, it was quite an elegant building.

As you stand facing the ruins, with the entrance to the Forum on your left, you'll see on your right three columns originally belonging to the:

❾ Temple of the Castors

This temple perpetuated the legend of Castor and Pollux, who appeared out of thin air in the Roman Forum and were observed watering their horses at the fountain of Juturna (still visible today), just as a major battle against the Etruscans turned in favor of Rome. Castor and Pollux, the heavenly twins (and the symbol of the astrological sign Gemini), are a favorite of Rome.

The next major monument is the circular:

❿ Temple of Vesta

Here dwelt the sacred flame of Rome and the Atrium of the Vestal Virgins. A Vestal Virgin was usually a girl of good family who signed a contract for 30 years. During that time she lived in the ruin you're standing in right now. Of course, back then it was an unimaginably rich marble building with two floors. There were only six Vestal Virgins at a time during the imperial period, and even though they had the option of going back out into the world at the end of their 30 years, few did. The cult of Vesta came to an end in A.D. 394, when a Christian Rome secularized all its pagan temples. A man standing on this site before then would have been put to death immediately.

Stand in the atrium with your back to the Palatine and look beyond those fragmented statues of the former vestals to the:

⓫ Temple of Antoninus and Faustina

It's the building with the free-standing colonnade just to the right of the ramp where you first entered the Forum. Only the colonnade dates from imperial times; the building behind it is a much later church dedicated to San Lorenzo.

After you inspect the beautifully proportioned Antoninus and Faustina temple, head up Via Sacra away from the entrance ramp toward the Arch of Titus. Pretty soon, on your left, you'll see the twin bronze doors of the:

⑫ Temple of Romulus

It's the doors themselves that are really of note—they're the original Roman doors, swinging on the same massive hinges they were mounted on in A.D. 306. In this case, the temple is not dedicated to the legendary cofounder of Rome, but to the son of its builder, Emperor Maxentius, who named his son Romulus in a fit of antiquarian patriotism. Unfortunately for both father and son, they competed with a general who deprived them of their empire and their lives. That man was Constantine, who, while camped outside Rome during preparations for one of his battles against Maxentius, saw the sign of the cross in the heavens with the insignia *In hoc signo vinces* (In this sign shall you conquer). Raising the standard of Christianity above his legions, he defeated Maxentius and became the first Christian emperor.

Those three gaping arches up ahead on your left were part of the:

⑬ Basilica of Constantine

At the time of Constantine's victory (A.D. 306), the great basilica was only half finished, having been started by the unfortunate Maxentius. Constantine finished the job and affixed his name to this, the largest and most impressive building in the Forum. To our taste, the delicate Greek-influenced temples are more attractive, but you have to admire the scale and engineering skill that erected this monument. The fact that portions of the original coffered ceiling are still intact is amazing. The basilica once held a statue of Constantine so large that his little toe was as wide as an average man's waist. You can see a few fragments from this colossus—the remnants were found in 1490—in the courtyard of the Conservatory Museum on the Capitoline Hill.

As far as Roman emperors went, Christian or otherwise, ego knew no bounds.

From Constantine's basilica, follow the Roman paving stones of Via Sacra to a low hill just ahead, where you'll find the:

⑭ Arch of Titus

Titus was the emperor who sacked the great Jewish temple in Jerusalem, and the bas-relief sculpture inside the arch shows the booty of the Jews being carried in triumph through the streets of Rome while Titus is crowned by Victory, who comes down from heaven for the occasion. You'll notice, in particular, the candelabrum, for centuries one of the most famous pieces of the treasure of Rome. In all probability, it lies at the bottom of the Busento River in the secret tomb of Alaric the Goth.

THE PALATINE HILL

When you've gathered your strength in the shimmering sun, head up the Clivus Palatinus—the road to the palaces of the Palatine Hill, or *Palatino*. With your back to the Arch of Titus, it's the road going up the hill to the left.

It was on the Palatine Hill that Rome first became a city. Legend tells us that the date was 753 B.C. The new city originally consisted of nothing more than the Palatine, which was soon enclosed by a surprisingly sophisticated wall, remains of which can still be seen on the Circus Maximus side of the hill. As time went on and Rome grew in power and wealth, the boundaries were extended and later enclosed by the Servian Wall. When the last of the ancient kings was overthrown (510 B.C.), Rome had already extended over several of the adjoining hills and valleys. As republican times progressed, the Palatine became a fashionable residential district. So it remained until Tiberius—who, like his predecessor, Augustus, was a bit too modest to call himself "emperor" out loud—began the first of the monumental palaces that eventually covered the entire hill.

It's difficult today to make sense out of the Palatine. First-time viewers might be forgiven for suspecting it to be an entirely artificial structure built on brick arches. Those arches, visible on practically every flank of the hill, are actually supports that once held imperial structures. Having run out of building sites, the emperors, in their fervor, simply enlarged the hill by building new sides on it.

The road goes on only a short way, through a small sort of valley filled with lush, untrimmed greenery. After about 5 minutes (for slow walkers), you'll see the ruins of a monumental stairway just to the right of the road. The Clivus Palatinus turns sharply to the left here, skirting the monastery of San Bonaventura, but we'll detour to the right and take a look at the remains of the:

⓫ Flavian Palace

As you walk off the road and into the ruins, you'll be able to discern that there were once three rooms here. But it's impossible for anyone but the most imaginative to comprehend quite how splendid they were.

The entire Flavian Palace was decorated in the most lavish of colored marbles and gold. Much of the decoration survived as late as the 18th century, when the greedy duke of Parma removed most of what was left. The room closest to the Clivus Palatinus was called the lararium and held statues of the divinities that protected the imperial family. The middle room was the grandest of the three. It was the imperial throne room, where sat the ruler of the world, the emperor of Rome. The far room was a basilica and was used for miscellaneous court functions, among them audiences with the emperor. This part of the palace was used entirely for ceremonial functions.

Adjoining these three rooms are the remains of a spectacularly luxurious peristyle. You'll recognize it by the hexagonal remains of a fountain in the middle. Try to imagine this fountain surrounded by marble arcades planted with mazes and

equipped with mica-covered walls. On the opposite side of the peristyle from the throne room are several other great reception and entertainment rooms. The banquet hall was here; beyond it, looking over the Circus Maximus, are a few ruins of former libraries. Although practically nothing remains except the foundations, every now and then you'll catch sight of a fragment of colored marble floor in a subtle, sophisticated pattern.

Toward the Circus Maximus, slightly to the left of the Flavian Palace, is the:

⓰ Domus Augustana

This is where the imperial family lived. The remains lie toward the Circus Maximus, slightly to the left of the Flavian Palace. The new building that stands here—it looks old to us, but in Rome it qualifies as a new building—is a museum. It stands in the absolute center of the Domus Augustana. In the field adjacent to the stadium, well into the present century stood the Villa Mills, a gingerbread Gothic villa of the 19th century. It was quite a famous place, owned by a rich Englishman who came to Rome from the West Indies. The Villa Mills was the scene of fashionable entertainment in Victorian times, and it's interesting to note, as H. V. Morton pointed out, that the last dinner parties that took place on the Palatine Hill were given by an Englishman. At any of several points along this south-facing gazebo of the Palatine Hill, you'll be able to see the faraway oval walls of the Circus Maximus.

Continue with your exploration of the Palatine Hill by heading across the field parallel to the Clivus Palatinus until you come to the north end of the:

⓱ Hippodrome, or Stadium of Domitian

The field was apparently occupied by parts of the Domus Augustana, which, in turn, adjoined the enormous stadium. The stadium alone is worth examination, although sometimes it's difficult to get down inside it. The perfectly proportioned area was usually used for private games staged for the amusement of the imperial family. As you look down the stadium from the north end, you can see, on the left side, the semicircular remains of a structure identified as Domitian's private box. Some archaeologists claim that this stadium was actually an elaborate sunken garden.

The aqueduct that comes up the wooded hill used to supply water to the Baths of Septimius Severus, whose difficult-to-understand ruins lie in monumental poles of arched brick at the far end of the stadium.

Returning to the Flavian Palace, leave the peristyle on the opposite side from the Domus Augustana and follow the signs for the:

⑱ House of Livia

They take you down a dusty path to your left. Although legend says that this was the house of Augustus's consorts, it actually was Augustus's all along. The place is notable for some rather well-preserved murals showing mythological scenes. But more interesting is the aspect of the house itself—it's smallish, and there never were any great baths or impressive marble arcades. Even though Augustus was the first emperor, he lived simply compared to his successors. His wife, Livia, was a fiercely ambitious aristocrat who divorced her first husband to marry the emperor (the ex-husband was made to attend the wedding, incidentally) and, according to some historians, was the true power behind Roman policy between the death of Julius Caesar and the ascension of Tiberius. She even controlled Tiberius, her son, since she had engineered his rise to power through a long string of intrigues and poisonings.

After you've examined the frescoes in Livia's parlor, head up the steps that lead to the top of the embankment to the north. Once on top, you'll be in the:

⑲ Orti Farnesiani (Farnese Gardens)

This was the 16th-century horticultural fantasy of a Farnese cardinal. They're constructed on top of the Palace of Tiberius, which, you'll remember, was the first of the great imperial palaces to be built on this hill. It's impossible to see any of it, but the gardens are cool and laid out nicely. You might stroll up to the promontory above the Forum and admire the view of the ancient temples and the Capitoline heights off to the left.

You've now seen the best of the Forum and the Palatine. To leave the archaeological area, continue walking eastward along the winding road that meanders steeply down from the Palatine Hill to Via di San Gregorio. When you reach the roaring traffic of that busy thoroughfare, walk north toward the ruins so famous that they symbolize the city itself:

⑳ The Colosseum

Its crumbling, oval bulk is the greatest monument of ancient Rome, and visitors are impressed with its size, its majesty, and its ability to conjure up the cruel games that were played out for the pleasure of the Roman masses. Visit it now or return later.

> **TAKE A BREAK**
> On a hill in back of the landmark Colosseum is the **Bar Martini**, Piazza del Colosseo 3B (✆ **06-7004431**), surrounded by flowery shrubs. Have your coffee, cool drink, plate of pasta, or simple sandwich outside at one of the tables and absorb one of the world's greatest architectural views: that of the Colosseum itself.

THE IMPERIAL FORUMS

Begun by Julius Caesar as an answer to the overcrowding of Rome's older forums during the days of the empire, the Imperial Forums were, at the time of their construction, flashier, bolder, and more impressive than the old Roman Forum, and as such represented the unquestioned authority of the Roman emperors at the height of their absolute power. After the collapse of Rome and during the Dark Ages, they, like many other ancient monuments, were lost to history, buried beneath layers of debris. Mussolini, in an egomaniacal attempt to draw comparisons between his fascist regime and the glory of ancient Rome, later helped restore the grandeur of Rome.

With your back to the Colosseum, walk westward along the:

㉑ Via dei Fori Imperiali

Keep to the right side of the street. It was Mussolini who issued the controversial orders to cut through centuries of debris and junky buildings to reveal many archaeological treasures and carve out this boulevard linking the Colosseum to the grand 19th-century monuments of Piazza Venezia. The vistas over the ruins of Rome's Imperial Forums from the northern side of the boulevard make for one of the most fascinating walks in Rome.

Some of the rather confusing ruins you'll see from the boulevard include the shattered remnants of the colonnade that once surrounded the Temple of Venus and Roma. Next to it, you'll see the back wall of the Basilica of Constantine.

Shortly, on the street's north side, you'll come to a large outdoor restaurant, where Via Cavour joins the boulevard. Just beyond the small park across Via Cavour are the remains of the:

㉒ Forum of Nerva

Your best view is from the railing that skirts it on Via dei Fori Imperiali. It was built by the emperor whose 2-year reign (A.D. 96–98) followed that of the paranoid Domitian. You'll be struck by just how much the ground level has risen in 19 centuries. The only really recognizable remnant is a wall of the Temple of Minerva with two fine Corinthian columns. This forum was once flanked by that of Vespasian, which is now completely gone. It's possible to enter the Forum of Nerva

from the other side, but you can see it just as well from the railing.

The next forum you approach is the:

㉓ Forum of Augustus

This was built to commemorate the emperor's victory over the assassins Cassius and Brutus in the Battle of Philippi (42 B.C.). Fittingly, the temple that once dominated this forum—its remains can still be seen—was that of Mars Ultor, or Mars the Avenger, in which stood a mammoth statue of Augustus that, unfortunately, has vanished completely. You can enter the Forum of Augustus from the other side (cut across the tiny footbridge).

Continuing along the railing, you'll see next the vast semicircle of:

㉔ Trajan's Market

Its teeming arcades, stocked with merchandise from the far corners of the Roman Empire, long ago collapsed, leaving only the ubiquitous cats to watch over things. The shops once covered a multitude of levels. In front of the perfectly proportioned semicircular facade, designed by Apollodorus of Damascus at the beginning of the 2nd century, are the remains of a great library. Fragments of delicately colored marble floors still shine in the sunlight between stretches of rubble and tall grass.

For most of 2007, the market will remain closed. However, here is the new admission policy for 2007. The exterior of the market can be visited Tuesday to Sunday 9am to 2pm for an admission of 3€ ($3.60). Entrance is at the Column of Trajan, a prominent landmark clearly visible.

㉕ Tower of the Milizie

This 12th-century structure was part of the medieval headquarters of the Knights of Rhodes. The view from the top (if it's open) is well worth the climb. From the tower, you can wander down to the ruins of the market, admiring the sophistication of the layout and the sad beauty of the bits of decoration that remain.

When you've examined the brick and travertine corridors, head out in front of the semicircle to the site of the former library; from here, scan the retaining wall that supports the modern road and look for the entrance to the tunnel that leads to the:

26 Forum of Trajan

It's entered on Via IV Novembre near the steps of Via Magnanapoli. Once through the tunnel, you'll emerge in the newest and most beautiful of the Imperial Forums, designed by the same man who laid out the adjoining market. There are many statue fragments and pedestals that bear still-legible inscriptions, but more interesting is the great Basilica Ulpia, with gray marble columns rising roofless into the sky. You wouldn't know it to judge from what's left, but the Forum of Trajan was once regarded as one of the architectural wonders of the world. Constructed between A.D. 107 and 113, it was designed by the Greek architect Apollodorus of Damascus.

Beyond the Basilica Ulpia is:

27 Trajan's Column

This column is in magnificent condition, with intricate bas-relief sculptures depicting Trajan's victorious campaign (although from your vantage point you'll be able to see only the earliest stages). The emperor's ashes were kept in a golden urn at the base of the column. If you're fortunate, someone on duty at the stairs next to the column will let you out there. Otherwise, you'll have to walk back the way you came.

The next stop is the:

28 Forum of Julius Caesar

This is the first of the Imperial Forums. It lies on the opposite side of Via dei Fori Imperiali, the last set of sunken ruins before the Vittorio Emanuele monument. Although it's possible to go right down into the ruins, you can see everything just as well from the railing. This was the site of the Roman stock exchange, as well as of the Temple of Venus, a few of

whose restored columns stand cinematically in the middle of the excavations.

ON TO THE CIRCUS MAXIMUS

From here, retrace your last steps until you're in front of the white Brescian marble monument around the corner on Piazza Venezia, the:

29 Vittorio Emanuele Monument

This flamboyant landmark, which has been compared to a frosted wedding cake or a Victorian typewriter, was constructed in the late 1800s to honor Italy's first king. An eternal flame burns at the Tomb of the Unknown Soldier. The interior of the monument has been closed to the public for many years.

Keep close to the monument and walk to your left, in the opposite direction from Via dei Fori Imperiali. You might like to pause at the fountain that flanks one of the monument's great white walls and splash some icy water on your face. Stay on the same side of the street and just keep walking around the monument. You'll be on Via del Teatro Marcello, which takes you past the twin lions that guard the sloping stairs and on along the base of the Capitoline Hill.

Keep walking along this street until you come to the:

30 Teatro di Marcello

It'll be on your right, and you'll recognize the two rows of gaping arches, which are said to be the models for the Colosseum. Julius Caesar is credited with starting the construction of this theater, but it was finished many years after his death (in 11 B.C.) by Augustus, who dedicated it to his favorite nephew, Marcellus. A small corner of the 2,000-year-old arcade has been restored to what presumably was the original condition. Here, as everywhere, numerous cats stalk around the broken marble.

The bowl of the theater and the stage were adapted many centuries ago as the foundation for the Renaissance palace of the Orsini family. The other ruins belong to old temples. To the right is the Porticus of Octavia, dating from the 2nd century B.C. Note how later cultures used part of the Roman structure without destroying its original character. There's another good example of this on the other side of the theater. Here you'll see a church with a wall that completely incorporates part of an ancient colonnade.

Keep walking along Via del Teatro Marcello away from Piazza Venezia for 2 more long blocks, until you come to Piazza della Bocca della Verità. The first item to notice in the attractive piazza is the rectangular:

③ Temple of Fortuna Virile

You'll see it on the right, a little off the road. Built a century before the birth of Jesus, it's still in magnificent condition. Behind it is another temple, dedicated to Vesta. Like the one in the Roman Forum, it is round, symbolic of the prehistoric huts where continuity of the hearth fire was a matter of survival.

About a block to the south you'll pass the facade of the Church of Santa Maria in Cosmedin, set on Piazza della Bocca della Verità. Even more noteworthy, a short walk east is the:

③ Circus Maximus

Its elongated oval proportions and ruined tiers of benches will make you think of *Ben-Hur*. Today a formless ruin, the victim of countless raids on its stonework by medieval and Renaissance builders, the remains of the once-great arena lie directly behind the church. At one time, 250,000 Romans could assemble on the marble seats, while the emperor observed the games from his box high on the Palatine Hill.

The circus lies in a valley formed by the Palatine Hill on the left and the Aventine

Hill on the right. Next to the Colosseum, it was the most impressive structure in ancient Rome, located certainly in one of the most exclusive neighborhoods. Emperors lived on the Palatine, and the great palaces of patricians sprawled across the Aventine, which is still a nice neighborhood. For centuries, the pomp and ceremony of imperial chariot races filled this valley with the cheers of thousands.

When the dark days of the 5th and 6th centuries fell on the city, the Circus Maximus seemed a symbol of the complete ruination of Rome. The last games were held in 549 on the orders of Totilla the Goth, who had seized Rome in 547 and established himself as emperor. He lived in the still-glittering ruins on the Palatine and apparently thought that the chariot races in the Circus Maximus would lend credence to his charade of an empire. The Romans of those times were caught between Belisarius, the imperial general from Constantinople, and Totilla the Goth, both of whom fought bloodily for control of Rome.

It must have been a pretty miserable show because the decimated population numbered something like 500 when Totilla recaptured the city. After the travesty of 549, the Circus Maximus was never used again, and the demand for building materials reduced it, like so much of Rome, to a great dusty field.

To return to other parts of town, head for the bus stop adjacent to the Church of Santa Maria in Cosmedin, or walk the length of the Circus Maximus to its far end and pick up the Metro to the Termini of anywhere else in the city that appeals to you.

WALKING TOUR 2 THE HEART OF ROME

Start:	Palazzo del Quirinale
Finish:	Piazza Santi Apostoli
Time:	3½ hours
Best Times:	Sunday mornings
Worst Times:	Morning and afternoon rush hours on weekdays

This walking tour will lead you down narrow, sometimes traffic-clogged streets that have witnessed more commerce and religious fervor than any other neighborhood in Rome. Be prepared for glittering and very unusual shops that lie cheek by jowl with churches dating back to A.D. 500.

Begin in the monumental, pink-toned:

❶ Piazza del Quirinale

Crowning the highest of the seven ancient hills of Rome, this is where Augustus's Temple of the Sun once stood (the steep marble steps that now lead to Santa Maria d'Aracoeli on the Capitoline Hill once serviced this spot), and part of the fountains in the piazza were built from the great Baths of Constantine, which also stood nearby. The palace, today home to the president of Italy, is open to the public only on Sunday mornings.

You can admire a nice view of Rome from the piazza's terrace, and then meander along the curiously lifeless streets that surround it before beginning your westward descent along Via della Dataria and your northerly descent along Via San Vincenzo to one of the most famous waterworks in the world, the:

❷ Trevi Fountain

Supplied by water from the Acqua Vergine aqueduct, and a triumph of the baroque style, it was based on the design of Nicolo Salvi (who is said to have died of illness contracted during his supervision of the project) and completed in 1762. On the southwestern corner of the fountain's piazza you'll see a somber, not particularly spectacular church (Chiesa SS. Vincenzo e Anastasio) with a strange claim to fame: In it are contained the hearts and intestines of several centuries' worth of popes. This was the parish church of the popes when they resided at

the Quirinal Palace on the hill above, and for many years each pontiff willed those parts of his body to the church. According to legend, the church was built on the site of a spring that burst from the earth after the beheading of St. Paul at one of three sites where his head is said to have bounced off the ground.

Throw a coin or two into the fountain to ensure your return to Rome, and then walk around to the right of the fountain along streets whose names will include Via di Stamperia, Via del Tritone, and Via F. Crispi. These lead to a charming street, Via Gregoriana, whose relatively calm borders and quiet apartments flank a narrow street that inclines upward to one of the most spectacular public squares in Italy:

❸ Piazza della Trinità dei Monti

Partly because of its position at the top of the Spanish Steps (which you'll descend in a moment), partly because of its soaring Egyptian obelisk, and partly because of its lavish and perfect baroque symmetry, this is one of the most theatrical piazzas in Italy. Flanking the piazza are buildings that have played a pivotal role in French (yes, French) politics for centuries, including the Church of Trinità dei Monti, begun by the French monarch Louis XII in 1502 and restored during Napoleon's occupation of Rome in the early 1800s. The eastern edge of the square, adjacent to Via Gregoriana, is the site of the 16th-century Palazzetto Zuccaro, built for the mannerist painter Federico

Walking Tour 2: The Heart of Rome

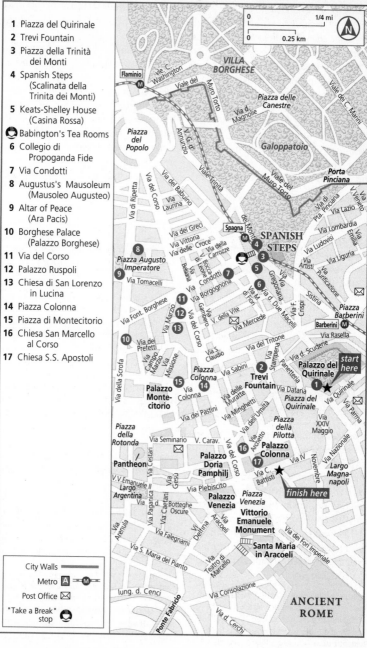

Zuccaro, with doorways and window openings fashioned into deliberately grotesque shapes inspired by the mouths of sea monsters. (It lies between Via Gregoriana, Via Sistina, and Piazza Trinità dei Monti.) In this building, at the dawn of the French Revolution, David painted the most politicized canvas in the history of France, *The Oath of the Horatii* (1784), which became a symbol of the Enlightenment then sweeping through the salons of Paris. Today the palazzetto is owned by the German Institute for Art History.

Begin descending the most famous staircase in the world, the:

❹ Spanish Steps

This azalea-flanked triumph of landscape design takes its name from the Spanish Embassy, which was in a nearby palace during the 19th century. The Spanish, however, had nothing to do with the construction of the steps. Designed by Italian architect Francesco de Sanctis between 1723 and 1725, they were funded almost entirely by the French as a preface to the above-mentioned French church, Trinità dei Monti.

The Spanish Steps are at their best in spring, when they're filled with flowers that seem to cascade down into Piazza di Spagna, a piazza designed like two interconnected triangles. Curiously, in the early 19th century, the steps were famous for the sleek young men and women who lined the travertine steps, flexing muscles and exposing ankles in hopes of attracting an artist and being hired as a model.

The boat-shape Barcaccia fountain, in the piazza at the foot of the steps, was designed by Bernini's father at the end of the 16th century.

There are two nearly identical houses at the foot of the steps on either side. One is the home of Babington's Tea Rooms (see "Take a Break," below); the other is the house where the English romantic poet John Keats lived—and died. That building, at 26 Piazza di Spagna, contains the:

❺ Keats–Shelley House

Keats died here on February 23, 1821, at the age of 25, during a trip he made to Rome to improve his failing health. Since 1909, when well-intentioned English and American aficionados of English literature bought the building, it has been a working library established in honor of Keats as well as Shelley, who drowned off the coast of Viareggio with a copy of Keats's work in his pocket. Mementos inside range from the kitschy to the immortal and are almost relentlessly laden with literary nostalgia.

>
> **TAKE A BREAK**
> **Babington's Tea Rooms,** Piazza di Spagna 23 (© 06-6786027), has been serving homemade scones and muffins, along with a good cuppa, ever since it opened in 1893 by Miss Anna Maria Babington, using her original recipes. Celebrities and thousands of visitors have stopped off here to rest in premises inspired by England's Victorian age. Prices are high, however.

In the past, the Piazza di Spagna area was a favorite of English lords, who rented palaces hereabouts and parked their coaches on the street. Americans now dominate the scene, especially since the main office of American Express is right on Piazza di Spagna and dispenses all those letters (and money) from home. Much to the dismay of many Romans, the piazza is also home to a **McDonald's;** however, it's not your average Golden Arches—we've never seen one so lavish, and it's a good place to duck in if you need a restroom.

To the extreme southern edge of the square— flanked by Via Due Macelli, Via Propaganda, and Piazza di Spagna—is an odd vestige of the Catholic church's sense of missionary zeal, the:

❻ Collegio di Propoganda Fide

Established in 1627 as the headquarters of a religious organization devoted to the training of young missionaries, this later became one of the most important centers for missionary work in the world. Owned and administered by the Vatican, it is therefore exempt from most of the laws and legalities of Italy. It contains design elements by two of the 17th century's most bitter artistic rivals, Bernini and Borromini.

The street that runs east–west as the logical continuation of the descent of the Spanish Steps is one of the most celebrated for style and fashion in Italy:

7 Via Condotti

It's lined with windows displaying the latest offerings from the Italian fashion industry. Even the least materialistic will enjoy window shopping along this impressive lineup of the most famous names in international design. (Via Condotti is only the most visible of several upscale shopping streets in the neighborhood. For more of the same temptations, detour onto a smaller but equally glamorous parallel street, Via della Croce, 2 blocks to the north, and wander at will with your platinum card in hand. You'll need to return to Via Condotti eventually for the continuation of this walking tour.)

Via Condotti ends at a shop-lined plaza, Largo Goldoni, where your path will fork slightly to the right onto Via Tomacelli. Staying on the right (northern) edge of the street, turn right at the second intersection into Piazza Augusto, site of the:

8 Augustus Mausoleum

Once covered with marble and cypress trees, this tomb housed the ashes of many of the emperors of the 1st century all the way up to Hadrian (who built what is now Castel Sant'Angelo across the river for his own tomb). The imperial remains stayed intact within this building until the 5th century, when invading barbarians smashed the bronze gates and stole the golden urns, probably emptying the ashes onto the ground outside. The tomb was restored by Mussolini, and although

you cannot enter the mausoleum itself, you can walk around it.

At the mausoleum's southwestern corner (Largo San Rocco), veer northwest until you reach the edge of the Tiber, stopping for a view of a bizarre, almost surreal compendium of ancient archaeological remnants restored and, in some cases, enhanced by Mussolini. It sits in an airy glass-and-concrete building beside the eastern banks of the Tiber at Ponte Cavour. Inside is one of the treasures of antiquity, the:

9 Altar of Peace (Ara Pacis)

The altar was built by the Senate as a tribute to Augustus and the peace he had brought to the Roman world. Look closely at the marble walls for portraits of Augustus's imperial family. Mussolini collected the few fragments of this monument that were scattered in museums throughout the world and gave his archaeological engineers a deadline for digging out the bulk of the altar, which remained underground—below the water table and forming part of the foundation of a Renaissance palace on the Corso. Fearful of failing Il Duce, the engineers hit on the idea of chemically freezing the water surrounding the altar and simply chipping the relic out in huge chunks of ice, building new supports for the palace overhead as they went.

Proceed southward along Via Ripetta, cross over Piazza di Porto di Ripetta, and then fork left, walking southeast along Via Borghese for a block until you reach the austere entrance to the:

10 Borghese Palace (Palazzo Borghese)

Although many of the art treasures that once graced its interior now form part of the Galleria Borghese collections (for details, see the listing on p. 168—you can't just duck in quickly on a whim), this huge and somewhat disjointed palazzo retains its status as the modern-day Borghese family's seat of power and prestige. Bought from another family in 1605 by the cardinal who later became Pope Paul V, it was later occupied by Pauline

Borghese, Napoleon's scandalous sister, a noted enemy of opera composer Rossini. Regrettably, the palace, carefully preserving its status as one of the most prestigious private homes in the world, is not open to the public.

From your vantage point, walk in a westerly direction along Via Fontanella Borghese back to a square you've already visited, Largo Goldoni, the western terminus of Via Condotti. The busy avenue on your right is one of the most richly stocked treasure troves of Italian merchandise in Rome:

⑪ Via del Corso

When compared with the many meandering streets with which it merges, the rigidly straight lines of Via del Corso are unusual. In the 18th century, residents of Rome commandeered the street to race everything from horses to street urchins, festooning the windows of buildings on either side of the narrow street with banners and flags. Although today its merchandise is not as chic (or as expensive) as what you'll find along Via Condotti, it's well worth a browse to see what's up in the world of Italian fashion.

Walk south along Via del Corso's western edge, turning right (west) after 1 block into Piazza San Lorenzo in Lucina. The severely massive building on the piazza's northern edge is the:

⑫ Palazzo Ruspoli

This is a 16th-century testament to the wealth of the Florentine Rucellai family. Family members commissioned the same architect (Bartolommeo Ammannati) who designed parts of the Pitti Palace in Florence to build their Roman headquarters. Today the building belongs to a private foundation, although it's occasionally open for temporary, infrequently scheduled exhibitions. The entrance is at Via del Corso 418A, although your best vantage point will be from Piazza San Lorenzo in Lucina.

On the piazza's southern edge rises the:

⑬ Chiesa di San Lorenzo in Lucina

Most of what you'll see today was rebuilt around 1650, although if you look carefully, the portico and most of the bell tower have survived almost unchanged since the 1100s. According to tradition, this church was built on the site of the mansion of Lucina, a prosperous Roman matron who salvaged the corpses of Christian martyrs from prisons and amphitheaters for proper burials. The church was founded by Sixtus III, who reigned for 8 years beginning in A.D. 432. Inside, look for the tomb of the French painter Poussin (1594–1665), which was carved and consecrated on orders of the French statesman Chateaubriand in 1830.

After your visit, retrace your steps back to Via del Corso and walk southward until you reach the venerable perimeter of:

⑭ Piazza Colonna

Its centerpiece is one of the most dramatic obelisks in town, the Column of Marcus Aurelius, a hollow bronze column rising 25m (83 ft.) above the piazza. Built between A.D. 180 and 196, and restored (some say "defaced") in 1589 by a pope who replaced the statue of the Roman warrior on top with a statue of St. Paul, it's one of the ancient world's best examples of heroic bas-relief and one of the most memorable sights of Rome. Beside the piazza's northern edge rises the Palazzo Chigi, official residence of the Italian prime minister.

Continue walking west from Piazza Colonna into another square a few steps to the east, and you'll find yourself in a dramatic piazza designed by Bernini:

⑮ Piazza di Montecitorio

This was the site during ancient times of the cremations of the Roman emperors. In 1792, the massive obelisk of Psammetichus II, originally erected in Egypt in the 6th century B.C., was placed here as the piazza's centerpiece. Brought to Rome

10

Shopping

Rome offers temptations of every kind. You might find hidden oases of charm and value in lesser-known neighborhoods, but in our limited space here, we've summarized certain streets known throughout Italy for their shops. Keep in mind that the monthly rent on these places is very high, and those costs will be passed on to you. Nonetheless, a stroll down some of these streets presents a cross-section of the most desirable wares found in Italy.

Although Rome has many wonderful boutiques, you'll find better shopping in Florence and Venice. If you're continuing on to either of these cities, hold off a bit.

Shopping hours are generally Monday from 3:30 to 7:30pm, and Tuesday through Saturday from 9:30 or 10am to 1pm and 3:30 to 7 or 7:30pm. Some shops are open on Monday mornings, however, and some shops don't close for the afternoon break.

1 The Shopping Scene

SHIPPING Shipping can be a problem, but—for a price—any object can be packed, shipped, and insured. For major purchases, you should buy an all-risks insurance policy to cover damage or loss in transit. Because these policies can be expensive, check into whether using a credit card to make your purchase will provide automatic free insurance.

TAX REBATES ON PURCHASES IN ITALY Visitors are sometimes appalled at the high taxes and add-ons that seem to make so many things expensive in Italy. Those taxes, totaling as much as 19% to 35% for certain goods, apply to big-ticket purchases of more than 155€ ($186) but can be refunded if you plan ahead and perform a bit of sometimes tiresome paperwork. When you make your purchase, get a receipt from the vendor. When you leave Italy, find an Italian Customs agent at the point of your exit from the country. The agent will want to see the item you've bought, confirm that it's physically leaving Italy, and stamp the vendor's receipt.

You should then mail the stamped receipt (keeping a photocopy for your records) back to the original vendor. The vendor will, sooner or later, send you a check representing a refund of the tax you paid. Reputable stores view this as a matter of ordinary paperwork and are very businesslike about it. Less honorable stores might lose your receipts. It pays to deal with established vendors on purchases of this size.

MAJOR SHOPPING STREETS

VIA BORGOGNONA This street begins near Piazza di Spagna, and both the rents and the merchandise are chic and ultra-expensive. Like its neighbor, Via Condotti, Via Borgognona is a mecca for wealthy, well-dressed men and women from around the world. Its storefronts have retained their baroque or neoclassical facades.

VIA COLA DI RIENZO Bordering the Vatican, this long, straight street runs from the Tiber to Piazza Risorgimento. Since the street is wide and clogged with traffic, it's best to walk down one side and then up the other. Via Cola di Rienzi is known for stores selling a wide variety of merchandise at reasonable prices—from jewelry to fashionable clothes and shoes.

VIA CONDOTTI Easy to find because it begins at the base of the Spanish Steps, this is Rome's poshest and most prominent shopping street—the Madison Avenue of Rome. Even the recent incursion of some less elegant stores hasn't diminished the allure of Via Condotti as a consumer's playground for the rich and super-rich. For us mere mortals, it's a great place for window-shopping and people-watching.

VIA DEL CORSO Not attempting the stratospheric image or prices of Via Condotti or Via Borgognona, Via del Corso boasts styles aimed at younger consumers. There are some gems scattered amid the shops selling jeans and sporting equipment. The most interesting stores are nearest the fashionable cafes of Piazza del Popolo.

VIA FRANCESCO CRISPI Most shoppers reach this street by following Via Sistina (see below) 1 long block from the top of the Spanish Steps. Near the intersection of these streets are several shops for unusual and less expensive gifts.

VIA FRATTINA Running parallel to Via Condotti, it begins, like its more famous sibling, at Piazza di Spagna. Part of its length is closed to traffic. Here the concentration of shops is denser, although some aficionados claim that its image is slightly less chic and prices are slightly lower than at its counterparts on Via Condotti. It's usually thronged with shoppers who appreciate the lack of motor traffic.

VIA NAZIONALE The layout recalls 19th-century grandeur, but the traffic is horrendous; crossing Via Nazionale requires a good sense of timing and a strong understanding of Italian driving patterns. It begins at Piazza della Repubblica and runs down almost to the 19th-century monuments of Piazza Venezia. You'll find an abundance of leather stores (more reasonable in price than those in many other parts of Rome) and a handful of stylish boutiques.

VIA SISTINA Beginning at the top of the Spanish Steps, Via Sistina runs to Piazza Barberini. The shops are small and stylish, and pedestrian traffic is less dense than on other major streets.

VIA VITTORIO VENETO Via Veneto is filled with expensive hotels and cafes and relatively expensive stores selling shoes, gloves, and leather goods.

BEST BUYS

Because of the Italians' consummate skills as manufacturers and designers, it's no surprise that consumers from all over the world flock to Italy's shops, trade fairs, and design studios to see what's new, hot, and salable back home.

The most obvious draw is **fashion.** Milan might be the center of the fashion industry, but Rome is a principal distribution center. There are literally hundreds of famous designers for both men and women, most of whom make eminently stylish garments. Materials include silks, leathers, cottons, synthetics, and wool, often of the finest quality.

Italian design influences everything from computer keyboards to kitchen appliances to furniture. The Italian studios of Memphis-Milan and Studio Alchimia are two of the leaders in this field, and many of their products (and rip-offs thereof) are now highly visible in machines and furnishings throughout the world. Alessi has

Ad Antiqua Domus **38**
Ai Monasteri **37**
Ai Monasteri **39**
Alberto di Castro **8**
Alfieri **3**
Anatrielio Argenteria Antica e Moderna Roma **12**
Antica Erboristeria Romana **44**

Arsenale **38**
Artimport **5**
Aston **55**
Bagagli **33**
Benetton **17**
Boutique Design **30**
Brighenti **25**
Brioni **56**
Buccone **2**
Bulgari **23**
Campanile **15**
Campo de Fiori **42**
Casagrande **31**
Castroni **1**
Coin **41**
Confetteria Mariondo e Gariglio **45**
c.u.c.i.n.a. **27**
Dalco' Nives **43**
Davide Cenci **59**
Degli Effetti **44**
Diego Percossi Papi **40**
Disfunzioni Musicali **58**
Ditta G. Poggi **46**
Dominici **4**
Emporio Armani **9**
Ex Ante **36**
Fausto Santini **24**
Federico Buccellati **20**
Feltrinelli Libri e Musica **44**
Fendi **6**
Ferragamo **14**
Fornari & Fornari **26**
Fragiacomo **20**
Francesco Rogani **16**
Fratelli Bassetti **41**
Giovanni B. Panatta Fine Art Shop **53**
Givenchy **19**

Grispigni **52**
Gucci **23**
La Città del Sole **35**
La Rinascente **28**
Laura Biagiotti **22**
Lavori Artigianali Femminili **49**
Liberia Babele **41**
Lily of Florence **54**
Lingerie D'elia **50**
The Lion Bookshop **7**
Livio di Simone **6**
Max Mara **21**
Mercato Andrea Doria **32**
Mercato dei Fiori **47**
Mercato delle Stampe **34**
Mercato di Testaccio **47**
Mercato di Via Sannio **59**
Mondello Ottica **42**
Officina Farmaceutica di Santa Maria Novella **39**
Pavoncello Angelo **41**
Pelletterie **41**
Piazza Vittorio Emanuele **59**
Porta Portese Flea Market **38**
Profumeria Materozzoli **18**
Renato Balestra **51**
Richard Ginori **48**
Savelli **32**
Schostal **29**
Siragusa **13**
Spazio Sette **44**
Stock Market **41**
Tad **11**
Trimani **57**
Valentino **23**
Valentino Sport **10**

become a world-renowned name in witty, innovative houseware design. You can preview many of Italy's new products and designs by reading a copy of *Domus,* a monthly magazine that reports on many different aspects of the country's design scene.

Food and wine never go out of style, and gourmets frequently bring some of Italy's bounty home with them. Many Roman shops sell chocolates, pastries, liqueurs, wines, and limited-edition olive oils. Keep in mind that there are restrictions against importing certain food products into North America, including anything fresh, such as fruit or prosciutto. Italian wines include many excellent vintages, and bottles of liqueurs (which are sometimes distilled from herbs and flowers) make unusual gifts. You can bring home only 1 liter of wine or spirits duty-free.

The **glassware** of Italy (and especially of Venice) is famous throughout the world and is sold all over Rome. It's fragile enough that you should look into shipping it directly home with insurance.

Italy's **porcelain** might be elegant and sought after, but personally we prefer the hand-painted rustic plates and bowls of thick-edged **stoneware** known as Laveggio. Done in strong and clear glazes and influenced by their rural origins, the bowls and plates are often used at the most formal dinners for their originality and style. The **tiles** and **mosaics** of Italy are virtually without equal in the world, whether used individually as drink coasters or decorative ornaments, or in groups set into masonry walls.

Nuns made **lace** in convents for many years. Venice became the country's headquarters. Handmade Italian lace is exquisite and justifiably expensive, crafted into tablecloths, napkins, clothing, and bridal veils. Beware of machine-made imitations; with a bit of practice, you'll soon be able to recognize the shoddy copies.

Paper goods, stationery, elegantly bound books, prints, and engravings are specialties of Italy. The engravings you find amid stacks of dozens of others will invariably look stately when framed and hanging on a wall back home.

Fabrics, especially silk, are made near Lake Como, in the foothills of the Italian Alps. Known for their supple beauty and their ability to hold color for years (the thicker the silk, the more desirable), these silks are rivaled only by the finest of India, Thailand, and China. Their history in Italy goes back to the era of Marco Polo, possibly much earlier.

Finally, Rome is the home to a **religious objects** industry. Centered on the streets near the Church of Santa Maria Sopra Minerva are dozens of shops selling pictures, statues, and reliefs of most of the important saints, the Madonna, Jesus, and John the Baptist. And some shops cross the line of good taste and into the realm of high camp—we've even seen snow globes of the pope blessing Rome.

2 Shopping A to Z

ANTIQUES

Some visitors to Italy consider the many antiques for sale the country's greatest treasure. But prices have risen to alarming levels as increasingly wealthy Europeans outbid one another in a frenzy. Any antiques dealer who risks the high rents of central Rome is acutely aware of valuations. So while you might find gorgeous pieces, you're not likely to find any bargains.

Beware of fakes, remember to insure anything you have shipped home, and for larger purchases—anything more than 155€ ($186) at any one store—keep your paperwork in order to obtain your tax refund (p. 70).

Via dei Coronari is buried in a colorful section of the Campo Marzio. To find the street, turn left out of the north end of Piazza Navona and pass the excavated ruins of Domitian's Stadium—it will be just ahead. There are more than 40 antiques stores in the next 4 blocks, offering inlaid secretaries, gilded consoles, vases, urns, chandeliers, marble pedestals, chaises, refectory tables—you name it. Bring your pocket calculator and keep in mind that stores are frequently closed between 1 and 4pm.

Via del Babuino is another major street for antiques in Rome, with some of the most prestigious stores found here, including Alberto di Castro (our favorite store for prints—see "Art," below), but many others as well.

A few minutes south of Piazza del Popolo, via Laurina lies midway between via del Corso and via del Babuino. It is filled with beautiful stores where you can find anything from an antique print to a 17th-century chandelier.

Ad Antiqua Domus   This shop practically feels like a museum of Italian furniture design through the ages. You'll find furniture from the days of Caesar through the 19th century for sale here. Via dei Coronari 41. ☎ **06-6861186.** Bus: 41, 46B, or 98.

ArtImport   An antiques shopper's dream, this bazaar always has something for sale that's intriguing and tasteful—if you can agree on a price. The store's motto is "In the service of the table," so there's an emphasis on silver, although the objects run the gamut. The goblets, elegant bowls, candlesticks, and candelabra sold here are almost without equal in Rome. Via del Babuino 150. ☎ **06-3221330.** Metro: Spagna.

ART

Alberto di Castro ★★   Alberto di Castro is one of the largest dealers in antique prints and engravings in Rome. You'll find depictions of everything from the Colosseum to the Pantheon, each evocative of the Mediterranean world, priced between 21€ to 7,967€ ($25–$9,560), depending on the age and rarity of the engraving. Via del Babuino 71. ☎ **06-3613752.** Metro: Spagna.

Giovanni B. Panatta Fine Art Shop   In business since 1890, this store is up the hill toward the Villa Borghese. Here you'll find excellent prints in color and black and white, covering a variety of subjects from 18th-century Roman street scenes to astrological charts. There's a good selection of attractive and reasonably priced reproductions of medieval and Renaissance art as well. Via Francesco Crispi 117. ☎ **06-6795948.** Metro: Spagna or Barberini.

BOOKSTORES

Feltrinelli Libri e Musica   Near the Pantheon, this is the Rome outlet for a chain of popular bookstores spread across Italy. It's been called the Italian Borders. This branch has a section of English titles, both fiction and nonfiction. There is an especially good section on travel, plus CD listening stations. Largo di Torre Argentina 5–6 (at Corso Vittorio Emanuele II). ☎ **06-68803248.** Bus: 30, 40, 62, 64, 70, or 87.

Libreria Babele   This is Rome's major gay and lesbian bookstore. Besides the usual stock, it sells a gay map of the city. Via dei Banchi Vecchi 116. ☎ **06-6876628.** Bus: 40, 62, or 64.

The Lion Bookshop   The Lion Bookshop is the oldest English-language bookshop in town, specializing in both American and English titles. It also sells children's books and photographic volumes on both Rome and Italy. English-language videos are for sale or rent. Closed in August. Via del Greci 33. ☎ **06-32654007.** Metro: Spagna.

CHINA, PORCELAIN & GLASSWARE

One of the city's most prestigious retail outlets for porcelain, both artworks and plates, contains a glittering assortment of the impeccably crafted porcelain of **Richard Ginori** ✸. Founded in 1735, it offers china and glassware as well. Anything you buy here can be shipped, but if you prefer to buy at Ginori's outlets in North America (which include Tiffany's in New York), you can at least check out the dozens of patterns. Piazza Trinità dei Monti 18B. ✆ **06-6793836.** Metro: Spagna.

CHOCOLATES

Confetteria Moriondo e Gariglio   There is no finer chocolatier in Rome than this family-run outlet that's mobbed at Easter and before Valentine's Day. The dark, liqueur-filled confections and other treats are molded and made right on-site. The staff also sells confections made out of almonds, chestnuts, and other nuts. Closed in August. Via di Pie' di Marmo 21–22. ✆ **06-6990856.** Bus: 40, 46, 64, or 119.

COSMETICS & PERFUMES

Ai Monasteri ✸✸   This shop, evoking a medieval apothecary, was founded here in 1892 and has since been managed by four generations of the Nardi family. It sells products from monastic orders around Italy, many of them based on centuries-old and closely guarded recipes. Merchandise ranges from liqueurs to "products from the beehive," rare oils and vinegar to some of the best tasting jams we've ever had. Expect to be dazzled by items that include some of the world's best chocolates to rare cosmetic products. Corso del Rinascimento 72. ✆ **06-68802783.** Bus: 87.

Antica Erboristeria Romana _(Finds)_   Charles Dickens might call it the curiosity shop. Since the 18th century it has been dispensing "wonders" from its tiny wooden drawers, some of which are labeled with skulls and crossbones. Scented aper, licorice, hellbane, and herbal remedies . . . it's all here and more. Via di Torre Argentina 15. ✆ **06-6879493.** Metro: Spagna or Barberini.

Officina Farmaceutica di Santa Maria Novella ✸   This highly scented perfumery and apothecary's shop is a branch of its more famous parent in Florence. The staff sells creams, exotic soaps and essences, and lotions based on formulas created in the 16th century by Dominican monks in Tuscany. The potpourri is a wonderful gift to take home. Closed 1 week in mid-August. Corso del Rinascimento 47. ✆ **06-6872446.** Bus: 62, 70, 116, or 492.

Profumeria Materozzoli ✸   This elegant _profumeria_ was founded in 1870 and has been satisfying Roman tastes in cosmetics and perfumes ever since. It is one of the best cosmetic shops in all of Italy, carrying many hard-to-find scents, including some from Britain and France. It's also known for body products, including bristle shaving brushes. Piazza San Lorenzo in Lucina 5. ✆ **06-68892686.** Metro: Spagna.

DEPARTMENT STORES

COIN   Close to the Vatican, this is hardly the Harrods of Rome, but might come in handy for any number of purchases. The store sells clothing of medium but affordable quality along with accessories, shoes, underwear, jewelry—you name it. If you shop carefully here, you can find some great buys. There is a good section of cosmetics, even a department for kids clothing and a good selection of Italian household wares. Via Copla di Rienzo 173 (at Via Poolo Emilio). ✆ **06-700020.** Metro: Ottaviano.

La Rinascente   This upscale department store offers clothing, hosiery, perfume, cosmetics, and other goods. It also has its own line of clothing (Ellerre) for men, women, and children. This is the largest of the Italian department-store chains. Piazza Colonna, Via del Corso 189. ✆ 06-6797691. Bus: 117.

DISCOUNT SHOPPING

Certain stores that can't move their merchandise at any price often consign their unwanted goods to discounters. In Italy, the original labels are usually still inside the garment, and you'll find some very chic labels strewn in with mounds of more generic garments. Know in advance that these pieces couldn't be sold at higher prices in more glamorous shops, and some garments are the wrong size, are the wrong look, or have a stylistic mistake. If you're willing to sift through a lot, you might find a gem.

Il Discount dell'Alta Moda *Value*   The honest and genuinely helpful staff here will help you pick through the constantly changing racks of women's and men's clothing, with discounts of up to 50% on such labels as Versace, Donna Karan, Armani, Krizia, and Ferré. The shop also sells irregulars and overstock at cut-rates. Near the Spanish Steps at Via di Gesù e Maria 16A. ✆ 06-3613796. Metro: Flaminio. Another branch is near Termini at Via Viminale 35 (✆ 06-47825672). Metro: Repubblica.

McArthurGlen Designer Outlet   Bargain hunters seeking major labels at prices 35% to 75% below normal head for the Roman hill town of Castel Romano 6 miles (10km) east of Rome. In a faux Roman setting, this shopping complex takes in nearly 90 stores. Here you'll have all your needs met in clothing, footwear, and accessories. Designer names include Versace, Dolce & Gabbana, Hilfiger, and Ferragamo. There is also a large playground here, along with restaurants and bars. Take the B line of the Metro to the Laurentina stop. From this point, catch a Cotral bus toward Pomezia-Latina to the Castel Romano stop. From this point, it's a 5-minute walk to Castel Romano Outlet. Via Ponte di Piscina Cupa 51, Castel Romano. ✆ 06-5050050.

EYEWEAR

Mondello Ottica   At Campo de' Fiori, this is one of the best places to shop for eyewear in all of Rome, with a wide selection ranging from sunglasses to prescription frames. A few steps from Corso Vittorio Emanuele II, it offers a very wide selection of both Italian and foreign brands of eyewear. Naturally, it's also well equipped to supply contact lenses. Via del Pellegrino 98. ✆ 06-6861955. Bus: 87.

FABRICS

Aston   Right on the tourist-trodden Via Veneto, this elegant outlet sells some of the finest Italian and continental fabrics, including silks. It also stocks fashionable ready-to-wear clothing for both men and woman. Sometimes remnants *(scampolia)* are sold, and these are true deals. Via Boncompagni 27. ✆ 06-42871227. Metro: Barberini. Bus: 52.

Fratelli Bassetti   About 300m (984 ft.) from Piazzo Campo de' Fiori, this antique *palazzo* is the showcase for a fabulous collection of exquisite Italian silks and other *couture* fashion fabrics. The Bassetti company also makes and sells sheets, bed coverings, rugs, tablecloths, curtains, and upholstery fabrics. Closed 2 weeks in August. Corso Vittorio Emanuele II, 73. ✆ 06-6892326. Bus: 40 or 64.

FASHION

See also "Department Stores," "Discount Shopping," "Leather," "Lingerie," and "Shoes."

FOR MEN

Brioni ⊛⊛ This is the finest men's clothing store in Rome, opening in 1945 and dressing ambassadors, actors, and presidents over the years. It numbers among its clientele a virtual who's who that includes Donald Trump, Clark Gable, John Wayne, Gary Cooper, and Luciano Pavarotti. Brioni even outfitted 007 in some of the James Bond films. The custom tailoring is impeccable, but you can also purchase ready-to-wear garments. Via Barberini 79. ℂ 06-484517. Metro: Repubblica. Bus: 175.

Emporio Armani This store stocks relatively inexpensive menswear crafted by the couturier who has dressed perhaps more stage and screen stars than any other designer in Italy. The designer's more expensive line—sold at sometimes staggering prices that are nonetheless up to 30% less than what you'd pay in the United States—is a short walk away at **Giorgio Armani,** Via Condotti 77 (ℂ **06-6991460**). Via del Babuino 140. ℂ 06-36002197. Metro: Spagna.

Schostal Dating to 1870, this is the clothing store for men who like their fashion conservative and well crafted. It features everything from underwear to cashmere overcoats. The prices are more reasonable than you might think. Via del Corso 158. ℂ 06-6791240. Bus: 117.

Valentino ⊛⊛⊛ If you can afford the high prices in this swank emporium, you'll be the most fashionable man in town. Valentino's women's haute couture is sold around the corner in an even bigger showroom at Via Bocca di Leone 15 (ℂ **06-6787585**). Via dei Condotti 13. ℂ **06-6790479**. Metro: Spagna.

FOR WOMEN

Arsenale ⊛ Most of the inventory displayed here is the creative statement of owner Patrizia Pieroni. Her design preferences include lots of ultra-rich fabrics, nothing too frilly or girlish, and a dignified kind of severity that many foreign visitors find captivating. Favorite colors include a spectrum of pinks, pale grays, and lilacs, with accents of bright orange, celadon green, Bordeaux, and off-whites. Via del Governo Vecchio 64. ℂ 06-6861380. Bus: 30, 81, or 87.

Benetton Despite the gracefully arched ceiling and its prized location, this branch of the worldwide sportswear distributor has down-to-earth prices and some of the same stock you'd find at branches around the world. Famous for woolen sweaters, tennis wear, blazers, and resort wear, this company (like every other clothier) has suffered from inexpensive copies of its designs. The men's line is also worth a look. Via del Corso Angolo 422–423, Via Tomacelli 164. ℂ 06-68102520. Metro: Spagna.

Givenchy ⊛ This is the Roman headquarters of one of the great design houses of France, a company known since World War I for its couture. In its Roman branch, the company emphasizes stylish ready-to-wear garments for women, appropriate for the warm Italian weather. Tasteful shirts and pullovers for men are also available. Via Borgognona 21. ℂ 06-6784058. Metro: Spagna.

Laura Biagiotti ⊛⊛ One of Rome's born-and-bred designers remains our favorite. Stylish *signoras* still come here to buy cashmere knits from a woman known as the "Queen of Cashmere." A Biagiotti dress fits casually, loosely, but flatteringly on a woman's frame and often contains topstitching and *ajourée,* or fretwork. She calls her own fashions "behavioral modern art." The designer also creates stylish fashions for men. Via Borgognona 43–44. ℂ 06-6791205. Metro: Spagna.

Max Mara   Max Mara is one of the best outlets in Rome for chic women's clothing. The fabrics are appealing, and the alterations are free. Via Frattina 28 (at Largo Goldoni). ℂ 06-6793638. Metro: Spagna. There is another branch at Via Nazionale 28–31. Bus: 117.

Renato Balestra   Rapidly approaching the stratospheric upper levels of Italian fashion is Renato Balestra, whose women's clothing exudes a lighthearted elegance. Via Sistina 67. ℂ 06-6795424. Metro: Spagna.

Tad   For one-stop shopping—perfume, accessories, shoes, fashion—this is the address. A textile line and a collection of home furnishings are only two features of what is called a "concept shop." Another section is devoted to music with a large CD collection. The Roman press has hailed Tad as the city's "coolest lifestyle store." The Tad Café serves breakfast, light lunches, and luscious desserts in an Asian-style inner courtyard. Via del Babuino 53. ℂ 06-36001809. Metro: Spagna.

FOR CHILDREN

Lavori Artigianali Femminili   Near Piazza di Spagna is an unusual clothing store for children and infants. The shop features what many a little Roman aristocrat might be wearing, including handmade velvet and chiffon lace-trimmed party dresses. They also sell embroidered crib and carriage linens. It's expensive and occasionally imprac- tical, but what a delight. Closed in August. Via di Capo Le Case 6. ℂ 06-6781100. Metro: Spagna.

CLASSICAL CLOTHING FOR MEN & WOMEN

Davide Cenci   This upscale specialty store opened in 1926 and has long been pop- ular with well-heeled locals. There's a wide choice of men's jackets (some in cashmere) and well-tailored shirts. Women gravitate to the beautifully tailored skirts and trousers, as well as the knitwear made of natural fibers. Even shoes and children's clothing are sold. Via Campo Marzio 1–7. ℂ 06-6990681. Metro: Colosseo.

Degli Effetti   Near the Pantheon, this funky but classic trio of designer boutiques stocks name labels. These are mostly from designers that can't afford their own show- case outlets. The store sells sophisticated menswear at number 75, chic women's apparel at 79, and unisex offerings at 93. The latter has the most high-quality apparel but at expensive prices. Piazza Capranica 75-79-93. ℂ 06-6790202. Bus: 87.

SPORTSWEAR FOR MEN & WOMEN

Valentino Sport   Specializing exclusively in sportswear, this is Valentino's least expensive line of clothing. His easy-to-wear, stylish clothing has warm climates in mind. In summer, there's more emphasis on women's clothes than men's, but the rest of the year the inventories are about equal. Via del Babuino 61. ℂ 06-36001906. Metro: Spagna.

FOOD

See also "Markets," below.

Castroni 𝕂𝕂   At this old-fashioned store, you'll find an array of unusual foodstuffs from around the Mediterranean. If you want herbs from Apulia, cheese from the Valle d'Aosta, or an obscure brand of balsamic vinegar, Castroni will have it. Filled to the rafters with the abundance of agrarian Italy, it also carries foods that are exotic in Italy but commonplace in North America, such as taco shells, corn curls, and peanut but- ter. Via Cola di Rienzo 196. ℂ 06-6874383. Bus: 32 or 81.

GIFTS

Ex Ante *(Finds)* You'll find some of the most exquisite and exotic gifts in Rome here, although they come with a hefty price tag. If you're looking for a gift from Italy, France, China, the Middle East, or some other faraway land, this is the place. Examples include handcrafted silver frames embedded with amber from Asia. There's another location at Via Vittoria 13 (*C* **06-32650534**), with smaller and more affordable items. Largo Toniolo 4. *C* **06-68801107.** Metro: Spagna. Bus: 70, 81, 119, or 170.

Grispigni Here you'll find a constantly changing array of gifts, including a large assortment of leather-covered boxes, women's purses, compacts, desk sets, and cigarette cases. Via Francesco Crispi 59 (at Via Sistina). *C* **06-6790290.** Metro: Spagna or Barberini.

HOUSEWARES

Bagagli Here you'll find a good selection of Alessi, Rose and Tulipani, and Villeroy & Boch china in a pleasantly kitschy old Rome setting complete with cobblestone floors. Via Campo Marzio 42. *C* **06-6871406.** Bus: 70 or 628.

c.u.c.i.n.a. This is a stainless-steel shrine to everything you need for a proper Italian kitchen, sporting designs that are as beautiful in their simplicity as they are utilitarian. Via Mario de' Fiori 65. *C* **06-6791275.** Metro: Spagna.

Spazio Sette This is far and away Rome's best housewares emporium, a design boutique of department-store proportions. It goes way beyond the Alessi tea kettles to fill three huge floors with the greatest names in Italian and international design. Via D. Barbieri 7, off Largo di Torre Argentina. *C* **06-6869747.** Metro: Colosseo.

Stock Market *(Value)* Here you'll find great prices on last year's models, overstock, irregulars, and artistic misadventures in design that the pricier boutiques couldn't move. Most is moderately funky household stuff, but you never know when you'll find a gem. Via D. Banchi Vecchi 51–52. *C* **06-6864238.** Bus: 40, 46, 62, or 64. Another location is near the Vatican at Via Tacito 60. *C* **06-36002343.** Metro: Ottaviano.

JEWELRY

Since the days when the ancient Romans imported amethysts and pearls from the distant borders of their empire, and the great trading ships of Venice and Genoa carried rubies and sapphires from Asia, Italians have collected jewelry. Styles range from the most classically conservative to neo-punk-rock frivolous—part of the fun is shopping for something you might never before have considered wearing.

Bulgari *(★★★)* Bulgari is the capital's most prestigious jeweler and has been since the 1890s. The shop window, on a conspicuously affluent stretch of Via Condotti, is a visual attraction in its own right. Bulgari designs combine classical Greek aesthetics with Italian taste. Over the years, Bulgari has managed to follow changes in style while still maintaining its tradition. Prices range from affordable to insane. Via Condotti 10. *C* **06-6793876.** Metro: Spagna.

Diego Percossi Papi *(★ Finds)* Look here for the ornate jewelry Lucrezia Borgia might wear if she were alive and kicking. Most of the designs are inspired by Renaissance themes, many crafted from gemstones and accented with iridescent patches of enameling. Jade, opal, and semiprecious gemstones are heavily featured. Via Sant'Eustachio 16. *C* **06-68801466.** Metro: Barberini or Colosseo. Bus: 64.

Federico Buccellati ✿✿✿   At this, one of the best gold- and silversmiths in Italy, neo-Renaissance creations will change your thinking about gold and silver designs. You'll discover the Italian tradition and beauty of handmade jewelry and holloware whose principles sometimes hark back to the designs of Renaissance gold master Benvenuto Cellini. Via Condotti 31. ✆ 06-6790329. Metro: Spagna.

LEATHER

Italian leather is among the very best in the world and, at its best, can attain buttersoft textures more pliable than cloth. You'll find hundreds of leather stores in Rome, many of them excellent.

Alfieri   Virtually every leather garment imaginable is sold in this richly stocked store. Established in the 1960s, with a somewhat more funky and counterculture slant than Casagrande or Campanile, Alfieri sells a wide range of jackets, boots, bags, belts, shirts, hats, and pants for men and women; shorts reminiscent of German lederhosen; and skirts in at least 10 different colors. Everything sold is made in Italy, but this place prides itself on reasonable prices rather than ultra-high quality. Check the stitching and zippers carefully before you invest. Via del Corso 1–2. ✆ 06-3611976. Bus: 117.

Campanile   Belying the postmodern sleekness of its premises, this outfit has a pedigree going back to the 1870s and an impressive inventory of well-crafted leather jackets, belts, shoes, bags, and suitcases for both men and women. Quality is relentlessly high (as are prices). Via Condotti 58. ✆ 06-6783041. Metro: Spagna.

Casagrande   If famous names in leather wear appeal to you, you'll find most of the biggies here—Fendi and its youth-conscious offspring, Fendissime, plus Cerruti, Mosquino, and Valentino. This well-managed store has developed an impressive reputation for quality and authenticity since the 1930s. Prices are more reasonable than in some other parts of town. Via Cola di Rienzo 206. ✆ 06-6874610. Bus: 81.

Fendi ✿✿✿   The House of Fendi is mainly known for its leather goods, but it also has furs, stylish purses, ready-to-wear clothing, and a new men's line of clothing and accessories. Gift items, home furnishings, and sports accessories are also sold here, all emblazoned with an F. It's closed Saturday afternoons from July to September. Via Borgognona 36–40. ✆ 06-696661. Metro: Spagna.

Francesco Rogani ✿   Francesco Rogani has become one of Rome's most famous leather stores, offering a wide selection of bags for every occasion. At Rogani, you'll find a good price-quality relation also for wallets, belts, and handmade ties. Via Condotti 47. ✆ 06-6784036. Metro: Spagna.

Gucci ✿✿✿   Gucci has been a legend since 1900, selling high-class leather suitcases, handbags, wallets, shoes, and accessories. It also has elegant men's and women's wear, including shirts, blouses, and dresses, as well as ties and scarves. *La bella figura* is alive and well at Gucci; prices have never been higher. Among the many temptations is Gucci's own perfume. Via Condotti 8. ✆ 06-6790405. Metro: Spagna. There is another location at Via Borgognona 7D. ✆ 06-69190661. Metro: Spagna.

LINGERIE

Brighenti ✿✿   Brighenti sells strictly lingerie di lusso, or perhaps better phrased, haute corseterie. You might run across a lacy, seductive fantasy you just have to have. Closed 2 weeks in August. Via Frattina 7–8. ✆ 06-6791484. Metro: Spagna.

One-of-a-Kind Shops

Alinari, Via Alibert 16A (*℃* **06-6792923;** Metro: Spagna), takes its name from the famed Florentine photographer of the 19th century. Original Alinari prints are almost as prized as paintings in national galleries, and they record the Rome of a century ago.

Siragusa, Via delle Carrozze 64 (*℃* **06-6797085;** Metro: Spagna), is more like a museum than a shop, specializing in unusual jewelry based on ancient carved stones or archaeological pieces mounted in 24K gold. Handmade chains, for example, often hold coins and beads discovered in Asia Minor that date from the 3rd and 4th centuries B.C.

Lingerie D'elia ✸   This shop offers delicately beautiful lingerie and negligees, all original designs of Luisa Romagnoli. Most of the merchandise is shimmery Italian silk; some is fluffy cotton or frothy nylon. Very revealing garments are sold ready to wear or custom-made. Via Sistina 119. *℃* **06-4881909.** Metro: Spagna or Barberini.

LUGGAGE

Livio di Simone   Unusual suitcases in many shapes and sizes into which handpainted canvas has been sewn are sold here. This outlet has one of the most tasteful yet durable collections in Rome. Via San Giacomo 23. *℃* **06-36001732.** Metro: Spagna.

MARKETS

Piles of fresh vegetables arranged above ancient pavements in the streaming Italian sunshine—well, what visitor can resist? Here's a rundown on the Roman markets known for fresh produce, uninhibited merchants, and long-running traditions.

Campo de' Fiori   During the Renaissance, this neighborhood contained most of the inns that pilgrims and merchants from other parts of Europe used for lodgings. Today its battered and slightly shabby perimeter surrounds about a hundred merchants who arrange their produce artfully every day. Campo de' Fiori. Bus: 46, 62, or 64.

Mercato Andrea Doria   After a visit to this open-air festival, you'll never look at frozen vegetables in the supermarket the same way again. Near the Vatican between Via Tunisi and Via Santamaura, the merchandise includes meats, poultry, eggs, dairy products, wines, an endless assortment of fruits and vegetables, and even some scruffy-looking racks of secondhand clothing. Via Andrea Doria. Metro: Ottaviano.

Mercato dei Fiori   Most of the week this vast covered market sells flowers only to retail florists, who resell them to consumers. Every Tuesday, however, the industrial-looking premises open to the public, who crowd in for access to exotic Mediterranean flowers at bargain-basement prices. Open to the public Tuesday from 10:30am to 1pm. Via Trionfale. Metro: Ottaviano.

Mercato delle Stampe   Virtually everything that's displayed in the dozens of battered kiosks here is dog-eared and evocatively ragtag. You'll find copies of engravings, books, magazines from the 1960s (or before), and prints and engravings that are either worthless or priceless, depending on your taste. If your passion is the printed word, this is your place, and bargaining is part of the experience. Monday to Saturday 7am to 1:30pm. Largo della Fontanella di Borghese. Bus: 81, 115, or 117.

Mercato di Testaccio   Because their stalls are covered from the wind, rain, and dust, the vendors here are able to retain an air of permanence about their setups that most outdoor markets simply can't provide. Inside you'll find fishmongers, butchers, cheese sellers, a wide array of dairy products, and the inevitable fruits and vegetables. Piazza Testaccio. Bus: 27 or 92.

Mercato di Via Sannio   If you like street fairs loaded with junky items but occasional nuggets of value or eccentric charm, this is the market for you. Regrettably, rare or unusual items are harder to find here because every antiques dealer in Italy seems to have combed through the inventories long ago. Despite that, you'll find some ragtag values. Via Sannio. Metro: S. Giovanni.

Piazza Vittorio Emanuele   Near Santa Maria Maggiore, the largest open-air food market in Rome takes place Monday through Saturday at Piazza Vittorio Emanuele. For browsing Roman style, head here any time between 7am and noon. Most of the vendors at this gigantic square sell fresh fruit, vegetables, and other foodstuffs, although many stalls are devoted to such items as cutlery, clothing, and other merchandise. The place has little to tempt the serious shopper, but it's great for discovering a slice of Roman life. Metro: Vittorio Emanuele.

Porta Portese Flea Market   On Sundays from 7am to 1pm, every peddler from Trastevere and the surrounding Castelli Romani sets up shop at the sprawling Porta Portese open-air flea market. Vendors are likely to sell merchandise ranging from secondhand paintings of Madonnas and termite-eaten Il Duce wooden medallions, to pseudo-Etruscan hairpins, rosaries, 1947 TVs, and books printed in 1835. Serious shoppers can often ferret out a good buy. If you've ever been impressed with the bargaining power of the Spaniard, you haven't seen anything until you've bartered with an Italian. As at any street market, beware of pickpockets. Near the end of Viale Trastevere. Bus: 75 to Porta Portese, and then a short walk to Via Portuense.

MOSAICS

Savelli ✾   This company specializes in the manufacture and sale of mosaics, an art form as old as the Roman Empire itself. Many objects in the company's gallery were inspired by ancient originals discovered in thousands of excavations throughout the Italian peninsula, including those at Pompeii and Ostia. Others, especially the floral designs, rely on the whim and creativity of the artists. Objects include tabletops, boxes, and vases. The cheapest mosaic objects begin at around $130 and are unsigned products crafted by art students at a school that is partially funded by the Vatican. Objects made in the Savelli workshops that are signed by the individual artists tend to be larger and more elaborate. The outlet also sells small souvenirs, such as key chains and carved statues. Via Paolo VI 27–29. ✆ 06-68307017. Metro: San Paola.

MUSIC

Disfunzioni Musicali   Sought out by vinyl lovers and used vinyl collectors from Europe and America, this shop has some serious goods. Come here for the rarities. Was that Mick Jagger we spotted searching old labels? Via Degli Etrushi 4–14. ✆ 06-4461984. Metro: Piazza Vittorio.

SHOES

Dalco' Nives *Finds* If you've ever suspected that a shoe fetish might be lurking deep inside you, a visit to this store will probably unleash it. Everything is handmade and usually can be matched to a handbag that provides a reasonably close approximation. Most of the shoes are low-key and conservative, but a few are wild, whimsical, and outrageous enough to appeal to RuPaul. But sorry, only women's shoes are stocked. Via Vittoria 65. *C* **06-6786536.** Metro: Spagna.

Dominici An understated facade a few steps from Piazza del Popolo shelters an amusing and lighthearted collection of men's and women's shoes in a rainbow variety of vivid colors. The style is aggressively young at heart, and the children's shoes are adorable. Via del Corso 14. *C* **06-3610591.** Bus: 117.

Fausto Santini ★★ This is the outlet for Rome's most celebrated designer of shoes for both men and women. Each pair of shoes is almost a work of art, and signs invite you to "please touch," since the feel of the shoes is a reward unto itself. Fausto Santini honors its commitment "to organic shapes and fundamental simplicity." Via Frattina 120. *C* **06-6784114.** Metro: Spagna. Bus: 61, 71, or 85.

Ferragamo ★★★ Ferragamo sells elegant and fabled footwear, plus women's clothing and accessories. The name became famous in America when such silent-screen vamps as Pola Negri and Greta Garbo began appearing in Ferragamo shoes. There are always many customers waiting to enter the shop; management allows them to enter in small groups. (Wear comfortable shoes for what could well be a 30-min. wait.) Via Condotti 66–73. *C* **06-6781130.** Metro: Spagna.

Fragiacomo Here you can buy shoes for both men and women in a champagne-colored showroom with gilt-touched chairs and big display cases. Via della Carrozze 28. *C* **06-6798780.** Metro: Spagna.

Lily of Florence This famous Florentine shoemaker now has a shop in Rome, with the same merchandise that made the outlet so well known in the Tuscan capital. Colors come in a wide range, the designs are stylish, and leather texture is of good quality. Shoes for both men and women are sold, and American sizes are a feature. Via Lombardia 38A (off Via Vittorio Veneto). *C* **06-4740262.** Bus: 60N or 63.

Pavoncello Angelo Pelletterie Near the Vatican, this store offers footwear in chic styles but at affordable prices. It also sells an assortment of handbags and other Italian leather goods and accessories. It's worth a detour out of your way to see the ever-changing repertoire. Piazza del Risorgimento 38. *C* **06-39737247.** Metro: Ottaviano–San Pietro.

SILVER

Anatriello Argenteria Antica e Moderna Roma ★ *Finds* This store is known for stocking new and antique silver, some of it the most unusual in Italy. New items are made by Italian silversmiths, in designs ranging from the whimsical to the formal and dignified. Also on display are antique pieces from England, Germany, and Switzerland. Via Frattina 27. *C* **06-6789601.** Metro: Spagna.

Fornari & Fornari This two-story showroom is filled with silver, lamps, porcelain, crystal, furniture, and upscale gift items from many manufacturers throughout Italy and Europe. Virtually anything can be shipped around the world. Closed in August. Via Frattina 133. *C* **06-6780105.** Metro: Spagna.

STATIONERS

Boutique Design ✿ This is the best shop for elegant writing paper and leather-bound notebooks if you wish to record a diary of your adventures in the Italian capital. The pen collection alone is dazzling, the kind you'd like to use to sign milestones in your life from marriage contracts to last wills and testaments. Via Campo Marzio 41 (at Piazza San Lorenzo in Lucina). ✆ **06-68807877.** Bus: 62, 63, 85, or 116.

Ditta G. Poggi ✿ The best art supply store in Rome has been selling to artists since 1825. That makes it too young to have come to the aid of da Vinci or Michelangelo, but many of the most famous artists of the 19th and 20th centuries shopped here for materials to aid them in their art. There are a lot of one-of-a-kind items of interest to artists. The staff also organizes painting courses taught by skilled Roman artists. Via del Gesù 74–75 (at Via Plebiscito). ✆ **06-6784477.** Bus: 87.

TOYS

La Città del Sole Other than the branch in Milan, this is the best stocked of any of the stores in its 40-member chain. It specializes in amusements for children and adults, with a wide range of toys and games that don't make beeping noises. Many games are configured in English, others in Italian. You'll find role-playing games, family games, and games that will challenge a young person and probably drive his parents crazy. Also for sale are such rainy-day distractions as miniature billiards tables and tabletop golf sets. Via della Scrofa 65. ✆ **06-6875404.** Metro: Spagna. Bus: 87 or 492.

WINES & LIQUORS

Ai Monasteri Italy produces a staggering volume of wines, liqueurs, and after-dinner drinks, and here you'll find a treasure trove of selections: liquors, honey, and herbal teas made in monasteries and convents all over Italy. You can buy excellent chocolates and other candies here as well. The shop will ship some items home for you. In a quiet atmosphere reminiscent of a monastery, you can choose your spirits as they move you. Piazza delle Cinque Lune 76. ✆ **06-68802783.** Bus: 70, 81, or 87.

Buccone This is a historic wine shop, right near Piazza del Popolo. Its selection of wines and gastronomic specialties is among the finest in Rome. Via Ripetta 19. ✆ **06-3612154.** Bus: 628 or 926.

Trimani Established in 1821, Trimani sells wines and spirits from Italy, with a selection of thousands of bottles. It collaborates with the Italian wine magazine *Gambero Rosso,* organizing wine lectures in which enthusiasts can improve their knowledge and educate their taste buds. Via Goito 20. ✆ **06-4469661.** Metro: Castel Pretorio. Bus: 38, 86, or 92.

11

Rome After Dark

When the sun goes down, lights across the city bathe palaces, ruins, fountains, and monuments in a theatrical glow. There are few evening pursuits as pleasurable as a stroll past the solemn pillars of old temples or the cascading torrents of Renaissance fountains glimmering under the blue-black sky.

Of these fountains, the **Naiads (Piazza della Repubblica),** the **Tortoises (Piazza Mattei),** and, of course, the **Trevi** are particularly beautiful at night. The **Capitoline Hill,** with its measured Renaissance facades, is magnificently lit after dark. The view of the **Roman Forum** from the rear of the trapezoidal Piazza del Campidoglio is the grandest in Rome, more so than even the Colosseum. Bus no. 84, 85, 87, 117, 175, 186, 271, 571, or 850 takes you here at night, or you can take a taxi. If you're across the Tiber, **Piazza San Pietro** (in front of St. Peter's Basilica) is particularly impressive at night. Illuminated architecture, Renaissance fountains, sidewalk shows, and art expos all enliven **Piazza Navona.**

Even if you don't speak Italian, you can generally follow the listings of special events and entertainment in *La Repubblica,* one of the leading Italian newspapers. The minimag *Wanted in Rome* (www.wantedinrome.com) has listings of jazz, rock, and such. The daily *Il Messaggero* lists current cultural news. *Un Ospite a Roma,* available free from the concierge desks of top hotels, is full of details on what's happening.

1 The Performing Arts

Rome's premier cultural venue is the **Teatro dell'Opera** (see below), which may not be Milan's legendary La Scala, but offers stellar performances nevertheless. The outstanding local troupe is the **Rome Opera Ballet** (see below).

Rome doesn't have a major center for classical music concerts, although performances of the most important orchestra, the **RAI Symphony Orchestra,** most often take place at the RAI Auditorium or the Academy of St. Cecilia.

Rome is a major stopover for international stars. Rock headliners often perform at **Stadio Flaminio, Foro Italico,** and in the EUR, at **Palazzo della Civiltà del Lavoro** or **Palazzo dello Sport.** Most concerts are at the Palazzo dello Sport.

CLASSICAL MUSIC

Parco della Musica ⊛   This is the largest concert facility in Europe, an ultramodern building constructed in 2002 by Renzo Piano, a world-famous architect. It has 40,000 sq. m (430,556 sq. ft.) of gardens and three separate concert halls, plus one massive open-air theater. In the summer, concerts are often outside, and you can listen to the strains of Brahms or Schumann under a star-studded sky. Viale de Coubertin 15. ② **06-802411.** Tickets and prices depend on the event. Bus: 53, 217, 231, or 910.

Opera at the Baths of Caracalla

After a long slumber (since 1993), opera has returned to the ancient **Baths of Caracalla** ☆☆☆, Via della Terme di Caracalla. Productions were shut down when it was feared that nightly audiences of 5,000 were damaging the open-air ruins. The season lasts only from July 9 to August 5, and tickets should be reserved as far in advance as possible. Conservation-minded officials have ordered that once-grandiose sets be scaled down and the stage moved to 39m (128 ft.) from the actual ruins, which are now a mere backdrop and not part of the scenery, as before. Only 2,000 spots on the wooden bleachers are now available. For tickets and information, call or go to the ticket office at Piazza Benjamino Gigli 1 (© **06-4881755**), open Tuesday to Saturday 9am to 5pm and Sunday 9am to 1:30pm. Ticket prices range from 25€ to 100€ ($30–$120).

Teatro Olimpico   Large and well publicized, this echoing stage hosts a widely divergent collection of singers, both classical and pop. Occasionally, the space is devoted to chamber orchestras or visits by foreign orchestras. The box office is open daily 11am to 7pm. Piazza Gentile Da Fabriano 17. © 06-3265991. Tickets 17€–50€ ($20.40–$60), depending on the event. Metro: Flaminio.

OPERA

Teatro dell'Opera   If you're in the capital for the opera season—usually October to June—you might want to attend a performance at the historic Rome Opera House, located off Via Nazionale. From July 9 to August 5, performances are held at the Teatro delle Terme di Caracalla (Metro: Circo Massimo). You can buy tickets at the box office (closed Mon), at any Banca di Roma bank, or by phone at © **800-907080.** Piazza Beniamino Gigli 1 off Via Nazionale. © 06-4881755. Tickets 9€–131€ ($10.80–$157). Metro: Termini.

BALLET & DANCE

Performances of the **Rome Opera Ballet** are given at the **Teatro dell'Opera** (see above). The regular repertoire of classical ballet is supplemented by performances of internationally acclaimed guest artists, and Rome is on the agenda for major troupes from around the world. Watch for announcements in the weekly entertainment guides to see what's happening at the time of your visit and to check on other venues, including the Teatro Olimpico and open-air performances.

2 The Club & Music Scene

NIGHTCLUBS/DANCE CLUBS

Alien   In a setting of exposed pipes and ventilation ducts, ▧ space-age dance floor, bathed in strobe lights and rocki house/techno music. Occasionally, an emcee will interject bri or comedy. The crowd tends to be young. It's open Tuesday t to 5am; closed mid-June to early September. Via Velletri 13–1 (including 1 drink) 16€–18€ ($19–$22). Bus: 38, 63, 80, or 92.

Alpheus ⊛ One of Rome's largest and most energetic nightclubs, Alpheus contains three sprawling rooms, each with a different musical sound and an ample number of bars. You'll find areas devoted to Latin music, to rock, and to jazz. Live bands come and go, and there's enough variety in the crowd to keep virtually anyone amused throughout the evening. Locals and visitors frequent this club, and the clients span a wide age range. It's open Tuesday through Sunday from 10pm to 4am. Via del Commercio 36. ⓒ 06-5747826. Cover 7€–13€ ($8.40–$16). Bus: 713.

Black Out If you're looking for a little counterculture edge where you might hear the latest indie music from the U.K., head for Black Out, which occupies an industrial-looking site. The recorded music includes punk, retro, R&B, grunge, and whatever else happens to be in fashion, plus rock, pop, new punk, and wave from the '70s and '80s. It's open Friday and Saturday from 10pm to 4am. This club lures a crowd, mainly Romans, in their 20s and 30s. Via Saturnia 18. ⓒ 06-70496791. Cover (including 1 drink) 5€–8€ ($6–$9.60). Metro: Re di Roma.

Blom In a palace from the 1400s, this venue is a combination restaurant and nightclub drawing a lot of young Roma to its precincts near the Piazza Navona. On some evenings, there's a live band; otherwise, a DJ spins dance music, often disco from the '70s. House music and jazz are also featured. It's open Monday, Tuesday, and Thursday to Saturday from 8:30pm to 2am, charging no cover; it's closed in August. Via del Teatro Pace 29–30. ⓒ 06-68802029. Bus: 40, 46, 63, 64.

Caruso Café de Oriente As the hippest district in Rome today, Testaccio attracts late-night revelers, many of whom turn up at Caruso. If you'd like to join Rome's beautiful people, head here, the later the better. Latin music, especially salsa, is played for the wildly gyrating dancers, stepping to the sounds of the Caribbean or Brazil. The average age of the patrons ranges from 25 to 40. Open Tuesday to Sunday 10pm to 4am. Via Monte Testaccio 36. ⓒ 06-5745019. Cover (including 1 drink) 8€–15€ ($9.60–$18). Metro: Piramide.

Gilda Named for Rita Hayworth's most famous movie role, Gilda is a combination of nightclub, disco, and restaurant known for its glamorous acts (past performances

---

Nocturnal Outdoor Entertainment

In summer, the streets of Rome become a kind of outdoor festival. Many Romans live in hot apartments without air-conditioning, and they spill into the cooler streets at night to enjoy evening concerts and other events.

The best of these occur along **Via di Monte Testaccio** in the Testaccio sector, which becomes a venue for jam sessions, jazz concerts, and other entertainment. Bars and restaurants overflow onto the streets, and there are food stalls, markets, and shops operating until late at night. From June until August, the street is blocked off from 8:30pm to 2am and entry is free.

It might not be Mexico, but music and spicy food will entertain you at **Fiesta,** a complex at Ippodromo delle Capannelle that opens every year from June 15 to August 15. Salsa music predominates, and major concerts sometimes feature big names such as José Feliciano. You'll find plenty of bars, shops, and food kiosks selling such specialties as fajitas, burritos, and enchiladas. Tickets cost ($12). For more information, call ⓒ 06-7182139. Take the Metro to Colli and then bus no. 664 to the end of the line.

include Diana Ross and splashy, Paris-type revues). The artistic direction ensures first-class shows, a well-run restaurant featuring international cuisine, and disco music played between the live acts. The disco offers music from the 60s to the present. The piano bar, **Swing,** features Italian and Latin music. The disco is open Tuesday through Sunday from midnight to 4am; the restaurant is open from 9:30pm. It's closed from July to mid-September. Via Mario de' Fiori 97. (©) 06-6784838. Cover (including 1 drink) 30€ ($36); meals from 35€ ($42). Metro: Spagna.

Gilda on the Beach

On a hot summer night, between May and September, many chic Romans escape the city heat and head for the resort of Fregene, 38.5km (24 miles) west of Rome and reached by Fregene bus no. 1 from the Lepanto Metro stop. The dance club here rocks nightly from 11pm to 4am, and the restaurant serves dinner from 8:30pm. There are four dance floors as well as a pool and private beach. To join the ultra-cool patrons, wear your most elegant swimwear. Gilda is *the* place on the summer see-and-be-seen circuit. Lungomare di Ponente 11. (©) 06-66560649. www.gildaonthe beach.it. Cover 20€ ($24).

Jackie O

Close to the American Embassy and Via Veneto, Jackie O is a glittery club that draws an affluent, over-30 crowd, mostly foreign. If you opt to go dancing here (it's not as frenzied as some might like), you might begin your evening with a drink at the piano bar and then perhaps end it in the restaurant. It's open Tuesday through Sunday from 8:30pm to 4am. Via Boncompagni 11. (©) 06-42885457. Cover (including 1 drink) 20€ ($24); meals 50€ ($60) without wine. Metro: Barberini.

Jonathan's Angels

This extraordinary space is decorated with colorful kitsch, pop art, and plastic furniture evoking Andy Warhol's famous old "Factory" in New York. Hip Romans come here for live piano music played by eccentric local musicians who often ask the audience to join in. This is one of the best night spots if you're in and around the Piazza Navona. Even if you don't have to go, check out the outlandish "loos" here, entered through a veritable pleasure garden. Take Via Pasquino from the Piazza Navona and turn right onto Via Parione, and then left on Via della Fossa. Open Monday to Friday 8pm to 3:30am, Saturday and Sunday 6:30pm to 3:30am. Via della Fossa 14–16. (©) 06-6893426. Beer 5€ ($6), cocktails 8€ ($9.60). No cover.

Locanda Atlantide

Don't be put off by the facade, which may make you think you've arrived for a Gestapo interrogation. This former warehouse is a nightclub, bar, concert hall, and theater. A different event is staged nightly; perhaps jazz on Tuesday, a play on Wednesday, or a concert on Thursday, giving way to dance club action on Friday and Saturday. The club is open Tuesday through Sunday from 10pm to 3:30am and is closed from June 15 to September 15. Via dei Lucani. (©) 06-44704540. Cover 2.50€–5€ ($3–$6), depending on the evening. Metro: Piazza Vittorio.

Magic Fly

Small-scale and somewhat cramped when it really begins to rock, this club lies about 5km (3 miles) to the northeast, outside the ring road that encircles the center of Rome. You'll need to take a taxi to get here. Music changes nightly; you might hear anything from salsa and meringue to rock or new wave. This club is elegant and posh, and you'll see many men in neckties. It's open Wednesday and Friday through Sunday from 10:30pm to dawn. Via Bassanello 15, Cassia-Grottarossa. (©) 06-33268956. Cover (including 1 drink) 5€–16€ ($6–$19).

Piper

This venue opened in 1965 in a former cinema and became the first modern disco of its kind in Italy. Many dances such as "the shake" were first introduced to Italy at this club. No longer what it was in those La Dolce Vita years, Piper is still going strong. Today it lures with fashion shows, screenings, some of the hottest parties in town, and various gigs, drawing a casual and mixed-age crowd. The pick-up scene here is hot and heavy. It's open Monday to Saturday 11pm to 4am. Via Tagliamento 9. ✆ 06-8555398. Cover (including 1 drink) 20€–25€ ($24–$30). Bus: 63.

Radio Londra Radio Londra aims for London-style hip. Everyone tries to look and act as freaky as possible. Because it is near the popular gay L'Alibi (see "Gay & Lesbian Clubs," below), the downstairs club attracts many brethren, although the young crowd is mixed, both Roman and foreign. Upstairs is a pub/pizzeria where bands often appear. Both are open Monday to Saturday 9pm to 3am. There's no cover; instead, you pay an annual membership fee. Via Monte Testaccio 67. ✆ 06-5750044. Annual Club membership (including 1 drink) 8€ ($9.60). Bus: 95.

JAZZ & OTHER LIVE SOUNDS

The places we've recommended appeal to a wide age group, especially the jazz joints.

Alexanderplatz At this leading jazz club, you can listen to the music or enjoy the cooking, everything from *pesto alla genovese* to Japanese cuisine. It's open Monday through Saturday from 9pm to 2am, with live music from 10:30pm. Via Ostia 9. ✆ 06-39742171. Club membership (valid for 1 month) 7€ ($8.40). Bus: 23.

Arciliuto This place reputedly once housed Raphael's studio, and is now home to one of the most romantic candlelit spots in Rome. The evening's presentation includes Neapolitan love songs, old Italian madrigals, and current hits from Broadway or London's West End. Highly recommended, it's hard to find, but it is within walking distance of Piazza Navona. It's open Monday through Saturday from 10pm to 1:30am and is closed July 20 to September 3. Piazza Monte Vecchio 5. ✆ 06-6879419. Cover (including 1 drink) 19€ ($23). Bus: 42, 62, or 64. From the west side of Piazza Navona, take Via di S. Agnese in Agone, which leads to Via di Tor Milliana; then follow this street to Piazza Monte Vecchio.

Big Mama Big Mama is a hangout for jazz and blues musicians, where you're likely to meet the up-and-coming jazz stars of tomorrow and sometimes even the big names. It's open Monday through Saturday from 9pm to 1:30am, and is closed July through September. Vicolo San Francesco a Ripa 18. ✆ 06-5812551. Cover 15€–30€ ($18–$36) for big acts (free for minor shows), plus 13€ ($16) seasonal membership fee. Bus: 75 or 170.

Fonclea Fonclea offers live music every night—jazz, Dixieland, rock, rhythm and blues, and funk. This is basically a cellar jazz bar that attracts folks from all walks of Roman life. There's also a restaurant that features moderately priced grilled meats, salads, and crepes; if you want dinner, it's best to reserve a table. Music usually starts at 9:15pm and lasts until about 12:30am. It's open daily from 7pm to 2am. The club is closed in July and August. Via Crescenzio 82A. ✆ 06-6896302. Cover Sat only 6€ ($7.20). Bus: 23, 34, or 492.

GAY & LESBIAN CLUBS

Degrado This is known as a sexual underground disco where hot boys perform in "cage-shows." With its maxi-screen videos, its free-for-all karaoke performances, and occasional theme nights, it's a hot, hot address in Rome for gay men, most of whom are under 40. Its special attraction is its semi-dark labyrinth and its sizzling dark room. It's open Friday and Saturday from 10:30pm to 5am. Via Ignazio Danti 20. ✆ 06-2753508. Bus: 052, 053, 054, or 056.

Edoardo This is the most popular gay restaurant and bar in Rome. With its top-rate food and drink, you can come here and make an evening of it. Seasonal products are used in the traditional Mediterranean dishes; there's also an excellent assortment of pastries. One cake, "the orgasm," features a hot heart of chocolate. This restaurant and bar attracts a young professional class of Romans. A trendy choice for a night out, the bar is named for the gay monarch himself. It's open Wednesday to Monday 7pm to midnight. Vicolo Margana 14. (C) 06-69942419. Bus: 117, 119, 170, or 175.

The Hangar Having survived since 1984, the Hangar is a landmark on the gay nightlife scene. It's on one of Rome's oldest streets, adjacent to the Forum. Each of The Hangar's two bars has an independent sound system. Women are welcome any night except Monday, when the club features videos and entertainment for men. The busiest nights are Saturday, Sunday, and Monday, when as many as 500 people cram inside. It's open Wednesday through Monday from 10:30pm to 2:30am. The Hangar is closed 3 weeks in August. Via in Selci 69. (C) 06-4881397. Annual club membership 7€ ($8.40). Metro: Cavour.

K-Men's Club There's no bar at this hard-core male-only leather S&M venue that quickly separates the S men from the M men. Its main attraction is its variety of well-equipped dark areas. Sometimes totally naked parties are thrown. Otherwise, a leather dress code is strictly enforced. This club is not for the faint of heart. It's open Sunday to Thursday 4pm to 4am, and Friday and Saturday 4pm to 5am. Via Amato Amati 6–8. (C) 03476220462. Bus: 50N or 105.

L'Alibi L'Alibi, which has an intimate setting in the Testaccio sector away from the heart of Rome, is a year-round stop on many a gay man's agenda. The crowd tends to be mixed: Roman and international, straight and gay, male and female. One room has a dance floor. L'Alibi is open Wednesday through Sunday from 11pm to 5am. From June to September, it is also open on Tuesday from 11pm to 5am. Via Monte Testaccio 44. (C) 06-5743448. Cover 7.50€–13€ ($9–$16). Bus: 30N.

Skyline Near Stazione Termini, this bar attracts a large crowd of gay men, along with a smaller group of lesbians. The Skyline gets quite rowdy at times and is amusing and fun. Porno movies are shown on Tuesday, and the second Saturday of every month is "Sexy Night," where anything goes. The bi-level bar has two backrooms where the action is. There are snacks available, and occasional live shows are presented. It's open Tuesday to Thursday and Sunday 10:30pm to 3am, and Friday and Saturday 11:30pm to 5am. Via degli Aurunci 26–28. (C) 06-4440817. Bus: 87, 117, or 141.

3 The Cafe & Bar Scene

It seems there's nothing Romans like better than sitting and talking over a beverage—usually wine or coffee. Unless you're dead set on making the Roman nightclub circuit, try what can be a far livelier and less expensive scene—sitting late at night on **Via Veneto, Piazza della Rotonda, Piazza del Popolo,** or one of Rome's other piazzas, all for the cost of an espresso, a cappuccino, or a Campari.

If you're looking for some scrumptious **ice cream,** refer to the listings below for Café Rosati and Giolitti, as well as the box titled "Take a Gelato Break," on p. 106.

CAFES
ON VIA VENETO

Back in the 1950s (a decade *Time* magazine gave to Rome, in the way it conceded the 1960s and later the 1990s to London), **Via Vittorio Veneto** rose in fame as the hippest street in Rome, crowded with aspiring and actual movie stars, their directors, and a fast-rising group of card-carrying members of the jet set. Today the beautiful

---

⟮Moments⟯ The Ruin to Beat All Ruins

There is no more dramatic sight in all of Rome at night than that of the Colosseum lit up. In the harsh light of day, it looks like a ruin, but at night your imagination goes into overdrive. Over the centuries, earthquakes, pollution, traffic, and pillage have taken a toll on the arena. But at night, Rome's greatest marvel emerges in its beauty.

---

people wouldn't be caught dead on touristy Via Veneto—but regardless, visitors flock here by the thousands. As one Roman cafe owner told us, "You can see Romans all over the city. But on Via Veneto, sit at one of our tables and catch people from all over the world go by. It's worth the price we charge for an espresso."

Café de Paris   This spot has been around for decades. It's popular in summer, when the tables spill right out onto the sidewalk and the passing crowd walks through the maze. This is the most famous cafe in all of Rome for people-watching along Via Veneto, although locals shun it. It's open Wednesday through Monday from 8am to 1:30am (Tues till midnight). Via Vittorio Veneto 91. ℭ 06-4815631. Metro: Barberini.

Harry's Bar   Sophisticated Harry's Bar is a perennial favorite of post-40 foreign visitors. Every major Italian city (such as Florence and Venice) seems to have one, and Rome is no exception, although this one has no connection with the others. In summer, tables are placed outside. If you want to dine outdoors but avoid the scorching sun, there's an air-conditioned sidewalk cafe open from May to November. Meals inside cost about double what you'd pay outside. In back is a small dining room serving some of the finest (and priciest) food in central Rome. The restaurant inside is open Monday through Saturday from 12:30 to 3pm and 7:30pm to 1am. Outside you can eat from noon to midnight. The bar is open Monday through Saturday from 11am to 2am (closed 1 week in mid-Aug), and the piano bar is open nightly from 9:30pm, with music starting at 11pm. Via Vittorio Veneto 150. ℭ 06-484643. Metro: Barberini.

NEAR THE TERMINI

Bar Marani   This century-old coffee bar by the marketplace attracts all kinds—students, visitors, Japanese tourists, shopkeepers, artists, pickpockets, and rock stars. Espresso is one of the lures, as is the delicious ice cream. Grab a table on the vine-covered terrace. Via dei Volsci 57. ℭ 06-490016. Metro: Termini.

Fiddler's Elbow   Fiddler's Elbow, near Piazza di Santa Maria Maggiore and the railway station, is reputedly the oldest pub in the capital. Sometimes, however, the place is so packed you can't find room to drink. It's open daily from 5pm to 2am. Via dell'Olmata 43. ℭ 06-4872110. Metro: Termini.

NEAR THE TREVI FOUNTAIN

San Crispino   At night we recommend a stroll by the Trevi Fountain, beautifully lit, followed by a stopover at this elegant ice-cream shop. Freshly made ice creams and sorbets come in such flavors as ginger and cinnamon, fresh walnut and dried fig, chestnut and rum, and even "ricotta soft." Sorbets are especially delectable, ranging from pear to Seville orange. Prices go from 1.70€ to 7€ ($2.05–$8.40); hours are Monday, Wednesday, Thursday, and Sunday noon to 12:30am, and Friday and Saturday noon to 1:30am. Via della Panetteria 42. ℭ 06-6793924. Metro: Barberini.

NEAR CAMPO DE' FIORI

Crudo This stylish bar, restaurant, and wine bar takes its name
served here—that is, such raw nibbles as delectable sushi or veal car
large and contemporary New York cocktail lounge, where recorded
jazz, or whatever, is provided each evening. You can order full meal
courses costing from 8€ to 16€ ($9.60–$19). Specialties include n
Piedmont with Mediterranean herbs, or else a special selection of cold cuts. Salads are
delectable, including one made with spinach, fresh salmon, peanuts, parmigiano, and
balsamic vinegar. Open Monday to Saturday 7:30pm to 2am. Via degli Speechi 6. ℃ 06-
6838989. Bus: 40.

NEAR PIAZZA NAVONA

Antico Caffé della Pace Head for the Antico Caffé della Pace, right off the heart-
beat of Piazza Navona. It's a wild scene on Saturday night, when it's packed with a gorgeous young crowd who comes to see and be seen. Via della Pace 3–5. ℃ 06-6861216. Bus:
40, 46, 62, 64.

Bar del Fico Sometimes it seems that everybody within walking distance of the
Piazza Navona and the Spanish Steps hangs out here. By 11pm, it's one of the busiest
bars in Rome—loud, raucous, and fun, with waiters scurrying about trying to serve
all the patrons. If you're walking around by day, you can drop in for drinks and light
meals. It's open daily from 7:30am to 1:30am. Piazza del Fico 27–28. ℃ 06-6865205. Metro:
Spagna.

Caffè della Pace Caffè della Pace has elegant neighbors, such as Santa Maria della
Pace, a church with sibyls by Raphael and a cloister designed by Bramante. The bar
dates from the beginning of the 20th century and is decorated with wood, marble, and
mirrors. It's open Monday 3pm to 3am, and Tuesday to Sunday 9am to 3am. Via della
Pace 3–5. ℃ 06-6861216. Bus: 64.

Vineria Reggio A long-established wine bar near Campo de' Fiori, Vineria Reggio
remains an enduring favorite in this heavily trafficked part of Ancient Rome. Interesting people show up here, anyone from students of history to movie stars. Wine, sold
by the glass, is affordably priced, and there are a number of beers on tap as well. Hours
are Monday to Saturday 8:30am to 2am; it's closed August 5 to 25. Campo de' Fiori 15.
℃ 06-68803268. Bus: 62 or 64.

NEAR THE PANTHEON

Piazza della Rotonda, across from the Pantheon, is the place to be after dark, especially in summer. Although it's touristy, locals come here, too, because it's a dramatic
place to be at night when the Pantheon is lit up.

Caffè Sant'Eustachio Strong coffee is liquid fuel to Italians, and many Romans
will walk blocks for what they consider to be a superior brew. Caffè Sant'Eustachio is
one of Rome's most celebrated espresso shops, where the water supply is funneled into
the city by an aqueduct built in 19 B.C. Rome's most experienced espresso judges claim
the water plays an important part in the coffee's flavor. Buy a ticket from the cashier
for as many cups as you want, and then leave a small tip (about .50€/60¢) for the
counter-person when you present your receipt. It's open Sunday through Thursday
from 8:30am to 1am, Friday from 8:30am to 1:30am, and Saturday from 8:30am to
2am. Piazza Sant'Eustachio 82. ℃ 06-68802048. Bus: 116.

i This stylish, breezy spot has a staff that's usually hysterically overbur-
d, with little time for small talk. But despite the fact that service might be slow,
crowd of midday office workers loyally returns for morning shots of espresso; affordable, filling salads at lunch; and tea in the afternoon. It's open daily from 7:30am to
9pm. Piazza San Lorenzo in Lucina 29. ✆ 06-6876606. Bus: 116.

Di Rienzo This is the top cafe at the Pantheon. In fair weather, try to snag one of
the sidewalk tables. In cooler weather, you can retreat inside, where the walls are inlaid
with the type of marble found on the Pantheon's floor. Many types of pastas appear
on the menu, as do *risotto alla pescatora* (fisherman's rice) and several meat courses.
You can also order pizzas. It's open daily from 7am to 1 or 2am. Piazza della Rotonda 8–9.
✆ 06-6869097. Bus: 116.

La Caffettiera In a comfortable, albeit bustling setting, you can enjoy a refresh-
ingly light meal, such as a sandwich or a slice of quiche, or just a quick fix of caffeine.
Lots of folks drop in for the Neapolitan-style ice-cream confections in the afternoon.
It's open Monday through Friday from 7am to 9pm, Saturday from 7:30am to 9pm,
and Sunday from 8am to 9pm. Piazza di Pietra 65. ✆ 06-6798147. Bus: 116.

Riccioli Café Formally known as Hemingway's Pub, this sleek night spot is a chic
oyster and champagne bar. In elegant yet informal surroundings, you can order drinks
as well as oysters on the half shell. It's a scene, but the food in the upscale loftlike wine
cellar is quite good. It's open daily 9am to 2am. Piazza delle Coppelle 10A. ✆ 06-68210313.
Bus: 64.

Riva Gauche This spot is the best of the new bars popping up in Rome to attract
yuppies who are deserting their traditional wine to sample one of the more than three
dozen types of whisky on sale here. As part of "Castro chic," people drink a variety of
rum-laced drinks as well. It's open daily from 8pm to 2:30am. Via dei Sabelli 43. ✆ 06-
4456722. Metro: Termini.

Solotto 42 Near the Pantheon, this is a "bookbar," furnished with sofas from the
1950s, Murano chandeliers from the early 1800s, marble balustrades from the 17th
century, and Art Nouveau decorations. Arguably, it is the most sophisticated bar in
the capital, and it's run by a Roman-Swedish alliance. The Swedish part is reflected in
the small plates offered here, a kind of small smorgasbord. The plates cost from 5€ to
10€ ($6–$12). Rome's chic denizens of the night come here to listen to live jazz
music, often provided in an outdoor setting when weather permits. Patrons range in
age from 25 to 40. The bar is open Tuesday to Saturday 10am to 2am, Sunday noon
to 6pm. Piazza di Pietra 42. ✆ 06-6785804. Bus: 85 or 850.

Tazza d'Oro This cafe is known for serving its own brand of espresso. Another specialty, ideal on a hot summer night, is *granità di caffè* (coffee that has been frozen,
crushed into a velvety slushlike ice, and placed in a glass between layers of whipped
cream). It's open daily from 7:30am to 1am. Piazza della Rotonda, Via degli Orfani 84. ✆ 06-
6789792. Bus: 116.

ON THE CORSO & PIAZZA COLONNA

Autogrill Autogrill is a monumental cafe that's often filled with busy shoppers.
There's a stand-up sandwich bar with dozens of selections and a cafeteria, both self-
and with a sit-down area. The decor includes high coffered ceilings, baroque wall
, globe lights, crystal chandeliers, and black stone floors. It's open daily from
11pm. Via del Corso 181. ✆ 06-6789135. Metro: Spagna.

Giolitti   Near Piazza Colonna, this is one of the city's most popular nighttime gathering spots and the oldest ice-cream shop. Some of the sundaes look like Vesuvius about to erupt. Many people take gelato out to eat on the streets; others enjoy it in the post-empire splendor of the salon inside. You can have your "coppa" daily 7am to 2am (closed at 1am in winter). Via Uffici del Vicario 40. © 06-6991243. Bus: 116.

ON OR NEAR PIAZZA DEL POPOLO

According to legend, the ashes of Nero were enshrined here until 11th-century residents began complaining to the pope about his imperial ghost. The Egyptian obelisk seen here today dates from the 13th century B.C.; it was removed from Heliopolis to Rome during the reign of Augustus (it originally stood at the Circus Maximus). The present piazza was designed in the early 19th century by Valadier, Napoleon's architect. Two almost-twin baroque churches stand on the square, overseeing the never-ending traffic.

Café Rosati   Café Rosati, which has been around since 1923, attracts guys and dolls of all persuasions, both foreign and domestic, who drive up in Maseratis and Porsches. It's really a combination of sidewalk cafe, ice-cream parlor, candy store, confectionery, and *ristorante* that has been swept up in the fickle world of fashion. The later you go, the more interesting the action. It's open daily from 7:30am to 11:30pm. Piazza del Popolo 5A. © 06-3225859. Bus: 117.

Canova Café   Although the management has filled it with boutiques selling expensive gift items, such as luggage and cigarette lighters, many Romans still consider Canova Café *the* place to be on the piazza. The Canova has a sidewalk terrace for people-watching, plus a snack bar, a restaurant, and a wine shop. In summer, you'll have access to a courtyard whose walls are covered with ivy and where flowers grow in terra-cotta planters. The restaurant is open daily from noon to 3:30pm and 7 to 11pm; the bar is open daily from 8am till midnight or 1am. Piazza del Popolo 16. © 06-3612231. Bus: 117.

NEAR THE SPANISH STEPS

Antico Caffè Greco ★★   Since 1760, this has been Rome's poshest coffee bar. Stendhal, Goethe, Keats, and D'Annunzio have sipped coffee here. Today you're more likely to see ladies who lunch and Japanese tourists, but there's plenty of atmosphere. In front is a wooden bar, and beyond is a series of small salons. You sit at marble-topped tables of Napoleonic design, against a backdrop of gold or red damask, romantic paintings, and antique mirrors. It was Giorgio De Chirico who suggested that this is the cafe where you sit and await the end. The house specialty is *paradisi,* made with lemon and orange. The coffee bar is open Sunday and Monday from 10:30am to 7pm, and Tuesday to Saturday from 9am to 7:30pm; it is closed 10 days in August (dates vary). Via Condotti 84. © 06-6791700. Metro: Spagna.

La Buvette   This place is both a cafe and an unpretentious restaurant. No one will mind if you come just for an espresso, but if you're hungry, consider ordering one of the meal-size salads, which serious shoppers from the nearby Via Condotti order as a pick-me-up in the heat and humidity of a hot Roman midday. More elaborate platters are also available. It's open daily from 8am to 11:30pm. Via Vittoria 44–47. © 06-6790383. Metro: Spagna.

IN TRASTEVERE

Several cafes in Trastevere, across the Tiber, are attracting crowds. Fans who saw Fellini's *Roma* know what **Piazza di Santa Maria in Trastevere** looks like at night. The square, filled with milling throngs in summer, is graced with an octagonal fountain and a 12th-century church. Children play on the piazza, and occasional spontaneous guitar fests break out when the weather's good.

Café-Bar di Marzio This warmly inviting place, which is strictly a cafe (not a restaurant), has narrow wood-paneled furnishings and outdoor tables at the edge of the square, with the best view of its famous fountain. Everybody from blue-collar workers to artists and writers goes here to see and be seen. The cafe is open daily from 7am to 2am and is closed on Mondays from October to March. Piazza di Santa Maria in Trastevere 15. ✆ 06-5816095. Bus: 44, 75, or 170.

Friends Art Café Named for the long-running American TV sitcom, this is one of our favorite hangouts in the historic district of Trastevere across the Tiber. It's an ideal place to hit on your pre-dinner rounds. Big glass windows overlook Piazza Trilussa, and the decor is modern with metal furnishings. The staff serves a cold vegetarian buffet and various cocktails, costing 3.50€ to 8€ ($4.20–$9.60). Piazza Trilussa 34, Trastevere. ✆ 06-5816111. Bus: 40 or 46.

NEAR TESTACCIO

Il Barone Rosso This is the biggest and best German beer garden in Rome, and on a summer night the "Red Baron" can be a lot of fun. Opened in 1996, this 380-seat club has a summer garden that always overflows in fair weather. The staff serves lots of beer and other drinks, along with Italian pizzas and German snacks, salads, and sandwiches. Beer costs 4.20€ ($5.05) a mug, and hours are daily 7pm to 3am. Via Libetta 13. ✆ 06-57288961. Metro: Garbatella.

WINE BARS

Enoteca Antica A drink in this dark, atmospheric spot is the perfect ending to a visit to the nearby Spanish Steps. Set behind a discreet facade in a chic shopping district, this is the city's best repository for Italian wines, brandies, and grappa. You can opt for a postage-stamp-size table in the back or stand at the bar with its impressive display of wines stacked in every available corner. It's open daily 11am to 2am. Via della Croce 76B. ✆ 06-6797544. Metro: Spagna.

Il Goccetto Set near Campo de' Fiori, Il Goccetto specializes in French and Italian wines by the glass at prices that range from 4€ ($4.80) for a simple Chianti to as much as 17€ ($20) for a glass of French champagne. Cold platters of food, including an extensive list of Italian cheeses and processed meats, especially salami and pâtés, as well as an occasional salad, are available. Overall, this place provides an excellent site for the *degustazione* of a wide assortment of unusual Italian wines, many of them from less well-known small producers. It's open Monday to Saturday from 11:30am to 2pm and from 6pm to midnight. Via dei Banchi Vecchi 14. ✆ 06-6864268. Bus: 46, 62, or 64.

La Bottega del Vino This old-fashioned setting comes complete with terra-cotta floors and long, battered wooden tables. Everything acts as a foil for the Italian and French wines served here. Priced at 5€ to 18€ ($6–$22) per glass, depending on the vintage, most come from well-known or obscure vineyards throughout Italy. Affordable snacks and cold platters are available as accompaniment. Lunch features dishes like crushed crabmeat served in a roulade of smoked salmon, but at other times the food is simpler, mostly salami, bread, and cheese. Lunch is served Tuesday to Saturday from 10am to 3:30pm; it is open in the evening Wednesday to Friday from 5:30pm to around midnight. Via del Teatro Valle 48–49. ✆ 06-6865970. Bus: 8.

12

Side Trips from Rome

Most European capitals are surrounded by a number of worthwhile attractions, but Rome tops them all for sheer variety. Just a few miles from Rome, you can go back to the dawn of Italian history and explore the dank tombs the Etruscans left as their legacy, or drink the golden wine of the towns in the Alban Hills (Castelli Romani). You can wander the ruins of Hadrian's Villa, the "queen of villas of the ancient world," or be lulled by the music of the baroque fountains in the Villa d'Este. You can loll on the beaches of Ostia di Lido or explore the remarkable ruins of Ostia Antica, Rome's ancient seaport.

If you have time, the attractions in the environs can fill at least 3 days. We've highlighted the best of the lot here.

1 Tivoli & the Villas ★★

32km (20 miles) east of Rome

Tivoli, known as Tibur to the ancient Romans, is 32km (20 miles) east of Rome on Via Tiburtina, about an hour's drive with traffic. If you don't have a car, take Metro Line B to the end of the line, the Rebibbia station. After exiting the station, board a CoTral bus (© 800-150008) for the trip the rest of the way to Tivoli. Generally, buses depart about every 20 minutes during the day. For information about the town, check with **Azienda Autonoma di Turismo,** Largo Garibaldi (© 0774-334522), Tivoli. Hours are Monday through Friday from 9am to 1pm and 3 to 5pm, and Saturday from 9am to 7pm.

EXPLORING THE VILLAS

Hadrian's Villa (Villa Adriana) ★★★ In the 2nd century A.D., the globe-trotting Hadrian spent the last 3 years of his life in grand style. Less than 6.5km (4 miles) from Tivoli, he built one of the greatest estates ever erected, and he filled acre after acre with some of the architectural wonders he'd seen on his many travels. Perhaps as a preview of what he envisioned for himself, the emperor even created a representation of hell. Hadrian was a patron of the arts, a lover of beauty, and even something of an architect. His staggering feat of building was more than a villa: It was a self-contained world for a vast royal entourage and the hundreds of servants and guards they required to protect them, feed them, bathe them, and satisfy their libidos.

Hadrian erected theaters, baths, temples, fountains, gardens, and canals bordered with statuary throughout his estate. He filled the palaces and temples with sculpture, some of which now rest in the museums of Rome. In later centuries, barbarians and popes, as well as anyone who needed a slab of marble, carted off much that made the villa so spectacular. But enough of the fragmented ruins remain for us to piece together the story. For a look at what the villa used to be, see the plastic model at the entrance.

One of the two most outstanding and evocative ruins is the **Canopo** ☆☆☆, or Canopus, a re-creation of the town of Canope with its famous Temple of the Serapis. The ruins of a rectangular area, **Piazza d'Oro,** are still surrounded by a double portico. Likewise, the **Sala dei pilastri dorici,** or Doric Pillared Hall, is still a delight, with its pilasters with Doric bases and capitals holding up a Doric architrave. The ruins of the **Baths** remain, revealing rectangular rooms with concave walls. The apse and the ruins of some magnificent vaulting are still found at the Great Baths. Only the north wall remains of the **Pecile,** or Poikile, which Hadrian discovered in Athens and had reproduced here. The other great ruin, **Teatro Marittimo** ☆☆☆, is a circular maritime theater in ruins with its central building enveloped by a canal spanned by small swing bridges. For a closer look at some of the items excavated, you can visit the museum on the premises and a museum and visitor center near the villa parking area.

Via di Villa Adriana. ℂ 06-39967900. Admission 6.50€ ($7.80). Daily 9am–sunset (about 7:30pm in summer, 5:30pm Nov–Mar). Closed Jan 1 and Dec 25. Bus: 4 from Tivoli.

Villa d'Este ☆☆   Like Hadrian centuries before, Cardinal Ippolito d'Este of Ferrara believed in heaven on Earth, and in the mid–16th century he ordered this villa built on a hillside. The dank Renaissance structure is not that noteworthy; the big draw for visitors are the **spectacular gardens** below (designed by Pirro Ligorio).

You descend the cypress-studded slope to the bottom and, on the way, are rewarded with everything from lilies to gargoyles spouting water, torrential streams, and waterfalls. The loveliest fountain is the **Ovato Fountain (Fontana dell Ovato),** by Ligorio. But nearby is the more spectacular achievement: the **Fountain of the Hydraulic Organ (Fontana dell'Organo Idraulico),** dazzling with its water jets in front of a baroque chapel, with four maidens who look tipsy. The work represents the genius of Frenchman Claude Veanard. The moss-covered **Fountain of the Dragons (Fontana dei Draghi),** also by Ligorio, and the so-called **Fountain of Glass (Fontana di Vetro),** by Bernini, are the most intriguing. The best walk is along the promenade, with 100 spraying fountains. The garden provides hours of exploration, but it's a lot of walking, with some steep climbs.

Piazza Trento, Viale delle Centro Fontane. ℂ 0774-312070. Admission 6.50€ ($7.80). Tues–Sun 8:30am to 1 hr. before sunset. Closed Jan 1, May 1, and Dec 25. Bus: Roma-Tivoli.

Villa Gregoriana ☆   The Villa d'Este dazzles with artificial glamour, but the Villa Gregoriana relies more on nature. The gardens were built by Pope Gregory XVI in the 19th century. At one point on the circuitous walk carved along a slope, you can stand and look out onto the most panoramic waterfall (Aniene) at Tivoli. The trek to the bottom on the banks of the Anio is studded with grottoes and balconies that open onto the chasm. The only problem is that if you do make the full descent, you might need a helicopter to pull you up again (the climb back up is fierce). From one of the belvederes, there's a panoramic view of the Temple of Vesta on the hill.

Largo Sant'Angelo. ℂ 0774-311249. Admission 4€ ($4.80). Apr 1–Oct 15 daily 10am–6:30pm; Mar and Oct 16–Nov 30 daily 10am–2:30pm. The bus from Rome stops near the entrance.

WHERE TO DINE

Albergo Ristorante Adriano ITALIAN   In a stucco-sided villa a few steps from the ticket office sits an idyllic stop for either before or after your visit Hadrian's Villa. It offers terrace dining under plane trees or indoor dining in a high-ceilinged room with terra-cotta walls, neoclassical moldings, and white Corinthian pilasters. The

Side Trips from Rome

Viterbo **1** **2** **3** Vignanello

2

Caprarola

Vetralla

Ronciglione

Blera

Cívita
Castellana

A1

Poggio
Mirteto

M O N T I   S A B A T I N I

M O N T I   S A B I N I

A1

Tiber

4

493

Lago di
Bracciano

Campagnano
di Roma

2

3

Bracciano

Anguillara

Monterotondo

4

Mentana

E80

E80

4

5
6 Cerveteri

A12

A24

18 **19**
Tivoli
17 **16**
Villa d'Este

5

R O M E

Palestrina
15

Fregene **7**

E80

7

Frascati
14

Tiber

Marino

**Castelli
Romani**

A1

Fiumicino

8 **Ostia Antica**

9

Castel Gandolfo **11** **13**

12 **Rocca di Papa**

Albano

10 **Nemi**

Lido di Ostia

Ariccia
Genzano

Pomezia

Velletri

601

Ardea

Aprília

7

Cisterna
di Latina

207

148

I T A L Y

Rome

Tyrrhenian
Sea

Nettuno

**To Naples &
Pompeii**

Latina

Anzio

Airport ✈

0 ——— 10 mi
0 ——— 10 km

N

cooking is home-style, and the menu includes roast lamb, saltimbocca (veal cooked with ham), grilled tuna with beans, deviled chicken, salads and cheeses, and simple desserts. They're especially proud of their homemade pastas.

Via di Villa Adriana 222. ℭ 0774-535028. Reservations recommended. Main courses 10€–30€ ($12–$36); fixed-price menus 15€–20€ ($18–$24). AE, DC, MC, V. Mon–Sat 12:30–4pm and 8–10pm; Sun 12:30–2:30pm and 8–10:30pm.

Antica Trattoria del Falcone ROMAN   One of the town's better choices lies in the historic core on the main artery leading off Largo Garibaldi. Because of its location, it attracts a lot of visitors, but that doesn't mean that it's a tourist trap. Far from it. The food is regionally inspired by a kitchen which specializes in market-fresh ingredients. Specialties include perfectly grilled fish from the sea as well as saltimbocca. Mixed roast meats, done over the coals, are our favorites. Another dish we like is homemade *crespella,* like a rolled pancake. It's stuffed with ricotta, nuts, and fresh spinach.

Via del Trivio 34. ℭ 0774-312358. Reservations recommended. Main courses 6€–10€ ($7.20–$12); fixed-price menus 13€–20€ ($16–$24). AE, DC, MC, V. Daily 11:30am–4pm and 6:30–11:30pm.

2 Palestrina

39km (24 miles) east of Rome

Like Tibur, ancient Preneste (as Palestrina was called) was a superb holiday spot. It was a favorite of Horace, Pliny, and even Hadrian, who maintained a villa here.

GETTING THERE

CoTral buses leave every 30 to 45 minutes during the day from Rome; departures are from the Anagnina Metro stop in Rome. It takes about an hour to reach Palestrina and costs about 2€ ($2.40).

If you're driving, take either Via Prenestina (much less trafficked than Via Tiburtina) or the Autostrada (A2), and get off at Valmontana; the latter route is much quicker.

EXPLORING THE TOWN

If you go out of Rome through the Porta Maggiore and travel on Via Prenestina for about 39km (24 miles), you'll eventually come to Palestrina, a medieval hillside town that overlooks a wide valley.

When U.S. airmen flew over in World War II and bombed part of the town, they never imagined their actions would launch Palestrina as an important tourist attraction. After the debris was cleared, a pagan temple (once one of the greatest in the world) emerged: the **Fortuna Primigenia,** rebuilt in the days of the empire but dating from centuries before. In Palestrina you'll also find a **Duomo** dating from 1100, with a mostly intact bell tower.

Palestrina predates the founding of Rome by several hundred years. It resisted conquest by the early Romans and later took the wrong side in the civil war between Marius and Sulla. When Sulla won, he razed every stone in the city except the Temple of Fortune and then built a military barracks on the site. Later, as a favorite vacation spot for the emperors and their entourages, it sheltered some of the most luxurious villas of the Roman Empire. Its most famous child was Pier Luigi da Palestrina, recognized as the father of polyphonic harmony.

Galleria Nazional d'Arte Antica in Barberini Palace 𝕲𝕲   High on a hill overlooking the valley, this palace was the work of both Bernini and Borromini, another landmark of papal patronage. It contains half of the National Gallery of Art, the other half found at the Corsini Palace in Rome. Today this palace houses Roman statuary found in the ruins, plus Etruscan artifacts (like urns) as fine as those in Rome's Villa Giulia. But worth the trip itself is the **Nile Mosaic** ★★★, a well-preserved ancient Roman work and the most remarkable ever uncovered. The mosaic details the flooding of the Nile, a shepherd's hunt, mummies, ibises, and Roman warriors, among other things. The museum also contains an array of paintings from not only Italian artists, but Dutch and Flemish works. The collection is mainly from the 13th to the 16th centuries, with works by Fra Angelico, Filippo Lippi, Lorenzo Lotto, Andrea del Sarto, Perugino, Caravaggio, Canaletto, Raphael, and Caravaggio. The most dazzling room is the Gran Salone, with its illusionist ceiling frescoes by Pietro da Cortona.

Palazzo Barberini. ✆ 06-32810. Admission 6€ ($7.20) adults, free for children ages 18 and under. Tues–Sun 8:30am–7:30pm. Follow the signs from the center to the top of the town.

WHERE TO STAY & DINE

Albergo Ristorante Stella (Restaurant Coccia)   A contemporary hotel and restaurant, the Stella is in the commercial district of town on a cobblestone square filled with parked cars, trees, and a small fountain. The soundproof bedrooms are rather basic but comfortable. All units contain bathrooms with shower/tub combinations. The simple lobby is filled with warm colors and contains curved leather couches and autographed photos of local sports heroes.

The sunny restaurant, open daily for lunch and dinner, serves affordable, zesty Roman cuisine.

Piazza della Liberazione 3, Palestrina, 00036 Roma. ✆ 06-9538172. Fax 06-9573360. www.hotelstella.it. 28 units. 60€ ($72) double; 100€ ($120) suite. AE, DC, MC, V. Parking .50€ (60¢). **Amenities:** Restaurant; bar; laundry service; dry cleaning; nonsmoking rooms. *In room:* A/C, TV, hair dryer.

3 The Castelli Romani ★★

For the Roman emperor and the wealthy cardinal in the heyday of the Renaissance, the **Castelli Romani (Roman Castles)** exerted a powerful lure, and they still do. The Castelli aren't castles, but hill towns—many of them with an ancient history and several producing well-regarded wines.

The ideal way to explore the hill towns is by car. But you can get a limited overview by taking one of the CoTral buses (costing 1.60€/$1.90) that leaves every 20 minutes from Rome's Subaugusta stop on Metro Line A.

MARINO

Marino, the closest to Rome (only 24km/15 miles away), is about 7km (4⅓ miles) off Via Appia Nuova, quite near Ciampino Airport. Much of Marino's original charm has fallen victim to modern builders, but the town is still the place to go each October during the **grape harvest.** Check with the Rome tourist office for the actual dates, which vary from year to year. At that time, the town's fountains are switched from water to wine, and everyone drinks for free.

ROCCA DI PAPA ★

The most attractive of the hill towns lies only some 9.5km (6 miles) from Marino. It's a lovely spot, on the slopes of Monte Cavo facing the Alban lakes. By car, the best route is 217 to the junction with 218, where you make a left turn. Before the intersection, you'll be high on a ridge above Lake Albano, where the views of the lake, the far woods, and the papal palace of Castel Gandolfo on the opposite mountain are superb.

Just before Rocca di Papa is the entrance to the toll road to **Monte Cavo.** A temple of Jove once stood on top of this mountain, and before that, the tribes of the area met with King Tarquin (the Proud) before Rome was a republic. At the top of the mountain is one of the most dramatic panoramic views in the hill towns, giving you a wide survey of the Alban Hills and the Castelli Romani. Down below, Rocca di Papa is a tangle of old streets and churches. A legend of dubious origin claims that Hannibal once camped just below the town in a wooded hollow.

NEMI

The Romans flock to **Nemi** in droves, particularly from April to June, for the succulent **strawberries** grown here, acclaimed by some gourmets as Europe's finest. In May, there's a strawberry festival. To reach Nemi by bus, go to the Anagnini Metro stop in Rome. From here, take the CoTral bus heading for Genzano. At Genzano, change buses, taking the one marked NEMI. Service is about every 30 minutes during the day.

Nemi was also known to the ancients. A temple to the huntress Diana was erected on **Lake Nemi** ⚐, which was said to be her "looking glass." In A.D. 37, Caligula built luxurious barges to float on the lake. The boats, lavishly fitted with bronze and marble, were sunk during Claudius's reign (he succeeded the insane Caligula) and were entirely forgotten until Mussolini drained the lake in the 1930s. Then the barges were found and set up in a lakeside museum; they remained as a wonder of ancient Rome until the Nazis burned them during their retreat.

At the **Roman Ship Museum (Museo delle Navi)** ⚐, Via di Diana 13 (© **06-39967900**), you can see two scale models of the ships destroyed by the Nazis. The major artifacts on display are mainly copies; the originals now rest in world-class museums. The museum is open daily from 9am to 7pm (daily 9am–5pm in winter). Admission is 2€ ($2.40). To reach the museum, head from the center of Nemi toward the lake.

The 15th-century **Palazzo Ruspoli,** a private baronial estate, is the focal point of Nemi, but the town itself invites exploration—particularly the alleyways the locals call streets and the houses with balconies jutting out over the slopes.

WHERE TO DINE

Ristorante Il Castagnone ⚐ ROMAN/SEAFOOD   This well-managed dining room in the town's best hotel takes definite pride in its Roman cuisine, emphasizing seafood above meat. The attentive formal service is usually delivered with a kind of gentle humor. Amid neoclassical accessories and marble, you can order delectable veal, chicken, beef, and fish dishes such as fried calamari, spaghetti with shellfish in garlicky tomato-based sauce, and roasted lamb with potatoes and Mediterranean herbs. As you dine, enjoy a sweeping lake view from the restaurant's windows.

In the Diana Park Hotel, Via Nemorense 44. © 06-9364041. Reservations recommended. Main courses 12€–20€ ($14–$24). AE, DC, MC, V. Tues–Sun noon–3pm and 8–11pm. Closed Nov (dates may vary).

EN ROUTE TO CASTEL GANDOLFO

The road to Gandolfo leads through a few worth-a-visit towns on the way. **Genzano,** on the other side of Lake Nemi, has views of the countryside and a 17th-century palace that belonged to the Sforza-Cesarini.

Ariccia is an ancient town that sent representatives to meet with Tarquin the Proud on top of Monte Cavo 2,500 years ago. After many centuries of changing hands, especially between medieval and Renaissance families, it has taken on a suburban look. The palace in the middle of town is still private and belongs to the Chigi family.

Albano practically adjoins Castel Gandolfo. It has a long history; this is the reputed site of Alba Longa, the so-called mother city of Rome, but it's quite built up and modern today. Trains going to Albano leave from Stazione Termini in Rome.

CASTEL GANDOLFO ✦

Now we come to the summer residence of the pope. The papal palace, a 17th-century edifice designed by Carlo Maderno, stands practically on the foundations of another equally regal summer residence, the villa of Emperor Domitian. Unfortunately, the palace, the gardens, and the adjoining Villa Barberini can't be visited. You'll have to content yourself with a visit to **Piazza della Libertà,** the piazza out front with its church, Chiesa di San Tomaso di Villanova, and fountain by Bernini.

If you're here for lunch, as many are, your best bet is **Antico Ristorante Pagnanelli,** Via Gramsci 4 (℗ **06-9360004**), which serves both regional and pan-Italian dishes, with meals starting at 9.50€ ($11) and a high of 18€ ($22) for the fresh seafood dishes. The restaurant is open Wednesday through Monday from noon to 3pm and 7pm to midnight.

FRASCATI ✦

About 21km (13 miles) from Rome on Via Tuscolana and some 322m (1,056 ft.) above sea level, Frascati is one of the most beautiful hill towns. It's known for the wine to which it lends its name, as well as for its villas, which were restored after the severe destruction caused by World War II bombers. To get here, take one of the CoTral buses leaving from the Anagina stop of Metro Line A in Rome. From there, take the blue CoTral bus to Frascati. Again, the transportation situation in Italy is constantly in a state of flux, so check your route at the station.

Although Frascati wine is exported and served in many of Rome's restaurants and trattorie, tradition holds that it's best near the vineyards from which it came. Romans drive up on Sunday just to drink it.

Stand in the heart of Frascati, at Piazza Marconi, to see the most important of the estates: **Villa Aldobrandini** ✦, Via Massala. The finishing touches to this 16th-century villa were added by Maderno, who designed the facade of St. Peter's in Rome. You can visit only the gardens, not the interior, but still, with its grottoes, yew hedges, statuary, and splashing fountains, it's a nice outing. The gardens are open Monday through Friday from 9am to 1pm and 3 to 5pm (to 6pm in summer), although you must go to the **Informazzione e Accoglienza Turistica,** Piazza Marconi 1 (℗ **06-9420331**), to ask for a free pass. The office is open in summer Monday to Saturday 8am to 2pm and Wednesday, Friday, and Saturday 4 to 7pm. Off-season hours are Monday to Saturday 8am to 2pm and Wednesday to Friday 3 to 6pm.

You also might want to visit the bombed-out **Villa Torlonia,** adjacent to Piazza Marconi. Its grounds have been converted into a public park whose chief treasure is the **Theater of the Fountains,** designed by Maderno.

If you have a car, you can continue about 5km (3 miles) past the Villa Aldobrandini to **Tuscolo,** an ancient spot with the ruins of an amphitheater dating from about the 1st century B.C. It offers what may be one of Italy's most panoramic views.

WHERE TO DINE

Cacciani Restaurant ROMAN   Cacciani is the top restaurant in Frascati, where the competition has always been tough. It boasts a terrace commanding a view of the valley, and the kitchen is exposed to the public. To start, we recommend the pasta specialties, such as pasta *cacio e pepe* (pasta with caciocavallo cheese and black pepper), or the original spaghetti with seafood and lentils. For a main course, the lamb with a sauce of white wine and vinegar is always fine. Of course, there is a large choice of wine. If you call ahead, the Cacciani family will arrange a visit to several of Frascati's wine-producing villas, along with a memorable meal at the restaurant.

Via Armando Diaz 13. ℂ **06-9420378.** Reservations required. Main courses 10€–16€ ($12–$19). AE, DC, MC, V. Tues–Sun 12:30–3pm and 7:30–10:30pm. Closed Jan 7–19 and Aug 16–26.

4 Ostia ⟨★

26km (16 miles) southwest of Rome

Ostia Antica is one of the area's major attractions, particularly interesting if you can't make it to Pompeii. If you want to see both ancient and modern Rome, grab your swimsuit, towel, and sun block, and take the Metro Line B from Stazione Termini to the Magliana stop. Change here for the Lido train to Ostia Antica, about 26km (16 miles) from Rome. Departures are about every half-hour, and the trip takes only 20 minutes. The Metro lets you off across the highway that connects Rome with the coast. It's just a short walk to the excavations.

Later, board the Metro again to visit the **Lido di Ostia,** the beach. Italy might be a Catholic country, but you won't detect any religious conservatism in the skimpy bikinis on display here. There's a carnival atmosphere, with dance halls, cinemas, and pizzerias. The Lido is set off best at Castelfusano, against a backdrop of pinewoods. This stretch of shoreline is referred to as the Roman Riviera.

Ostia Antica's Ruins ★★   Ostia was the port of ancient Rome and a city in its own right. The currents and uneven bottom of the Tiber prevented Mediterranean shipping from going farther upstream, so merchandise was transferred to barges for the remainder of the trip. Ostia's fate was tied closely to that of the empire. At the peak of Rome's power, the city had 100,000 inhabitants—hard to imagine looking at today's ruins. Ostia was important enough to have had a theater, numerous temples and baths, great patrician houses, and a large business complex. Successive emperors, notably Claudius and Trajan, enlarged and improved the facilities. A prosperous city developed, full of temples, baths, theaters, and patrician homes.

Ostia flourished for about 8 centuries before it began to wither away. By Constantine's time (4th c. A.D.), the worm had turned. The barbarian sieges of Rome in the 5th century spelled the end of Ostia. Gradually, it became little more than a malaria bed, a buried ghost city that faded into history. A papal-sponsored commission launched a series of digs in the 19th century; however, the major work of unearthing was carried out under Mussolini's orders from 1938 to 1942 (the work had to stop because of the war). The city is only partially dug out today, but it's believed that all the chief monuments have been uncovered. Quite a few visible ruins have been unearthed, so this is no dusty field like the Circus Maximus.

These principal monuments are clearly labeled. The most important spot is **Piazzale delle Corporazioni,** an early version of Wall Street. Near the theater, this square contained nearly 75 corporations, the nature of their businesses identified by the patterns of preserved mosaics. Greek dramas were performed at the **ancient theater,** built in the early days of the empire. The classics are still aired here in summer (check with the tourist office for specific listings), but the theater as it looks today is the result of much rebuilding. Every town the size of Ostia had a forum, and during the excavations a number of pillars of the ancient **Ostia Forum** were uncovered. At one end is a 2nd-century B.C. temple honoring a trio of gods, Minerva, Jupiter, and Juno (little more than the basic foundation remains). In addition, in the enclave is a well-lit **museum** displaying Roman statuary along with some Pompeii-like frescoes. Also of special interest are the ruins of **Thermopolium,** which was a bar; its name means "sale of hot drinks." The ruins of **Capitolium and Forum** remain; this was once the largest temple in Ostia, dating from the 2nd century A.D. A lot of the original brick remains, including a partial reconstruction of the altar. Of an insula, a block of multiparty apartments, **Casa Diana** remains, with its rooms arranged around an inner courtyard. There are perfect picnic spots beside fallen columns or near old temple walls.

Viale dei Romagnoli 717. (✆ **06-56358099.** Admission 4€ ($4.80). Nov–Feb Tues–Sun 8:30am–6pm; Mar Tues–Sun 8:30am–5pm; Apr–Oct Tues–Sun 8:30am–6pm. Metro: Ostia Antica Line Roma–Ostia–Lido.

5 Fregene ✭

38.5km (24 miles) west of Rome

The fame of this coastal city north of the Tiber dates back to the 1600s, when the land belonged to the Rospigliosi, a powerful Roman family. Pope Clement IX, a member of that wealthy family, planted a forest of pine that extends along the shoreline for 4km (2½ miles) and stands half a mile deep to protect the land from the strong winds of the Mediterranean. Today the wall of pines makes a dramatic backdrop for the golden sands and luxurious villas of the resort. If you'd like to see an Italian beach, head here instead of to the more polluted beaches along Ostia's Lido.

GETTING THERE

You can catch the CoTral bus to Fregene, which leaves from the Lepanto Metro stop in Rome and carries passengers to the center of Fregene. A ticket costs 2.50€ ($3), and travel time is 1 hour.

If you're driving, follow Autostrada 1 (also known as Via Aurelia Malagrotta) heading west, crossing over the bypass that encircles Rome. After Castello di Guido, 23km (14 miles) west of Central Rome, exit onto the secondary road marked MACCARESE-FREGENE. Then continue southwest for another 16km (10 miles), following the signs to Fregene. There is no tourist information office.

WHERE TO STAY & DINE

La Conchiglia ✭ La Conchiglia means "The Shell," and it's an appropriate name for this beachfront hotel and restaurant, with views of the water and the pines. It features a circular lounge with curving wall banquettes facing a cylindrical fireplace. Guest rooms are comfortable and well furnished, ranging from medium to spacious, each with a fine mattress and a bathroom equipped with a shower/tub combination.

It's also possible to stop by just for a good moderately priced meal. Try, for example, spaghetti with lobster and grilled fish, or one of many excellent meat dishes. Meals start at 7€ ($8.40). The restaurant is open daily for lunch and dinner.

Lungomare di Ponente 4, Fregene, 00050 Roma. (✆ **06-6685385.** Fax 06-66563185. www.laconchiglia.it. 36 units. 85€–121€ ($102–$145) double. Rates include breakfast. AE, DC, MC, V. Free parking. **Amenities:** Restaurant; lounge; room service (breakfast, lunch, and dinner but not 24 hrs.). *In room:* A/C, TV, dataport (in some), minibar, hair dryer, safe.

6 Etruscan Historical Sights

CERVETERI (CAERE)

As you walk through Rome's Etruscan Museum (Villa Giulia), you'll often see CAERE written under a figure vase or sarcophagus. This is a reference to the nearby town known today as Cerveteri, one of Italy's great Etruscan cities, whose origins could date from as far back as the 9th century B.C.

Of course, the Etruscan town has long since faded, but not the **Necropolis of Cerveteri** ★★ (© **06-9940001**). The effect is eerie; Cerveteri is often called a "city of the dead." When you go beneath some of the mounds, you'll discover the most striking feature: The tombs are like rooms in Etruscan homes. The main burial ground is the Necropolis of Banditacca. Of the graves thus far uncovered, none is finer than the **Tomba Bella (the Reliefs' Tomb),** the burial ground of the Matuna family. Articles such as utensils and even house pets were painted in stucco relief. Presumably, these paintings were representations of items that the dead family would need in the world beyond. The necropolis is open daily from 8:30am to 1 hour before sunset. Admission is 4€ ($4.80) for adults and 2€ ($2.40) for children.

Relics from the necropolis are displayed at the **Museo Nazionale Cerite,** Piazza Santa Maria Maggiore (© **06-9941354**). The museum, housed within the ancient walls and crenellations of Ruspoldi Castle, is open daily from 8:30am to 7:30pm. Admission is 4€ ($4.80).

You can reach Cerveteri by bus or car. If you're driving, head out Via Aurelia, northwest of Rome, for 45km (28 miles). By public transport, take Metro Line A in Rome to the Lepanto stop; from Via Lepanto, you can catch a CoTral bus to Cerveteri; the trip takes about an hour and costs 2.80€ ($3.35). You can visit their website at www.cotralspa.it. Once you're at Cerveteri, it's a 2km (1¼-mile) walk to the necropolis; follow the signs pointing the way.

TARQUINIA ★

If you want to see tombs even more striking and more recently excavated than those at Cerveteri, go to Tarquinia, a town with medieval turrets and fortifications atop rocky cliffs overlooking the sea. It would seem unusual for a medieval town to have an Etruscan name, but actually, Tarquinia is the adopted name of the old medieval community of Corneto, in honor of the major Etruscan city that once stood nearby.

The main attraction in the town is the **Tarquinia National Museum** ★, Piazza Cavour (© **0776-856036**), devoted to Etruscan exhibits and sarcophagi excavated from the necropolis a few miles away. The museum is housed in the Palazzo Vitelleschi, a Gothic palace from the mid–15th century. Among the exhibits are gold jewelry, black vases with carved and painted bucolic scenes, and sarcophagi decorated with carvings of animals and relief figures of priests and military leaders. But the biggest attraction is in itself worth the ride from Rome: the almost life-size pair of **winged horses** ★★ from the pediment of a Tarquinian temple. The finish is worn here and there, and the terra-cotta color shows through, but the relief stands as one of the greatest Etruscan masterpieces ever discovered. The museum is open Tuesday through Sunday from 8:30am to 7:30pm, and charges 4€ ($4.80) admission adults, 2€ ($2.40) 18 to 25 years old, under 18 free. *Note:* It is possible to buy a combined ticket for the Tarquinia National Museum and the Etruscan Necropolis. It costs 6.50€ ($7.80). The museum is closed Christmas, January 1, and May 1.

A fee of 4€ ($4.80) fee (adults), 2€ ($2.40) (ages 18–25, under 18 free) admits you to the **Etruscan Necropolis** ✹✹ (© **0766-856308**), covering more than 4km (2½ miles) of rough terrain near where the ancient Etruscan city once stood. Thousands of tombs have been discovered, some of which have yet to be explored to this day. Looters discovered many, of course, but although countless pieces now reside in museums and private collections, many treasures remain. The **paintings** on the walls of the tombs have helped historians reconstruct the life of the Etruscans—a heretofore impossible feat without a written history. The paintings depict feasting couples in vivid colors mixed from iron oxide, lapis lazuli dust, and charcoal. One of the oldest tombs (6th c. B.C.) depicts young men fishing while dolphins play and colorful birds fly high above. Many of the paintings convey an earthy, vigorous sexuality among the wealthy Etruscans. The tombs are generally open Tuesday through Sunday from 8:30am to 1 hour before sunset. You can reach the gravesites by taking a bus from the Barriera San Giusto to the Cimitero stop. Or, try the 20-minute walk from the museum. Inquire at the museum for directions. It is closed Christmas, January 1, and May 1.

To reach Tarquinia by car, take Via Aurelia outside Rome and continue on the autostrada toward Civitavecchia. Bypass Civitavecchia and continue another 21km (13 miles) north until you see the exit signs for Tarquinia. As for public transport, a *diretto* (direct) train from Roma Ostiense station takes 50 minutes. Eight buses a day leave from the Via Lepanto stop in Rome for the 2-hour trip to the town of Barriera San Giusto, 2.5km (1½ miles) from Tarquinia. Bus schedules are available at the **tourist office** in Barriera San Giusto (© **0766-856384**), open Monday through Saturday from 8am to 1pm.

7 Viterbo ✦

98km (61 miles) north of Rome

The 2,000 years that have gone into the creation of the city of Viterbo make it one of the most interesting day trips from Rome. Although it traces its history back to the Etruscans, the bulk of its historical architecture dates from the Middle Ages and the Renaissance, when the city was a residence (and hideout) for the popes. The old section of the city is still surrounded by the thick stone walls that once protected the inhabitants from papal (or antipapal, depending on the situation at the time) attacks.

ESSENTIALS
GETTING THERE   Take a direct train from Rome (at the Ostiense Statin or Roma Trastevere) to Viterbo. The trip takes 1¾ hours, costing 4.10€ ($4.90) one-way.

If you're driving, take Autostrada 2 north to the Orte exit.

VISITOR INFORMATION   **Tourist information** is available at Via Mariano Romiti (inside the Porta Romana train station; © **0761-304795**); the office is open Monday to Thursday 9:30am to 1pm and 3 to 6pm, Friday to Saturday 9:30am to 1pm.

SEEING THE SIGHTS
The only way to see Viterbo properly is to wander through the narrow cobblestone streets of the medieval town. **Piazza del Plebiscito,** dominated by the 15th-century town hall, impresses visitors with the fine state of preservation of Viterbo's old buildings. The courtyard and fountain in front of the town hall and the 13th-century governor's palace are favorite meeting places for townsfolk and visitors alike.

Just down Via San Lorenzo is **Piazza San Lorenzo** 🕸🕸, the site of Viterbo's cathedral, which sits atop a former Etruscan acropolis. The **Duomo,** dating from 1192, is a composite of architectural styles, with pagan foundations, a Renaissance facade, and a Gothic bell tower. Next door is the 13th-century **Palazzo Papale** 🕸🕸, which was built as a residence for the pope but also served as a hideout when he was in exile. The exterior staircase and the colonnaded loggia combine to make up one of the finest examples of civil Roman architecture from the Gothic period.

The best example of medieval architecture in Viterbo is the **San Pellegrino Quarter** 🕸🕸, reached from Piazza San Lorenzo by a short walk past Piazza della Morte. This quarter, inhabited by working-class Viterboans, is a maze of narrow streets, arched walkways, towers, steep stairways, and ornamental fountains.

Worth a special visit is the **Convent of Santa Maria della Verita,** dating from 1100. The church contains 15th-century frescoes by Lorenzo da Viterbo, a student of Piero della Francesca.

Park of the Monsters (Parco dei Mostri) 🕸 About 13km (8 miles) east of Bagnaia at Bomarzo lies the Park of the Monsters. Prince Vicino Orsini had it built in a deep valley that's overlooked by the Orsini Palace and the houses of the village. On the other side of the valley are stone cliffs. Prince Orsini's park, Bosco Sacro (Sacred Wood), is filled with grotesque figures carved from natural rock. Nature and art have created a surrealistic fantasy: the Mouth of Hell (an ogre's face so big that people can walk into its gaping mouth), a crude Hercules slaying an Amazon, nymphs with butterfly wings, a huge tortoise with a statue on its shell, a harpy, a mermaid, snarling dogs, lions, and much, much more.

Villa delle Meraviglie, Bomarzo. ✆ 0761-924029. Admission 8€ ($9.60). Daily 8am–dusk. Bus: Take a CoTral bus from Viterbo.

Villa Lante 🕸🕸 The English author Sacheverell Sitwell called Villa Lante, located in Bagnaia, a suburb of Viterbo, "the most beautiful garden in Italy." Water from Monte Cimino flows down to the fountains of the villa, running from terrace to terrace until it reaches the central pool of the regal garden, with statues, stone banisters, and shrubbery. Two symmetrical Renaissance palaces make up the villa. The gardens that adjoin the villa, however, can be visited only on a guided tour. (The gatekeeper at the guard house will show you through, usually with a group that has assembled.) The interiors of the twin mansions can't be visited.

Via Giacopo Barrozzi 71, Bagnaia. ✆ 0761-288008. Admission 2€ ($2.40). Nov–Mar Tues–Sun 8:30am–4:30pm; early Apr and Sept–Oct 9am–5:30pm; mid-Apr to Aug 8:30am–6:30pm. Bus: Take a CoTral bus from Viterbo.

WHERE TO STAY & DINE

Grand Hotel Salus e delle Terme Whether you'd like to stay overnight or just drop in for lunch, the best place in Viterbo is this rather elegant modern hotel. Almost every room opens onto a loggia with a panoramic view. Bedrooms are furnished in a streamlined modern format, with well-groomed bathrooms with tub/shower combinations. The hotel's swimming pool is partially indoors so that it can also be used in winter, but the main draw is the Termal Centre, a top-rated spa. There's also a solarium. The severely modern restaurant serves some of Viterbo's finest Italian cuisine, with main courses costing 12€ to 30€ ($14–$36).

Strada Tuscanese 26–28, 01100 Viterbo. ✆ 0761-3581. Fax 0761-354262. www.grandhoteltermesalus.com. 100 units. 175€ ($210) double; 290€ ($348) suite. AE, DC, MC, V. **Amenities:** 2 restaurants; bar; 2 pools (1 indoor heated); health club; spa; Jacuzzi; room service (7am–10pm); laundry service; dry cleaning; nonsmoking rooms; rooms for those w/limited mobility. *In room:* A/C, TV, dataport, minibar, hair dryer.

Appendix A:
Rome in Depth

Rome, according to legend, was built on seven hills. These hills rise from the marshy lowlands of the Campagna and are mostly on the left bank of the Tiber River. They include the Quirinale (seat of the modern Italian government), Esquiline, Viminal, Caelian, and Aventine—and all combine to form a crescent-shape plateau of great historical fame. In its center rises the Palatine Hill, the all-powerful seat of the imperial residences of ancient Rome, which looks down on the ancient Forum and the Colosseum. To the northwest rises the Capitoline Hill. Some historians have suggested that Rome's geography—set above a periphery of marshy and swelteringly hot lowlands—contributed to the fall of the Roman Empire because of its propensity to breed malaria-carrying mosquitoes.

The modern city of Rome is composed of 22 districts, covering an area of nearly 26 sq. km (10 sq. miles). The Tiber makes two distinct bends within Rome, below Ponte Cavour, one of the city's major bridges, and again at the history-rich island of Tiberina.

With bloodlines that include virtually every race ever encompassed by the borders of the ancient Roman Empire, the people of Rome long ago grew accustomed to seeing foreign influences come and go. Picking their way through the architectural and cultural jumble of Rome, they are not averse to complaining (loudly) of the city's endless inconveniences, yet they are the first to appreciate the historical and architectural marvels that surround them. Cynical but hearty and warm, modern Romans propel themselves through life with an enviable sense of style.

The crowds of pilgrims and the vast numbers of churches and convents exist side by side with fleshier and more earthbound distractions, the combination of which imbues many Romans with an overriding interest in the pleasures and distractions of the moment. This sense of theatricality can be seen in Roman driving habits; in animated conversations and gesticulations in restaurants and cafes; in the lavish displays of flowers, fountains, food, and architecture, the nation's trademark; and in the 27 centuries of building projects dedicated to the power and egos of long-dead potentates.

Despite the crowds, the pollution, the heat, and the virtual impossibility of efficiency, Romans for the most part take life with good cheer and *pazienza*. Translated as "patience," it seems to be the frequently uttered motto of modern Rome and an appropriate philosophy for a city that has known everything from unparalleled glory to humiliation and despair. Romans know that since Rome wasn't built in a day, its charms should be savored slowly and with an appreciation for the cultures that contributed to this panoply.

1 Rome Past & Present

Many of the key events that shaped the rich and often gory tapestry of Italian history originated in Rome. Although parts of Italy (especially Sardinia and Sicily) were inhabited as early as the Bronze Age, the region around Rome was occupied relatively late. Some historians claim that the presence of active volcanoes in the region during the Bronze Age prevented prehistoric tribes from living here, but whatever the reason, Rome has unearthed far fewer prehistoric graves and implements than have neighboring Tuscany and Umbria.

THE ETRUSCANS   Among the early inhabitants of Italy, the most significant were the Etruscans—but who were they? No one knows, and the many inscriptions they left behind (mostly on graves) are of no help, since the Etruscan language has never been deciphered by modern scholars. It's thought they arrived on the eastern coast of Umbria several centuries before Rome was built, around 800 B.C. Their religious rites and architecture show an obvious contact with Mesopotamia; the Etruscans might have been refugees from Asia Minor who traveled westward about 1200 to 1000 B.C. Within 2 centuries, they had subjugated Tuscany and Campania and the Villanova tribes who lived there.

While the Etruscans built temples at Tarquinia and Caere (present-day Cerveteri), the few nervous Latin tribes that remained outside their sway gravitated to Rome, then little more than a sheepherding village. As its power grew, however, Rome increasingly profited from the strategically important Tiber crossing where the ancient Salt Way (Via Salaria)

turned northeastward toward the central Apennines.

From their base at Rome, the Latins remained free of the Etruscans until about 600 B.C. But the Etruscan advance was inexorable, and though the tribes concentrated their forces at Rome for a last stand, they were swept away by the sophisticated conquerors. The new overlords introduced gold tableware and jewelry, bronze urns and terra-cotta statuary, and the best of Greek and Asia Minor art and culture; they also made Rome the governmental seat of all Latium. Roma is an Etruscan name, and the kings of Rome had Etruscan names: Numa, Ancus, Tarquinius, and even Romulus.

Under the combined influences of the Greeks and the Mesopotamian east, Rome grew enormously. A new port was opened at Ostia, near the mouth of the Tiber. Artists from Greece carved statues of Roman gods to resemble Greek divinities. From this enforced (and not always peaceable) mixture of Latin tribes and Etruscans grew the roots of what eventually became the Republic of Rome.

The Etruscans ruled until the Roman revolt around 510 B.C., and by 250 B.C., the Romans and their Campania allies had vanquished the Etruscans, wiping out their language and religion. However, many of the former rulers' manners and

---

Dateline

- **Bronze Age** Tribes of Celts, Teutonics, and groups from the eastern Mediterranean inhabit the Italian peninsula.
- **1200 B.C.** The Etruscans migrate from the eastern Mediterranean (probably Mesopotamia) and occupy territory north and south of Rome.
- **800 B.C.** Sicily and southern Italy (especially Naples) flourish

under Greek and Phoenician protection; independent of most outside domination, Rome evolves as an insignificant community of shepherds with loyalties divided among several Latin tribes.

- **753 B.C.** Rome's traditional founding date.
- **660 B.C.** Etruscans occupy Rome as the capital of their empire; the city grows rapidly and a major seaport (Ostia)

opens at the mouth of the Tiber.

- **510–250 B.C.** The Latin tribes, still centered in Rome, maintain a prolonged revolt against the Etruscans; alpine Gauls attack the Etruscans from the north, and Greeks living in Sicily destroy the Etruscan navy.
- **250 B.C.** The Romans and their allies finally purge the Etruscans from Italy; Rome flourishes as a republic and

beliefs remained, assimilated into the culture. Even today, certain Etruscan customs and bloodlines are believed to exist in Italy, especially in Tuscany.

The best places to see the legacy left by these mysterious people are in Cerveteri and Tarquinia, outside Rome. Especially interesting is the Etruscan necropolis, just 6.5km (4 miles) southeast of Tarquinia, where thousands of tombs have been discovered. See chapter 12, "Side Trips from Rome," for details on all these sites. To learn more about the Etruscans, visit the National Etruscan Museum (Museo Nazionale di Villa Giulia) in Rome itself (see chapter 8, "Exploring Rome").

THE ROMAN REPUBLIC Gauls from the alpine regions invaded the northern Etruscan territory around 600 B.C., and the Latin tribes revolted in about 510 B.C., toppling the Etruscan-linked rulers from their power bases and establishing the southern boundary of Etruscan influence at the Tiber. Greeks from Sicily ended Etruscan sea power in 474 B.C. during the battle of Cumae off the Italian coastline just north of Naples. By 250 B.C., the Romans and their allies in Campagna had vanquished the Etruscans, wiping out their language and religion.

Tempered in the fires of military adversity, the stern Roman republic was characterized by belief in the gods, the necessity of learning from the past, the strength of the family, education through books and public service, and, most important, obedience. The all-powerful Senate presided as Rome defeated rival powers one after the other in a steady stream of staggering military successes.

As the population grew, the Romans gave to their Latin allies and then to conquered peoples partial or complete Roman citizenship, always with the obligation of military service. Colonies of citizens were established on the borders of the growing empire and were populated with soldiers/farmers and their families. Later, as seen in the history of Britain and the European continent, colonies began to thrive as semi-autonomous units on their own, heavily fortified and linked to Rome by well-maintained military roads and a well-defined hierarchy of military command.

The final obstacle to the unrivaled supremacy of Rome was the defeat, during the 3rd century B.C., of the city-state of Carthage during the two Punic Wars. An ancient Phoenician trading post on the coast of Tunisia, Carthage had grown into one of the premier naval and agricultural powers of the Mediterranean, with strongly fortified positions in Corsica, Sardinia, and Spain. Despite the impressive victories of the Carthaginian general Hannibal, Rome eventually eradicated Carthage in one of the most famous defeats in ancient history. Rome was able

---

begins the accumulation of a vast empire.

- **250–50** B.C. Rome obliterates its chief rival, Carthage, during two Punic Wars; Carthage's defeat allows unchecked Roman expansion into Spain, North Africa, Sardinia, and Corsica.
- **44** B.C. Julius Caesar is assassinated; his successor, Augustus, transforms Rome from a city of brick to a city of marble and solidifies

Rome's status as a dictatorship.

- **40** B.C. Rome and its armies control the entire Mediterranean world.
- **3rd century** A.D. Rome declines under a series of incompetent and corrupt emperors.
- **4th century** A.D. Rome is fragmented politically as administrative capitals are established in such cities as Milan and Trier, Germany.

- **395** The Empire splits: Constantine establishes a "New Rome" at Constantinople (Istanbul); Goths invade Rome's provinces in northern Italy.
- **410–55** Rome is sacked by barbarians—Alaric the Goth, Attila the Hun, and Gaiseric the Vandal.
- **475** Rome falls, leaving only the primate of the Catholic church in control; the pope

continues

to immediately expand its power into North Africa, Sardinia, Corsica, and Iberia.

THE ROMAN EMPIRE   By 49 B.C., Italy ruled the entire Mediterranean world either directly or indirectly, with all political, commercial, and cultural pathways leading directly to Rome. The wealth and glory to be found in Rome lured many there but drained other Italian communities of human resources. As Rome transformed itself into an administrative headquarters, imports to the city from other parts of the Empire hurt local farmers and landowners. The seeds for civil discord were sown early in the Republic's existence, although, because Rome was embellished with temples, monuments, and the easy availability of slave labor from conquered territories, many of its social problems were overlooked in favor of expansion and glory.

No figure was more towering during the Republic than Julius Caesar, the charismatic conqueror of Gaul—"the wife of every husband and the husband of every wife." After defeating the last resistance of the Pompeians in 45 B.C., he came to Rome and was made dictator and consul for 10 years. He was at that point almost a king. Conspirators led by Marcus Junius Brutus stabbed him to death in the Senate on March 15, 44 B.C. Beware the ides of March.

Marc Antony then assumed control by seizing Caesar's papers and wealth. Intent on expanding the Republic, Antony met with Cleopatra at Tarsus in 41 B.C. She seduced him, and he stayed in Egypt for a year. When Antony eventually returned to Rome, still smitten with Cleopatra, he made peace with Caesar's willed successor, Octavius, and, through the pacts of Brundisium, soon found himself married to Octavius's sister, Octavia. This marriage, however, didn't prevent him from openly marrying Cleopatra in 36 B.C. The furious Octavius gathered western legions and defeated Antony at the Battle of Actium on September 2, 31 B.C. Cleopatra fled to Egypt, followed by Antony, who committed suicide in disgrace a year later. Cleopatra, unable to seduce his successor and, thus, retain her rule of Egypt, followed suit with the help of an asp.

Born Gaius Octavius in 63 B.C., Augustus, the first Roman emperor, reigned from 27 B.C. to A.D. 14. His reign, called "the golden age of Rome," led to the Pax Romana, 2 centuries of peace. He had been adopted by and eventually became the heir of his great-uncle Julius Caesar. In Rome you can still visit the remains of the Forum of Augustus, built before the birth of Christ, and the Domus Augustana, where the imperial family lived on the Palatine Hill.

---

slowly adopts many of the responsibilities and the prestige once reserved for the Roman emperors.

■ **731** Pope Gregory II renounces Rome's spiritual and political link to the authorities in Constantinople.

■ **800** Charlemagne is crowned Holy Roman Emperor by Pope Leo III; Italy dissolves into a series of small warring kingdoms.

■ **1065** The Holy Land falls to the Muslim Turks; the Crusades are launched.

■ **1303–77** A papal schism occurs when a rival pope is established at Avignon.

■ **1377** The "antipope" is removed from Avignon, and the Roman popes emerge as sole contenders to the legacy of St. Peter.

■ **Mid-1400s** Originating in Florence, the Renaissance blossoms throughout Italy;

Italian artists receive multiple commissions from the ecclesiastical communities of Rome.

■ **1508** Ordered by the pope, Michelangelo begins work on the ceiling of the Vatican's Sistine Chapel.

■ **1527** Rome is attacked and sacked by Charles V, who—to the pope's rage—is elected Holy Roman Emperor the following year.

On the eve of the birth of Jesus, Rome was a mighty empire whose generals had brought the Western world under the influence of Roman law, values, and civilization. Only in the eastern third of the Mediterranean did the existing cultures—notably, the Greek—withstand the Roman incursions. Despite its occupation by Rome, Greece permeated Rome more than any culture with new ideas, values, and concepts of art, architecture, religion, and philosophy.

The emperors, whose succession started with Augustus's principate after the death of Julius Caesar, brought Rome to new, almost giddy, heights. Augustus transformed the city from brick to marble, much the way Napoleon III transformed Paris many centuries later. But success led to corruption. The emperors wielded autocratic power, and the centuries witnessed a steady decay in the ideals and traditions on which the Empire had been founded. The army became a fifth column of barbarian mercenaries, the tax collector became the scourge of the countryside, and for every good emperor (Augustus, Claudius, Trajan, Vespasian, and Hadrian, to name a few) there were three or four debased heads of state (Caligula, Nero, Domitian, Caracalla, and more).

The ideals of democratic responsibility in the heart of the Empire had begun to break down. The populace began to object violently to a government that took little interest in commerce and seemed interested only in foreign politics. As taxes and levies increased, the poor emigrated in huge and idle numbers to Rome and the rich cities of the Po Valley. Entire generations of war captives, forced into the slave-driven economies of large Italian estates, were steeped in hatred and ignorance.

Christianity, a new and revolutionary religion, probably gained a foothold in Rome about 10 years after Jesus's crucifixion. Feared far more for its political implications than for its spiritual presuppositions, it was at first brutally suppressed before moving through increasingly tolerant stages of acceptability.

After Augustus died (by poison, perhaps), his widow, Livia—a crafty social climber who had divorced her first husband to marry Augustus—set up her son, Tiberius, as ruler through a series of intrigues and poisonings. A long series of murders ensued, and Tiberius, who ruled during Pontius Pilate's trial and crucifixion of Christ, was eventually murdered in an uprising of landowners. In fact, murder was so common that a short time later, Domitian (A.D. 81–96) became so obsessed with the possibility of assassination that he had the walls of his palace covered in mica so he could see behind him at all times. (He was killed anyway.)

■ **1796–97** Napoleon's military conquests of Italy arouse Italian nationalism.

■ **1861** Rome is declared the capital of the newly established Kingdom of Italy; the Papal States (but not the Vatican) are absorbed into the new nation.

■ **1929** A concordat between the Vatican and the Italian government delineates the rights and responsibilities of both parties.

■ **1935** Italy invades Abyssinia (Ethiopia).

■ **1941** Italy invades Yugoslavia.

■ **1943** General Patton lands in Sicily and soon controls the island.

■ **1945** Mussolini killed by a mob in Milan.

■ **1946** Rome is established as the capital of the newly created Republic of Italy.

■ **1960s** Left-wing terrorist groups rise; flight of capital from Italy begins; continuing problems of the impoverished south cause an exodus from the countryside into such cities as Rome.

■ **1980s** *Il Sorpasso* imbues Rome (and the rest of Italy) with dreams of an economic rebirth.

■ **1994** Right-wing forces win in Italian national elections.

■ **1996** Dini steps down as prime minister, as the president

continues

Excesses and scandal ruled the day: Caligula (a bit overfond of his sister Drusilla) appointed his horse a lifetime member of the Senate, lavished money on foolish projects, and proclaimed himself a god. Caligula's successor, his uncle Claudius, was deceived and publicly humiliated by one of his wives, the lascivious Messalina (he had her killed for her trouble); he was then poisoned by his final wife, his niece Agrippina, to secure the succession of Nero, her son by a previous marriage. To thank her, Nero murdered not only his mother, but also his wife, Claudius's daughter, and his rival, Claudius's son. The disgraceful Nero was removed as emperor while visiting Greece; he committed suicide with the cry, "What an artist I destroy."

By the 3rd century A.D., corruption was so prevalent that there were 23 emperors in 73 years. There were so many emperors that it was common, as H. V. Morton tells us, to hear in the provinces of the election of an emperor together with a report of his assassination. How bad had things gotten? So bad that Caracalla, to secure control of the Empire, had his brother Geta slashed to pieces while lying in his mother's arms.

As the decay progressed, Roman citizens either lived on the increasingly swollen public dole while spending their days at gladiatorial games and imperial baths, or were disillusioned patricians at the mercy of emperors who might murder them for their property.

The 4th-century reforms of Diocletian held the Empire together, but at the expense of its inhabitants, who were reduced to tax units. He reinforced imperial power while paradoxically weakening Roman dominance and prestige by dividing the Empire into east and west halves and establishing administrative capitals at outposts such as Milan and Trier, Germany. Diocletian instituted not only heavy taxes, but also a socioeconomic system that made professions hereditary. This edict was so strictly enforced that the son of a silversmith could be tried as a criminal if he attempted to become a sculptor instead.

Constantine became emperor in A.D. 306, and in 330 he made Constantinople (or Byzantium) the new capital of the Empire, moving the administrative functions away from Rome altogether, an act that sounded a death knell for a city already threatened by the menace of barbarian attacks. The sole survivor of six rival emperors, Constantine recognized Christianity as the official religion of the Roman Empire and built an entirely new, more easily defended capital on the banks of the Bosporus. Named in his honor (Constantinople, or Byzantium), it was later renamed Istanbul by the Ottoman

Turks. When he moved to the new capital, Constantine and his heirs took with them the best of the artisans, politicians, and public figures of Rome. Rome, reduced to little more than a provincial capital controlling the threatened western half of the once-mighty empire, continued to founder and decay. As for the Christian church, although the popes of Rome were under the nominal auspices of an exarch from Constantinople, their power increased slowly and steadily as the power of the emperors declined.

THE EMPIRE FALLS The eastern and western sections of the Roman Empire split in 395, leaving Italy without the support it had once received from east of the Adriatic. When the Goths moved toward Rome in the early 5th century, citizens in the provinces, who had grown to hate and fear the bureaucracy set up by Diocletian and followed by succeeding emperors, welcomed the invaders. And then the pillage began.

Rome was first sacked by Alaric in August 410. The populace made no attempt to defend the city (other than trying to buy off the Goth, a tactic that had worked 3 years before); most people simply fled into the hills or headed to their country estates if they were rich. The feeble Western emperor Honorius hid out in Ravenna the entire time.

More than 40 troubled years passed until the siege of Rome by Attila the Hun. Attila was dissuaded from attacking, thanks largely to a peace mission headed by Pope Leo I in 452. Yet relief was short-lived: In 455, Gaiseric the Vandal carried out a 2-week sack that was unparalleled in its pure savagery. The empire of the West lasted for only another 20 years; the sackings and chaos finally destroyed it in 476, and Rome was left to the popes, under the nominal auspices of an exarch from Byzantium (Constantinople).

The last would-be Caesars to walk the streets of Rome were both barbarians:

The first was Theodoric, who established an Ostrogoth kingdom at Ravenna from 493 to 526; and the second was Totilla, who held the last races in the Circus Maximus in 549. Totilla was engaged in a running battle with Belisarius, the general of the Eastern emperor Justinian, who sought to regain Rome for the Eastern Empire. The city changed hands several times, recovering some of its ancient pride by bravely resisting Totilla's forces but eventually being entirely depopulated by the continuing battles.

THE HOLY ROMAN EMPIRE A ravaged Rome entered the Middle Ages with its once-proud population scattered and unrecognizable in rustic exile. A modest population started life again in the swamps of the Campus Martius, while the seven hills, now without water since the aqueducts were cut, stood abandoned and crumbling.

After the fall of the Western Empire, the pope took on more imperial powers, yet there was no political unity. Decades of rule by barbarians and then Goths were followed by takeovers in different parts of the country by various strong warriors, such as the Lombards. Italy was thus divided into several spheres of control. In 731, Pope Gregory II renounced Rome's dependence on Constantinople and thus ended the twilight era of the Greek exarch who had nominally ruled Rome.

Papal Rome turned toward Europe, where the papacy found a powerful ally in Charlemagne, a king of the barbarian Franks. In 800, he was crowned emperor by Pope Leo III. The capital he established at Aachen (Aix-la-Chapelle in French) lay deep within territory known to the Romans a half millennium ago as the heart of the barbarian world. Though Charlemagne pledged allegiance to the church and looked to Rome and its pope as the final arbiter in most religious and cultural affairs, he launched northwestern

Europe on a course toward bitter political opposition to the meddling of the papacy in temporal affairs.

The successor to Charlemagne's empire was a political entity known as the Holy Roman Empire (962–1806). The new empire defined the end of the Dark Ages but ushered in a period of long, bloody warfare. The Lombard leaders battled Franks. Magyars from Hungary invaded northeastern Lombardy and were defeated, in turn, by the increasingly powerful Venetians. Normans gained military control of Sicily in the 11th century, divided it from the rest of Italy, and altered forever the island's racial and ethnic makeup and its architecture. As Italy dissolved into a fragmented collection of city-states, the papacy fell under the power of Rome's feudal landowners. Eventually, even the process for choosing popes came into the hands of the increasingly Germanic Holy Roman emperors, although this power balance would very soon shift.

Rome during the Middle Ages was a quaint rural town. Narrow lanes with overhanging buildings filled many areas that had once been showcases of ancient imperial power, such as the Campus Martius. The forums, mercantile exchanges, temples, and theaters of the Imperial Era slowly disintegrated and collapsed. The decay of ancient Rome was assisted by periodic earthquakes, centuries of neglect, and, in particular, the growing need for building materials. Rome receded into a dusty provincialism. As the seat of the Roman Catholic church, the state was almost completely controlled by priests, who had an insatiable need for new churches and convents.

By the end of the 11th century, the popes shook off control of the Roman aristocracy, rid themselves of what they considered the excessive influence of the emperors at Aachen, and began an aggressive expansion of church influence and acquisitions. The deliberate organization of the church into a format modeled on the hierarchies of the ancient Roman Empire put it on a collision course with the Holy Roman Empire and the other temporal leaders of Europe, resulting in an endless series of power struggles.

THE MIDDLE AGES The papacy soon became essentially a feudal state, and the pope became a medieval (later Renaissance) prince engaged in many of the worldly activities that brought criticism on the church in later centuries. The fall of the Holy Land to the Turks in 1065 catapulted the papacy into the forefront of world politics, primarily because of the Crusades, most of which were judged to be military and economic disasters and many of which the popes directly caused or encouraged. During the 12th and 13th centuries, the bitter rivalries that rocked the secular and spiritual bastions of Europe took their toll on the stability of the Holy Roman Empire, which grew weaker as city-states buttressed by mercantile and trade-related prosperity grew stronger. In addition, France emerged as a strong nation in its own right during this period. Each investiture of a new bishop to any influential post became a cause for endless jockeying for power among many political and ecclesiastical factions.

These conflicts achieved their most visible impasse in 1303 with the full-fledged removal of the papacy from Rome to the French city of Avignon. For more than 70 years, until 1377, viciously competing popes (one in Rome, another under the protection of the French kings in Avignon) made simultaneous claims to the legacy of St. Peter, underscoring as never before the degree to which the church was both a victim and a victimizer of European politics.

The seat of the papacy was eventually returned to Rome, where a series of popes proved every bit as fascinating as the

Roman emperors they replaced. The great families—Barberini, Medici, Borgia—enhanced their status and fortunes impressively whenever one of their sons was elected pope.

In the mid–14th century, the Black Death ravaged Europe, killing a third of Italy's population. Despite such setbacks, northern Italian city-states grew wealthy from Crusade booty, trade with one another and with the Middle East, and banking. These wealthy principalities and pseudorepublics ruled by the merchant elite flexed their muscles in the absence of a strong central authority.

THE RENAISSANCE The story of Italy from the dawn of the Renaissance in the 15th century to the Age of Enlightenment in the 17th and 18th centuries is as varied and fascinating as that of the rise and fall of the Empire.

Despite the centuries that had passed since the collapse of the Roman Empire, the age of siege wasn't yet over. In 1527, Charles V, king of Spain, carried out the worst sack of Rome ever. To the horror of Pope Clement VII (a Medici), the entire city was brutally pillaged by the man who was crowned Holy Roman Emperor the next year.

During the years of the Renaissance, the Reformation, and the Counter-Reformation, Rome underwent major physical changes. The old centers of culture reverted to pastures and fields, and great churches and palaces were built with the stones of ancient Rome. This construction boom did far more damage to the temples of the Caesars than any barbarian sacking had done. Rare marbles were stripped from the imperial baths and used as altarpieces or sent to lime kilns. So enthusiastic was the papal destruction of imperial Rome that it's a miracle anything is left.

This era is best remembered for its art. The great ruling families, especially the Medicis in Florence, the Gonzagas in Mantua, and the Estes in Ferrara, not only reformed law and commerce, but also sparked a renaissance in art. Out of this period arose such towering figures as Leonardo da Vinci and Michelangelo. Many visitors come to Italy to view what's left of the art and glory of that era, including Michelangelo's Sistine Chapel ceiling at the Vatican.

THE MOVE TOWARD A UNITED ITALY During the 17th, 18th, and 19th centuries, the fortunes of Rome rose and fell with the general political and economic situation of the rest of Italy. Since the end of the 13th century, Italy had been divided into a series of regional states, each with mercenary soldiers, its own judicial system, and an interlocking series of alliances and enmities that had created a network of intensely competitive city-states. (Some of these families had attained formidable power under such *signori* as the Este family in Ferrara, the Medici in Florence, and the Sforza in Milan.) Rome, headquarters of the Papal States, maintained its independence and (usually) the integrity of its borders, although some of the city's religious power had been diluted as increasing numbers of Europeans converted to Protestantism.

Napoleon made a bid for power in Italy beginning in 1796, fueling his propaganda machines with what was considered a relatively easy victory. During the 1815 Congress of Vienna, which followed Napoleon's defeat, Italy was once again divided among many different factions: Austria was given Lombardy and Venetia, and the Papal States were returned to the popes. Some duchies were put back into the hands of their hereditary rulers, whereas southern Italy and Sicily went to a newly imported dynasty related to the Bourbons. One historic move, which eventually assisted in the unification of Italy, was the assignment of the former republic of Genoa to Sardinia (which at the time was governed by the House of Savoy).

By now, political unrest had become a fact of Italian (and Roman) life, at least some of it encouraged by the rapid industrialization of the north and the almost total lack of industrialization in the south. Despite these barriers, in 1861 the Kingdom of Italy was proclaimed, and Victor Emmanuel II of the House of Savoy, king of Sardinia, became head of the new monarchy. In 1861 the designated capital of the newly united country, following a 2,000-year-old precedent, became Rome.

Garibaldi, the most respected of all Italian heroes, must be singled out for his efforts, which included taking Sicily, then returning to the mainland and marching north to meet Victor Emmanuel II at Teano, and finally declaring a unified Italy (with the important exception of Rome itself). It must have seemed especially sweet to a man whose efforts at unity had caused him to flee the country fearing for his life on four occasions. It's a tribute to the tenacity of this red-bearded hero that he never gave up, even in the early 1850s, when he was forced to wait out one of his exiles as a candlemaker on Staten Island in New York.

In a controversial move that engendered resentment many decades later, the borders of the Papal States were eradicated from the map as Rome was incorporated into the new nation of Italy. The Vatican, however, did not yield its territory to the new order, despite guarantees of nonintervention proffered by the Italian government, and relations between the pope and the political leaders of Italy remained rocky until 1929.

WORLD WAR II & THE AXIS On October 28, 1922, Benito Mussolini, who had started his Fascist Party in 1919, knew the time was ripe for change. He gathered 50,000 supporters for a march on Rome. Inflation was soaring and

workers had just called a general strike, so rather than recognizing a state under siege, King Victor Emmanuel III recognized Mussolini as the new government leader. In 1929, Il Duce defined the divisions between the Italian government and the Vatican by signing a concordat granting political and fiscal autonomy to Vatican City. It also made Roman Catholicism the official state religion—but that designation was removed in 1978 through a revision of the concordat.

During the Spanish Civil War (1936–39), Mussolini's support of Franco's Fascist Party, which staged a coup against the democratically elected government of Spain, helped encourage the formation of the "Axis" alliance between Italy and Nazi Germany. Despite its outdated military equipment, Italy added to the general horror of the era by invading Abyssinia (Ethiopia) in 1935. In 1940, Italy invaded Greece through Albania, and in 1942 it sent thousands of Italian troops to assist Hitler in his disastrous campaign along the Russian front. In 1943, Allied forces, under the command of U.S. Gen. George Patton and British Gen. Bernard Montgomery, landed in Sicily and quickly secured the island as they prepared to move north toward Rome.

In the face of likely defeat and humiliation, Mussolini was overthrown by his own cabinet (Grand Council). The Allies made a separate deal with Victor Emmanuel III, who had collaborated with the fascists during the previous 2 decades and now easily shifted allegiances. A politically divided Italy watched as battalions of fanatical German Nazis released Mussolini from his Italian jail cell to establish the short-lived Republic of Salò, headquartered on the edge of Lake Garda. Mussolini had hoped for a groundswell of popular opinion in favor of Italian fascism, but events quickly proved this nothing more than a futile dream.

In April 1945, with almost half a million Italians rising in a mass demonstration against him and the German war machine, Mussolini was captured by Italian partisans as he fled to Switzerland. Along with his mistress, Claretta Petacci, and several others of his intimates, he was shot and strung upside-down from the roof of a Milan gas station.

MODERN ROME   Disaffected with the monarchy and its identification with the fallen fascist dictatorship, Italian voters in 1946 voted for the establishment of a republic. The major political party that emerged following World War II was the Christian Democratic Party, a right-of-center group whose leader, Alcide De Gasperi (1881–1954), served as premier until 1953. The second-largest party was the Communist Party; however, by the mid-1970s it had abandoned its revolutionary program in favor of a democratic form of "Eurocommunism" (in 1991, the Communists even changed their name to the Democratic Party of the Left).

Although after the war Italy was stripped of all its overseas colonies, it quickly succeeded in rebuilding its economy, in part because of U.S. aid under the Marshall Plan (1948–52). By the 1960s, as a member of the European Community (founded in Rome in 1957), Italy had become one of the world's leading industrialized nations, prominent in the manufacture of automobiles and office equipment.

But the country continued to be plagued by economic inequities between the prosperous industrialized north and the economically depressed south. It suffered an unprecedented flight of capital (frequently aided by Swiss banks only too willing to accept discreet deposits from wealthy Italians) and an increase in bankruptcies, inflation (almost 20% during much of the 1970s), and unemployment.

During the late 1970s and early 1980s, Italy was rocked by the rise of terrorism, instigated both by neofascists and by left-wing intellectuals from the Socialist-controlled universities of the north.

THE 1990s & INTO THE NEW MILLENNIUM   In the 1990s, some 6,000 businesspeople and politicians were implicated in a billion-dollar government graft scandal. Such familiar figures as Bettino Craxi, former head of the Socialist party, and Giulio Andreotti, a seven-time prime minister, were accused of corruption.

Hoping for a renewal after all this exposure of greed, Italian voters in March 1994 turned to the right wing to head their government. In overwhelming numbers, voters elected a former cruiseship singer turned media billionaire, Silvio Berlusconi, as their new leader. His Forza Italia (Go, Italy) party formed an alliance with the neofascist National Alliance and the secessionist Northern League to sweep to victory. These elections were termed "the most critical" for Italy in 4 decades. The new government was beset with an almost hopeless array of new problems, including destabilization caused by the Mafia and its underground economies. When the Northern League defected from the coalition in December 1994, Berlusconi resigned.

Treasury Minister Lamberto Dini, a nonpolitical international banker, replaced him. Dini signed on merely as a transitional player in Italy's topsy-turvy political game. His austere measures enacted to balance Italy's budget, including cuts in pensions and health care, were not popular among the mostly blue-collar Italian workers or the very influential labor unions. Pending a predicted defeat in a no-confidence vote, Dini also stepped down. His resignation in January 1996 left beleaguered Italians shouting *"Basta!"* ("Enough!"). This latest shuffling in Italy's political deck prompted President Oscar Scalfaro to dissolve both houses of the Italian Parliament.

Once again Italians were faced with forming a new government. Elections in April 1996 proved quite a shocker, not only for the defeated politicians, but also for the victors. The center-left coalition known as the Olive Tree, led by Romano Prodi, swept both the Senate and the Chamber of Deputies. The Olive Tree, whose roots stem from the old Communist party, achieved victory by shifting toward the center and focusing its campaign on a strong platform protecting social benefits and supporting Italy's bid to become a solid member of the European Union. Prodi followed through on his commitment when he announced a stringent budget for 1997 in a bid to be among the first countries to enter the monetary union.

The year 1997 saw further upheavals as the Prodi government continued to push ahead with cuts to the country's generous social security system. In the autumn of 1997, Prodi was forced to submit his resignation when he lost critical support in Parliament from the Communist Refounding party, which balked at further pension and welfare cuts in the 1998 budget. The party eventually backed off with its demands, and Prodi was returned to office.

In December 1999, under Prime Minister Massimo D'Alema, Italy received its 57th new government since 1945. But it didn't last long. In April 2000, former Prime Minister Giuliano Amato, a one-time Socialist, returned to power.

As 1999 neared its end, Rome rushed to put the finishing touches on its many monuments, including churches and museums, and everybody was ready for the scaffolding to come down before the arrival of 2000. Italy spent all of 2000 welcoming Jubilee Year visitors from around the world, as its political cauldron bubbled. One particularly notable clash in 2000 pitted the church and social conservatives against more progressive young Italians, as the pope lashed out at the World Gay Pride rally held in the summer of 2000. His condemnation sparked much debate in the media, but the actual event went off without a hitch and, in fact, was labeled as rather tame when compared to more raucous Gay Pride rallies elsewhere around the globe.

In May 2001, with right-wing support, the richest man in Italy, billionaire media tycoon Silvio Berlusconi (owner of three private TV networks) swept to victory as prime minister a second time. Calling for a "revolution" in Italy, Berlusconi promised a million and a half new jobs, pension hikes, epic tax cuts, anticrime bills, and beefed-up public works projects.

In 2002, Italians abandoned their long-beloved lire and began trading in euros along with their neighbors to the north, including France and Germany—a total of 12 countries (but not Britain). As the new currency went into effect, counterfeiters and swindlers had a field day; one elderly woman in Rome who was cashing a benefit check, unwittingly paid the equivalent of 600 U.S. dollars for a cup of cappuccino. But in general, the transition went relatively smoothly, especially among businesses.

Unlike France and Germany, Prime Minister Berlusconi proved to be a valuable ally of the United States when it went to war against Iraq in 2003. Berlusconi has attacked "Saddam apologists" who want to try to regain power through terrorist activity. A great deal of Italy, however, does not take the position of its prime minister and is highly critical of the way the U.S. has handled the war in Iraq.

In the Italy elections in April of 2006, Berlusconi was ousted by a narrow vote, losing to Romano Prodi. The new prime minister faces difficult challenges in that he may have a hard time keeping together nine parties that range from moderate Catholics to Communists.

Appendix B:
Molto Italiano

1 Basic Vocabulary

English	Italian	Pronunciation
Thank you	**Grazie**	*graht*-tzee-yey
You're welcome	**Prego**	*prey*-go
Please	**Per favore**	*pehr* fah-*vohr*-eh
Yes	**Si**	see
No	**No**	noh
Good morning or good day	**Buongiorno**	bwohn-*djor*-noh
Good evening	**Buona sera**	*bwohn*-ah *say*-rah
Good night	**Buona notte**	*bwohn*-ah *noht*-tay
How are you?	**Come sta?**	*koh*-may *stah*
Very well	**Molto bene**	*mohl*-toh *behn*-ney
Goodbye	**Arrivederci**	ahr-ree-vah-*dehr*-chee
Excuse me (to get attention)	**Scusi**	*skoo*-zee
Excuse me (to get past someone)	**Permesso**	pehr-*mehs*-soh
Where is . . . ?	**Dovè . . . ?**	doh-*vey*
the station	**la stazione**	lah stat-tzee-*oh*-neh
a hotel	**un albergo**	oon ahl-*behr*-goh
a restaurant	**un ristorante**	oon reest-ohr-*ahnt*-eh
the bathroom	**il bagno**	eel *bahn*-nyoh
To the right	**A destra**	ah *dehy*-stra
To the left	**A sinistra**	ah see-*nees*-tra
Straight ahead	**Avanti** (*or* **sempre diritto**)	ahv-vahn-tee (*sehm*-pray dee-*reet*-toh)
How much is it?	**Quanto costa?**	*kwan*-toh *coh*-sta?
The check, please	**Il conto, per favore**	eel kon-toh *pehr* fah-*vohr*-eh
When?	**Quando?**	*kwan*-doh
Yesterday	**Ieri**	ee-*yehr*-ree
Today	**Oggi**	*oh*-jee
Tomorrow	**Domani**	doh-*mah*-nee

English	Italian	Pronunciation
Breakfast	**Prima colazione**	*pree*-mah coh-laht-tzee-*ohn*-ay
Lunch	**Pranzo**	*prahn*-zoh
Dinner	**Cena**	*chay*-nah
What time is it?	**Che ore sono?**	kay *or*-ay *soh*-noh
Monday	**Lunedì**	loo-nay-*dee*
Tuesday	**Martedì**	mart-ay-*dee*
Wednesday	**Mercoledì**	mehr-cohl-ay-*dee*
Thursday	**Giovedì**	joh-vay-*dee*
Friday	**Venerdì**	ven-nehr-*dee*
Saturday	**Sabato**	*sah*-bah-toh
Sunday	**Domenica**	doh-*mehn*-nee-kah

Numbers

1	**uno** (*oo*-noh)	22	**venti due** (*vehn*-tee *doo*-ay)
2	**due** (*doo*-ay)	30	**trenta** (*trayn*-tah)
3	**tre** (tray)	40	**quaranta** (kwah-*rahn*-tah)
4	**quattro** (*kwah*-troh)	50	**cinquanta** (cheen-*kwan*-tah)
5	**cinque** (*cheen*-kway)	60	**sessanta** (sehs-*sahn*-tah)
6	**sei** (say)	70	**settanta** (seht-*tahn*-tah)
7	**sette** (*set*-tay)	80	**ottanta** (oht-*tahn*-tah)
8	**otto** (*oh*-toh)	90	**novanta** (noh-*vahnt*-tah)
9	**nove** (*noh*-vay)	100	**cento** (*chen*-toh)
10	**dieci** (dee-*ay*-chee)	1,000	**mille** (*mee*-lay)
11	**undici** (*oon*-dee-chee)	5,000	**cinque milla** (*cheen*-kway *mee*-lah)
20	**venti** (*vehn*-tee)	10,000	**dieci milla** (dee-*ay*-chee *mee*-lah)
21	**ventuno** (vehn-*toon*-oh)		

2 A Glossary of Architectural Terms

Ambone   A pulpit, either serpentine or simple in form, erected in an Italian church.

Apse   The half-rounded extension behind the main altar of a church; Christian tradition dictates that it be placed at the eastern end of an Italian church, the side closest to Jerusalem.

Atrium   A courtyard, open to the sky, in an ancient Roman house; the term also applies to the courtyard nearest the entrance of an early Christian church.

Baldacchino (also ciborium)   A columned stone canopy, usually placed above the altar of a church; spelled in English *baldachin* or *baldaquin*.

Baptistry   A separate building or a separate area in a church where the rite of baptism is held.

Basilica   Any rectangular public building, usually divided into three aisles by rows of columns. In ancient Rome, this architectural form was frequently used for places of public assembly and law courts; later, Roman Christians adapted the form for many of their early churches.

Caldarium   The steam room of a Roman bath.

Campanile   A bell tower, often detached, of a church.

Capital   The top of a column, often carved and usually categorized into one of three orders: Doric, Ionic, or Corinthian.

Castrum   A carefully planned Roman military camp, whose rectangular form, straight streets, and systems of fortified gates quickly became standardized throughout the Empire; modern cities that began as Roman camps and that still more or less maintain their original forms include Chester (England), Barcelona (Spain), and such Italian cities as Lucca, Aosta, Como, Brescia, Florence, and Ancona.

Cavea   The curved row of seats in a classical theater; the most prevalent shape was that of a semicircle.

Cella   The sanctuary, or most sacred interior section, of a Roman pagan temple.

Chancel   Section of a church containing the altar.

Cornice   The decorative flange defining the uppermost part of a classical or neo-classical facade.

Cortile   Courtyard or cloisters ringed with a gallery of arches or lintels set atop columns.

Crypt   A church's main burial place, usually below the choir.

Cupola   A dome.

Duomo   Cathedral.

Forum   The main square and principal gathering place of any Roman town, usually adorned with the city's most important temples and civic buildings.

Grotesques   Carved and painted faces, deliberately ugly, used by everyone from the Etruscans to the architects of the Renaissance; they're especially amusing when set into fountains.

Hypogeum   Subterranean burial chambers, usually of pre-Christian origins.

Loggia   Roofed balcony or gallery.

Lozenge   An elongated four-sided figure that, along with stripes, was one of the distinctive signs of the architecture of Pisa.

Narthex   The anteroom, or enclosed porch, of a Christian church.

Nave   The largest and longest section of a church, usually devoted to sheltering or seating worshipers and often divided by aisles.

Palazzo   A palace or other important building.

Piano Nobile   The main floor of a palazzo (sometimes the 2nd floor).

Pietra Dura   Richly ornate assemblage of semiprecious stones mounted on a flat decorative surface, perfected during the 1600s in Florence.

Pieve   A parish church.

Portico   A porch, usually crafted from wood or stone.

Pulvin   A four-sided stone that serves as a substitute for the capital of a column, often decoratively carved, sometimes into biblical scenes.

Putti   Plaster cherubs whose chubby forms often decorate the interiors of baroque chapels and churches.

Stucco   Colored plaster composed of sand, powdered marble, water, and lime, either molded into statuary or applied in a thin concretelike layer to the exterior of a building.

Telamone   Structural column carved into a standing male form; female versions are called *caryatids*.

Thermae   Roman baths.

Transenna   Stone (usually marble) screen separating the altar area from the rest of an early Christian church.

Travertine   The stone from which ancient and Renaissance Rome was built; it's known for its hardness, light coloring, and tendency to be pitted or flecked with black.

Tympanum   The half-rounded space above the portal of a church, whose semicircular space usually showcases a sculpture.

3 Italian Menu Terms

Abbacchio   Roast haunch or shoulder of lamb baked and served in a casserole and sometimes flavored with anchovies.

Agnolotti   A crescent-shape pasta shell stuffed with a mix of chopped meat, spices, vegetables, and cheese; when prepared in rectangular versions, the same combination of ingredients is identified as ravioli.

Amaretti   Crunchy, sweet almond-flavored macaroons.

Anguilla alla veneziana   Eel cooked in a sauce made from tuna and lemon.

Antipasti   Succulent tidbits served at the beginning of a meal (before the pasta), whose ingredients might include slices of cured meats, seafood (especially shellfish), and cooked and seasoned vegetables.

Aragosta   Lobster.

Arrosto   Roasted meat.

Baccalà   Dried and salted codfish.

Bagna cauda   Hot and well-seasoned sauce, heavily flavored with anchovies, designed for dipping raw vegetables; literally translated as "hot bath."

Bistecca alla fiorentina   Florentine-style steaks, coated before grilling with olive oil, pepper, lemon juice, salt, and parsley.

Bocconcini   Veal layered with ham and cheese, and then fried.

Bollito misto   Assorted boiled meats served on a single platter.

Braciola   Pork chop.

Bresaola   Air-dried spiced beef.

Bruschetta   Toasted bread, heavily slathered with olive oil and garlic and often topped with tomatoes.

Bucatini   Coarsely textured hollow spaghetti.

Busecca alla Milanese   Tripe (beef stomach) flavored with herbs and vegetables.

Cacciucco ali livornese   Seafood stew.

Calzone   Pizza dough rolled with the chef's choice of sausage, tomatoes, cheese, and so on and then baked into a kind of savory turnover.

Cannelloni   Tubular dough stuffed with meat, cheese, or vegetables and then baked in a creamy white sauce.

Cappellacci alla ferrarese   Pasta stuffed with pumpkin.

Cappelletti   Small ravioli ("little hats") stuffed with meat or cheese.

Carciofi   Artichokes.

Carpaccio   Thin slices of raw cured beef, sometimes in a piquant sauce.

Cassatta alla siciliana   A richly caloric dessert that combines layers of sponge cake, sweetened ricotta cheese, and candied fruit, bound together with chocolate buttercream icing.

Cervello al burro nero   Brains in black-butter sauce.

Cima alla genovese   Baked filet of veal rolled into a tube-shape package containing eggs, mushrooms, and sausage.

Coppa   Cured morsels of pork filet encased in sausage skins, served in slices.

Costoletta alla milanese   Veal cutlet dredged in bread crumbs, fried, and sometimes flavored with cheese.

Cozze   Mussels.

Fagioli   White beans.

Fave   Fava beans.

Fegato alla veneziana   Thinly sliced calves' liver fried with salt, pepper, and onions.

Focaccia   Ideally, concocted from potato-based dough left to rise slowly for several hours and then garnished with tomato sauce, garlic, basil, salt, and pepper, and drizzled with olive oil; similar to a deep-dish pizza most popular in the deep south, especially Bari.

Fontina   Rich cows' milk cheese.

Frittata   Italian omelet.

Fritto misto   A deep-fried medley of whatever small fish, shellfish, and squid are available in the marketplace that day.

Fusilli   Spiral-shape pasta.

Gelato (produzione propria)   Ice cream (homemade).

Gnocchi   Dumplings usually made from potatoes *(gnocchi alla patate)* or from semolina *(gnocchi alla romana),* often stuffed with combinations of cheese, spinach, vegetables, or whatever combinations strike the chef's fancy.

Gorgonzola   One of the most famous blue-veined cheeses of Europe—strong, creamy, and aromatic.

Granita   Flavored ice, usually with lemon or coffee.

Insalata di frutti di mare   Seafood salad (usually including shrimp and squid) garnished with pickles, lemon, olives, and spices.

Involtini   Thinly sliced beef, veal, or pork rolled, stuffed, and fried.

Minestrone   A rich and savory vegetable soup usually sprinkled with grated parmigiani and studded with noodles.

Mortadella   Mild pork sausage, fashioned into large cylinders and served sliced; the original lunchmeat bologna (because its most famous center of production is Bologna).

Mozzarella   A nonfermented cheese, made from the fresh milk of a buffalo (or, if unavailable, from a cow), boiled, and then kneaded into a rounded ball, served fresh.

Mozzarella con pomodori (also "caprese")   Fresh tomatoes with fresh mozzarella, basil, pepper, and olive oil.

Nervetti   A northern Italian antipasto made from chewy pieces of calves' feet or shins.

Osso buco   Beef or veal knuckle slowly braised until the cartilage is tender and then served with a highly flavored sauce.

Pancetta   Herb-flavored pork belly, rolled into a cylinder and sliced—the Italian bacon.

Panettone   Sweet yellow bread baked in the form of a brioche.

Panna   Heavy cream.

Pansotti   Pasta stuffed with greens, herbs, and cheeses, usually served with a walnut sauce.

Pappardelle alle lepre   Pasta with rabbit sauce.

Parmigiano   Parmesan, a hard and salty yellow cheese usually grated over pastas and soups but also eaten alone; also known as *granna*. The best is *parmigiano reggiano*.

Peperoni   Green, yellow, or red sweet peppers (not to be confused with pepperoni).

Pesci al cartoccio   Fish baked in a parchment envelope with onions, parsley, and herbs.

Pesto   A flavorful green sauce made from basil leaves, cheese, garlic, marjoram, and (if available) pine nuts.

Piccata al marsala   Thin escalope of veal braised in a pungent sauce flavored with marsala wine.

Piselli al prosciutto   Peas with strips of ham.

Pizza   Specific varieties include *capricciosa* (its ingredients can vary widely, depending on the chef's culinary vision and the ingredients at hand), *margherita* (with tomato sauce, cheese, fresh basil, and memories of the first queen of Italy, Marguerite di Savoia, in whose honor it was first made by a Neapolitan chef), *napoletana* (with ham, capers, tomatoes, oregano, cheese, and the distinctive taste of anchovies), *quatro stagione* (translated as "four seasons" because of the array of fresh vegetables in it; it also contains ham and bacon), and *siciliana* (with black olives, capers, and cheese).

Pizzaiola   A process in which something (usually a beefsteak) is covered in a tomato-and-oregano sauce.

Polenta   Thick porridge or mush made from cornmeal flour.

Polenta de uccelli   Assorted small birds roasted on a spit and served with polenta.

Polenta e coniglio   Rabbit stew served with polenta.

Polla alla cacciatore   Chicken with tomatoes and mushrooms cooked in wine.

Pollo alla diavola   Highly spiced grilled chicken.

Ragù   Meat sauce.

Ricotta   A soft bland cheese made from cow's or sheep's milk.

Risotto   Italian rice.

Risotto alla milanese   Rice with saffron and wine.

Salsa verde   "Green sauce," made from capers, anchovies, lemon juice and/or vinegar, and parsley.

Saltimbocca   Veal scallop layered with prosciutto and sage; its name literally translates as "jump in your mouth," a reference to its tart and savory flavor.

Salvia   Sage.

Scaloppina alla Valdostana   Escalope of veal stuffed with cheese and ham.

Scaloppine   Thin slices of veal coated in flour and sautéed in butter.

Semifreddo   A frozen dessert; usually ice cream with sponge cake.

Seppia   Cuttlefish (a kind of squid); its black ink is used for flavoring in certain sauces for pasta and also in risotto dishes.

Sogliola   Sole.

Spaghetti   A long, round, thin pasta, variously served: *alla bolognese* (with ground meat, mushrooms, peppers, and so on), *alla carbonara* (with bacon, black pepper, and eggs), *al pomodoro* (with tomato sauce), *al sugo/ragù* (with meat sauce), and *alle vongole* (with clam sauce).

Spiedini   Pieces of meat grilled on a skewer over an open flame.

Strangolaprete   Small nuggets of pasta, usually served with sauce; the name is literally translated as "priest-choker."

Stufato   Beef braised in white wine with vegetables.

Tagliatelle   Flat egg noodles.

Tonno   Tuna.

Tortelli   Pasta dumplings stuffed with ricotta and greens.

Tortellini   Rings of dough stuffed with minced and seasoned meat, and served either in soups or as a full-fledged pasta covered with sauce.

Trenette   Thin noodles served with pesto sauce and potatoes.

Trippe alla fiorentina   Beef tripe (stomach).

Vermicelli   Very thin spaghetti.

Vitello tonnato   Cold sliced veal covered with tuna-fish sauce.

Zabaglione/zabaione   Egg yolks whipped into the consistency of a custard, flavored with Marsala, and served warm as a dessert.

Zampone   Pig's trotter stuffed with spicy seasoned pork, boiled and sliced.

Zuccotto   A liqueur-soaked sponge cake, molded into a dome and layered with chocolate, nuts, and whipped cream.

Zuppa inglese   Sponge cake soaked in custard.

Appendix C:
Useful Toll-Free Numbers
& Websites

AIRLINES

Aer Lingus
☎ 800/474-7424 in the U.S.
☎ 0818/365000 in Ireland
www.aerlingus.com

Air Canada
☎ 888/247-2262
www.aircanada.ca

Air France
☎ 800/237-2747 in U.S.
☎ 0820-820-820 in France
www.airfrance.com

Air Malta
☎ 866/357-4155 in U.S.
☎ 356/2169-0890 in Malta
www.airmalta.com

Air New Zealand
☎ 800/262-1234 in the U.S.
☎ 0800/737-000 in New Zealand
www.airnewzealand.com

Airtran Airlines
☎ 800/247-8726
www.airtran.com

Alitalia
☎ 800/223-5730 in U.S.
☎ 06/65644 in Italy
www.alitalia.it

American Airlines
☎ 800/433-7300
www.aa.com

American Trans Air
☎ 800/225-2995
www.ata.com

Austrian Airlines
☎ 800/843-0002 in U.S.
☎ 43/05-1789 in Austria
www.aua.com

BMI
No U.S. number
☎ 0870/6070-222 in Britain
www.flybmi.com

British Airways
☎ 800/247-9297
☎ 0870/850-9-850 in Britain
www.ba.com

Continental Airlines
☎ 800/525-0280
www.continental.com

Delta Air Lines
☎ 800/221-1212
www.delta.com

Easyjet
No U.S. number
www.easyjet.com

Iberia
☎ 800/772-4642 in U.S.
☎ 902/400-500 in Spain
www.iberia.com

Icelandair
☎ 800/223-5500 in U.S.
☎ 354/50-50-100 in Iceland
www.icelandair.com

Jet Blue Airlines
☎ 800/538-2583
www.jetblue.com

KLM
℡ 020/4-747-747 in Netherlands
www.klm.nl

Lufthansa
℡ 800/645-3880 in U.S.
℡ 49/0-180-5-838426 in Germany
www.lufthansa.com

Meridiana
℡ 892-928 in Italy
℡ 39/0789-52682 worldwide
www.meridiana.it

Northwest KLM Airlines
℡ 800/225-2525
www.nwa.com

Olympic Airways
℡ 800/223-1226 in U.S.
℡ 80/111-444-444 in Greece
www.olympicairlines.com

Qantas
℡ 800/227-4500 in the U.S.
℡ 612/131313 in Australia
www.qantas.com

RyanAir
℡ 0871-0246-0000 worldwide
www.ryanair.com

Scandinavian Airlines
℡ 800/221-2350 in U.S.
℡ 0070/727-727 in Sweden
℡ 70/10-20-00 in Denmark
℡ 45/32-32-68-00 in Finland
℡ 915/05-400 in Norway
www.scandinavian.net

Singapore Airlines
℡ 800/742-3333 in U.S.
℡ 65/6223-8888 in Singapore
www.singaporeair.com

Swiss International Airlines
℡ 877/359-7947 in U.S.
℡ 0848/85-2000 in Switzerland
www.swiss.com

TAP Air Portugal
℡ 800/221-7370 in U.S.
℡ 351/707-205-700 in Portugal
www.tap-airportugal.pt

Tarom Romanian
www.tarom.ro

Thai Airways International
℡ 212/949-8424
www.thaiair.com

Turkish Airlines
℡ 800/874-8875 in U.S.
℡ 90-212-444-0849 in Turkey
www.flyturkish.com

United Airlines
℡ 800/241-6522
www.united.com

US Airways
℡ 800/428-4322
www.usairways.com

Virgin Atlantic Airways
℡ 800/821-5438 in Continental U.S.
℡ 0870/574-7747 in Britain
www.virgin-atlantic.com

CAR-RENTAL AGENCIES

Advantage
℡ 800/777-5500
www.arca.com

Alamo
℡ 800/462-5266
www.alamo.com

Auto Europe
℡ 888/223-5555
www.autoeurope.com

Avis
℡ 800/331-1212 in Continental U.S.
℡ 800/TRY-AVIS in Canada
www.avis.com

Budget
℡ 800/527-0700
www.budget.com

Dollar
℡ 800/800-3665
www.dollar.com

Enterprise
© 800/261-7331
www.enterprise.com

Hertz
© 800/654-3131
www.hertz.com

Kemwel Holiday Auto (KHA)
© 800/678-0678
www.kemwel.com

National
© 800/227-7368
www.nationalcar.com

Payless
© 800/729-5377
www.paylesscarrental.com

Rent-A-Wreck
© 800/944-7501
www.rentawreck.com

Thrifty
© 800/847-4389
www.thrifty.com

Index

See also Accommodations, Restaurant, and Cafe indexes, below.

FROMMER'S® COMPLETE TRAVEL GUIDES

Alaska
Amalfi Coast
American Southwest
Amsterdam
Argentina & Chile
Arizona
Atlanta
Australia
Austria
Bahamas
Barcelona
Beijing
Belgium, Holland & Luxembourg
Belize
Bermuda
Boston
Brazil
British Columbia & the Canadian
  Rockies
Brussels & Bruges
Budapest & the Best of Hungary
Buenos Aires
Calgary
California
Canada
Cancún, Cozumel & the Yucatán
Cape Cod, Nantucket & Martha's
  Vineyard
Caribbean
Caribbean Ports of Call
Carolinas & Georgia
Chicago
China
Colorado
Costa Rica
Croatia
Cuba
Denmark
Denver, Boulder & Colorado Springs
Edinburgh & Glasgow
England
Europe
Europe by Rail
Florence, Tuscany & Umbria

Florida
France
Germany
Greece
Greek Islands
Hawaii
Hong Kong
Honolulu, Waikiki & Oahu
India
Ireland
Israel
Italy
Jamaica
Japan
Kauai
Las Vegas
London
Los Angeles
Los Cabos & Baja
Madrid
Maine Coast
Maryland & Delaware
Maui
Mexico
Montana & Wyoming
Montréal & Québec City
Moscow & St. Petersburg
Munich & the Bavarian Alps
Nashville & Memphis
New England
Newfoundland & Labrador
New Mexico
New Orleans
New York City
New York State
New Zealand
Northern Italy
Norway
Nova Scotia, New Brunswick &
  Prince Edward Island
Oregon
Paris
Peru
Philadelphia & the Amish Country

Portugal
Prague & the Best of the Czech
  Republic
Provence & the Riviera
Puerto Rico
Rome
San Antonio & Austin
San Diego
San Francisco
Santa Fe, Taos & Albuquerque
Scandinavia
Scotland
Seattle
Seville, Granada & the Best of
  Andalusia
Shanghai
Sicily
Singapore & Malaysia
South Africa
South America
South Florida
South Pacific
Southeast Asia
Spain
Sweden
Switzerland
Tahiti & French Polynesia
Texas
Thailand
Tokyo
Toronto
Turkey
USA
Utah
Vancouver & Victoria
Vermont, New Hampshire & Maine
Vienna & the Danube Valley
Vietnam
Virgin Islands
Virginia
Walt Disney World® & Orlando
Washington, D.C.
Washington State

FROMMER'S® DAY BY DAY GUIDES

Amsterdam
Chicago
Florence & Tuscany

London
New York City
Paris

Rome
San Francisco
Venice

PAULINE FROMMER'S GUIDES! SEE MORE. SPEND LESS.

Hawaii

Italy

New York City

FROMMER'S® PORTABLE GUIDES

Acapulco, Ixtapa & Zihuatanejo
Amsterdam
Aruba
Australia's Great Barrier Reef
Bahamas
Big Island of Hawaii
Boston
California Wine Country
Cancún
Cayman Islands
Charleston
Chicago
Dominican Republic

Dublin
Florence
Las Vegas
Las Vegas for Non-Gamblers
London
Maui
Nantucket & Martha's Vineyard
New Orleans
New York City
Paris
Portland
Puerto Rico
Puerto Vallarta, Manzanillo &
  Guadalajara

Rio de Janeiro
San Diego
San Francisco
Savannah
St. Martin, Sint Maarten, Anguila &
  St. Bart's
Turks & Caicos
Vancouver
Venice
Virgin Islands
Washington, D.C.
Whistler

FROMMER'S® CRUISE GUIDES

...ska Cruises & Ports of Call	Cruises & Ports of Call	European Cruises & Ports of Call

FROMMER'S® NATIONAL PARK GUIDES

...onquin Provincial Park	National Parks of the American West	Yosemite and Sequoia & Kings
...ff & Jasper	Rocky Mountain	Canyon
...nd Canyon	Yellowstone & Grand Teton	Zion & Bryce Canyon

FROMMER'S® MEMORABLE WALKS

...don	Paris	San Francisco
...w York	Rome	

FROMMER'S® WITH KIDS GUIDES

...cago	National Parks	Toronto
...waii	New York City	Walt Disney World® & Orlando
...Vegas	San Francisco	Washington, D.C.
...don		

SUZY GERSHMAN'S BORN TO SHOP GUIDES

...nce	London	Paris
...ng Kong, Shanghai & Beijing	New York	San Francisco
...y		

FROMMER'S® IRREVERENT GUIDES

...sterdam	London	Rome
...ton	Los Angeles	San Francisco
...icago	Manhattan	Walt Disney World®
...Vegas	Paris	Washington, D.C.

FROMMER'S® BEST-LOVED DRIVING TOURS

...stria	Germany	Northern Italy
...tain	Ireland	Scotland
...ifornia	Italy	Spain
...nce	New England	Tuscany & Umbria

THE UNOFFICIAL GUIDES®

...venture Travel in Alaska	Hawaii	Paris
...yond Disney	Ireland	San Francisco
...lifornia with Kids	Las Vegas	South Florida including Miami &
...ntral Italy	London	the Keys
...icago	Maui	Walt Disney World®
...uises	Mexico's Best Beach Resorts	Walt Disney World® for
...sneyland®	Mini Mickey	Grown-ups
...gland	New Orleans	Walt Disney World® with Kids
...rida	New York City	Washington, D.C.
...rida with Kids		

SPECIAL-INTEREST TITLES

...ens Past & Present	Frommer's Exploring America by RV
...st Places to Raise Your Family	Frommer's NYC Free & Dirt Cheap
...Ranked & Rated	Frommer's Road Atlas Europe
...Places to Take Your Kids Before They Grow Up	Frommer's Road Atlas Ireland
...mmer's Best Day Trips from London	Great Escapes From NYC Without Wheels
...mmer's Best RV & Tent Campgrounds	Retirement Places Rated
...n the U.S.A.	

FROMMER'S® PHRASEFINDER DICTIONARY GUIDES

...nch	Italian	Spanish

Parla italiano?

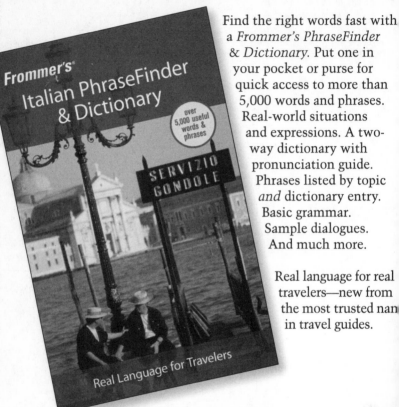

Find the right words fast with a *Frommer's PhraseFinder & Dictionary*. Put one in your pocket or purse for quick access to more than 5,000 words and phrases. Real-world situations and expressions. A two-way dictionary with pronunciation guide. Phrases listed by topic *and* dictionary entry. Basic grammar. Sample dialogues. And much more.

Real language for real travelers—new from the most trusted nam in travel guides.

Also available:
Frommer's French PhraseFinder & Dictionary
Frommer's Spanish PhraseFinder & Dictionary

Available wherever books are sold.

The best conversations start here.

Frommer's
A Branded Imprint of WI
Now you know.